Terry and Jan Todd Series on Physical Culture and Sports

Edited by Sarah K. Fields, Thomas Hunt, Daniel A. Nathan, and Patricia Vertinsky

ALSO IN THE SERIES:

Thomas Hunt, *Drug Games: The International Olympic Committee
and the Politics of Doping, 1960–2008*

John D. Fair, *Mr. America: The Tragic History of a Bodybuilding Icon*

John Hoberman, *Dopers in Uniform:
The Hidden World of Police on Steroids*

Kevin Robbins, *Harvey Penick: The Life and Wisdom of
the Man Who Wrote the Book on Golf*

Jason P. Shurley, Jan Todd, and Terry Todd, *Strength Coaching in America:
A History of the Innovation That Transformed Sports*

NO WAY BUT TO FIGHT

GEORGE FOREMAN

and the Business of Boxing

Andrew R. M. Smith

UNIVERSITY OF TEXAS PRESS

AUSTIN

Requests for permission to reproduce material
from this work should be sent to:
Permissions
University of Texas Press
P.O. Box 7819
Austin, TX 78713-7819
utpress.utexas.edu/rp-form

♾ The paper used in this book meets the minimum requirements of
ANSI/NISO Z39.48-1992 (R1997) (Permanence of Paper).

Library of Congress Cataloging-in-Publication Data

Names: Smith, Andrew R. M., author.
Title: No way but to fight : George Foreman and the business of boxing /
Andrew R. M. Smith.
Other titles: Terry and Jan Todd series on physical culture and sports.
Description: First edition. | Austin : University of Texas Press, 2020. |
Series: Terry and Jan Todd series on physical culture and sports |
Includes bibliographical references and index.
Identifiers: LCCN 2019019899 | ISBN 978-1-4773-1976-5 (cloth : alk. paper) |
ISBN 978-14773-1977-2 (library e-book) |
ISBN 978-1-4773-1978-9 (nonlibrary e-book)
Subjects: LCSH: Foreman, George, 1949– | Boxers (Sports)—
United States—Biography.
Classification: LCC GV1132.F65 S65 2020 | DDC 796.83092 [B] —dc23
LC record available at https://lccn.loc.gov/2019019899

doi:10.7560/319765

For Erika, Sophie, and Phoebe

Contents

No Way but to Fight

Prologue

CROSSROADS

"This isn't artistic," Howard Cosell told viewers who tuned into ABC's broadcast of George Foreman versus Ron Lyle on January 24, 1976, "but it is slugging." As Cosell described these heavyweights trading blows, it escaped him that the artistry was not in the fight but in its production. Two of the hardest hitters in the sport stood toe to toe, landing punches and scoring knockdowns, right inside Caesars Palace. "The way the public wants it," Cosell added with a hint of derision, but he was right—and it wasn't a coincidence. This was a carefully planned, made-for-television event designed to provide the "public" with what it wanted and sow the seeds for the future of prizefighting.

Foreman straddled the sport's past and future. Many believed that his best days were behind him, but few could point to a better successor should the current heavyweight champion, Muhammad Ali, follow through on his threats to retire. Foreman had originally signed on to fight Pedro Lovell—who made a bigger imprint on the sport as an actor playing the club fighter "Spider" Rico in the *Rocky* saga than he did as a prizefighter—at the Las Vegas Convention Center, a nod to Foreman's early career, when he traveled around the country knocking out lesser-known competitors in small-time venues. The music and television promoter Jerry Perenchio had a different vision for professional boxing. He had orchestrated the first fight between Joe Frazier and Muhammad Ali, in 1971, in the traditional home of championship boxing, New York City's Madison Square Garden (MSG). When tradition, among other things, stalled his attempts to promote a rematch between Ali and Frazier, he looked elsewhere, first to the growing population of California before proposing a marriage of prizefighting and legalized gambling in Nevada. Promoters before him, including "Tex" Rickard (not a native Texan) and "Doc" Kearns (not a practicing physician), had tried to move the sport's biggest events from the "Mecca of Boxing" to the "Gomorrah of the Desert" without sustained success. In the mid-1970s, Perenchio sought to leverage the medium that had made him rich as well as the heightened competition between sprawling casino-hotels in order to pull big-time prizefights into Sin City's orbit. He convinced Foreman to renege on fighting Lovell at the convention center in order to take on a better-known opponent at a more attractive venue.[1]

A pioneer of the opulence that dotted the Las Vegas Strip, Caesars wagered that hosting boxing matches would fill up its rooms while adding to the take not only at its sports book but at the slots and tables as well. Its Roman motif transformed a bout between two desperate contenders for Ali's heavyweight championship into a gladiatorial contest. They might as well have worn ox-hide *caestus*. Every punch came through eight-ounce gloves, thinner than those required in states such as New York or California, and since Caesars' "Sports Pavilion" accommodated only a seventeen-square-foot ring, there wasn't much room to avoid them either. The deck was stacked to ensure more brawling than boxing. A sellout was virtually guaranteed, since seating capacity was limited to about five thousand. The full house and fast action made for a great picture on TV, with ample opportunity to air slow-motion replays of fists pounding flesh, all while hiding the preproduction warts. Behind the scenes, the main event came off in a makeshift ring thrown up in the middle of a tented tennis court. At the signal, Foreman marched to it from his "dressing room"—a trailer in the parking lot.[2]

Cosell described it as a "crossroads fight." Both boxers needed a decisive victory in order to stay in contention for a title shot. Another contender for the heavyweight crown, Ken Norton, joined Cosell at the broadcaster's table. Both acknowledged Foreman as the favorite—betting fans could get odds of 3–1 to 5–1 without leaving the building—but they agreed that if Lyle could "survive the first five rounds," he was "the better bet to win." To their surprise, Lyle jumped out at the first bell and fired off something Cosell described as a "wild, almost amateurish right," making it clear that he did not intend to play a long game. Foreman, under the direction of new trainers Gil Clancy and "Kid" Rapidez, had recently been trying to downplay his reputation as a slugger and prove his merit as a boxer instead. In their prefight banter, Cosell asked Norton whether a fighter like Foreman could change his style to such a degree. "In the gym," Norton snorted, before suggesting that after taking a punch, Foreman would likely revert to what he knew best. It didn't take long. Lyle came out of a break with an overhand right that crashed down onto Foreman, followed by hooks and uppercuts that sent him grasping for something to keep him upright. The Houston sports reporter Ralph Cooper saw that Foreman "came out trying to box," but after he "got hit upside the head," that plan changed: "It became a street fight." Cosell screeched that Foreman was "in trouble ... wobbling back toward his corner," and Lyle tried to keep up the momentum in the next round, opening again with an errant swing. Norton pointed out that Lyle was "giving Foreman no respect," just before a three-punch combination led Cosell to warn, "That could be a mistake, Kenny." Foreman became the aggressor, pinning Lyle against the ropes before the bell sounded. Since it was only two minutes into the round, the signal came as a surprise to many, but a very pleasant one for Lyle. He might not have stood up to another sixty seconds.[3]

With most scorecards awarding one round to each fighter, the match settled into a pattern. Foreman, ignoring the advice of Clancy, who yelled, "Hook to the body!" until his voice went hoarse, prodded for an opening to score a big head shot. Cosell reminded his audience that "Foreman can end the fight at any time." Lyle could, too. He waited for Foreman to throw those haymakers so that he could land the counterpunches that represented his best weapons. In the fourth round, Foreman overextended himself and Lyle countered with a combination that swung the momentum. "Remember how invincible George Foreman looked through forty bouts?" Cosell asked Norton and the wider TV audience. "What happened to him?" Lyle worked himself into a frenzy until he knocked Foreman down. But Foreman jumped to his feet without so much as looking at his corner or the referee. One minute later he delivered a "magnificent right" that sent Lyle down to one part of the canvas and his mouthpiece to another. Still, Lyle beat the count and got back in the fray, landing a combination that stunned Foreman and following up with a huge right hand. "Foreman goes down! Foreman goes down!" Cosell cried, recycling a more polished version of perhaps his most memorable boxing call from a few years earlier. "But Foreman gets up. Foreman is up. What a fight, Kenny!"

As Cosell was bawling his thoughts into the microphone, Foreman told a reporter later there was only one thing running through his mind: "I'll be God-damned if somebody is going to knock me out!" Once he was considered the savior of the fight game. Now he was on the mat, at the end of a round, in a state where no one can be saved by the bell. Foreman pulled himself up before Charlie Roth could count him out, and staggered back to Clancy. Lyle likewise had trouble getting to his corner until Roth pointed him in the right direction. Yet Cosell repeated that "most people" believed if the fight crested into the fifth round, as the next bell would signal, Lyle's chances would be "materially improved." Norton said, "The question is if George can recover," and opined, "I think Lyle has the mental edge right here." Forty-five seconds later, Lyle struck a thundering left that buckled Foreman's knees and seemed to prove Norton correct. "Here we go, Howard!" he called out as Foreman's legs weakened and his hands fell to his waist. "No bounce in the legs," Cosell noted, and Norton added, "Foreman's hands are down, if you notice." While the commentators sized Foreman up like undertakers, Lyle failed to administer last rites. At the two-minute point of the fifth round, Foreman landed a couple of short, snappy punches and then hurled another one that knocked out Lyle's mouthpiece again while pinning him into a corner. Foreman suddenly unleashed a bombardment of, in one ringside account, at least twenty lefts and rights before stepping back and watching Lyle "sag to the canvas . . . like a submarine slipping under ocean waters." He did not resurface before Roth said, "Ten!"[4]

Foreman had barely weathered the stormy fourth round but stayed on course for a heavyweight championship bout. Even if he did not necessarily prove his skill as a boxer, he silenced the critics who said the big brawler couldn't take a punch. As Pat Putnam of *Sports Illustrated* attested, "He took them by the dozens"—and had a three-inch cut inside his mouth to prove it. In a postfight interview, Foreman dismissed the nicks and bruises that Lyle inflicted, calling them a consequence of his "rust." Then he credited Cosell and ABC executives, who disparaged his last performance on their network, for his determination to keep on fighting. "I'm never going to give up," he said, "I'll *die* before I give up." He had one goal and one path toward it. "There are no short cuts," on his road back to the heavyweight championship. "No way but to fight."[5]

★

Fighting was perhaps not the only way, but at least one of the very few ways available for someone from the urban working poor to make it in postwar America. For George Foreman, it was not as simple as punching his way to fame or fortune. It required fighting on multiple fronts, from the streets of Houston to stadiums around the world. He has been a foot soldier in the War on Poverty, the Cold War, and America's culture wars, all while battling through prize-fights watched by millions as well as working behind the scenes of what the boxing writer and analyst Larry Merchant once called "the last of the unregulated, free-enterprise sports." The fight game demands not just a sharp punch or a strong jaw but also a sharp persona and strong sense of self-promotion. In that unique climate, Foreman's most challenging conflicts were internal ones as he wrestled with personal beliefs and public images to position himself for the next big fight. "Boxing was invented for me," he said after nearly thirty years in the sport. "There's nobody been born meant to wake up in the morning and put on the 'bruising suit' [like me] . . . this is what I do. All I do. This is my business."[6]

Foreman has been in business, publicly, for fifty years: from the 1968 Summer Olympics to the final episode of *Better Late Than Never* in 2018. During that half century of public life, the most consistent aspect of his career remains the ability to adapt and reshape his image. He tried to borrow Muhammad Ali's rhymes, wear Jim Brown's sideburns, and replicate Walt Frazier's cool pose, all in the effort to look like a heavyweight champion before he wore the belt. As a sports superstar, he once sought to withdraw from the media, but then not only opened up but also worked as a broadcaster beside Howard Cosell, all while he campaigned for another shot at the championship. Foreman employed humor and wit, threats and intimidation, as well as occasional southern colloquialisms to stand out in the high tide of athletic celebrity. He was his own man, even if his vision of masculinity—he was never as brash as Ali, not quite as terse as Brown, and certainly not as flamboyant as Frazier—kept changing as the soul era gave way to disco and he left the prize ring for the pulpit.[7]

Like his strategic use of down-home expressions, Foreman sporadically dropped religious references, even if he did not seem like a true believer. Raised in the shadows of multiple churches, most of them Baptist, the young Foreman gave irregular, not necessarily obligatory, thanks to God or Jesus after some early success—predominantly in the Houston papers that his family might read. But as a mature heavyweight trying to gain momentum for a title shot against a Muslim champion, he started to emphasize his Christian identity. Before that rematch came to fruition, however, a "born again" experience pushed him out of boxing and into the ministry. Though never exactly out of the public eye, for a decade Foreman generally appeared in a religious role. Yet when he announced a return to the prize ring, he doused the fire and brimstone while fashioning an image that reached the broadest possible cross section of Americans. That version of Foreman, with a skyrocketing Q rating, was thrust into the competition for the title again and simultaneously launched into a television career.

In the mid-1990s, the two-time champion's success in the ring and on TV surprised Madison Avenue as much as sportswriters or fight fans. Amid many endorsement deals, he was handpicked, almost browbeaten into becoming the pitchman for a floundering kitchen appliance. Foreman proved that he could sell more than just himself. Particularly in the unscripted platform of the infomercial, a middle-aged overweight prizefighter with broad likability and deep marketing acumen—a "Miracle of Reinvention" according to Richard Hoffer—drove sales to unimaginable levels, inextricably linking him to an electric grill that still bears his name. He proved to be most convincing when he was allowed to just be himself, and that realization coincided with the rise of reality television. A loosely scripted medium was the perfect fit for a natural performer who had learned how to crack jokes for a camera from Bob Hope. His presence on the small screen kept him relevant, even after he had stepped out of his "bruising suit" and retired from the ring, to Baby Boomers through the iGeneration.[8]

Since becoming well known during the "long 1960s," Foreman has been captured in numberless snapshots. Blowing up those still frames over time has reified images that run the gamut from celebratory to defamatory but are usually oversimplified. The panoramic view is much more complicated. Under a microscope for many years, Foreman's life and times might be better seen through a telescope that is not just fixed on one superstar but also shines some light on the shadowy characters orbiting "Big George." A full picture would account for the bright lights and the dark spots, his big wins and hard losses in the ring as well as outside the ropes. Two impressive stints as a prizefighter, in 1969–1977 and again in 1987–1997, cannot be divorced from his troubled early life, unorthodox amateur pathway, the tumultuous decade between his professional careers, or his much more lucrative exploits as an ex-champ. This book is the first to follow all the iterations of George Foreman across eight decades, from the Fifth Ward of Houston to the Boxing Hall of Fame and into the pantheon of pop culture, charting his tacks and jibes as he navigated the realpolitik of the prize ring around the world while staying afloat in the crosscurrents of the "American Century" and making it in the sordid business of boxing.[9]

Fruits of the Fifth Ward

If you can't catch the blues in Houston,
man, you can't catch them anywhere.

TOWNES VAN ZANDT, quoted in Kathleen
Hudson, *Telling Stories, Writing Songs*, p. 69

There wasn't much for George Foreman to see in the early 1960s. "I didn't know there was another place in the world but Houston," he recalled. More specifically, he did not look too far outside the Fifth Ward, where he lived—albeit in many different addresses—from infancy through adolescence. Foreman's view extended for about five square miles: east to west from Lockwood to Jensen Drive; hemmed in by Buffalo Bayou on the south up to Liberty Road. Liberty was an ironic name for its northern boundary, since the economic circumstances that brought nearly fifty thousand residents into the poorest section of Houston precluded them from leaving it anytime soon. New highways, including Interstate 10, abutted old ones such as US 59 and circumscribed much of the neighborhood in concrete before the end of the 1950s. By then, the core of the ward, once the Lyons Avenue Commercial District, had eroded into a dangerous thoroughfare simply known as Lyons Ave. When Foreman was old enough to walk there, it was unsafe to do so after dark. But if he made it to the western edge, he could look up at the overpass and watch the cars speeding away on roads to anywhere but there. He could see both sides of US 59 and imagine folks going northeast, maybe as far as the town of Marshall, where he was born; or southwest, perhaps through Sugar Land and past its notorious prison, where a self-described "delinquent of all delinquents" might end up. He could not imagine what he would see in that spot a half century later.[1]

Visible from both directions along the newly minted I-69, formerly US 59, is a fifty-foot-long mural entitled *Fruits of the Fifth Ward*. Built by students from nearby Phillis Wheatley High School, and overseen by the Museum of Cultural Arts Houston with a $10,000 seed grant from the History Channel, roughly fifteen thousand mosaic tiles form four panels depicting twenty-one of the most notable people to affect—or come right out of—the "Bloody Fifth." On the far side of the last panel is a picture of George Foreman with a playful smile above a huge fist cocked just below his chin. The lone fighter alongside artists, politicians, and educators, including Wheatley.[2]

★

"Tenaha!" echoed from the heart of Reconstruction-era Texas across oceans in the middle of the twentieth century. Sometimes it came with more emphasis on the first syllable: TEN-aha! Or it might get a long, drawn-out middle that sounded like "Tennnnnny-ha." But never too strong on the back end—"ha"—because this was no laughing matter. Anyone shooting dice in the Lone Star State who needed to roll a ten could call out the name of this obscure little town in Shelby County for some good luck.

When new soldiers and ex-sharecroppers took part in the Great Migration out of the rural South, colloquialisms followed. Popular culture could grease the wheels, too, and this common "tex-clamation" gained traction with a recording of "Tenaha, Timpson,

Bobo and Blair" by a singing cowboy named Tex Ritter. So while the world was at war, GIs from anywhere in the country might be passing the time on bases stateside or on ships at sea, stationed somewhere in Europe or Asia, by appealing to Texan dice karma if a pile of cash was just one set of double-fives away from their pocket. Tenaha![3]

George Foreman first heard "Tenaha" in its original context: as one of four quick stops in Shelby County along the Houston East and West Texas (HE&WT) Railway. Those stations came up so fast that the conductor did not have time to announce each town individually, so "Ten'ha-Tim'son-Bobo-'n-Bla-yaaaah!" sprayed out like buckshot at the door of each car as the conductor rushed off to the next one. In the summer of 1949, Tenaha flew right past the Foreman family. They were not stopping there, not quitting generations of sharecropping around Marshall, in Harrison County, for more of the same just a couple counties down. And they were not riding the old HE&WT either. Instead, they were following the family patriarch, J. D. Foreman, on the Southern Pacific Railway. When the Southern Pacific bought out the HE&WT, with designs on expanding service across the burgeoning Sunbelt region, it offered rural workers like J.D. steady employment and better pay to build and maintain tracks around the growing urban center of Houston. This was no longer the railway whose initials, Tex Ritter said, were an abbreviation for "Hell Either Way You Take it"; rather, this was meant to be a trip to the promised land, two hundred miles south.[4]

Passing through Tenaha, from Marshall en route to Houston, was still a gamble. Being stuck in the cyclical indebtedness of sharecropping was a bad hand, to be sure, but no one knew what was coming up after the turn to Houston. Anything seemed possible, yet nothing was guaranteed, in a self-proclaimed boomtown still trying to shed its swampy image as the Bayou City and rebrand itself as the "Golden Buckle of the Sunbelt." Nancy Foreman took the risk, claimed free passage on the Southern Pacific for an employee's family, and piled five children on the train: her oldest son, three daughters, and a six-month-old baby named George. The possibilities may have seemed infinite, but Foreman's family remained fixated on two things: "big wages, and indoor plumbing."[5]

Neither of those two criteria was readily available to tenant farmers in northeastern Texas. Foreman described the family homestead there as a "shotgun house" because you could fire from one end to the other of the long, narrow-roofed rectangle and not hit anything of substance—no rooms, no appliances, no wiring, no plumbing. Nothing. He heard stories of desperation and want. His grandparents tried to raise a family large enough to form a free male workforce, but were "cursed" with nine daughters before having a son. "People would come from miles around to watch those girls," he was told, with their hair up in do-rags and "big shoulders," performing hard labor like clearing the fields and pulling out stumps. But it did not change the family's fortunes. When an aunt from Louisiana came to visit, she refused to extend her stay because, more than a full generation after the Emancipation Proclamation, the view from Harrison County convinced her that slavery was still legal in Texas.[6]

The "push factors" to get out of Marshall were not limited to poverty. Whispers about baby George—who did not look much like his brother or sisters, and who was given the nickname "Mo'head" because, it seemed, his large cranium predicted that he would outgrow them all soon—were the kind of "non-economic motives" that disproportionately affected women. For Nancy Foreman, these factors augmented the desire she shared with thousands of families across the rural South to leave small towns and big fields for a new life in urban America. But for the truly poor, those desires were not actionable without the kind of "pull factors" that might provide resources. Specifically, transportation and accommodation, which were no small matters for a mother with a troubled marriage, five children, and no cash. The fringe benefit of free train fare afforded by J.D.'s new job enabled the family to leave Marshall, and they relied on Nancy's sisters who already lived in Houston's Fifth Ward for a place to stay. This was not a romance. It was the reality of sharecroppers trying to escape poverty in postwar America, sometimes only to discover another form of it in a different environment.[7]

Houston attracted as many, and maybe more, newcomers as some northern cities, and plenty of them, like the Foremans, never crossed state lines to get there. The traditional methods of researching internal migration, however, concentrate on interstate travel. It is harder to account for in-state migrants. Yet tens of thousands of black, white, and brown people from rural Texas had been steadily funneling into Houston for more than a century. Since the city's founding in 1836, its population had doubled every twelve years. Then, after Lieutenant Governor Richard Hubbard addressed the Centennial Exposition in Philadelphia with a speech entitled "Come to Texas," it tripled over the next fourteen. Even though Hubbard's invitation targeted middle-class white northerners and hoped to quiet their fears of "redeemers" in a former Confederate state, the message held great appeal to recently emancipated slaves in Texas and echoed to the sharecropping descendants of those freedmen in the years to come.[8]

The image of African Americans leaving the Jim Crow South by the millions for more freedom and opportunity in the urban North still captures the American imagination. Two distinct waves of the Great Migration, interrupted only by reduced mobility during the Great Depression, forever changed the demographics of the nation—and heavyweight boxing history, too. The trek toward world titles for iconic champions like Joe Louis and Joe Frazier started with the determination to leave Alabama and South Carolina for Detroit or Philadelphia. As full-fledged members of the working class, they had access to organized recreation, including boxing, and pursuing those inclinations to their fullest potential became a possibility. But not everyone who migrated experienced greatness.[9]

During the period considered the first wave, more than thirty thousand African Americans chose Houston over New York or Chicago. The Great Depression did not interrupt the exodus from Texas's rural periphery to Houston as it did the more famous northern trajectory of relocation. The city's black population rose by another twenty thousand during even the worst years of economic decline. More than forty thousand claimed residence in the next decade. In fact, there were no waves of migrants in Houston because a riptide from the vast expanses of the Texas countryside pulled more and more people toward the Gulf coast and straight into one of the fastest-growing cities in the nation.[10]

The Foremans shared an optimism that had attracted families like them to Houston for decades. Jobs were plentiful. The federal government invested millions of dollars in Houston during the 1930s, which staved off the worst effects of the Depression. When the Second World War erupted, forty-five Houston companies were awarded defense contracts, which stimulated the local economy through the 1940s. In addition to a booming oil business, billions of dollars from private investors buttressed a chemical industry that supported more than six hundred factories in Harris County alone, which already laid claim to having the most cattle of any Texas county, and the third-highest number of hogs and chickens. Moreover, Houston had become a shipping hub second only to New York City by the end of the war. Between the oil, chemical, defense, and agriculture industries, as well as the ports that moved all their products around the country and beyond, Houstonians' economic well-being was pervasive. *Time* magazine called Houston "one of the few places left in the world where millionaires hatch seasonally." The Works Project Administration estimated that residents of Harris County had a buying power of more than $300 million. Just a few months before the Foremans arrived, one of those million-aires, Glenn McCarthy, opened his Shamrock Hotel. Frank Lloyd Wright compared the eighteen-story monolith, which was painted in no less than sixty-three shades of green, to the inside of a juke-box. Yet its grand opening, on St. Patrick's Day 1949, attracted 175 film stars and at least 50,000 fans, who drowned out the live re-cording of a Dorothy Lamour radio show. Regardless of questions of taste, McCarthy and the Shamrock were further proof that there was plenty of money flowing through Houston. Many rural folks like the Foremans came there intending to catch some of it.[11]

"Houston is spreading like a spilled bucket of water," a French journalist observed. "There is no plan. I am horrified." There were some visible consequences of Houston's unrestrained and in-equitable growth. Pilots flying into the city simply followed the "mile-wide plume of industrial haze." Buffalo Bayou, the source of Houston's previous moniker, became a dumping ground for slaughterhouses, chemical plants, and the raw sewage from an overextended treatment station. Its waters became so polluted that some Houstonians suggested that the rats might start drinking gin instead. The inadequacy of Houston's infrastructure was felt most heavily at the bottom of its socioeconomic structure. Tens of thou-sands lived in "substandard" housing without access to electricity, running water, paved streets, or clean wells. Some other dwellings stood in such bad repair that they posed safety hazards. Yet in 1940, Houston had only one public housing project, San Felipe Courts, which contained one thousand apartments, exclusively for white tenants. By the end of the decade, there were a few more projects, but they remained racially segregated, and the number of families in need—across racial groups—continued to rise. In the search for adequate and affordable housing, Foreman remembers his family moving roughly every four months: "We'd pack up quickly and go from one place to the next." But the next residence was unlikely to be much better than the last. Formerly immobilized in Marshall, they could not stop moving around the Fifth Ward.[12]

Other cities combatted housing crunches with federal assistance. Houston's unwavering refusal to accept federal zoning regulations, however, quashed that option. "One thing about Houstonians is that very few of them fit a pattern," the *Houston Post*'s George Fuermann wrote in 1951. "Unless individualism is a pattern." Ironically, the same folks who courted millions of dollars in defense contracts from the federal government during the late 1930s and early 1940s were vehemently opposed to accepting money from Washington for urban renewal after the war. And yet in the mid-1950s, they aggressively lobbied for funding to build new highways as part of President Eisenhower's interstate system. The construction of I-45 and I-10 allowed more people and products to move in and out of Houston faster and more efficiently. But as they slashed through the Third, Fourth, and Fifth Wards, effectively walling these neighborhoods off from one another, the new interstates limited the movement of Houstonians living in those areas. They contributed to the evolution of "second ghettoes"—most notoriously, the "Bloody Fifth"—and despite their value to local businesses, many of the poorest residents saw them as roads to nowhere.[13]

In 1900, more than 80 percent of the African American population in Texas lived in rural areas like Harrison and Shelby Counties. When Nancy Foreman and her children got off the train in the middle of 1949, however, 65 percent of black Texans lived in urban centers—particularly Houston. The city already boasted more than a hundred black churches, three newspapers that targeted an African American readership, close to thirty public schools for black children, and one university, Texas Southern, where they could pursue higher education. There were more black-owned businesses in Houston than in any other southern city at midcentury, and the growing African American population there deposited an estimated $7 million in local banks.

But the vibrancy of Houston's black community was largely due to necessity. Despite changes of image and income, Houston was still segregated. The Foremans added a handful to the roughly 125,000 black Houstonians, most of whom resided in the Third, Fourth, or Fifth Ward neighborhoods, which traditionally housed people of color. The last, where the Foremans settled, was a "black poverty pocket" housing approximately 45,000 people, nearly 90 percent of them African American. There were no luxury hotels or towering office buildings in that part of town, no indicators of a city where industrial products grew in value at a rate of $500 million each year, nor of the place that a *Houston Post* writer said "uses dollars as Niagara Falls uses water." The Fifth Ward did not make it into the *Time* magazine story either. Hidden behind the highly publicized success of a modern boomtown were the crowded, impoverished ghettoes of "Invisible Houston," where George Foreman grew up.[14]

Although they made the trip from Marshall on the Southern Pacific's dime—as well as occasional return trips to visit grandparents, usually without enough seats for the whole family and once requiring George to spend the entire ride in a women's restroom—they did not get much more than train tickets from the railroad. Foreman remembers that his mother might not see J.D. at all "unless she found him early on a Friday night," and little if any of his paycheck made it back to them. She cleaned houses for other families before finding more regular work as a short-order cook at the OST Café in midtown Houston. Her job required a bus ride across the city and back, augmenting an already long workday.[15]

George was always within walking distance of a school in the Fifth Ward, like Charles H. Atherton Elementary, but it might as well have been a death march. As he recalled years later, "What I remember about school is, I hated it." Most of his time there was spent "looking for a nice, quiet desk to take a nap" in a crowded classroom. Home was not much quieter. Shouts of "Mo'head" rang out as older siblings riled him up, and two younger brothers, Roy and Kenneth, were born in Houston, stretching the family's resources even thinner. There were eight mouths to feed on the low wages— about $26 a week—of a de facto single parent. On the rare occasion Nancy could smuggle a hamburger home from work, everyone got only a small bite. "All I remember about the Fifth Ward," Foreman says, "is a lot of fond memories. And a lot of hunger."[16]

Despite earning only about 25 percent of the newly determined "poverty threshold" annual income in 1959, set at $4,849 for a family of seven or more, Nancy did not qualify for "assistance" programs. She tried to apply for the programs designed to help families in need, but she had a job and was still legally married. She told Foreman: "They'd ask, 'Where's your husband?' and I wasn't gonna lie to them. Sure I had a husband. But he didn't give me anything." The available assistance programs in 1950s Houston did not account for such nuances. "They were asking personal questions," Foreman recalls, and "she was not going to deal with that." They were hardly an anomaly, since restrictive access, underfunded programs, and personal pride kept many families like them languishing in a purgatory between a living wage and public assistance: the working poor.[17]

To survive, they relied a great deal on informal, private charity. Friends who did qualify for free commodities might share their allotment if Nancy agreed to hold their place in the excruciatingly long line. Hours of waiting could earn the family some cheese, flour, or flavorless yellow cornmeal. "To this day," Foreman maintained, "I hate yellow cornmeal." But whatever came home, he said, "I'd clean it up in two days." His mother recalled an even quicker turnaround when she was able to do grocery shopping. George would wait for her on the front steps, not moving, not playing, just waiting, as she did in the commodities line. After she unloaded, he would start pillaging the refrigerator, cabinets, everything. In her later years, Nancy would tell the story to others, with her son in the room, still referring to him in the third person: "He would not leave until it was all gone. I couldn't stop him. He would not *move* until everything is gone."[18]

The pervasive hunger no doubt contributed to Foreman's negative experience in school as well as his apparent lethargy in class. But that could be kept hidden. Filling up a paper bag with his own hot air, and even going a step further to rub it in some grease, may have fooled some into believing he could afford to bring a lunch. But he literally had to wear his poverty on his sleeves, as well as on his legs and, certainly, his big feet. Old, ill-fitting, stained, or frayed clothes on top of oversized, sometimes mismatched shoes were not the outfits of a child from the burgeoning class of black professionals, or even from the solidly working-class families of longshoremen, oil riggers, nurses, or chemical plant workers—at least not anymore. His clothes, which came from donation bags, instantly marked him as poor. Worse than poor, in fact: po'. Just not officially poor enough to get any help. "One kid got free clothes and a voucher for lunch every day," he remembered. Everyone knew why kids like that had clothes and food, and they all knew precisely why kids like Foreman did not. "They had a stigma on them. I didn't care if they put *that* stigma on me." Even among those who looked like him and lived in the same undesirable part of town, he felt marginalized. Although Texas officially integrated its public schools in 1961, policies as restrictive as those for food or financial assistance limited student movement. Of 177,000 black schoolchildren in Houston, only 12 "qualified" for transfer to a previously all-white school. He could try to hide his hunger, but it was impossible to hide his poor clothes, limited vocabulary, and below-average literacy. Being taller than his classmates led to the perception that he had been held back a grade or two, and made him seem hopeless to overworked teachers.[19]

Ironically, Foreman's favorite book was a nationally reprinted early-reader anthology entitled *Roads to Everywhere*. That is, if a nearly illiterate student who disliked school could have a favorite book. At least the many illustrations of children in bucolic scenes provided a temporary escape. There were not many of those, at school or home. When he visited an aunt who had a television, he could lose himself in favorite cowboy shows such as *The Lone Ranger* or the short dramas that played on *The Loretta Young Show*. If he was near a radio during the afternoon, he would listen intently to the vivid descriptions in *The Romance of Helen Trent*—so vivid, he recalled, that other men stared at the radio, conjuring up the images behind the voices. If he passed in front of the speakers, they would yell, "Boy, get out the way!"[20]

He elongated those escapes by simply skipping school. To get away with it required the ten-year-old Foreman to engineer a route from his house that started toward school but veered from the building before he could be seen, and then detoured away from any neighbors that might notice him and report back to his mother. It brought him home well after everyone else was gone for the day, where he sneaked through a window and returned to bed. Yet he was careful to wake up in time to hop back out the same window, reverse his course almost exactly, and rejoin the mass of other students heading back home after dismissal. Playing hooky necessitated the kind of effort, thoughtfulness, and attention to detail that his teachers never saw, even when he was present. But it was also a slippery slope toward more serious offenses. Always quick to make friends in his neighborhood, despite frequently moving, Foreman fell in with a group predisposed to shoplifting. After he accompanied them a few times, it was his turn to steal. He was not very smooth or particularly fast, though, and the shopkeeper easily chased him down. Foreman learned that he did not really want to steal, and it joined a long list of things he knew he did not want to do as the 1960s started.[21]

★

His uncertainty was coupled with a general sense of fear that he felt in his house and around the neighborhood as a historic presidential election drew nigh. Although Foreman was too young to follow politics at the time, and unsure of the issues, he later clearly recalled his friends' and family's anxiety throughout a long, divisive campaign. Fears of communism, racism, and, now, Catholicism reverberated around the Fifth Ward as they did the rest of Houston and most of the country. Rumors of the consequences that the election of either candidate meant for his community heated up right through November—and beyond. Then fear and anxiety struck closer to home. Nancy contracted tuberculosis and spent the better part of the next two years in hospitals. Foreman moved in with his oldest brother, Robert Earl, whom they affectionately called "Sonny." He looked up to Sonny, who had a steady job as a mover for Wald Transfer and Storage, which enabled him to have his own place and, most importantly, a car. But widespread political uncertainty and reduced parental supervision during these formative years were unlikely to pull an almost-teenage Foreman out of the tailspin: begrudgingly walking toward school each morning, head down, unsure whether he would go to class, go back home, or get caught up in something worse.[22]

The new president, John F. Kennedy, came to Houston in 1962 with a plan to pull everyone's head up. He stood in the center of Rice University's football stadium and addressed not just the forty thousand faces in the stands but also millions more through the television cameras and radio microphones. Broadly, he implored Americans to seek out new knowledge. "We meet in an hour of challenge and change," he proclaimed, "in a decade of hope and fear, in an age of both knowledge and ignorance," his *r*'s dropping like rocket stages off a Saturn V—a sight that would become commonplace in Apollo launches half a dozen years later. "The greater our knowledge increases, the greater our ignorance unfolds." His goal was to gain public support for America's space program. He boiled down a vast transatmospheric policy to one clear goal: "put a man on the moon" by the end of the decade. That dictum echoed through the stadium, the rest of the three hundred acres that Rice occupied, and the three thousand more that the school had already donated to a toddler-age National Aeronautics and Space Administration (NASA). Foreman didn't hear any of it. He met plenty of challenge and change, had both knowledge and ignorance. But Rice University, on the opposite corner of Houston, could have been on another planet in a different galaxy. Foreman's whole universe remained the five square miles of the Fifth Ward, and the stars were pretty dim there.[23]

A glimmer of hope appeared, however, when Foreman moved to E. O. Smith Junior High School. Occupying the shell of the original Phillis Wheatley High School, which itself had filled the remains of an all-white school from the 1910s, the first incarnation of E. O. Smith did not have much. But it did have sports. Football, in particular, appealed to Foreman. And for a student struggling financially, academically, and socially, the opportunity to play, compete, and earn some recognition on the gridiron may have been the key to keeping him in school. A generation later, a student large for his age, and undeniably athletic for his size, might have been nurtured by teachers and administrators, possibly shepherded between the disparate worlds of underfunded public schools and a multibillion-dollar college sports industry. But in the Fifth Ward of the early 1960s, he was left to a roughneck coach who did not preach so much as enforce discipline, with "an almost sadistic penchant for using a paddle."[24]

Foreman was no stranger to corporal punishment, but he did not have much discipline, and no experience in organized sports. In fact, no one in Foreman's family had played organized sports before he found himself under the direction of Coach James Bryant—"Bear" to his players. Even in the loosely regulated pickup games he might play on the street or on a patch of grass off the freeway, Foreman strayed outside the lines. The future Oakland Raider Lester Hayes, a little younger than Foreman and a resident of the Fifth Ward, remembered him as "a bully per se," although Hayes was quick to dissociate himself from "guys in [Foreman's] neighborhood" who "lived off other kids' hush money." Hayes applied his "neighborhood ball" skills to the Wheatley High School team, on which he starred as a defensive end. He then became a standout linebacker for Texas A&M and eventually a Pro Bowl cornerback in the NFL. Foreman might have used athletics as his path out of the Bloody Fifth as well, but he needed more help finding the way.[25]

"Hey, George," the familiar voice of his coach pierced through the chatter after school one fall afternoon, "I see that cigarette." This was not on the field or even on the school grounds. Foreman was strolling outside a drugstore on Lyons Ave. that housed a soda fountain in back that he visited nearly every day to buy or bum some combination of soda and smokes. And there he came face-to-face with the Bear. He was speechless. The coach liked Foreman. He gave him nicknames such as "Hardnose" and "Monkeyman"—great leaps forward from "Mo'head," which he still heard at home. But he was in clear violation of a team rule against cigarettes. "When he caught someone," Foreman affirmed, "by the time he got through, the cigarette wasn't the only thing smoking." All his potential on the field would not mitigate the punishment to be meted out to "Hardnose," in a much softer region, the next time he met his coach. The sentence was never carried out, however. Not because of mercy or clemency, but because the accused failed to appear. Foreman did not return to football practice and essentially dropped out of E. O. Smith. He had been challenged; he left unchanged.[26]

By the time his mother was discharged from the hospital, Foreman already seemed like a lost cause. One cousin, herself unemployed and out of school, told him: "It doesn't matter. Nobody in this family is ever going to be anything anyway.... You may as well go back to bed." Nancy, on the other hand, went back to work. Pooling resources with her employed children, they were able to make payments on a television. Foreman could sit back and watch *The Beverly Hillbillies*, laughing at the show's rural folksiness, forgetting that he was less than fifteen years removed from a sharecropper's shotgun house and still hungry: "I was always thinking about food because there was so little of it."[27]

It might have been easier to get drunk on Lyons Ave. than full at home. Underage but oversized, George moved from delinquency to felonies, from shoplifting or throwing rocks to fighting and mugging. He could briefly escape the sights and sounds of the Bloody Fifth by watching sitcoms on TV or listening to Motown music emanating from radios. He listened to "anything that made you dance" but never really paid attention to the lyrics. When Harry Belafonte recorded a new version of an old blues riff from Huddie "Lead Belly" Ledbetter, with a young Bob Dylan on the harmonica, he should have been listening.[28]

If you ever go to Houston, boy, you'd better walk right
And you better not stagger, and you better not fight

Bason and Brock will arrest you
Payton and Boone'll take you down
The judge will sentence you
And you Sugarland bound.

Ledbetter had not, in fact, been arrested in Houston. The murder for which he served time occurred in De Kalb, three hundred miles north. But while in the charge of the state penal system, he wound up at the Central Unit Prison—or "Central Farm"—which peered over the town of Sugar Land for a century. During his stay, Ledbetter adapted a traditional prison song to fit the experience of many other residents at the Farm. Plenty came straight from Houston, just thirty miles away. In the 1920s, Detectives George Payton and Johnnie Boone worked parts of the city like the Bloody Fifth for Chief A.W. Brock. A visit from Payton and Boone often precipitated a not-so-great migration of black men from Houston to Sugar Land. By 1963, Foreman was headed in the same direction, fast.[29]

Nancy had not given up on her troubled middle son. She made a last-ditch effort to stop the gravitational pull toward Sugar Land by launching him straight there—as a guest. Sonny obliged, packing Foreman into his "nice old Chevrolet" to "get a lesson" by visiting a cousin already doing time there. The fourteen-year-old admittedly learned something, but not exactly the message his family had intended to teach him. As the inmates came into view, he vividly remembered that in "a sea of guys" in uniform, only "one stood out." He wasn't very tall or very big, but he rose above the crowd. Surrounded by messy hair and shaggy beards, his head and face were shaved clean, reflecting all the light available in the old state prison. While everyone else was draped in oversized prisoner's garb, his fit snug around bulging muscles. In a mass of slouching, slumping bodies, he stood straight with his head held high. Foreman stared.

Then he turned to Sonny and asked who that was. "He's a slugger," the older brother drawled. "Slugger?" "Yeah, a boxer." Foreman had never seen a boxing match, but he developed a sudden fascination with the sport—or at least with its rewards, which were more than pecuniary to a fledgling teenager who had never known anything but poverty. "Of all the men in that place, he was the only one that had self-esteem." Foreman had never felt that kind of confidence. He knew immediately: "That's the man I wanted to be."[30]

★ 2 ★

Corpsman's Call

The dish pit is not exactly a cauldron where self-confidence is forged. While the slugger in Sugar Land kept his head high, George Foreman's nose was down in the sink. But since he was not going to school, he needed a job, and the easiest entry to the working world was by washing dishes at the same restaurant where his mom cooked. There, the fifteen-year-old could earn a little cash by scrubbing during the day. Just not as much as he could make at night by assaulting people on Lyons Ave. and stealing their money.[1]

For a junior high school dropout, there did not seem to be much opportunity other than low-paying work or outright thievery, either menial jobs or midnight fistfights. Like his aunts working the farm in Marshall decades earlier, Foreman was impressive to look at—well over six feet tall, his shoe size running neck and neck with his age—but that did not change his bleak circumstances. Unlike Lester Hayes, Foreman did not stay in school long enough to have a chance to excel in team sports. Despite his recent fascination with a boxer in jail, none of the punches that Foreman threw on Lyons Ave. were gloved. The fact that he might take someone's wallet after knocking him out did not exactly qualify him as a prizefighter when

29

he gathered with Sonny and coworkers from Walds one night to hear some boxing on the radio.

There was not a lot of sympathy for underdogs in the Bloody Fifth because they usually didn't last long. So when an Olympic light heavyweight challenged a true heavyweight, the "baddest" champion in a long time, the gang from Walds was probably not pulling very hard for Cassius Clay. Their coworker, on the other hand, shared a nickname with the reigning champ, Sonny Liston. And since Clay's political views had not yet become public information, no extraneous considerations distracted from the pure physicality of the contest. This was going to be a fight, though not likely a good one, but they would be listening to it anyway.[2]

For weeks the "Louisville Lip" had been poking the Bear—almost literally—while beating the drum for media attention on him and the upcoming bout. Sportswriters obliged, but the dominant narrative was one of Clay's demise. If Foreman and his friends had looked through the local papers beforehand, they would have seen that the *Houston Post* had Liston a 7–1 favorite and predicted a third-round knockout. The only question that remained for them was, as one headline put it, "Will Clay Still Talk On His Way Down?" In the end, it lasted more than twice as long as the *Post*'s prediction and resulted in a new heavyweight champion, soon to be renamed Muhammad Ali. Foreman later did not recall a clear rooting interest in the room as they listened to the blow-by-blow from Les Keiter on ABC radio, but he said, "The look on my brother's face when Sonny Liston lost" spoke volumes. A seismic shift occurred in the boxing world, shaking it out of a second "Dark Age" for heavyweight fighters, burying the International Boxing Club era in rubble, and laying a foundation for national interest, global appeal, and million-dollar purses.[3]

Foreman cashed in, too—he got hired by Wald to move furniture with his brother, earning a little more than a dollar an hour. He was on his way—not yet out of the Fifth Ward, but at least to his own place in it, and maybe into his own car. For now, he still lived in his mom's house. And he still had a nightlife. He continued drinking, fighting, and stealing. When a late night caused him to sleep through a shift at Walds, he was fired immediately. There were few second chances in the Bloody Fifth. Losing that job only deepened his dangerous cycle of stealing money to buy cheap liquor to conjure up the courage to steal again. One night he stumbled in drunk and passed out on top of his bed. He woke up the next day with nothing on him except his underwear and a pamphlet titled *I Am an Alcoholic*.[4]

Foreman hit rock bottom at the right time. He became a statistic just at the moment when such statistics mattered to policy makers. He factored into the 75 percent of black, Latino, and Chicano Texans who lived in urban centers like Houston, and he fell into the majority of that population living below the poverty line. Already out of school, Foreman was part of another majority: 70 percent of African Americans in Texas did not complete high school, and more than 90 percent would never attend college. The postwar boom left a fallout of poverty as more people lived closer together with fewer resources and even less hope for the future. But this demographic shift coincided with an ideological change that had deep roots in Texas.[5]

"Writers facing the problem of Texas find themselves foundering in generalities," John Steinbeck observed in the early 1960s. "Texas is a state of mind, Texas is an obsession. Above all, Texas is a nation in every sense of the word." In the presidential election a couple of years later, Lyndon Johnson carried almost every county in that nation within a nation, even though New Dealers like him did not typically fare well in the Lone Star State. The same election witnessed another liberal Democrat, Ralph Yarborough, narrowly retain a crucial Senate seat from a challenge by a political novice, George H. W. Bush. In both cases, the Texan nationalism that Steinbeck identified seems to have played a significant role. Johnson rode home-state support to a margin of victory that no Democrat has achieved since the birth of modern conservatism, which Johnson's opponent, Barry Goldwater, helped kick-start. Meanwhile, Yarborough framed his challenger as a "carpetbagging" northeastern émigré to Houston's oil industry. It remained uncertain, however, what this sudden progressive swing would mean for the people represented by all those statistics—let alone the ones like Foreman, who were not eligible to vote.[6]

In 1964, President Johnson announced his own moon shot, which, for people like Foreman, was much more down to earth. He intended to form a Great Society by waging a War on Poverty. Although Johnson's rhetoric may have soared over the Fifth Ward, his appointed "poverty czar," R. Sargent Shriver, clarified that the crux of this ambitious slate of programs would be subsidized job training. Even a sixteen-year-old "street corner wino" heard the message and drew the connection between better work, better pay, better housing, and a better life. Foreman walked into the local employment center to claim his free training. He was told the program accepted only adults, even though he towered over most of them. But the staff told him about another initiative for young people: the Job Corps.[7]

Johnson and Shriver considered this a domestic version of JFK's Peace Corps and wanted it to be the flagship program of their agenda. The Job Corps took young people out of urban ghettoes or rural isolation and provided basic education and paid vocational training in one of the many rural camps or urban centers sprinkled across the country. After graduating, these new "Corpsmen" could return to their community with the requisite skills and credentials for good-paying jobs as well as a check from Uncle Sam to help them get started. More Texans took advantage of the Job Corps than youth from any other state, and only California spent more on its

Job Corps programming. And that made Texas a battleground for the War on Poverty. Republicans like Bush, who rebounded from his Senate loss to win a seat in Congress, questioned spending levels; the Yale grad accused the government of spending more than a year's tuition at Harvard to train each Corpsman. Yarborough countered that spending on a more skilled workforce now would return the investment via greater tax revenue. The need for the Job Corps was even more hotly contested at a local level. Black community activists worried that large-scale government programs would take control of already scarce resources. Latino advocates feared disproportionate emphasis on ghettoes over barrios. Others, including Mrs. C. O. Wade, who wrote to both Bush and Yarborough, felt that "none of L. B. Johnson's poverty programs ... include help for needy white people." The flagship struggled through choppy waters.[8]

The complexity of these debates over who and how the Job Corps served could not be incorporated into a commercial. Celebrities— notably, the professional football superstars Johnny Unitas and Jim Brown—pitched the program on televisions across the country. Opportunity. Jobs. Free. The message permeated the rough exteriors of the Fifth Ward generally and of George Foreman specifically. He and a neighborhood friend, Roy Harrison, applied to the Job Corps together. They were both accepted, "but you gotta leave town," they were told. "No option." They were not privy to the machinations behind this condition. The complaints of folks like Mrs. Wade grew louder and threatened to undermine the Job Corps, so its director, Dr. Otis A. Singletary, began compiling demographic data and implementing a secret quota system. The closest center to Houston, in San Marcos, had too many black Corpsmen. African American applicants from the Houston area, including Foreman and Harrison, were strategically deployed to centers that looked more racially balanced or simply did not get looked at. Fort Vannoy, tucked away in the southwestern corner of Oregon, met both criteria of being integrated and invisible. It was two thousand miles farther than either had intended to move, but they both got on the airplane. Foreman remembers his mother crying as he left, but not completely from sorrow.[9]

Fort Vannoy was a world away from the Bloody Fifth, but there was something familiar about it. He had seen this before, just not in person. The pages from *Roads to Everywhere* came to life in front of him. "There were rivers!" Foreman remembered thinking as they descended into the Oregon wilderness. And more importantly, there was food: "Every problem I ever had was over. I had three meals in one day." The camp was far from perfect. It was not even complete. Foreman, like almost everyone else at Fort Vannoy, was there to learn carpentry and bricklaying, but soon discovered that this was a blend of general and on-the-job job training as they finished building the facility. Amenities were few; the camp lacked the recreational space and organized activities available at other, bigger, more established sites. Downtime could be rough, both figuratively and literally.[10]

"At home in Houston, I drank and fought," Foreman said later, but in Oregon, without access to alcohol, he "just fought." Wrestling with change and identity in a new environment, Foreman fell back on what he knew best. But it was not the same as in the Bloody Fifth, where it could seem necessary to fight for self-defense or as his source of income. "This was the least threatening place I'd ever been," he acknowledged, but he still manufactured reasons to start fights that he knew he could finish. Foreman fought everywhere from the barracks to the dining hall, using a dinner tray as a weapon if he was tired of using his fists. Even his hometown friend distanced himself from someone who seemed like a soon-to-be-former Corpsman. His actions might have been better suited for Sugar Land than Fort Vannoy, and despite reprimands from Job Corps counselors or shaming from kitchen workers whom he strategically befriended, the behavior continued. As he put it, "I wasn't fighting to live, I was living to fight."[11]

It took a "down-and-out hippie" from Tacoma to disarm the bully from the Bloody Fifth. Richard Kibble was nowhere near Foreman's size, but was well above taking his crap. When Foreman was too loud, Kibble told him to be quiet. When Foreman challenged him to a fight, Kibble simply refused. Kibble, in essence, stood up to Foreman while staying seated, and shouted him down without raising his voice. "He was so much [more] mature than me," Foreman remembered. And he should have been, since Kibble was already in his early twenties and up against the age limit for the Job Corps program. Their unlikely friendship was critical to Foreman's progress. Kibble encouraged him to not just hear music but also listen to lyrics, particularly Bob Dylan, and think about the world around him. He got Foreman to apply some of the general-education skills they practiced in the Job Corps—such as reading—when they were in the barracks. Foreman first read a book cover to cover there, and even though it was a racy romance novel, it was a gateway. Foreman started reading newspapers, magazines, and each fresh copy of the *Corpsman*, which arrived every two weeks with stories from Job Corps centers all around the country. Just as importantly, Kibble became Foreman's conduit to social interaction in a small camp where violence had been isolating him.[12]

Foreman's attempt to open up included sending some money home to his mother and asking her to send back a real LBJ-style Stetson hat. He thought wearing the hat and embracing his Texan heritage might be a conversation piece. But the "Hey, Tex!" calls it engendered only enraged Foreman. The disapproving looks and comments he got not only from Kibble but also from Mrs. Moon, who adjudicated the extra helpings in the cafeteria, started to quell his violent reactions. He began to talk instead. With Kibble as facilitator, Foreman started to loosen up and participate in the less-than-witty yet socially important banter of teenage boys from other states, some from as far away as New York. The Job Corps actively promoted a message of national unity over regional disparity. The camp invited the former bodybuilding champion Carl Hempe—the medium-height-class winner of the 1939 America's Finest Physique Contest, later renamed the Mr. America competition—to address the Corpsmen. The second-generation German immigrant and World War II veteran had moved from bodybuilding to competitive pistol shooting, and served on the Contra Costa County Sheriff's posse in California. He worked actively with the Job Corps to establish a facility in Alameda County, just below Contra Costa. Between guns, those on his biceps as well as in his holster, Hempe cut an imposing image. He met Foreman at his own level, in many ways, when he preached: "You fight because you call each other names. But you're an American. That's your name." Foreman put away the Stetson.[13]

Nationalism and fisticuffs dovetailed in a common area at Fort Vannoy when Foreman gathered around a radio with a group of young men waiting to hear the blow-by-blow of a heavyweight championship bout. Floyd Patterson had leapfrogged a host of deserving contenders to challenge Muhammad Ali, more on cultural than pugilistic grounds. After Ali joined the Nation of Islam, Patterson deemed it "unfit" for a "Black Muslim" to hold the title, and the devout Catholic sought to regain boxing's championship for (Christian) America. "I'm going to do my best to beat Clay and give the title back to the United States," he told reporters. The politico-cultural context may not have permeated the coterie of Corpsmen who wanted to consume a meaningful sporting event and also get a little taste of legalized violence. Local papers made Ali a 3–1 favorite and predicted the fight would go no more than six rounds. That it went twelve, even if they were all terribly one-sided, was a blessing for those sequestered in Fort Vannoy. The slow march toward a cer-

tain outcome left plenty of time for trash talk. Some of Foreman's
new friends jabbed him as sharply as Ali stuck Patterson when they
quipped that if he was really tough, he ought to try boxing.[14]

In another time and place, Foreman would have hit back. But
as he grappled with old habits and new experiences in Oregon, he
just absorbed the blow, for now, and considered that they were
right. He still remembered that slugger in Sugar Land. There was
no organized boxing at Fort Vannoy, but he knew from reading the
Corpsman and talking to counselors that other facilities had robust
recreational activities. In fact, the one that Carl Hempe worked
on—the Parks Job Corps Center in Pleasanton, California—had its
own magazine, *Corpsman's Call*, which touted its organized boxing
program. Current Corpsmen were permitted to request a transfer
to any of the urban centers, like Parks, where the Job Corps was
looking to boost its numbers. Only six months into his stay, Foreman felt it was time for a change. His friend and unofficial mentor,
Kibble, had lasted only four months before deciding to leave the Job
Corps, even if he could not decide whether to go home or "hitch-
hike anywhere." As 1965 drew to a close Foreman knew where his
next stop would be. He submitted his request for a transfer to Pleasanton, where he could learn electrical assembly and, more importantly, keep fighting, legally.[15]

Charles Broadus could be hard to see, but he was easy to find. The
short, stocky, gruff character closely resembled a bulldog, with a
commensurate malocclusion. Yet he cast a long shadow around
Parks—he managed elements of camp security, dining, and athletics, especially the boxing program. He had no medical training,
but everyone called him "Doc." It didn't take a full day for George
Foreman to find him. "I want to be a boxer," the nervously excited

teenager blurted out. Broadus craned his neck up to say, "You're big enough," then added, "And you're ugly enough. Come on down to the gym." By the time Foreman got around to visiting the gym, Broadus was out. He found another coach and told him about Doc's invitation, but it did not make much of an impression. Surrounded by a full complement of Corpsmen skipping rope, sparring, and shadowboxing, the coach had no time to walk a newcomer around the place. Foreman felt a blend of disappointment and relief. "I didn't want part of that anyway," he thought as he left the rec center.[16]

Broadus did not forget, however. The next time he saw Foreman, he marched right up and said, "Hey, I thought I told you to come down to the gym." Caught off guard, Foreman mumbled an explanation. Doc cut through it and set a time to meet. He stoically monitored Foreman's first clumsy attempts at hitting a bag and punching air. He did not seem very impressed by what he saw, and yet he wanted to see some more—live. Two weeks into his time at Parks, Foreman found himself face-to-face with another Corpsman and actively encouraged to fight him. In his excitement, Foreman told everyone he knew to come down and see his first tilt in the ring. Even his hometown friend Roy Harrison, who had transferred to Parks for its welding program, came to watch. As Foreman threw awkward punches, slipped all over the mat, and ate up jabs every time he tried to inch closer, he could hear them all laughing. Harrison, trying not to further bruise his friend's ego, pretended he hadn't seen the debacle that appeared to be the first and last boxing match fought by George Edward Foreman.[17]

Foreman might have retired after that, but Broadus, a veteran of more than a hundred amateur bouts and a short professional stint, was not done. He tracked Foreman down and started barking: "Why haven't you been down?" He answered his own question with another: "Scared?" Foreman, surprised again by Doc's pointed interrogations, grasped for excuses and pulled one from his childhood: "I don't have any shoes." Doc told him to sit and wait, and Foreman did not move. In a matter of minutes, he returned with a brand-new pair of canvas shoes—a matching pair that fit his huge feet. He was out of excuses and back in the gym.[18]

Working with Broadus on the fundamentals of boxing became another regular part of Foreman's life at Parks, alongside taking remedial academic courses for a GED and learning the basics of electrical assembly. He seemed more inclined to apply the lessons from class—he eventually built a small transistor radio—than those from the gym. Every time Broadus offered up live competition, Foreman demurred. Instead, he engaged in the kinds of fights he knew how to win. He challenged Corpsmen for allegedly stealing things from him or just for offending his honor. But these attacks did not occur in the darkness of Lyons Ave. or the isolation of Fort Vannoy. Now he was one of roughly two thousand Corpsmen, living alongside a huge staff of teachers, coaches, and counselors—many of whom, including Broadus, were military veterans. The lights were always on at Parks, and nothing stayed a secret. Police visited, Litton industries asked questions, and the administration intervened. Foreman's place in the Job Corps hung in the balance. He had few advocates, but Broadus may have been chief among them. And Doc had a habit of getting his way. After some deliberation, officials gave Foreman one last chance to remain in the Job Corps, on the condition that he work out in the boxing gym every day.[19]

Doc got what he wanted. His protégé now had to spend plenty of time boxing. Getting Foreman over the hump of evading live competition, however, did not come easily. When Parks hosted a boxing tournament in April, an invitational mainly for Corpsmen from Parks and the Alder Springs Center in Glenn County, northwest of Sacramento, Foreman hesitated. Broadus insisted that he compete in the tournament and signed him up, but Foreman never showed;

neither did any other heavyweights. Broadus made sure that Foreman knew he would have won his division and received a trophy just for walking in the gym. When Parks sponsored the "Diamond Belt Tournament" in January 1967, Foreman arrived to collect his prize. This time, however, another heavyweight showed up. Foreman would have to earn this trophy. Recent matches at Parks had exposed how much the teenager still had to learn. "I was so mad," he remembered, after realizing that he needed to get back in the ring. But he directed the anger toward his opponent and knocked out an unprepared Marion Jones in the first round. The accolades were addictive, and Broadus had carte blanche to enter Foreman in more tournaments. He did not waste any time.[20]

A couple of weeks later, they were at the Winterland Ballroom in San Francisco for the Golden Gloves regional tournament. One month removed from his eighteenth birthday, Foreman qualified for the junior division. As in other tournaments, the heavyweight field was short—particularly in a three-division setting—and Foreman's decision victory over Bob Winter let him waltz out of the Winterland as the junior champion. The next week, Broadus entered him in the open division of the regional Golden Gloves tournament in Las Vegas. Once again, Foreman bested his heavyweight opponent, Thomas Cook. He won three consecutive tournaments in 1967, and only a year after his introduction to boxing, he had a ticket punched for one of its most prestigious amateur tournaments: the National Golden Gloves.[21]

The pace would have been dizzying for anyone except, perhaps, an eighteen-year-old in the eye of the storm. Foreman wrapped up the Las Vegas regionals on February 23; contestants for the national tournament were expected to arrive in Milwaukee on the next day, ready for weigh-ins, physical exams, and the first round of action on February 25. A delayed start for the heavyweight division and a first-round bye for Foreman may have appeared fortunate—or it might have undercut his momentum. Winning three tournaments in one month had left little time to think. Now he had a little too much time, surrounded by more than three hundred boxers from thirty-one cities across twenty-two states. When he finally climbed back in the ring on Monday night, the pent-up energy released in his punches far exceeded the absorption capacity of his canvas shoes. On the fading rosin of a well-used ring, he stumbled all over the place. Thomas Gamble, representing Salt Lake City, patiently bobbed and weaved through the long, slow misfires, occasionally tagging Foreman but generally letting his undisciplined opponent beat himself. Another slip, with assistance from Gamble, was ruled a knockdown. If there were any questions about the scoring, that appeared to answer them, and the judges awarded Gamble the decision.[22]

All the Las Vegas fighters that Foreman traveled with lost in the early rounds except for the welterweight Jesse Lopez. Because Lopez made it to the finals, held on Wednesday night, Foreman and the rest of the team had to stay for the duration of the tournament. Although Lopez got outpointed in his 147-pound championship bout, Foreman focused on the heavyweight ring, where a big Californian named Clay Hodges held court. As tall as Foreman but infinitely more mature, Hodges could move, box, and pack a punch. When Foreman lost to Gamble, he recognized the difference between a boxer and a puncher. Hodges took on Gamble in the finals and systemically dismantled him, winning by knockout in the second round. "I wanted to be a street fighter, not a boxer," Foreman said. Seeing a real boxer in the ring only confirmed that. He returned to Parks with his regional Golden Gloves trophies, but he was already looking past the gym and the Job Corps.[23]

Broadus always thought ahead, but he was gazing in the opposite direction. Not long after the 1967 amateur-boxing championship circuit concluded, recruiters from the air force descended on

Parks, looking for its promising heavyweight. Like other branches of the armed services, the air force had a strong presence in amateur boxing. Seventeen of the contestants in the Las Vegas Golden Gloves came directly from Hamilton Air Force Base, which tied for the team championship. Foreman had no specific qualms about military service—many of his friends from home and the Job Corps enlisted or received their draft notices around the same time. He would have considered signing up, but Broadus, a former air force sergeant, would not hear of it. "He knew them all by name," Foreman remembered, but to his surprise, Doc called them many different ones; "Broadus caught them half-way and cussed them out and drove them away."[24]

Doc believed in the military, just not for Foreman. He drove Foreman to Oakland to take the induction tests, rather than to suburban Pleasanton, because he thought that doing so would decrease his chances of being drafted. Sure enough, after a physical exam, the officers "came back looking like they felt sorry for" him and classified him "lower than 1-A." He never heard from the Selective Service again. It was part of Doc's plan. The Job Corps might have been Foreman's ticket out of the Bloody Fifth, and now Foreman appeared to be Broadus's ticket out of the Job Corps. And he would not let anyone—military or civilian—take that chance away.[25]

The only thing obstructing Doc's plan for Foreman was, in fact, Foreman. His blueprint never changed. After two years in Job Corps, he had gained the basic education he had avoided in Houston, received technical training in electrical assembly, and had a few boxing trophies to brag about. He could return home, get a job, find his own place, and maybe buy a car; he could hold his head high, like the slugger from Sugar Land. Broadus envisioned a long journey together, but Foreman already had one foot out the door. Broadus made a last, desperate plea to keep him in California. He had backers that he said would cover expenses and pay a salary if Fore-man turned pro. This was the model that a group of businessmen in Louisville, Kentucky, had used to launch the career of Cassius Clay, and a Philadelphia conglomerate incorporated as Cloverlay had a similar relationship with Joe Frazier. Foreman didn't buy it. "Or," Broadus added, "if you want to go to the Olympics, we'll work on that." Doing the same thing for no money was even less appealing. They could not see eye-to-eye on the future, so Foreman decided not to see him at all. He signed his graduation papers, collected his $1,200 "readjustment allowance," and left Parks without even say-ing good-bye to Broadus.[26]

Before George Foreman's triumphant return, however, a more fa-mous boxer had moved to Houston. The heavyweight champion Muhammad Ali became a resident in February as he prepared to face off against Ernie Terrell in his second consecutive bout at the Astrodome. "I'm a Texan now, so saddle up my horse and git my gun," he hollered to the press corps. Ali's draft status had been re-classified to 1-A in 1966, and eventually he was "summoned" for induction into the armed services. That is why he reported to the Armed Services Examining and Entrance Center on San Jacinto Street, in downtown Houston, on April 28, 1967, and made one of the biggest steps no one ever took. He restated a conscientious objection to serving in the military. Charged with draft evasion, he began preparing for a trial in the Houston courts, but the New York State Athletic Commission did not wait for the justice system. Within the hour, the commission's chairman, Eddie Dooley, or-dered press releases to confirm it had suspended his boxing license in New York, precipitating similar declarations from most of the significant governing bodies in professional boxing. At perhaps the prime of his career, Ali lost his job. He picked up speaking engagements, particularly at college campuses, for some cash as he navigated his first real experience with unemployment in America.[27]

Foreman shared that experience during the summer of 1967. "I think it was discrimination," he told a reporter, "but I can't prove it." He recognized the addition of equal-employment-opportunity notices in job ads and knew they meant employers "had to accept any applicants." But it became apparent that in fact employers did not have to hire any of them. Across town, Allen Matusow, a history professor at Rice and critic of the War on Poverty, acknowledged that the Job Corps deserved "ever-lasting credit" for taking in those "from a clientele that nearly every other institution in America had abandoned." Yet the data suggested that "only a minority emerged notably more employable," and six months after graduation, less than 30 percent had found work related to their training, and another 30 percent did not work at all. That disparity, combined with a shortage of seasonal jobs that year, led the *Texas Observer* to report that many of those who needed help most "say they haven't even heard of a poverty war."[28]

Although Foreman was "oblivious" to Ali's presence in Houston at the time, his brother pointed out the posters advertising a "succession tournament" for the now-vacant heavyweight crown. Daydreams of recovering his brief glory in the ring blunted the frustration of not working. So, too, did alcohol—something that had been unavailable to him in Oregon or California but proved easy to find back on Lyons Ave. It fermented in a cocktail of rage that spilled over into late-night brawls. While Ali faced indictment by a federal grand jury and later stood trial in a Houston courtroom for refusing to fight, Foreman reported to the police station to answer charges for assault. In less than twenty minutes, an all-white jury convicted Ali of violating Selective Service laws (a fact he never contested), and Judge Joe Ingraham meted out the maximum penalty the same day. Ali posted bail to keep out of prison. Foreman did the same on a much smaller scale, paying a $100 fine so that he could avoid jail time. Both remained technically free but increasingly trapped.[29]

Nancy Foreman knew it, too. In fact, with George's readjustment allowance having already evaporated and no new source of income in sight, his mom had to pay his fine at the police station. When his old boxing coach from California called to check on his favorite pupil, who had left without saying good-bye, she did not mince any words. "Mr. Broadus, can you help my son?" she asked. "Please. Take him and do something with him. Just get him out of here." Broadus cashed his paycheck to buy Foreman a one-way airplane ticket from Houston to Oakland. Nancy, for the second time, cried with mixed emotions as her son escaped the Bloody Fifth.[30]

California had its fair share of traps for a poor black teenager with a history of violence. Watts had erupted in riots during the summer of 1965, and in the next few years street gangs like the Crips and their rivals, the Bloods, germinated in the high schools and housing projects around Los Angeles. In the Bay Area, the Black Panther Party for Self-Defense organized in Oakland and brought firearms to the state capitol in Sacramento. Meanwhile, student-athletes in San Jose considered agitating for change by refusing to compete. Such forms of protest attracted many kinds of Americans who felt frustrated and powerless in the 1960s, and these currents of dissatisfaction and anger swirled around the Parks Job Corps Center in Pleasanton, to which Broadus hastily drove Foreman.[31]

Broadus immediately unveiled a new plan to keep them both happy. Rather than throwing Foreman into the world of private backers and professional fights, Broadus offered a compromise. He leveraged his role in dining services to get Foreman a job in the kitchen. After all, Foreman had experience with washing dishes. But in his off hours, he would be at the gym. They had until the end of the year to finish a crash course before the next Golden Gloves tournaments kicked off. In 1968, the goal was bigger than a trophy: amateur boxing champions got a shot at making the United States Olympic boxing team. Broadus intended to get this raw, undisciplined, and inexperienced teenager into the Summer Games in Mexico City. Foreman went along for the ride. He earned about the same as he might have at the OST Café, but he had a purpose at Parks. He mopped the floors "for fun." Although he was still in the dish pit, his future looked brighter than ever.[32]

★ 3 ★
God Bless the Puncher

Foreman progressed from being a client of the Office of Economic Opportunity to being an employee, from a beneficiary of the War on Poverty to one of its foot soldiers. For two years, "big" liberal government had worked for him and now, in 1967, he worked for it. This experience instilled a fierce loyalty to not only the fellow Texan pushing these programs from the White House but also the institution of government generally, and the traditional nation-state as well. Working among so many former service members at Parks buttressed these feelings. Only one thing frustrated him: "not enough time to train."[1]

Maybe Broadus forgot just how raw Foreman was in the ring. Perhaps they both underestimated how much energy a full day in the kitchen could drain out of an eighteen-year-old. Regardless, it became very apparent very fast that a few hours before or after work would not be enough time to turn a street fighter into an Olympian. Doc stepped in. Foreman earned a promotion to "avocation in-structor." It came with a pay increase—up to $63 biweekly—as well as a private room in the bachelor's quarters and, of course, all the food he could eat. His primary responsibility became opening and closing recreational facilities. The hours in between were his own. Or more accurately, they belonged to Broadus. Foreman still faced a lot of obstacles to making the Olympics. He had not yet reached his full height, let alone filled out his growing frame, and he had only a handful of bouts under his belt. He would be one of the youngest boxers vying for a spot on the Olympic team, and possibly the least experienced.[2]

Doc sought to bridge the experience gap by calling up some old connections in the Bay Area fight game. Dick Sadler managed a stable of fighters out of Hayward, about a twenty-minute jaunt down I-580 from Parks. To showcase them, he worked closely with the Oakland promoter Henry C. Winston—who typically included the middle initial when he bellowed his name—and Winston's matchmaker-*cum*-publicist, Bill Caplan. In 1967, Sadler had not only managed the California state welterweight champion Charlie Shipes, a contender for a world title, but also Sonny Liston's campaign to regain the heavyweight championship he lost to the now-exiled Ali. Sadler and Winston could get Foreman some real experience, real fast.[3]

It didn't get much more real than taking shots from Sonny Liston. Foreman was a big, young, mobile heavyweight who insisted on working for free as a sparring partner for the former heavyweight champion. Winston and Sadler offered him five dollars at the end of a sparring session, but Foreman, as part of his Olympic preparation, had read a biography of Jim Thorpe. It made him paranoid about taking cash or anything else that might jeopardize his amateur status. So he absorbed the beatings for free—almost. He gave a few good shots to the Bear and even staggered him once. Winston boomed, "If this was a championship fight, you'd be the champion of the world!" Foreman was getting stronger, smarter, and more confident, but he was still—like most rational human beings—afraid of Liston. He thought, "Please shut up."[4]

Foreman's performance as a sparring partner impressed Winston and Sadler enough that they maneuvered to put him on a pro card as soon as possible. They wanted first dibs on the promising young fighter. The fight would not affect his amateur status, because California allowed promoters to tack amateur bouts onto professional events as long as they were in accordance with the state's amateur rules and preceded an intermission. Shipes was already booked for a Winston promotion in Oakland at the end of January, and now Foreman, a Houston transplant with hardly any competitive fights to his name, was being marketed as "local heavyweight sensation" in his first taste of prizefighting—as long as they could find him an opponent.[5]

Sadler went out and booked a champion. The reigning National Golden Gloves champion, in fact. Foreman and Broadus remembered Clay Hodges from Milwaukee, where they saw firsthand his long reach and the "stinging" left jabs that he could punctuate with hard right straights if you gave him an opening. Hodges had been a fixture in West Coast amateur circles since 1964, when he won the Olympic trials for the western region and set his sights on the Tokyo games. Looking up at him, however, was a short, stocky powerhouse named Joe Frazier. Before they were through, Frazier was looking down at a prostrate Hodges. Although Frazier lost the finale to Buster Mathis, an injury paved the way for him to represent the United States in Tokyo and take home the gold medal. At the turn of 1968, Frazier and Mathis were about to face off for the world heavyweight championship. Hodges had had years to ruminate over his last, lost opportunity. He seemed a strong favorite to compete for that Olympic heavyweight spot this year, if no more Joe Fraziers were lying in wait.[6]

Hodges, a law student at Long Beach State and a reserve in the National Guard, downplayed the idea of a professional career, despite his mounting success in amateur rings: "My big goal is to make the Olympics," he told reporters directly after winning the 1967 Golden Gloves. Foreman had shared that goal with him for only a few months. As they prepared to meet, in a prelude to the 1968 amateur tournaments and Olympic trials, Foreman got distracted. Some of his coworkers at Parks were protesting unfair hiring and advancement practices, and he decided to join them on the picket line before heading into Oakland. They were now friends and colleagues, rather than rivals or targets, and he later recalled them telling him to go. He could be a source of pride for Parks; they might read about him in the center's newsletter, the *Corpsman's Call*. He wanted to be supportive as long as he could, especially since rumors swirled about Job Corps centers being closed because of cuts in the federal budget. He nonetheless left to kick off his Olympic campaign. At Parks, the scene escalated to violence on the picket line and fires being set in the barracks, but Foreman was gone by then.[7]

Broadus and Foreman knew that Hodges could dish it out, but from their brief glimpse the previous year, they did not know whether he could take it. They intended to find out. When the bell rang, Foreman threw a "blizzard" of punches and sent Hodges to the canvas while bringing the spectators to their feet. Hodges got up at the count of five, and the crowd remained standing. Only Foreman began to tire. Hodges hit his stride, picking apart a wilting opponent. Foreman could not answer: "I couldn't hold my head up." Bill Caplan, working as Winston's ring announcer, declared Hodges the winner in a unanimous decision. Foreman came to a realization: "He could outbox me every day of the week!" In late 1967, he had stood toe-to-toe with a former champion of the world; now he could not keep up with a good amateur.[8]

There was a clear path to the Olympics for any amateur boxer that year. Berths in the US Olympic Boxing Team Trials, scheduled for early September, went to winners of the National Golden Gloves tournament and the Amateur Athletic Union (AAU) tournament.

Contestants could secure a place in one or both of those two national tournaments in the spring by winning a regional tournament. But the regionals started soon. Foreman's loss to Hodges was just another course in his fast-tracked vocational education in boxing. He did not have much time to study before the next exam: the San Francisco Golden Gloves.

It could have been a replay. Foreman had won the junior division of the same tournament the previous year by defeating the one other heavyweight in attendance. This year, entered in the senior division, only L. C. Brown stood in his way—but not for long. Foreman won in a "spectacular" knockout and looked ahead to the national tournament. Doc had a narrower field of vision. Just as before, he shepherded Foreman to the Las Vegas Golden Gloves directly after the San Francisco version. More than a hundred fighters representing five states converged on the Las Vegas Convention Center. Just one mattered to Foreman: Clay Hodges. Fresh off an upset loss to Herman "Bunky" Akins at the Golden Gloves regional in Los Angeles, Hodges needed to win in Vegas in order to continue toward the Olympics. Tom Diskin of the *Las Vegas Sun* anticipated their potential meeting as the tournament kicked off, and he did not have to wait long to see it: Foreman drew Hodges in the first round. Their fight looked eerily familiar. Foreman came out strong and knocked Hodges down. Hodges waited until the referee counted to five, and then hopped up. Foreman tired; Hodges became energized. By the end of three rounds, Hodges had proved to be the better boxer again. He went on to win the tournament. For the second time in six weeks, Foreman took a long trip back to Pleasanton with the imprint of Clay Hodges's fist on his face.[9]

The second defeat in three matches cast a pall over Foreman's upcoming trip to Maumee, Ohio, for the National AAU tournament. The USOB would take only one heavyweight, and Hodges clearly had Foreman's number. A self-acknowledged slow starter, he took

Foreman's best shot in the first round of both meetings before coming to life, as he said later: "When I got up from the knockdowns
and showed him I wouldn't quit, all the fire seemed to leave him." If
the bout had gone another round or two, Hodges was pretty sure he
would have knocked out the exhausted Foreman. "I beat him like an
ugly sister," he remembered. And Foreman knew it. To make matters worse, Hodges would not be defending his title at the National
Golden Gloves tournament in Salt Lake City, which commenced
the week after their meeting in Vegas. Instead, a twenty-four-year-
old marine named Al Wilson tore through the competition to earn
the first berth in the USOB Team Trials. If Hodges was going to
make the Olympics, which he called "the ultimate in sports activ-
ity," he would have to win the AAU. As Foreman prepared to travel
two thousand miles to Ohio, he was afraid that it would look the
same as it had in Oakland or Vegas when he squared off against
Hodges for a third time.[10]

From the moment he entered the Lucas County Recreation Center, in the suburbs of Toledo, Foreman scoured the faces of more
than two hundred boxers, looking for his nemesis. Hodges was hard
to miss, but Foreman could not find him. He looked some more. He
asked around: "Hodges here?" He wasn't. Someone told him that
Hodges's reserve unit of the National Guard was on duty the last
weekend of March, and so he could not make it to the tournament.
Regardless of the reason for Hodges's absence, and the end of his
Olympic dream, Foreman's path to the USOB Team Trials looked
much clearer. He thought, "I can win this thing."[11]

In actuality, Hodges was not indestructible. The surprising loss
to Bunky Akins in February was not an aberration. Before winning
the Western Regional qualifier to make the 1964 USOB Team Trials, in which he lost to Frazier, Hodges got knocked out in the first
round of a match against Al Wilson—the same marine who had already qualified for the 1968 USOB trials. Even after coming up short

against Joe Frazier in 1964 and losing a contestable decision versus Jerry Quarry in 1965, Hodges had his fair share of slipups. In 1966, already established as one of the best amateur heavyweights in the country and a "prime favorite" to win that year's National Golden Gloves, Hodges suffered a second-round TKO against James Howard in the finals and also lost to a little-known Italian, Giorgio Bambino, in an exhibition match. Despite winning the 1967 National Golden Gloves, the twenty-three-year-old was eliminated from the AAU tournament by seventeen-year-old Forest Ward. Hodges's style, length, and experience gave Foreman a lot of trouble in 1968. But his absence gave Foreman a decisive psychological boost on the eve of the AAU tournament.[12]

Riding a wave of new confidence, Foreman crashed the heavyweight division from top to bottom. He started with the tournament's biggest contender, six-four 256-pound "Bobo" Renfrew, and left him "bloody and groggy" after a third-round TKO. Then he moved onto Billy Thompson of Joliet, Illinois, and knocked him out in the first. For his finale, Foreman beat the shortest heavyweight, five-ten Henry Crump, by decision. What he lacked in skill or experience, he made up for in power and determination. Hodges remembered Foreman as uniquely strong, noting, "He swung from the floor.... When he caught you on the arms, it moved you back." In Maumee, he added a relentlessness that overwhelmed all his opponents effectively, even if not aesthetically.[13]

"We got a couple of good exciting fighters down there," one friend in Ohio wrote to a former Golden Gloves champion, Emmanuel Steward. Although he had left the ring to work as an electrician for Edison in Detroit, Steward still liked to talk boxing. His friend passed along information about amateurs such as "that kid named Al Jones," a Detroit native whom Steward knew. Also, "a real sharp boxer named Ronnie Harris," who, en route to his third straight AAU title, was a strong favorite to compete at the Olympics.

"But the funniest thing," according to Steward's correspondent, "is we got a big clumsy heavyweight kid, I think from the Job Corps. He will miss a punch, spin all the way around, and still hit the guy with the punch. He's falling all over the place, but he's winning the fights." Steward had to see that for himself. He drove down to catch the end of the tournament. After watching Foreman decision Crump and take home the AAU trophy as well as the Olympic tryout that came with it, the future Hall of Fame trainer concluded: "No skills at all."[14]

"I just listen to my trainers," Foreman told the *Toledo Blade*. "I haven't been in this game very long." Before the USOB Team Trials, scheduled for early September, he needed to improve. In Foreman's case that meant more fights. Two weeks after winning the AAU, he was scheduled to appear on an amateur card in Los Angeles against, yet again, Clay Hodges, and Dick Sadler wanted him to spar with Liston some more as he ramped up his chase for Joe Frazier's title. But as one of the eighty-eight boxers competing for a spot on the Olympic team, Foreman was property of the USOB. The organization wanted him to get not just more amateur fights but also some international experience if he were to have any hope of making the team, let alone winning a match in Mexico City. Hodges, who subsequently lost in the western regional Olympic-qualifying tournament, retired from amateur boxing and left law school for law enforcement. Instead of representing his country at the Olympics, he represented his precinct at the "Police Olympics" in Los Angeles that year.[15]

Foreman was the lone American heavyweight sent to West Germany for a match. He did not impress officials from either country as he once again slipped all over the ring while throwing wild punches that rarely hit their target and too many times landed, illegally, on the back of the head. His opponent, Dieter Renz, sat back in a low crouch and let Foreman disqualify himself. Foreman developed an awareness of the politics of international competition, believing that international rules and referees "cheated" American fighters. But, he later admitted, he did not learn a thing about boxing during the trip: "All I could do was punch."[16]

In some instances, pure punching could be enough to win. In fact, before Broadus and Foreman's odyssey began, Doc predicted, "[Foreman will] stop everybody in sight because he's a natural. God bless the puncher!" While that may have been true for prizefighters, it became clearer that international amateur boxing—particularly in a high-altitude location like Mexico City—favored those with more skill and stamina. Fortunately, the USOB Team Trials took place closer to home, and relatively close to sea level, back at the Lucas County Recreation Center in Maumee. Foreman entered the place with a little more confidence this time, since there was no chance of meeting Clay Hodges. But the winner of the tournament that sent Hodges home, Stoney Land, would be the first hurdle on the last leg of his dash to the Olympics. Foreman won a decision but did not win over skeptics. His next match, against the all-army champion, Otis Evans, would be a significant test. Evans matched Foreman in size and strength and had the benefit of experience—a veteran of almost a hundred fights as well as military-issue conditioning. They traded blows through two rounds, and the Associated Press report had Evans winning on points as the bout drew to a close. With only fifteen seconds left, Foreman landed a thunderous uppercut that floored Evans and won the fight. He was out of breath, and he didn't have time to celebrate. Al Wilson waited for him in the final.[17]

Wilson had nearly qualified for the Olympic team in 1964, and had knocked out Clay Hodges in the process. He had boxed consistently on marine bases from the Carolinas to Hawaii since then, regularly appearing in the interservice championships. In 1968, he flew through the National Golden Gloves tournament and did the same in the first two rounds of the Olympic trials. Foreman said that his family did not really believe he was a boxer until they saw this fight on ABC. Some who watched might not have called him a boxer either. He grabbed, pushed, and pulled Wilson as much as the referee would allow while continually slipping in worn canvas shoes over thinning rosin. God bless the puncher. In the second round, one of Foreman's wild swings soared over Wilson's head, but the follow-through knocked him over. It was ruled a slip, but Wilson looked shaken. Gravity seemed to pull everything from his headgear to his hands a little farther down. Foreman, growing either savvier or just more tired, exercised some patience. He maneuvered Wilson into a corner, and when he couldn't land a clean punch, just leaned on him instead. Wilson broke free, but Foreman marshaled him into another corner and hammered him with a right to the gut, quickly followed by a left hook flush to the head. A second left sent Wilson down directly into a right uppercut already in motion. There was no need for a count because Wilson was not getting up; his Olympic aspirations stayed with him on the canvas. Foreman moved one step closer to Mexico City: the USOB training camp in New Mexico.[18]

The games' opening ceremonies were only one month away, but the USOB was not ready to commit to a slate of boxers. It brought twenty-five of them to Santa Fe for two weeks of training before holding a series of "box-offs" that would determine the team's representative in each of the eleven weight classes. To challenge Foreman, they chose Otis Evans. After all, he had been beating Foreman in Maumee until one lucky punch caught him just before the final bell. Moreover, Evans was an active-duty soldier, and there was definite appeal to having service members compete and, even better, win on the international stage during the Vietnam era. After two weeks of roadwork, instruction, and sparring at St. John's College and the New Mexico School for the Deaf, the boxers got ready to face off in the decisive matches in Albuquerque. Although the USOB hadn't committed to that either. On the eve of the finals there remained uncertainty over just how "final" the upcoming bouts would be. Perhaps if a Team Trials winner from Maumee lost a box-off in Albuquerque, he would get a rematch in Santa Fe; maybe it would turn into a best-of-three series; or the team might be decided by the coaches after they looked at the cumulative performances. Not even the boxers knew what would happen after the box-offs. But Evans knew it was his last chance to get off an army base and into the Olympics. He would not let his guard down at the end of the fight again. Foreman knew he had to win decisively to offset any favoritism; he couldn't wait until the last round. In the first, he threw the same uppercut that had KO'd Evans in Maumee. It knocked Evans down, but this time he got up. Like Clay Hodges, he took Foreman's best shot early and came back swinging. But this time Foreman did not punch himself out by trying to finish the job. He and Evans, as in their first meeting, traded heavy blows back and forth over two more fairly even rounds. In the end, the early knockdown made the difference, and Foreman—like all the Team Trials winners—won his box-off by decision and cemented his place on the squad for the Nineteenth Olympiad.[19]

Foreman was not only a little more experienced when he won a spot on the USOB team, but also under new direction. The team's assistant coach, Raymond Rogers, a marine drill sergeant, provided him close technical instruction, since sparring opportunities were limited—no one in camp was near his size. In particular, Rogers emphasized the left jab to set up everything else in Foreman's powerful arsenal. The head coach, Robert "Pappy" Gault, another former marine, took care of the inspiration. The first black head coach in USOB history, Gault peered down over a large gold medallion that read "Sock It To Me" and performed two primary responsibilities, Foreman recalled: "cuss and motivate." Probably in that order. He paid significant attention to physical conditioning, running the boxers all through the New Mexico hills to build up their stamina and get them acclimated to the thinner air at high altitudes (Mexico City is 7,382 feet, or 1.4 miles, above sea level). He paired that with mental conditioning, drilling into them the nuances of international boxing after running them to exhaustion. Gault declared: "The boys from foreign countries don't have us abilitywise. They have us gentleman wise. We've gotten beat on the rules. . . . They say the foreigners are cheating us. We're cheating ourselves." He refused to believe the popular perception of his team as an underdog in the Olympics—even Al Jones felt that most observers considered the boxers "one of the weaker teams"—yet Gault predicted that his eleven fighters would win as many as seven medals. He challenged them to follow his lead. He told a reporter from a black newspaper, "My fighters believe in me. They do what I say."[20]

Gault was uniquely suited to building a team for an individual sport. He had the "skills of getting everyone together and making them feel important," Foreman noted. He could connect with them. One of the few African Americans in a position of authority on the Olympic team, he coached nine black and two Latino boxers. He could speak the "militarese" understood by servicemen, who made up more than half the group. Foreman was the youngest team member and one of the few with no military experience. He may have been the biggest impediment to Gault's team culture, especially in front of the media.[21]

Surveying the lowly regarded USOB team for one good story before it left training camp, Gil Rogin from *Sports Illustrated* gravitated toward the unheralded heavyweight, more for his personality than his boxing ability. Fighters like Al Jones (middleweight) and Ronnie Harris (lightweight), who had clearly stood out in every tournament since the AAU championships, bought into Gault's team-first philosophy and quietly trained for their moment in Mexico. Foreman was just coming out of his shell. He garnished his shadow-boxing with short verses for Rogin. "I'm a lover, a gamer, a woman tamer," he rapped. "Fight a little, talk a lot." Of course, he had been precisely the opposite for most of his nineteen years, but Rogin did not know that. Foreman feared he would not be noticed without a little showmanship, so he mimicked the best in recent memory, Muhammad Ali, and delivered pithy couplets between punches:

I can move to your right
Stick all night
Move to your left
Cause your death.

Rogin lapped it up. Much to Foreman's surprise, he became the centerpiece of Rogin's story, which featured his "proclivity for near rhymes," a feature that extended to his robe adorned with large uppercase letters: GEORGE FOREMAN, THE FIGHTING CORPS-MAN. Rogin concluded by labeling this Olympic heavyweight the "spiritual descendent of Ali."[22]

The irony of identifying with the Great Society's flagship program while parroting boxing's most outspoken critic of the American government was lost on Foreman and Rogin. It probably bothered the hell out of Gault. "Boxing is usually considered an individual sport," he barked at Rogin. "I'm trying to make it a team sport. I don't want any stars or individualists." Ali's style did not jibe with the kind of culture Gault had fashioned for his team. Moreover, someone else had already claimed and even canonized Ali in the buildup to the 1968 Olympics. Harry Edwards anointed him the "saint of this revolution," which became known as the revolt of the black athlete. Edwards, a professor and coach at San Jose State University, inspired black student-athletes to use their platform as a lever to bring about change—to boycott competitions until college administrators provided black students with equal housing, representation on student government, and appropriate academic programs, for example. The movement soon spread across the country, and black and white student-athletes withheld their services in order to challenge their institution or highlight racist policies at other schools. Ali visited many of those campuses, collecting speaking fees while unable to earn money in the ring. Foreman's only college experience came from sleeping in the St. John's dorms on the road to the Olympics.[23]

The revolt of the black athlete may never have crossed Foreman's path, since he did not attend college, but its corollary, the Olympic Project for Human Rights (OPHR), headed directly to Mexico City when he did. Edwards pivoted from domestic colleges to international sporting events, and many black amateur athletes—especially collegiate student-athletes—went with him. Rumblings that the International Olympic Committee (IOC) and its American president, Avery Brundage, planned to reinstate South Africa before the games began propelled the OPHR to push for an Olympic boycott by African American athletes. They would not compete against a nation that codified racism in its apartheid policy, or perform in events that generated revenue for the IOC if it implicitly condoned apartheid by inviting South Africa. Professional athletes such as Ali and Jim Brown supported Edwards. The best college basketball player in the country, UCLA's Lew Alcindor, refused to play for the Olympic team. More than thirty nations had already threatened to boycott the games if South Africa participated. As the pressure mounted, the OPHR issued its demands to Brundage and the IOC: ban South Africa from international competition; seat African American representatives in the United States Olympic Committee (USOC); and replace Brundage. While the IOC reversed course on South Africa, influenced not only by the OPHR but also by the other possible boycotts and some strong lobbying from Mexico to prevent any interruption to a very expensive production, the other OPHR demands were tabled until after the next

Olympics. The partial victory drove a wedge between the OPHR's constituents. To many, restoring the prohibition of South Africa was the definitive task. Edwards admitted that after news of the ban of South Africa reached the OPHR, support for the boycott fell by half. Since a fractured movement could not produce more than a fissured protest, the OPHR gave up on its goal of a total boycott. Instead, Edwards urged every successful African American athlete to perform a demonstration of protest on the podium, reducing his vision for a mass demonstration by a nation within a nation to representative protests by only the most committed athletes who were also talented enough to medal in their events.[24]

The USOB did not hear much from the OPHR. When it gathered with the rest of the US Olympic team before crossing into Mexico, the boxers had the option of hearing a variety speakers, some of whom represented the OPHR or promoted demonstrations or protests, but Foreman did not recall being approached by them—"They passed us by the way a freight train would a hobo." Yet the team heard a lot from Pappy Gault. "We are never individualists when we support the US," the coach reaffirmed, perhaps directing particular attention to the "fun-lovin'" Foreman. Even if USOB members had been interested in alternative viewpoints, they may not have gained access to them. Instead, they received warnings about the student protests in Mexico City, the threat of violence outside of the Olympic Village, and the digestive risks of drinking tap water there. When they arrived in Denver for some even higher-altitude acclimation, as well as vaccinations and visas, the boxers seemed to be exemplars of the apolitical amateurism projected by Brundage's IOC. Both areas grayed, however, before the team headed to Mexico.[25]

Foreman's first direct experience with politics came in Denver when representatives for the presidential candidate Richard Nixon sought him out and asked him to support the Republican nominee.

Though not generally interested in politics, one issue stuck with him: the Job Corps. He heard that Nixon planned to cut the Job Corps if elected, and Foreman would not support that. For him, politics remained very personal. Likewise, amateurism could be relative. An unattached teenager was not concerned about taking time off work to train for the Olympics, getting little more than food and sleeping arrangements in exchange. But his older teammates with families found it much harder. He noticed that when other boxers asked coaches or officials for some cash to send home, they usually had their requests filled—quietly. Sponsors also muddied the waters of amateurism for Olympic athletes. In Foreman's case, Adidas offered him new, rubber-soled boxing shoes. While some of his teammates demurred, either on practical or moral grounds, Foreman had a long memory of missing or mismatched shoes back home as well as of slipping all over boxing rings in the canvas shoes Doc Broadus had given him. It was "the most amazing thing," and he gladly took the free shoes. The USOC launched an investigation into whether these sporting goods companies gave athletes cash as well, but no one came for Foreman's shoes as he walked into the Olympic Village.[26]

The boxers had plenty of time to prepare before the tournament started. That gave Foreman a chance to break in his new boxing shoes and get used to the conditions in Mexico City. He did not need any time to adjust to his roommate, because he was fortunate to draw Al Jones, who had shared a room with him in Santa Fe as well as on their trip to Germany before that. But there was a fair amount of time to dwell on uncertainties and inadequacies. The high-altitude training in the United States had not prepared him for the much higher altitude of Mexico City. During workouts, he felt himself running out of air "midway through the second round." Combined with his inexperience—barely twenty legitimate fights— and the prospect of squaring off against fully matured opponents, some with more than a hundred amateur bouts under their belts, he lost some confidence. When the draw came out, it got worse. "What I feared most of all," Foreman said, "was left-handers." Foreman's first-round opponent, Lucjan Trela, represented a perfect composite of his fears.[27]

Seven years older than Foreman and a veteran of more than 140 matches, Poland's left-handed heavyweight threatened to truncate Foreman's Olympic experience. Worse, Trela fought out of the same awkward defensive crouch that Dieter Renz had used to draw Foreman into a disqualification. It was only Foreman's third time facing a southpaw in the ring. The trepidation negated any advantage his new boxing shoes might provide. Trela, on the other hand, looked comfortable with the slow-paced action, relying on short right hooks to try and score points without giving up too much room for the heavy-hitting Foreman. Restrained by memories of his disqualification in West Germany, Foreman nervously tried to find openings for his nascent left jab. They were few and far between as the bout dragged into its third round. Sensing the ticking clock, Foreman finally opened up and connected with a powerful hook that knocked Trela to the canvas. The referee ruled it a slip, however, and Foreman once more felt like the victim of an international conspiracy. He skulked back to his corner after the final bell to await the judges' verdict. To his surprise, they awarded him the split decision—perhaps taking the "slip-down" into consideration or penalizing Trela for a lack of action—and Foreman earned his first Olympic victory.[28]

The afterglow was cut short when Foreman discovered that his next opponent would be another older and more experienced fighter. His coaches insisted he come out with the jab again. And although that plan hadn't worked against Trela, in the bout with Ion Alexe of Romania, the jab landed. It hurt, too. He learned that it could do more than just score points or give him some distance from his opponent when he jabbed Alexe right off of his feet and advanced to the semifinals. Yet when he tried the same thing against Giorgio Bambini, it did not yield the same results. The wily Italian southpaw, who claimed victories against both Dieter Renz and Clay Hodges, glided in and out of Foreman's range and appeared to score at will throughout the first round. In the second, a frustrated Foreman lowered his guard and looked for a fight. Bambini pounced, landing a straight left flush on Foreman's nose and causing him to temporarily lose his senses. Then the Bloody Fifth kicked in. Foreman threw wild punches in all directions. Bambini, caught off guard, dropped his hands while dodging the haymakers. He didn't see the last one before it hit him on the jaw. Foreman regained his composure before the referee raised his arm and catapulted the puncher into the gold-medal match.[29]

Foreman's place in the finals came as a surprise to many. Even he had acknowledged at the start of the tournament that he was not the favorite to win. But Tommie Smith and John Carlos qualifying for the 200-meter sprint final was a foregone conclusion. Both were members of San Jose State's "Speed City"—which could have competed as its own country in the Olympics and landed just outside the top ten in the medal count—and they had been tested in international competition and put themselves ahead of the pack. As protégés of Harry Edwards, they were also some of the most committed members of the OPHR. When they both medaled, they made their protest from the podium. Remembered largely for the black gloves raised during the playing of the American national anthem, their symbolism went all the way down to their socks, which represented poverty. Brundage tried to make a symbol out of them. True to his warnings that protestors would be punished, he dismissed both athletes from the Olympics and stripped them of their medals immediately. Foreman sympathized with Smith and Carlos even if he was not totally sympathetic to their demonstration.

After all, his experience with poverty was more than just symbolic. Moreover, the three boxing coaches in his short career had all been servicemen. Litton Industries had even brought Doc Broadus to the finals so that all of them would be present for Foreman's gold-medal match. Rogers stuffed a miniature American flag in Foreman's pocket before he faced off against the Soviet champion, Ionas Chepulis.[30]

Chepulis was a heavy favorite. The native Lithuanian was a full decade older than his challenger, and while Foreman had enjoyed some months of easy living and heavy training at Parks, Chepulis had the support of the USSR's comprehensive athletic infrastructure. The difference was obvious in their path to the gold-medal match—Foreman won a narrow split decision over Trela and nearly succumbed to Bambino. Chepulis stopped all three of his opponents before the final bell, including his foe in the semifinal, when he knocked out hometown favorite, Joaquin Rocha, for which the Mexican fans would not forgive him. Even though the odds favored Chepulis, at least Foreman felt a certain amount of home-field advantage while being urged on by a cacophony of "Spanglish" support in the Arena México.[31]

For the thousands of spectators and millions more watching on television, the 1968 Olympic boxing heavyweight gold-medal match still evokes a powerful image—just not one from the fight. In the moment, it was less than five minutes of decidedly amateur boxing. At the bell, a nervous Foreman planted his feet in the middle of a canvas that could have been mistaken for wet sand. Chepulis cautiously circled, flicking lefts that he hoped would score points. Gault pleaded, "You've got to use the jab. Jab, jab, jab." But Foreman's big left arm did not always snap like a jab so much as linger like a battering ram. Both heavy hitters grew impatient and began to follow up with straight rights. Midway through the first round, however, they were both losing to the altitude. Backs hunched, gloves drooped, and the straights arched. As they turned to two-fisted attacks, the melee favored Foreman. Each looked tired at the break, but Chepulis was covered in his own blood.[32]

Foreman left all pretense of boxing in his corner. He came out for the second stanza looking to end the fight before he ran out of air. There were no more jabs, just long, looping haymakers from either hand. Chepulis's circles became backpedals. Less than a minute into the round, the referee, from Ghana, forced the Soviet to take a standing count. Over the next minute, Foreman launched punches that might have carried him off balance if Chepulis hadn't caught them with his face. Before the end of the round, the referee stopped the fight. Chepulis walked back to his corner, dejected; Foreman had to be directed back to his corner, exhausted. It took another full minute before the announcer proclaimed Foreman—still clutching the ropes for support—the gold medalist. He reached into his "Fighting Corpsman" robe, fumbled around the good-luck beads a girlfriend had given him, and pulled out Rogers's tiny flag, which he delicately flicked with thickly taped wrists. After catching his breath, he came back to life and began an elaborate version of the traditional bow at each corner. Foreman did not merely bow; rather, he danced in and out of a slight bend at each corner before juking his way to the next. He seemed far more concerned with his bowing than his flag-waving. But in the charged context of debates over racism and nationalism, heightened by Carlos's and Smith's demonstration three days earlier, the tiny flag became a lightning rod.[33]

★ 4 ★
Eatin' Money

"I just do my own thing," Foreman told Howard Cosell after winning the gold and waving the flag. He wanted to stay out of the storm that was billowing as the "problem Olympics" in Mexico drew to a close. But even the closing ceremonies became politicized. After accusations that rowdy athletes had disrespected officials and authorities during the closing ceremonies in 1964, the IOC voted to reinstate the regulation that each nation delegate a maximum of seven representatives to participate in the finale. The USOC moved to make Foreman one of its delegates, even though the ceremony started only hours after his final match. Instead, he went to a hotel with Litton's Barney Oldfield to call family and friends back home. They all basked in the glow of his victory and expressed their pride in the unexpected success of a "delinquent" from the Bloody Fifth. The reaction outside his family, however, was more complicated. He may have sensed that from the interview with Cosell, in which Foreman emphasized: "I am no Uncle Tom."[1]

Harry Edwards fumed that waving the flag was a "blatant political act," but the IOC and USOC celebrated Foreman, unlike Smith and Carlos, because his act was "in the interests of the establishment."

On the other hand, A. S. "Doc" Young complained that Foreman did not receive as much attention as Smith and Carlos in the aftermath of the Olympics. The *Sporting News* reprinted Edwards's statement when the book *The Revolt of the Black Athlete* came out the next year. Shortly after the Olympics, however, the same magazine published an article that piggybacked on Young's comments by bemoaning the disproportionate attention devoted to protests rather than to athletic accomplishments. Likewise, the *Los Angeles Sentinel*, a newspaper intended mainly for an African American readership, revealed divisions between its sports editor, Brad Pye, and staff sportswriters regarding the transformation of Olympic podiums to soapboxes. Pye denounced politicking at the Olympics, whereas several staff writers congratulated Smith and Carlos for their courageous stand. Across town at the *Los Angeles Times*, John Hall sided with Pye, adding, "Foreman's stand is really the majority stand."[2]

Foreman insisted that his actions were just about "identity"—not politics—but during a heated presidential election campaign, everything was political. The Office of Economic Opportunity immediately collected and disseminated a package of press clippings about Foreman and the flag to every House and Senate member as a subtle plug for its signature program, which had already borne significant cuts and had become a divisive talking point on the campaign trail. One report from St. Louis about a factory owner who decided to integrate his workforce after watching Foreman's performance made its way into President Johnson's "night reading" and the pages of *Jet* magazine several weeks later. That story did not align with the platform of George Wallace, the candidate of the American Independent Party, but the other two men vying to take Johnson's place, Hubert Humphrey and Richard Nixon, recognized the political cachet that Foreman could bring to their campaigns and promptly reached out to him for support.[3]

Although not old enough to vote, Foreman became popular with politicians. He still intended to return to Pleasanton and work at Parks while starting college and considering when, or if, to pursue a professional boxing career. Oldfield suggested hiring him to travel between Job Corps centers to build morale and generate publicity—something like an interdepartmental goodwill tour. Just days after the Olympics, the OEO created the "Job Corps Award of Achievement" and, unsurprisingly, chose Foreman as the first recipient. So deciding between Vice President Humphrey, proponent of the Great Society, and Nixon, who, Foreman heard, would terminate programs like the Job Corps if elected, was easy. He appeared at Humphrey rallies up until Election Day, stumping for the Democratic nominee, extolling the virtues of his party's antipoverty programs, and, of course, waving miniature American flags, to great applause.[4]

Nixon used Foreman's name to get applause, even without his support. He referred to the patriotic display of "a nineteen-year-old Negro boxer" at a rally at Madison Square Garden on Halloween. A week later, he rode a 1 percent margin of victory in the popular vote to win the presidency by more than a hundred electoral college votes. The following week, Foreman visited the White House to meet President Johnson. LBJ had previously declined a suggestion to invite all the American Olympic medalists—including Smith and Carlos—but he approved the request to host the first Job Corps Achievement Award winner. When they finally met for a handshake and photo op, Foreman presented the president with an award of his own, a plaque that read: "In appreciation for fathering the Job Corps program which gave young Americans like me hope, dignity, and self-respect."[5]

After the Olympics, Foreman seemed to get warm receptions everywhere. He heard cheers at Humphrey rallies and kind words from celebrities such as Chubby Checker, Lee Majors, and Gene

Barry, whom Foreman admired as the TV version of Bat Masterson. Vince Lombardi introduced himself at a restaurant in DC on the same weekend that Foreman visited the White House. Back home, however, not much had changed.[6]

His mother's place on Dan Street, just a couple of blocks up from Lyons Ave., felt crowded with siblings. Foreman wore the gold medal around his neck constantly, but it did not make the house bigger, the neighborhood nicer, or the food on the table more plentiful. The medal did not generate any income, and the social capital it provided in other places was absent in the Bloody Fifth. Elementary school kids looked up to him—literally and figuratively—when he visited the buildings that he had desperately tried to avoid at their age. Yet old friends and neighbors still looked at him sideways. He felt them glaring at him in disappointment, even disapproval. He noticed the posters of Smith and Carlos hanging in other people's houses. He wondered, "How could I protest against 'the establishment' when that establishment had created the Job Corps for guys like me?" Foreman lost interest not only in politics, but in Houston as well. When he noticed some green marks on his gold medal, he stopped at a jeweler to get it cleaned up. It wasn't dirt; the gold plating had worn off. His Olympic medal, he realized, was gilded.[7]

Solid or not, the medal attracted some new friends. Ambitious boxing trainers, managers, and promoters vied for "rights" to the potential heavyweight contender. His experience on *The Dating Game* hardly compared with the wooing he received from this carousel of suitors. Sports moguls—or at least their kids—saw that Foreman would be a great investment if they could get in on the ground floor. Jimmy Iselin, son of the New York Jets' owner Philip Iselin, dabbled in boxing and horse racing. He currently promoted Buster Mathis, and adding Foreman would make him a promotional force in the heavyweight division. He wooed Foreman and his mother by dangling cash and promising to take care of the whole family.

Locally, Fred Hofheinz, whose father had not only established a major league baseball team in Houston but also developed its signature venue, the Astrodome, made a strong pitch as well. Hofheinz partnered with one of Ali's lawyers, Bob Arum, to promote fights as well as project them on closed-circuit television. They needed a star they could put in the ring and on the screen, and Foreman's knockout potential promised that. They even offered the services of Ali's trainer, Angelo Dundee, as part of the deal. But when Dundee called him, Foreman felt he "wasn't enthusiastic enough," although that might have been one of his greatest strengths as a cornerman. Cus D'Amato, who had guided Floyd Patterson to a heavyweight championship, found many similarities between the ex-champ and this championship hopeful. Foreman's inherent skepticism would not have meshed with the Spartan-Victorian blend of the "kindly paranoiac," however. In fact, that skepticism—which Foreman credited to his Job Corps training, though it may have been well developed before he left the Bloody Fifth—inhibited him from signing with any of them. Still unsure whether he wanted to turn pro, he knew damn well he did not want to be owned.[8]

As the speculation and reports about his future gained momentum, Foreman stalled. *Ring* magazine put him on the cover and ran a feature article titled "Foreman, 19, Aspires to Success as Pro Champ," though he went back to Pleasanton, where he could earn a fair wage—plus room and board—without the pressure or the politics surrounding his Olympic afterglow. But those things crossed state lines too. Nixon kept his campaign promises about slashing antipoverty programs. The Parks Job Corps Center was one of many "country clubs for delinquents" swept away in a political sea change.[9]

With the closing of Parks, Doc Broadus put together another one of his plans. He had wanted Foreman to turn pro in 1967. And even before then, he had persuaded Foreman to sign a quasi contract making him the boxer's manager and, of course, granting him an appropriate cut of any earnings when that day came. Now Broadus latched onto the contract and prepared for Foreman's transition from amateur bouts to the prize ring. But the boxer held back. Increasingly wary of people trying to buy or claim pieces of him, and confident that a piece of paper signed by a seventeen-year-old was not exactly a legally binding document, he refused. Broadus made a last-ditch plea to retain a place in Foreman's corner, but Foreman looked down and said, "That's not gonna be."[10]

If it was going to be, it was going to be on his terms—no contracts or loans. Not many investors, promoters, or established managers would accept that kind of arrangement. But Dick Sadler was a throwback to a bygone era of boxing. His fistic lineage could be traced all the way to Jack "Doc" Kearns, the Machiavellian manager who spent nearly a decade shaping Jack Dempsey, a scrapper from the West Coast mining camps, into the heavyweight champion of the world—all without ever having a formal contract between them. When Foreman bumped into Sadler at the Oakland airport and asked about working out with him again or taking some more exhibition fights, Sadler quickly agreed. Details could be worked out later, but he recognized a rare opportunity. "Just exhibitions," Foreman emphasized. "Exhibitions," Sadler confirmed before adding some of his flare: "We'll spread your name and fame!"[11]

True to his word, Sadler welcomed Foreman into his stable with no apparent strings attached. So did Liston, who liked him as a sparring partner almost as much as he enjoyed having Foreman carry his bags. Rather than giving him a car or a place to live and then treating them as advances against future purses, thereby linking them together, Sadler helped Foreman rent an apartment within walking distance of the gym. He trained, sparred, and talked boxing all the time; he did everything like a professional except earn any money. Sadler covered his expenses, but arranged only exhibition fights for Foreman while trying to blaze Liston's trail back to the heavyweight championship. The path was not a straight line to New York City, still the center of the boxing universe, but a circuitous route around the country with stops in cities small and large, east and west, where Liston could build up his record and generate some publicity. Along the way, Foreman learned a lot more than ring tactics. Liston showed him how to dress like a champion, including regular haircuts and shoe shines. Sadler taught him how to comport himself—and hand out tips—like a champ when they ate in restaurants or stayed in hotels. Liston let Foreman read his contract, less as a teacher than a student, because he wanted someone with better literacy skills to verify that he and Sadler had agreed to a fifty-fifty split. Sadler revealed to Foreman the business of boxing as he connected with promoters—sometimes invoking his connection with Doc Kearns—to arrange the kind of fights that would get the results he wanted people to see in the next day's paper.[12]

What happened in the ring might have been sport, but turning a fighter into a champion was an art. For that, Sadler had apprenticed under one of the masters. During the Great Depression, Sadler, a "tap-dancing, piano-tinkling, one-time hobo" from Ohio, struck off for California, where he could pursue—and hopefully profit off— entertainment or boxing. They were closely related. He had worked with some boxers in Columbus and tried to make it as a professional fighter. Between 1939 and 1942, he had seven prizefights and lost all but one. As a trainer, however, he caught Doc Kearns's attention. Kearns, then managing the championship contender Archie Moore, brought Sadler into the corner. As they moved around the country, taking strategic bouts in select venues and making indelible impressions, Sadler watched and listened to two of the greatest self-promoters in the fight game. He learned boxing's twin peaks of barnstorming and ballyhoo. The man who had cast Jack Dempsey as either a hero or a villain—depending on which persona would be the most profitable—taught Sadler the importance of not just making fights but also creating characters. As Kearns got older, he traveled less; he could set fights across the country by phone, and he let Sadler take the reins. Kearns died in 1963, and soon thereafter Sadler was employing the techniques of "neo-Kearnsianism" to keep Liston's hopes alive. But the Bear was a finished work and starting to show cracks. Foreman, on the other hand, was a big brick of moldable clay.[13]

After two years of resisting the urge to get paid for throwing punches, Foreman decided, with remarkable nonchalance, to turn pro. Sadler could get him a slot on the undercard of a hotly anticipated bout between Joe Frazier and Jerry Quarry; Madison Square Garden offered a $5,000 purse. If there was a time, this was it. The Garden was firmly entrenched as the premier prizefighting venue in the world, with a pay scale reflecting its position, so any opportunity to fight there could be golden. An event like this, headlined by an interracial heavyweight championship bout, promised to fill the recently built fourth incarnation of the Garden, along with many more seats in over a hundred locations with the closed-circuit television feed. There was no better moment to debut. But there was a catch. Sadler told Foreman that their informal and unsigned agreement would not hold up in New York. He presented Foreman with a standard contract, which Foreman immediately noticed had a different division of finances from the one in Liston's agreement: only a third of Foreman's purse would go to Sadler. He agreed to turn pro, take the fight, and commit to Sadler, all at once—although he couldn't actually sign off on the deal. They had to send a copy to Houston for Nancy Foreman's signature before her son could legally climb into a prize ring.[14]

His opponent hardly mattered. This was Frazier and Quarry's show, along with a little prelude of up-and-coming contenders, including Quarry's younger brother, the light heavyweight Mike

Quarry, and the reigning Olympic heavyweight gold medalist, Foreman. The Garden, like Sadler, recognized potential and sought to cultivate stars. Fair fights did not always accomplish that. The venue's operators put more effort and emphasis on Foreman's pre-fight publicity than on his role in the ring. Teddy Brenner, MSG's matchmaker at the time, selected a former Golden Gloves light-heavyweight champion named Don Waldhelm. Reporters wrote that he "looked like a middleweight" next to Foreman. The result seemed to be a foregone conclusion. But the Garden's stalwart publicity man, John F. X. Condon, went to work. He capitalized on Foreman's Olympic image by orchestrating photo ops showing him distributing miniature American flags in front of the arena. The bet was that the pictures outside would outlast the scene inside the ring. Over sixteen thousand uninhibited spectators valued a good fight more than small flags, though. They freely expressed displeasure with the three one-sided rounds, loosely refereed by a former professional baseball and basketball player, Zach Clayton. Those eight minutes of boxing constituted Foreman's first and Waldhelm's last. More than half played out under a chorus of boos as the Garden crowd impatiently awaited the main event. Even if that fight was not much better than this prelim, at least it would be meaningful as part of the saga of establishing Ali's rightful successor.[15]

The $5,000 check—or what remained after Sadler's cut and other expenses—meant a lot to Foreman. He took it back to Houston, just as he had done with his Job Corps readjustment check a couple of years earlier, but this time he spent it downtown instead of in the Fifth Ward. In fact, he went straight to Mosk's for Men, beside Battelstein's department store, on Main Street. Eyeing Liston's closet over the past year had raised Foreman's awareness of fine clothing; "a suit for every day of the week." A single twenty-year-old at the end of the 1960s wanted more. Foreman found "the most wonderful pair of bell bottoms and a nice white jacket" at Mosk's—the perfect look for an aspiring celebrity in the soul era. More importantly, he strolled out of the store with a brand-new outfit and onto the streets where he had grown up wearing other people's discarded clothes. Sadler liked to spend money, too, but he had to caution the eager Foreman. He arranged another fight, just a week after their debut, at the Sam Houston Coliseum, only a few blocks from Mosk's and Battelstein's. The purse, however, might not be enough for another shopping trip. Sadler could get a lot of action, but not all venues paid like the Garden. He couldn't promise a lot of money early on, but pledged, "I can teach you how to fight." Foreman bought in. He took care of business in Houston with a first-round knockout of Fred Askew, and the two embarked on their own barnstorm.[16]

The experience opened Foreman's eyes. Sadler's were already wide open—even if he could see out of only one—but traveling with Foreman rejuvenated him. Liston had been accustomed to a champion's schedule, taking just a few fights a year and preferring to remain near his home in Las Vegas. Foreman, by contrast, could handle multiple fights in a month and let Sadler take them anywhere they could get a good match. In turn, Sadler made Foreman feel like a partner in selecting opponents. This arrangement contrasted starkly with those endured by boxers like Ali in his early years or Joe Frazier on his championship run, who were "owned" by conglomerates. Sadler might have taken more than one-third of the winnings, as stipulated in their contract, but he did more than just arrange the fights, too. He handled everything from footwork and training to negotiating and publicity, even washing Foreman's clothes and ironing his robe before a fight. Foreman "just had to put the gloves on and go get 'em"—and he more than lived up to his end of the agreement.[17]

After a fight at a racetrack in Oxon Hill, Maryland, that never saw a second round, they received a second invitation to the Garden for a multiheavyweight card that would take place the day after Woodstock officially ended. Perhaps sensing a shark, they threw Foreman a bleeder—the "Bayonne Bleeder"—New Jersey's Chuck Wepner. Predictably, the young challenger laid into the journeyman tomato can. Multiple cuts on his face caused the referee to call a TKO early in the third round. Foreman once again left the Garden with a nice paycheck, for even less work than his debut, but without winning over the fans. Boos from New York seemed to follow him around the nation. They headed west, to Seattle, and then returned to Houston for a couple of weeks, where Liston had a match with Sonny Moore and Foreman could fight a couple of times. During the month, Foreman won three bouts in a cumulative nine minutes of action. Even an ostensibly hometown audience jeered Foreman as he beat up on subpar competitors and looked friendly with one of the sport's pariahs, Liston.[18]

When Foreman made his third appearance at the Garden, as part of an all-heavyweight Halloween event, he finally went the distance in a professional fight. It just meant that he heard the boos for all eight scheduled rounds. At the end of a long, frustrating match against the crafty Peruvian veteran Roberto Davila, who staved off the attack without returning many punches, Muhammad Ali enunciated the palpable frustration echoing through the arena. He said Foreman "showed promise" but that his manager was "nursing him along." There was no time to refute Ali's charges, since Sadler had Foreman fighting a 190-pound novice at the Catholic Youth Center in Scranton, Pennsylvania, just five days later. Those four rounds with Leo Peterson, on the heels of his eight-round decision over Davilla, meant that he had fought twelve rounds in one week. By comparison, Foreman's first seven pro bouts combined for only thirteen total rounds over three months. Sadler's neo-Kearnsianism called for a flurry of short matches, allowing them to amass an impressive record very quickly. So they squeezed in one more performance at the Sam Houston Coliseum before meeting up with Liston in Las Vegas.[19]

Sadler still devoted energy to Liston's championship aspirations even while spending a lot of time on the road with Foreman. The World Boxing Council (WBC) had yet to solve its post-Ali questions, and so to move things along, Sadler staged an event that would force one of the two active claimants for the heavyweight championship—New York State Athletic Commission champ Joe Frazier or the last man standing from the World Boxing Association's elimination tournament, Jimmy Ellis—to give Liston another shot. First, Sadler manipulated the air of uncertainty around the title to lobby for the creation of a North American Boxing Federation title. Run by the California Athletic Commission, the NABF happily intervened in the dispute between NYSAC and the WBA. Since Nevada was one of the eight states supporting the NABF, the decision to host its inaugural championship bout in Las Vegas and arrange for a Sin City resident like Liston to "win" the title was an easy call. So easy, in fact, that the brand-new International Hotel and Casino agreed to put on the show. This nominal title match at the country's newest megaresort made it more than a fight: it would be a sporting *event*. ABC's *Wide World of Sports* sent Cosell and his crew to cover it for national television. The table was set; all Liston had to do was to eat.[20]

"You can't win them all. Nobody wins them all. You hear that, George?" Liston's wife, Geraldine, tried to cut through the gloom at her postfight party. Planned as a victory celebration for the first NABF champion, it took on a much more somber tone after Leotis Martin caught Liston with a three-punch combo that knocked him out in the ninth round. Martin never defended his title, because the Bear had detached his retina earlier in the fight. In fact, Liston led on all three scorecards, but that was never going to be a consideration. He was the "house fighter" in Vegas at the time—his and Geraldine's designer home on a golf course in the trendy Paradise Palms subdivision was only five minutes from the Strip. Sadler often reminded Foreman of the advantage that house fighters enjoyed with judges and referees. That was why he insisted that Foreman, who often took on challengers in their own backyards, let his fists adjudicate. That night they rendered their decision on Bob Hazleton in less than ninety seconds. It was Foreman's eleventh straight victory in less than six months of prizefighting. He offered consoling words and a soda to the ex-champ, but had to take Geraldine's warning with a grain of salt, since his career and Liston's were obviously moving in opposite directions. "Everybody loses," she yelled, "but you can't just die!" Her last point was especially ominous. Foreman left the party—he had a fight in Miami ten days later. Liston took six months and then flew to New Jersey and gashed Wepner, just as Foreman had done the year before. Six months after that, in early January 1971, Geraldine found him dead in their bedroom. In the year that elapsed between their final meeting and Liston's death, Foreman fought fourteen more bouts. He won them all, including twelve by knockout, and established himself as something of a house fighter in a much more prestigious venue than Las Vegas, which was a distant satellite of professional boxing at the end of the 1960s.[21]

As Liston declined, Foreman became Dick Sadler's primary charge. They continued touring the nation, racking up knockouts and building publicity. Along the way, they developed habits and even rituals. For example, Foreman did not drink any water the day before a fight. As he got ready to take the ring, Sadler would give him a little ice and one small sip, medical science about hydration and athletic performance be damned. "It was a ceremony," Foreman said. One they performed at least once a month—sometimes more often—and he kept winning. He usually didn't fight long enough to get dehydrated. Foreman received on-the-job training as they traveled. Sadler taught him a lot about boxing, but even more about the fight game. Through his deep stockpile of stories, he revealed to Foreman a dark underworld that often governed the barely regulated sport, a side of prizefighting that Foreman had never seen while rising through amateur and Olympic tournaments and then easing onto professional cards. Sadler told him about Charlie Powell, a former NFL player turned heavyweight contender who had the look of a champion. Certain interests made Sadler aware that they intended to see him win the title. So when Sadler found himself in an opposite corner from Powell, he knew the arrangement. One challenger who recognized that Powell wasn't a very good boxer came back to the corner and told Sadler, "I can whup this guy," and threatened to call off the deal. Sadler knew that it could cost both of them in blood. "If you do it, I will kill you myself," he shot back. Powell won, and Sadler lived to become Kearns's protégé and Archie Moore's cornerman.[22]

That relationship blew up, Sadler told Foreman, when Moore took his last big payday against the rising Cassius Clay. After the third round, Moore came back to the corner and instead of sitting on the stool, he stood and kicked it. That was a sign, Sadler recognized, that Moore was about to take a dive—coincidentally, in the round that Clay had predicted he would stop the "Old Mongoose." Sadler glared as Moore returned to the center of the ring, took some more punches, and fell three times before the referee stopped the bout. While it is unlikely that Moore, at nearly fifty years of age, could have beat Clay in any scenario, it is pretty certain that a bet on Clay in the fourth round that night would have generated a nice return. Bookies had whittled Clay down to a 2–1 favorite, even a little shorter, by the first bell as "smart money" started moving toward

Moore. Odds for a KO in the fourth grew longer. Sadler did not talk to Moore for a decade, not because he believed he threw the fight—that was hardly taboo in 1960s boxing—but because Moore didn't let Sadler know beforehand so that he could place a bet, too.[23]

Sadler's experience in professional boxing during one of its darkest eras, marred by the influence of organized crime and the domination of James Norris's International Boxing Club of New York, made him highly skeptical of the machinations behind prizefighting. Those concerns dovetailed with Foreman's intrinsic cynicism. Particularly when they fought in someone else's hometown, Sadler did not want to jeopardize their perfect record by having a house fighter steal a decision from them. Although they did not have a home base of their own, they started to spend more time in New York City, cozying up to the powerbrokers of boxing and angling for more opportunities at the Garden, for the exposure as well as the purses. While in town, Sadler hooked up with other acquaintances in the fight game. Foreman could work out at the gym run by Gil Clancy—a highly regarded trainer and manager in the Big Apple—and have former champions like Sandy Saddler (no relation to Dick Sadler) in his corner. It became an immersive program in pugilism, and Sadler made it clear that Foreman should keep his boxing in the gym; bouts were for punching. When the bell rang, he wanted a knockout. A quick one. They were not yet in a position to trust referees and judges. Fast knockouts remained their security, for now, but the best safeguard would be to install Foreman as a house fighter somewhere. Despite their West Coast roots, they worked on Brenner to get more fights at the Garden in 1970.[24]

In January, they got another shot, albeit one on an underwhelming Monday-night card. Foreman gave up a few inches and at least twenty pounds to "Giant" Jack O'Halloran, the biggest opponent he had faced as a pro, but he disposed of him in five rounds and showed a little chin in the process. It was enough. Brenner wanted them back at the Garden in two weeks as part of the undercard for Frazier and Ellis's unification match. To fight in the top prelim bout, or "semifinal," Foreman required a legitimate opponent. They all agreed on Gregorio Peralta, a former light-heavyweight contender who had moved up a weight class as he crested into his midthirties. The WBA ranked Peralta as the ninth-best heavyweight in the sport after fighting to a draw against Oscar Bonavena, and then Ellis cancelled a date with him. Peralta was fifteen years older than Foreman, twenty pounds lighter, and ranked in the top ten, so a fight with him probably couldn't hurt. Another decisive win in front of a sold-out Garden and tens of thousands of closed-circuit viewers in multiple countries might propel him into the top ten himself—or at least earn him some cheers. The *Newark Star-Ledger*'s Jerry Izenberg told readers, "Watch Foreman closely. Tonight we should learn if he can fight."[25]

Izenberg's readers got ten rounds of evidence on which to base their decision. Peralta did not run away but remained flat-footed, just out of reach, and then moved in and clutched before Foreman could get inside. Although Foreman landed some good shots early on, and again in the last two rounds, for most of the bout he looked frustrated. Midway through, Peralta opened up a cut over his eye, which made the spectators' perception of a bad fight even worse. Sadler aimed to capitalize on the event and finally get a crowd behind Foreman by dressing him in bright blue trunks with a red waist and white stripes—a patriotic persona set against a foreign opponent. Instead, they heard the familiar chorus of boos until the end of the fight. Then it got worse. The ring announcer, Johnny Addie, caught the microphone that dropped from the ceiling and read the scores in his matter-of-fact tone. Tony Castellano had it 5–4, with one even round, in Foreman's favor, and the crowd roared its disapproval; Jack Gibbons gave Foreman seven rounds, and the din increased a few more decibels. Addie persevered to announce that referee Mark Conn scored it 9–1 for Foreman, and the place went crazy. The result did not exactly work out as Sadler had envisioned, but they left the Garden with some cause for optimism. Foreman believed that the win, even if a contestable decision instead of a decisive knockout, put him "in contention." And getting awarded seven of the rounds from one judge, let alone nine from the referee, certainly looked like a house fighter's advantage at the Garden.[26]

Still, Brenner opined that it would be at least a year before Foreman could challenge for the title. He amassed an impressive record against forgettable opponents such as "Hobo" Wiler, Charley Polite, and "Scrap Iron" Johnson, but that hardly endeared Foreman to fight fans—and he barely earned any money. He and Sadler stood to make a little more from the gate by taking on challengers in their hometowns, like the New Yorker James J. Woody at the Felt Forum, and the Philadelphia local Roger Russell at the Spectrum. But after pinning Woody against the ropes and knocking Russell unconscious, Foreman was met by torrents of boos in both locations. Still undefeated, he seemed to lose popularity with each lopsided matchup and did not exactly grow rich by knocking out palookas for purses that he described as "eatin' money."[27]

During his first year as a professional prizefighter, Foreman won twenty consecutive matches. Seventeen times in twelve months he beat an opponent unconscious or into submission, or left him imploring the referee for mercy. On paper, it was a sterling record, but wins and losses were only part of the equation in an age when television revenue was beginning to outweigh gate receipts. The major networks and the new closed-circuit outfits vied for the rights to broadcast boxing matches. One manager acknowledged that with the added pressure of Nielsen ratings, "you're developing matinee idols first and fighters second." Despite Mays Andrews's comparison of Foreman to the legendary Joe Louis for his combination of punching power and patriotism, Foreman's record against unimpressive competitors and his Olympic image did not excite crowds or, for that matter, many sportswriters. Sadler and Foreman needed to change course if the second year of their partnership was going to be more memorable than the first—and more profitable.[28]

★ 5 ★
Sculpting
George Foreman

Levi "Superfly" Forte had fought forty bouts in almost a decade of prizefighting before getting caught up in the whirlwind of George Foreman's first year as a pro. "He broke three of my ribs," Forte remembered. "He's a heavy hitter, but not the heaviest. George *Chuvalo* hit the hardest." Forte would know—he fought Chuvalo twice and never made it out of the second round. He went the distance against Foreman on a Tuesday-night card in Miami Beach, the kind of event designed to get the up-and-coming contender another knockout and keep his name in the paper. But Forte went off script. He took all of Foreman's shots and stood tall until the end of the tenth round, even though the referee and both judges scored every single stanza for Foreman.[1]

Forte might have been inspired by Chuvalo, who just a few days earlier had upset the boxing world when he refused to lose. Since the mid-1960s, Chuvalo had squared off against some of the best heavyweights in the world and never gone down. But he never won those big fights either. Chuvalo lost decisions to Floyd Patterson, Ernie Terrell, and Muhammad Ali. Joe Frazier stopped him in the fourth round, though Chuvalo stayed on his feet despite multiple cuts on his face and a broken bone competing with them from the inside out. His manager, Irv Ungerman, called Chuvalo a "trial horse" for future heavyweights after Frazier nearly skinned him—though he considered that a positive: "Every kid on the way up is gonna want a piece of Georgie boy." As the owner of a meatpacking plant in Toronto, Ungerman knew a lot more about selling animal flesh than he did about boxing. But Chuvalo was not yet resigned to that fate. Ungerman and Brenner served him up to Jerry Quarry, who needed to add a few knockouts to his record before he could challenge Frazier again. "The two toughest white men on the planet" traded blows and drew blood, as expected, but when Chuvalo landed a short left to Quarry's temple, it sent shockwaves up his arm and through the sport. Quarry, the young, good-looking, highly ranked contender, was out. Chuvalo, the old trial horse, vaulted over him to become the third-ranked heavyweight by both the WBA and *Ring* magazine. Dick Sadler leapt into action.[2]

Foreman thought Chuvalo was a "scary guy," but Sadler's only fear was of missing the moment when a well-known veteran was basking in the glow of a knockout during the twilight of his career. Others recognized the opportunity, too. Brenner immediately tried to arrange a rematch with Quarry, the popular Irish American who was becoming another house fighter at the Garden, but Chuvalo refused to do it for less than $100,000. "The KO dramatically changed my bargaining position," he wrote. Moreover, when he heard that the referee and one judge had him way down on points in a fight he thought he was winning, Chuvalo recognized he would have to replicate the performance; he would not get a decision over Quarry in New York. Instead, Chuvalo coveted a rematch with Ali; it was becoming clear that he would soon regain a boxing license and get back in the ring. Chuvalo, "the highest-ranked white heavyweight on the planet," could wait for that lucrative opportunity. But Ungerman, Brenner, and Sadler did not have that kind of patience. They convinced Chuvalo that Ali was months, maybe years away from a return, and that a second tilt against Quarry would not sell enough tickets or television rights to guarantee him $100,000. They could, however, promise him $50,000 to headline a Garden card against Foreman, who had just cracked the top ten. Chuvalo reluctantly took the deal. Foreman and Sadler were more enthusiastic for less than half the money: $17,500 was their biggest purse so far. But the prestige was more valuable. Foreman knew that the Chuvalo fight—a bout against a top-three contender in a first-rate venue— was "the most important" of his young career.[3]

Its importance to the general public and boxing fandom, how- ever, remained ambiguous. The higher-ranked fighter, Chuvalo, came in as an underdog at between 3–2 and 7–5, depending on the bookie's mood. Their Tuesday-night meeting sold over twelve thousand tickets, generated a gate in excess of $100,000, and could be seen on television in thirty-two states outside the ninety-mile blackout radius. But an interracial slugfest between top-ten heavy- weights should have sold out the Garden's twenty thousand seats. To Chuvalo's chagrin, Ali regained his license and chose the other white hope, Quarry, for his "trial horse." Their Monday-night bout, with 17–5 odds, grossed $4 million, largely thanks to an inter- national television audience of 100 million viewers, and Quarry got $400,000 to take a three-round beating. Neither Chuvalo nor Foreman commanded the drawing power of Ali or even Quarry in the summer of 1970. Whoever came out of the Garden victorious needed public relations as much as pugilism.[4]

Not that anyone watching Foreman versus Chuvalo was looking for pugilism. They expected a brawl. Sadler and Foreman's strategy was the same as always—go for the knockout. It hardly mattered who was on the other side of the ring. In the age before widespread access to video footage, Chuvalo and his trainer, Teddy McWhorter, used their network of friends in the fight game to get information on Foreman. They heard plenty, and not much of it was positive.

He was a "converted southpaw" that Chuvalo could confuse into "thinking left-handed" if he slipped his jabs and got to the inside. When the bell rang, that was exactly how Chuvalo approached things. He tried to keep away from Foreman's jab and throw his left hook down to the body. When Chuvalo had to, he uncharacteristically backed into the ropes or lunged in for a clutch. He underestimated Foreman's strength. A minute in, Foreman got frustrated and threw the roughly 215-pound Chuvalo from the middle of the ring into the ropes. As soon as the second-round bell rang, Foreman launched a wild haymaker, signaling his intention to end the fight soon. Chuvalo slid to the other side of the ring. Don Dunphy, calling the blow-by-blow, suggested that Chuvalo probably hoped that Foreman would "punch himself out," but he admitted "those big telephone-pole arms" kept jabbing and taking their toll.[5]

In the third stanza, Chuvalo slowed down while Foreman ratcheted up the intensity. "He cut off the ring and cracked me with as good a left hook to the jaw as I was ever hit with," Chuvalo said. Propelled into the ropes, he rebounded back into a merciless two-fisted barrage. He was spitting blood by the middle of the round. Foreman herded him into his corner and teed off. Chuvalo hunched over and weathered the storm, letting him "throw punches out the window" and waiting for him to get tired. His seconds did not see it the same way. According to ringside witnesses, Chuvalo's trainer, manager, or wife—perhaps all of them—screamed at the referee, Arthur Mercante, to stop the fight. When he stepped in between them and waved Foreman off, one reporter noticed Chuvalo's lips moving, but couldn't make out the words in all the commotion. Chuvalo recalled that it was a question: "Are you fucking nuts?" He felt that Mercante stopped it far too early. Those watching, who saw him "impressed, literally and figuratively, by Foreman's fists," might have asked Chuvalo the same question.[6]

After Mercante raised Foreman's arm and Sadler led him back down into the bowels of the Garden, Foreman found the jazz legend Miles Davis "waiting at [his] door like a little fan." Davis, who followed boxing religiously, wanted to meet the rising heavyweight. Foreman might have felt like a celebrity, but by the time he met with reporters after the bout, he was playing the same notes of modesty, humility, and youth that had struck so many chords during his Olympic coda. When asked about the fight, he simply said, "It was work all the way," and admitted, "I was hoping he'd go down." Then he added, for a chuckle, "I was hoping he wouldn't even show up." The next morning, someone asked him why he threw Chuvalo across the ring in the first round. "You can't take chances with old George," he replied with a big grin, while pantomiming a head butt. Sadler used the same blend of humor and humility as he officially launched their championship campaign. "We are interested in any fight that would help us get closer to the title," he announced. "If everybody cooperates by letting us win, then we'll be happy."[7]

The joke fell flat. Cooperation and happiness were not commonly found in prizefighting. Sadler and Foreman took great pains to parlay his Olympic image into that of a popular, likable boxer. Ironically, no one, from the fight fans to the powerbrokers of boxing, liked that very much. His public persona remained tethered to patriotism. Two weeks after he beat Chuvalo, *Sports Illustrated* ran an article titled "Salute the Grand Old Flag-Raiser George F." Yet the preparations for the Munich Olympics in 1972 superseded the waning memories of Mexico City. His patriotic shtick became a target as soldiers returning from Vietnam swelled the ranks of professional boxing. The former marine Ken Norton rifled off sixteen consecutive wins, and Jim Elder, a navy veteran with an undefeated record, brought the comparison into sharp relief: "While he was waving that flag around, I was busy fighting for it." Foreman's persona factored into matchmaking and the heavyweight rankings. Quarry traded shots with Chuvalo for seven rounds and got knocked out; Foreman disarmed him in about seven minutes. But many, including *Ring* magazine, still ranked Quarry ahead of Foreman. Both had become regulars at the Garden, but Quarry could fill the house. Brenner's boss, Harry Markson, issued a dictum: Foreman had not yet shown enough for a title shot; but the Garden might consider matching him and Quarry.[8]

Markson's edict did not sit well with Sadler. After all, Quarry hadn't held a boxing title since the 1965 Golden Gloves. His place in the rankings had more to do with his popularity than his ability—and it was a kind of popularity that someone with Foreman's level of melanin could not attain in Nixon's America. Quarry was the current Great White Hope. Sadler and Foreman opted for the "New White Hope" instead, Boone Kirkman. His reputation as a towering knockout artist from the Pacific Northwest derived from the incessant promotion of Jack Hurley, Kirkman's septuagenarian manager. Hurley was cut from the same mold as Doc Kearns and ballyhooed with the best of them. Seeing the financial success of white hopes like Quarry and even the aging Chuvalo gave Hurley to impetus to find—or create—one of his own. He called Kirkman his "last fighter" and "last chance."[9]

More than eighteen thousand spectators crowded the Garden to see Foreman take on "Boom Boom" Kirkman, as well as the closed-circuit telecast of Frazier defending his title against Bob Foster, which followed. Theater Network Television's first "electronic double-header" showed Foreman-Kirkman in New York and then Frazier-Foster in Detroit to viewers in either location or a hundred others. The closed-circuit-television revenue helped offset a remarkably low gate in the Motor City, which was dealing with an auto strike and looked skeptically at the chances of a light heavyweight like Foster standing up to the champion. But there was still some intrigue around the other feature; at least the two fighters were about the same size. An estimated half-million viewers in more than twenty countries had paid for the privilege of watching. Roughly one million eyes, then, may have widened at the first bell, when Foreman tore out of his corner and rather than throw a punch, threw Kirkman—right onto the seat of his pants and back into the corner he came from. It was uncharacteristically aggressive, but it was more than an early psychological ploy. Foreman did not relent. Before the end of the round, he scored a legitimate knockdown. On the restart, he peppered Kirkman with lefts and rights before throwing him onto the canvas again. Arthur Mercante deducted a point for the "palpable foul," but it did not appear that points would play a significant role in the fight. Seconds later, the timekeeper signaled the end of the first round, and the stunned Kirkman finally got a break. He was no more prepared than the spectators were for this new Foreman.[10]

In reality, Kirkman was not prepared for any kind of Foreman. Nor was Hurley. Their hopes had dissipated through the painful first round and were completely dashed in the second. Giving up all pretense of practicing the sweet science, Foreman hurled haymakers. Kirkman folded up and fell down. It took less than twenty seconds. He tried to avoid the mandatory eight count and get back into the fray, but his legs had not caught up with his body. Foreman poured on the punches and Kirkman lapped them up until he "did a drunken stumble along the ropes" and then plummeted to the canvas again. Mercante started his count while shooing Foreman away, but after taking a good look at Kirkman he gave up and called off the fight. So did Hurley. He retired to Seattle's Olympic Hotel and stayed out of the fight game. Kirkman did, too—he waited three full years, until after Hurley died, to climb back into the ring. In Hurley's obituary, Dan Daniel stated, "[He] never got over that debacle. He simply withered, pined away and in two years went to his grave. . . .

No manager suffered so intensely from a protégé's collapse as Hurley did after Kirkman's complete defeat." Sadler put it succinctly, "George wrecked Boone Kirkman's career in two rounds." Foreman, on the other hand, had reached a turning point. His fights began looking increasingly Hobbesian—nasty, brutish, and short.[11]

While the Garden was transitioning from a boxing arena to a movie theater for the telecast of Frazier versus Foster, a makeshift medical station appeared in Kirkman's corner. Foreman paid his respects and then started to praise his outmatched opponent in a post-fight interview. Sadler tried to redirect the conversation by pitching their new business venture, a microfilm company that used federal funding to retrain minority workers. But in subsequent interviews about the Kirkman bout, which often focused on Foreman's aggressive tactics, the fighter's responses sharpened. They went from "I wanted to establish myself" to "I wanted him to know who was the boss." Harry Markson took note of Foreman's new style, as did boxing fans and sportswriters. Markson's opinion of Foreman suddenly improved, and he acknowledged that Foreman "may be only two fights away from being in the thick of it."[12]

Those next two fights included first-round knockouts of Mel Turnbow and, it appeared, Phil Smith. Turnbow was huge—Foreman's height and carrying an extra thirty pounds—and had had a promising start in the mid-1960s. But when he stood eye to eye with Foreman, it had been more than three years since his last victory. In a repeat of the Kirkman opening, at the first bell Foreman "rushed Turnbow like a comet racing through the sky" and beat him down to the canvas. As soon as he got up, the increasingly aggressive Foreman "charged him like a stone flung out of a slingshot" and pummeled him some more. This referee, Whitey Domstad, didn't let it go into the second round. Like Kirkman, Turnbow took an extended hiatus after facing the new George Foreman and did not return to action for eighteen months. Phil Smith, on the other hand, didn't even show up for his bout with Foreman. Instead, Charlie Boston fought under Smith's name for two unspectacular minutes before a right uppercut dropped him. After two fights lasting a total of two rounds, against a barely-has-been and a literal never-was, the WBA catapulted Foreman over Jimmy Ellis, Oscar Bonavena, and Jerry Quarry to rank him as the number-one contender for Joe Frazier's heavyweight championship.[13]

The WBA purposefully ignored Muhammad Ali in its rankings, even though Frazier had agreed to defend his title against him in March 1971. Years in the making, the most coveted boxing match in recent memory shattered records and oozed superlatives. Some called it the "Fight of the Century," but that moniker had been used at least a couple of times already since 1900. The "Super Fight" seemed more appropriate, given the exceptional largesse of the event. An undefeated champion and his undefeated challenger would split $5 million down the middle. With a sellout virtually guaranteed, the Garden considered pricing its top tickets as high as $250 each. But the biggest purse in prizefighting history would have to be paid for by the television revenue. Jerry Perenchio, chief architect of the deal that made the Super Fight a reality, estimated a gross of more than $10 million from television—if they didn't raise those ticket prices, too—so reeling in $20 million to $30 million from the live gate and ancillaries seemed possible. Frazier and Ali's first encounter reset the bar for championship boxing. Yet just as Markson predicted, Foreman was "in the thick of it."[14]

The Super Fight attracted such interest because it would be fought for more than just a bejeweled belt. Ali had been an icon of the Black Power movement since he converted to Islam and discarded his "slave name" of Clay in 1964, briefly adopting Cassius X before accepting a "full Muslim name" from the Nation of Islam leader, Elijah Muhammad. Frazier, on the other hand, was a devout Christian with an equally strong faith in capitalism. In many ways,

Frazier reflected the most moderate arm of the civil rights movement, whereas Ali stood on the leading edge of its radical wing. The fight program included a poem by the Pulitzer Prize winner Gwendolyn Brooks; it conveyed a sense that the brutality of their boxing would be mitigated by their mutual "black love." But Frazier and Ali's growing rivalry represented intensifying inter- and intraracial conflict in America.[15]

Black sportswriters such as Brad Pye magnified the conflict by writing that Frazier was "the blackest White Hope in history." In response, Frazier challenged Ali's authenticity, first claiming that Ali was "no leader of black people" and then dredging up the politics of pigment—"I'm blacker than he is. There ain't a black spot on his whole body"—and finishing with a class-based argument: "Clay is a phony. He never worked. He never had a job. He don't know nothing about life for most black people." The Young and Rubicam advertising agency incited the rivalry further when it televised a tense phone conversation—the "Commercial of the Century"—between Frazier and Ali. The unscripted ad ended when Frazier's percussion-like repetition of "Clay, Clay, Clay" spurred Ali to scream, "Even white people call me Muhammad now.... You're known as the Tom in this fight!" Foreman knew the sting of being called an Uncle Tom, too, but he learned that it really upset Frazier because he feared people would think he ran around peeping in windows. The politics of the Super Fight, however, gave Foreman an opportunity to further distance himself from his 1960s Olympian image and fashion something more marketable in the 1970s.[16]

Beginning in the fall of 1970, Foreman started to move from an affable persona dressed in relatively plain clothes to a more aloof demeanor clad in increasingly expressive attire. He began to choose his words as carefully as his wardrobe. Short, pointed quips were paired with a carefully styled Afro. On top he did not wear a Stetson or a black beret but instead sported a fashionably oversized driving cap. He thought he looked the part when soul-era celebrities flocked to New York for the Super Fight. According to Foreman, that prefight party was a formative experience because of two short and utterly disappointing encounters. First, he spotted the New York Knicks' all-star point guard Walt Frazier. Nicknamed "Clyde" for his wide-brimmed hats and sharp suits, which drew comparisons to Warren Beatty's outfits in *Bonnie and Clyde*, Frazier was a paragon of black masculine style. And he had completed an image transition very similar to Foreman's. Once a quiet member of Southern Illinois University's unheralded basketball program, Frazier had become the NBA's most dynamic personality. From his perfectly picked Afro to the fastidiously laced canvas shoes that Puma paid him to endorse, he epitomized the soul aesthetic that Foreman was growing into. But Clyde already had it down. He interrupted Foreman's awkward attempt at an introduction—"I've seen you do your thing, you've seen me do mine"—and coolly strutted away, leaving Foreman somewhere between starstruck and awestruck.[17]

Foreman redoubled his efforts when Jim Brown came into view. Foreman showed his admiration for Brown by sporting mutton-chops modeled after those Brown wore as Lyedecker in the film *100 Rifles*. Yet Brown played it as cool in the club as he did on-screen: he did not make eye contact, let alone conversation, and offered Foreman nothing more than a limp handshake while gazing off in the distance. The freshly minted contender suffered two quick knockouts from sports heavy hitters of the soul era. He went to work perfecting the "cool pose" used by Brown and described by Frazier several years later in his *Rockin' Steady: A Guide to Basketball and Cool*. The March issue of *Sport* magazine included a feature titled "The Walt Frazier Style," and Foreman got a preview of it in Harlem.[18]

"Soul style" was characterized by "radiating an aura of aloofness, detachment, and emotional invulnerability," and Jim Brown and Walt Frazier were *it*. Foreman was still in flux. He declined an invitation from the Congress of Racial Equality to watch the Super Fight at the 142nd Street Armory, the only spot in Harlem with a close-circuit feed, and dress in the colors of black liberation: black, green, and red. Rather, he chose to see it live, decked out with the panache of a soul brother. He wore stark-white bellbottoms, a tight-fitting denim shirt, and a brown felt cap. At the weigh-in on the morning of the fight, Foreman eschewed the cliché of a top contender demanding a title shot with whoever came out on top that night. Instead, he wryly offered a challenge to the loser, since, he said, "you can't rush success." But when Brenner asked whether he would step into the ring for an introduction before the fight, Foreman responded: "Are you crazy? I'm not going up in that ring!" He had not yet achieved the "emotional invulnerability" of a soul aesthetic, even if he looked the part.[19]

Emotions ran high that night as Frazier and Ali battled to the end of fifteen brutal rounds. The open weeping of Ali's cornerman and stalwart supporter Drew Bundini Brown forecast the unanimous decision in Frazier's favor. Scorecards did not change hearts or minds, however. Some writers scrambled to reify the caricatures they had drawn before the fight. Bryant Gumbel penned a cover story for *Boxing Illustrated* that questioned whether Frazier was a "White Champion in a Black Skin." *Jet* magazine sustained the image of Frazier as a "white created champion" and called Ali "one of the few Black heroes still alive." Foreman tried to stay cool. "It sure wasn't the fight of any century," he said. "I didn't see much skill demonstrated by either fighter." But no bad-mouthing of the skill on display was going to affect the demand for a rematch. The Super Fight lived up to its hype and only hardened battle lines. Foreman would have to wait until the completion of Frazier and Ali's saga before getting a shot. Dick Sadler tried to speed up the time line.[20]

In an interview with *Ring*'s Ted Carroll, Sadler implored Foreman to assume a "take charge" attitude regardless of whom he got his shot against. Sadler insisted that Foreman could beat either Frazier or Ali if he dominated the ring. The subtext suggested a recognition that Foreman had to sell himself as a champion before anyone would give him the chance to fight for the title. "Taking charge" and "dominating" as Joe Frazier did, or Sonny Liston used to, was one thing. But Foreman in the early 1970s was significantly more complicated than just "Sonny Liston redux." He was not mean, but cool; he was rough in the ring and sharp outside of it. Foreman's terse comments and hip clothes were part of the new image he had fashioned in the months leading up to the Super Fight—one that diverged from the Frazier-Ali dichotomy because it was more rooted in popular culture than in traditional politics.[21]

"I lived in *Playboy* magazine," Foreman said. Not only for the provocative photos but also for the intellectually provocative cartoons, the men's fashion (which played to his interest in clothes), and the interviews with famous men. "You had to be someone to be interviewed," he pointed out. Foreman wasn't yet enough of a someone to rate a spot in the magazine's pages, but his next bout after the Super Fight came off at the first Playboy Club Hotel, on Lake Geneva in Wisconsin. He barely broke a sweat while knocking five-eleven Stamford Harris around for a little over five minutes. It was more like a dessert for Hugh Heffner's $50-a-plate dinner party than a prizefight. The photos of Foreman surrounded by Playboy Bunnies burnished his growing persona.[22]

Ironically, Ali was also in Wisconsin that week. As he spoke on college campuses, talking about politics under bright lights beaming onto his conservative jacket and tie, he probably perspired more than Foreman did while taking on Harris. Frazier was also in the state—he appeared at the Playboy Club during Foreman's visit—but as a musical talent rather than a fistic one. His band, the Knockouts, performed a synthesis of pop and gospel music that projected a curious blend of Old Testament religion and postwar consumption.

They represented Motown at a time when its popularity was waning. Foreman, on the other hand, looked like the new cadre of musicians who rejected Berry Gordy's heavy hand. The images emanating from Lake Geneva, which came on the heels of pictures showing
Foreman's outdoor training sessions with rocks and wheelbarrows,
contrasted sharply with those of both Frazier and Ali.[23]

In the wake of the Playboy event, Foreman prepared to meet Gregorio Peralta again, this time for the North American Boxing Federation championship, which had been claimed a couple of times
by different boxers but never defended. Frazier was preparing, too,
but not for the rematch with Ali; the Knockouts had a gig at the Felt
Forum (a venue beneath the Madison Square Garden arena), which
would be preceded by a lively hot-pants contest. A stalwart of the
New York Amsterdam News, the columnist Les Matthews suggested
that boxing itself had degenerated into a "hot pants contest." But
people liked hot-pants contests, and new data suggested they liked
boxing again, too. Nat Fleischer cited a Harris poll that found boxing's popularity had risen significantly in the past year, though the
spike was largely due to the buildup toward the Super Fight. Foreman and Peralta's second tilt, part of a closed-circuit triple-header
that included Jimmy Ellis and George Chuvalo fighting in Toronto,
as well as Ernie Terrell and Luis Pires in Chicago, drew only five
thousand spectators to the Coliseum Arena in Oakland. Foreman's
$20,000 purse took more than half the gate. The title of an article
in *Ring* called the entire event a "Fistic and Financial Failure" and
suspected all the promoters lost money. Foreman was a clear winner in the ring, although it took him ten rounds to secure a TKO
and earn him the title nobody seemed to want. Noticeably frustrated with the performance, Sadler said that Foreman "had gone
stale and needed a long layoff." He stayed out of the prize ring for
four months, his longest hiatus since turning pro. During Foreman's
break, Sadler started to mix it up.[24]

"We need some fights, so I'm gonna sign with these guys," Sadler told Foreman. "They'll get [you] some publicity." Despite some suspicions, Foreman still trusted Sadler's direction in the business of boxing. After all, Sadler had piloted him to the top of the heavyweight rankings without Forman having to face any bona fide contenders. For his efforts, the Boxing Writers Association of America named Sadler "Manager of the Year" and presented him with the Al Buck Memorial Award at the annual BWAA dinner in late June 1971. That night Sadler and Foreman introduced Marty Erlichman to "boxing society." Erlichman had no experience in the fight game, although the heavyweight championship may not have been predicated on boxing anyway. Most notable as the publicist and manager for Barbra Streisand, Erlichman had also found Bette Midler and turned his typist, Joan Rivers, into a comedian. He likely saw similarities between his entertainer clients and a heavyweight contender. Most importantly, he had the bankroll to buy his way in. For a reported $500,000 up front, split by him and David Miller from Philadelphia, they would get half of all Foreman's ancillary revenues. The deal excluded purses and gate receipts, but included television proceeds and any endorsement deals that, presumably, Erlichman would facilitate. All parties shared a common interest in making the new George Foreman as marketable as possible, inside and outside the prize ring. In retrospect, Foreman thought Sadler had mortgaged their future for some quick cash, but at the time, Erlichman—whom Foreman called "the second most impressive human being I had ever met"—made the boxer "feel like a celebrity" after his encounters with Walt Frazier and Jim Brown. More importantly, Erlichman promised promotional opportunities with huge names such as Streisand to ensure that Foreman stayed in the public eye and ultimately looked like a champion.[25]

Looks were critical in the venal world of prizefighting. "To earn my title shot," Foreman believed, "I had to look, even in street clothes, like I deserved that title more than Frazier . . . or Ali." He did not, however, live out the image in the way some of his contemporaries did. Jim Brown faced accusations of playing out his action roles offscreen; Walt Frazier embraced his playboy lifestyle and invited *Jet* magazine into his apartment for a frank discussion of his busy romantic life. By contrast, Foreman did not fight for free anymore, and he was about to marry his girlfriend, a Minneapolis businesswoman named Adrienne Calhoun, in a small private service before the end of the year. Sadler disapproved on principle, even though he had introduced them the previous year. He need not have worried. Foreman stayed focused on their goal: "There was never a moment when I considered marriage more sacred than the heavyweight championship."[26]

In only three years under the spotlight of American sport celebrity, Foreman had gone through two public personae—a brash, poetic carbon copy of Ali before the Olympics, and a jovial hyperpatriotic gold medalist afterward—and now he constructed a third. At the same time, a glut of music, movies, and television programs targeted the growing demographic of young African American consumers. In these media, especially blaxploitation films, the "radical" separatists and conservative "accommodationists," which Ali and Frazier signified, were both subject to ridicule when contrasted with strong, cool, fashionable, yet aloof black antiheroes. Foreman tapped into this cultural sea change to market himself as a profitable opponent against either Ali or Frazier. "These were the days when I was sculpting George Foreman," he recalled. "I shaped the clay to match what Sadler taught; manipulated it to resemble characters in books and movies; and squeezed it to copy heroes."[27]

It worked. Floyd Patterson said that Foreman was "the only man left in the top ten capable of . . . stirring up some interest," and the formerly skeptical Teddy Brenner now called him "the best title prospect since Joe Louis." Les Matthews pointed out that Foreman might ascend to the heavyweight throne after Frazier and Ali's "finale." As the boxing world waited for a second Super Fight, Foreman went back to work. He won four fights in two months, the last of which ended after four rounds when Luis Pires stayed in his corner, nursing an elbow and a nose that had both been broken by Foreman's heavy punches. Matthews called him "star material" despite the boos that echoed through the Garden. Foreman returned to Houston in time to catch Ali's match with Jimmy Ellis and, under the auspices of *Boxing Illustrated* as a "guest reporter," got into Ali's dressing room. "I'm the leading contender," he told Ali, "I'm before Ellis." Ali jabbed at his press credentials: "Who are you, a colored Howard Cosell?" But Foreman slipped it and countered with a shot to Ali's masculinity: "When you gonna move up to me, boy?" drawing out the last word into two pronounced syllables embedded with centuries of meaning. "I'll get you. You don't have to worry about that," the former champ replied as he ratcheted up the intensity. Foreman ended the conversation: "Bye, bo-y." The freshly sculpted Foreman believed he "was definitely the number one contender," but the heavyweight division remained gridlocked by Frazier and Ali's unsettled scores.[28]

★ 6 ★
Better Must Come

In its final issue of 1971, *Ring* magazine, the self-styled "Bible of Boxing," preached some fire and brimstone: "The heavyweight division is in a state of virtual lethargy." The champion, Frazier, took his Knockouts on a European tour in mid-May and did not fight again that year. Both top contenders, Foreman and Ali, stayed busy but kept far away from each other. The high tide of boxing popularity that had crested with the Super Fight receded after a year of inactivity. In early 1972, the editor of *Boxing Illustrated*, Bert Sugar, referred to a new Gallup poll indicating that only 1 percent of Americans still followed boxing. Although writers and fighters often later remembered the first half of the 1970s as a "golden era" for heavyweight prizefighting, there were moments when even its biggest proponents would have seen it as an age of fool's gold.[1]

After the tumultuous 1960s, which included several boxing-induced deaths, most notably of Davey Moore and Benny Paret, the rumored influence of organized crime on fighters, especially Sonny Liston, and the interference of religion and politics, primarily with regard to Muhammad Ali, the fight game seemed moribund. Then Super Fight breathed life back into it. More than twenty thousand spectators had jammed the Garden, and the $1,352,951 gate set a new record for gross receipts at an indoor boxing match. But ticket sales amounted to merely a garnish on the entrée of closed-circuit-TV revenue, funded by approximately three hundred million viewers in theaters and stadiums around the world. Jerry Perenchio emerged as the undisputed winner that night, and the Garden appeared to solidify its position as the "Mecca of Boxing."[2]

While Foreman tried to undermine Frazier and Ali's rivalry by questioning their skills, a new tax policy did more to jeopardize the rematch. Typically, Madison Square Garden was taxed at a rate of 5 percent of the gross receipts, and in this case, Harry Markson received his expected bill for $292,000. Then unexpected invoices for $348,246.50 each were sent directly to Frazier and Ali. Before they squared off, the New York State Tax Commission had decided to invoke its nonresident tax on boxers for the first time. Months of negotiations and increasingly negative press did not bring about any policy change from the cash-strapped state. The *New York Times* feared that this development would "threaten the extinction of big time New York boxing," and Markson claimed, "It effectively puts us out of business."[3]

Nat Fleischer, the founding editor of *Ring*, led the crusade against the tax commission from his office two blocks east of the Garden. Only a few years earlier, however, those offices had been inside the venue. The bible of boxing and the mecca of boxing had been intricately linked for half a century, from the time when the building was actually in Madison Square and Fleischer was editing the sport pages of a couple of penny papers. In 1922, the dominant fight promoter and Garden lessee George "Tex" Rickard planned to tighten his grip on the sport by building a third incarnation of the Garden farther uptown, and as part of the deal, he and a group of partners, including Frank Coultry, the secretary-treasurer of the Garden, agreed to underwrite a boxing-centric magazine for Fleischer to edit. The gravitational pull of a modern venue in a prime location with a magazine dedicated to its endeavors drew many of the biggest prizefights to New York City. Rickard did not live through the 1920s, but Fleischer, known as "Mr. Boxing," carried the torch through some of the sport's darkest ages. Then a fourth version of the Garden, erected right above Penn Station, the success of the Super Fight, and the anticipation of a Super Sequel all signaled a renaissance for boxing. The newly revived tax threatened that progress, and Fleischer gave voice to the resistance throughout 1971.[4]

The voice of the Garden, Johnnie Addie, died before the end of the year. After announcing more than a hundred fights across three decades in melodious tones, he had become part of the Garden's promotion. Few would have guessed that Foreman's victory over Pires marked his final address; fewer still that it would be Foreman's last performance there, too. The rebirth of boxing had been interrupted by life's two great certainties: death and taxes. After a year without a resolution or even a reduction in the nonresident tax, Fleischer wrote in exasperation that "the tax people are voracious to no end." His lead writer at the time, Dan Daniel, added that it might take a Supreme Court ruling to break this stranglehold keeping significant prizefights from the Big Apple. But Daniel, looking to the future, acknowledged that "big time boxing no longer counts heavily on live gate finance," because of the huge revenues derived from paid-television broadcasts. *Ring* recalled a prognostication from Mike Jacobs, who had picked up Rickard's mantle and dominated the promotion of prizefights in New York during the 1930s: "You will see big fights televised all over the world, and boxers paid not on the basis of what a promoter figured he could draw at the gate, but on the basis of his boxer's magnetic powers as figures of world interest." Jacobs reportedly suggested, "You might even see a world championship battle being televised from a studio. The . . . financial success of a fight will depend entirely on closed circuit television." Meaning that watching a fight would not require making a pilgrimage to the Garden. The nonresident tax lived through the legislative session, and the eighty-four-year-old Mr. Boxing died that summer. Given the de facto moratorium on marquee prize-fights in New York, some people may have been ready to clean out *Ring*'s offices, pluck the hand-me-down ring from the center of the newest Garden incarnation, and throw it all on Fleischer's funeral pyre.[5]

The combination of New York state taxes and worldwide tele-vision feeds fueled two new certainties in the world of boxing circa 1972: Frazier and Ali's encore would not happen anytime soon, and when Frazier did defend his title again, it would not be at the Gar-den. In contrast to the seismic shifting of boxing's tectonic plates, its heavyweights laid dormant on the surface. Frazier engaged in two defenses against lackluster challengers; Ali fought three opponents who would not even be classified as heavyweights when the weight classes were redrawn a few years later; and Foreman took five bouts against older, lighter boxers that all ended in second-round knock-outs. When *Ring* called the division lethargic at the end of 1971, it might have been optimistic; heavyweight prizefighting was nearly comatose. Yet *Ring* found reason for optimism: "There we stand in this year 1972, no longer bemused by White Hopes, no longer disturbed by racial rivalries." And indeed the latest cohort of white hopes—George Chuvalo, Jerry Quarry, and Boone Kirkman—had largely been discredited. It was not the absence of interracial ri-valry, however, but an intensifying intraracial conflict that prom-ised to resuscitate the sport.[6]

To that end, Foreman's most significant confrontation of 1972 was not any of his Hobbesian bouts against forgettable opponents such as "Mustang" Joe Goodwin, who had not won a fight since his debut in 1960; rather, it was an impromptu clash with the leviathan of race in the ring. Ali's rematch against Jerry Quarry, at the Las Vegas Convention Center, also featured Quarry's younger brother

Mike in a light-heavyweight tilt opposite Bob Foster. The event was sold as "Soul Brothers versus Quarry Brothers," even if the conservative dress and ascetic lifestyle prescribed by the Nation of Islam did not exactly jibe with soul culture. Neither fight was very good, but after the lethargic Ali beat the listless Quarry, the winner became rejuvenated, telling a gaggle of interviewers in the ring, "I want Frazier," while parrying Howard Cosell's questions about his recent and future opponents, including the nearly forty-year-old Floyd Patterson. "George Foreman's not old!" Ali countered, spying the heavyweight hopeful at ringside. Both Cosell and Ali invited Foreman to the mat, and perhaps to their surprise, he accepted. When Foreman got close, Ali stuck a hand in his face and started a soliloquy on whupping. Foreman interrupted him with the same invective he had doled out the year before: "I want Frazier, I don't want no *bo-y*." "Boy? Boy?!" Ali erupted, looking around for affirmation before throwing punches down at Foreman on the other side of the ropes. Foreman snapped a quick jab back near Ali's chin and then left. No blows connected, but the performance reinforced the perception that Foreman was, in the parlance of the era, a "bad mother."[7]

The scene from Las Vegas reverberated in New York. Murray Goodman quickly offered Ali $500,000 to meet Foreman inside the ring of his recently constructed Nassau Coliseum on Long Island. Markson acknowledged that Frazier-Ali II "had to wait," but he was not ready to throw in the towel on hosting premier prizefights at the Garden. He began angling for a Frazier-Foreman title bout, which would promise, in one writer's opinion, nothing short of "opulent fiscal possibilities." Although Foreman and Ali were developing a personal feud—Foreman accused him of "jiving in training" and said that he looked "overweight and shaky-like"—Frazier and Foreman mirrored a cultural-generational divide. Foreman's wardrobe could have come from the closets of Isaac Hayes, Curtis Mayfield, or Marvin Gaye, in a much larger size. Frazier openly derided such "hippie clothes" while riding his motorcycle adorned with an American flag. The boxing literati still wrote about a "Foreman controversy" and asked whether he deserved a title fight or posed any real threat to Frazier. But they had to acknowledge Foreman's enormous "box office, and closed-circuit television potential." Predictably, *Ring* ran a story with a title that connected the Garden with the biggest-available prizefight: "Madison Square Garden Hotly Interested in Matching George with Champion." Assumptions about the Garden enjoying a privileged bargaining position with two house fighters, however, proved false. There was not just one reason for the Garden to worry but, as Foreman recalled, "about 350,000" of them. When Albany decided it wanted "a bigger piece" of prizefighting's pie, Foreman knew "that was the death sentence for MSG." The Garden's hegemony over heavyweights slackened as discussions over Frazier and Foreman ratcheted up. The subsequent bidding war for Frazier versus Foreman sent the boxing world scrambling for its atlases.[8]

Frazier started the trend when he asked aloud: "Oklahoma? Where's that at?" He was responding to the Oklahoma Boxing Commission's decision to rescind his heavyweight championship in July for failing to defend against "bona fide" challengers. The commission exercised little influence, however, and only one other state commission—in Massachusetts—followed its lead. Because the Oklahoma commission announced that it would bestow its now-vacant championship title on the winner of a proposed fight between Foreman and Oscar Bonavena in Boston, the Bay State had a vested interest in defrocking Frazier. A fight between a rising star and an aging veteran, held in Boston only because Dick Sadler owed a favor to Bonavena's promoter, had garnered tepid interest up to that point. But if it could be construed as a title fight, stakeholders hoped that Foreman-Bonavena would quickly become a heavy-weight championship *event*, perhaps filling the vacuum left by New York's decline and establishing Boston as the next mecca of boxing.[9]

Murray Goodman sought to usurp the Garden's role while keeping the sport's biggest events in the state. For a defense against Foreman, he offered Frazier the same $500,000 purse that he had dangled in front of Ali. But Goodman's venue remained within reach of the New York State Tax Commission. Jack O'Connell, president of the Astrodome, matched Goodman's offer, in a much more tax-friendly state. Frazier's manager, Yank Durham, told O'Connell plainly that a half million was now "inadequate" for Frazier's services. Las Vegas promoters then upped the ante to $750,000. Gambling money also backed a Philadelphia bid as John J. Finley, the president of Eagle Downs Racing Association, promised to top any offer on the table and secure a third hometown defense for Frazier at the five-year-old Spectrum. A formal proposal from Finley never materialized, but O'Connell was quick to call the raise from Las Vegas. In response, Markson and the Garden marshaled their resources to increase the bid by $20,000. Publicly, at least, Durham and Frazier were still "mulling" the deal when O'Connell went all in. His newest offer of $800,000 to Frazier, and nearly half that amount to Foreman, pushed the other promoters out of the game.[10]

The bidding war engendered so much press that it took the form of a public auction, with readers of mainstream newspapers and boxing magazines attentively following each raise of the paddle. It became clear that the tax commission in New York would not budge on its nonresident tax, and that Foreman was going to blow off the Bonavena fight in Boston now that a title bout with Frazier appeared certain. The stadium that the Reverend Billy Graham called the "Eighth Wonder of the World" and that the Texas-born writer Larry McMurtry described as "the working end of a gigantic roll-on deodorant" suddenly became a decided favorite to host Frazier-Foreman in 1972, possibly replace the Garden as the main stage for boxing's biggest events, and signal a redirection of major sporting events from the wilting Northeast to the blossoming Sunbelt.[11]

Just as the heavyweight division shook itself free from the "paralysis" of New York state taxes, it became entangled in a web of litigation. Bonavena's representatives sued Foreman for reneging on their contracted fight, as did the Baltimore heavyweight Larry Middleton, who contended there was an agreement in place for him to meet Foreman before the negotiations for a Frazier-Foreman title fight became public. For both Bonavena and Middleton, a bout with the suddenly anointed top contender for the title became too valuable to give up. Sadler, too, recognized the appreciation of Foreman's stock—and started to sell. On top of the agreement he made with Erlichman and Miller, Sadler sold Foreman futures to what became a Philadelphia-based conglomerate called George Foreman Associates (GFA). Although Foreman understood that GFA worked with Erlichman, it was not part of the negotiations with Frazier and Durham. With the stakes increasing for Foreman's first—and maybe only—championship match, Erlichman and Miller filed suit against Foreman and Sadler to secure their percentages of the revenue; Foreman and Sadler sued Erlichman for a breach of contract, citing a lack of promotional appearances. Not to be left out, Frazier and Durham sued Erlichman and Miller for interfering with Frazier's career. Regardless of what venue in which city earned the right to host Frazier versus Foreman, multiple requests for injunctions stood in the way of a deal. Those obstacles turned into fertile soil, however, for new and highly improbable alliances. A Peruvian promoter in Paris, a Chinese Jamaican bookie in New York, and a "gofer" in the Philadelphia fight game facilitated a proposal that did more than just make a fight—it ushered in a new era for heavyweight boxing.[12]

★

Word of Frazier and Foreman's stalemate reached Alex Valdez, the music promoter responsible for the Knockouts' recent tour of Europe. Although that endeavor was an abysmal failure, Valdez earned Frazier's trust by telling him otherwise. Frazier liked to hear good news, and now Valdez wanted to deliver more. Likewise, Lucien Chen, who had reputedly parlayed his income as a waiter on Long Island into the House of Chen restaurant back on his home island of Jamaica, wanted to bring some optimism to a nation caught in the throes of a global depression. Chen's restaurant was not as lucrative as the bookkeeping business he ran out of it, which snowballed into 120 offtrack betting parlors, a thriving casino conveniently located above the House of Chen, and sporadic boxing promotions in Kingston. He had sunk deep roots into the Jamaican sports industry, and Valdez held a branch to the heavyweight champion. Fortunately for them, they connected at the dawn of Michael Manley's administration.[13]

The Manley family was a Jamaican equivalent of America's Kennedys. Each clan had a strong interest in, and acumen for, both politics and sports. Norman Manley had been a "schoolboy champion" in sprinting, enjoyed boxing, and developed a love for cricket before turning his energy toward securing Jamaica's independence and self-government. His second son, Michael, may have been less gifted than his father but more passionate. Also a standout athlete in Jamaican schools, he followed West Indian cricket from abroad while studying at the London School of Economics, and later wrote a history of Jamaica's relationship with a quintessentially British sport. While his father led the People's National Party (PNP) in Jamaica, Michael Manley reportedly bankrolled one of Chen's boxing promotions in Kingston. Shortly after Norman Manley died in

1969, Michael Manley shifted his passion for sports toward politics. He began a protracted campaign for prime minister, in a general election still a few years away. Focusing on unity and optimism, he courted Rastafarians and evangelical Christians, farmers and industrial workers, corporate owners and trade unions, engendering an "awesome popularity" that manifested at the polls. He was swept into office in March 1972, along with a large majority of seats in parliament and a mandate to fulfill his campaign slogan, "Better Must Come."[14]

Two of the areas targeted for betterment early in Manley's first term included sports and tourism. The government announced that October would be "Tourism Month." The news came just as National Sports Limited (NSL), the government-funded company charged with managing the National Stadium in Kingston, underwent a reorganization. A multimillion-dollar venue barely a decade old, the National Stadium had deteriorated prematurely and required increasing subsidies just to pay its bills. It was a questionable destination for locals—cars were routinely vandalized in the parking lot during events, fights often broke out in the stands, and a professional soccer player was brazenly sucker punched in the tunnel at halftime of a tournament match—let alone an attraction for tourists. When Manley's secretary for sport, Seymour Mullings, addressed the new fifteen-member board of the NSL in September, he gave it a mandate to make the National Stadium "financially self-supporting," and echoed the calls of Jamaican sportswriters to use it for "big international events drawing large crowds." Mullings's directive that NSL make money off international crowds came, coincidentally, just a few weeks before Tourism Month kicked off with a series of full-page ads in the *Jamaica Daily Gleaner* trumpeting the economic potential of foreign travelers, under the tagline "Tourism is my business—yours too." Within forty-eight hours of being nominated as the new chairman of the NSL, a twenty-nine-year-old Kingston attorney named Paul Fitzritson formed a three-man committee that promised to review solicitations and suggestions for just two weeks before unfurling a plan to make Jamaica "a real sports Mecca."[15]

The selection of the committee indicated the direction in which the NSL was headed. Mike Fennell, president of the Jamaica Boxing Board of Control, joined Fitzritson and the outgoing chair, Arthur Scholefield, as part of the triumvirate that would review proposals for the NSL's 1973 program. Meanwhile, Valdez and Chen were pulling strings around the island, and the *Gleaner* picked up a Reuters story that the WBC's president, Ramon Velasquez, had threatened to strip Frazier of the title if he did not schedule a defense against a ranked opponent. Frazier and Durham weighed the competing offers while Foreman and Sadler waited for court rulings. But when the WBC council issued an ultimatum to Frazier and Foreman to set the match or give up their rankings, the *Gleaner*'s sport section devoted fully one-third of a page to the block-letter headline "MOVE TO GET WORLD TITLE FIGHT HERE."[16]

The offer materializing offshore matched the Astrodome's purse and promised freedom from not only taxes but also the pending injunctions. Foreman and Sadler were ready to pack their bags, but Yank Durham didn't move, so Frazier stayed idle. All the underground machinations and governmental influence that went into the Jamaican proposal would mean nothing if the champ wouldn't accept it. Durham would not let Frazier fight in New York under the current tax structure and allegedly did not want to hold the bout in California for fear of earthquakes; now some wondered whether he just refused to let Frazier defend against Foreman period. The Jamaican press published regular updates on the status of negotiations and listed the benefits of hosting a major international sporting event in Kingston. The *New York Times* did not acknowledge Jamaica's bid for three weeks. Because of its delayed publication schedule, the *Ring* took three months to finally cover the story. None of them, according to Foreman, told the "inside truth" about how the deal got done.[17]

Doc Kearns's boxing alliances extended across the country, even after his death, and Sadler had used those connections to navigate Foreman from an amateur to the number-one contender. In Philadelphia, where Foreman once bludgeoned Roger Russell at the Spectrum, one of their Kearns connections was Norman Henry. Not a fighter and only occasionally listed as anything else of record, Henry was known as a reliable "gofer," but he functioned almost as an attaché of the Quaker City fight game. Henry had worked for Kearns and also Archie Moore, knew Sadler well, had been friends with Joe Louis, and became friends with the local boxer turned world champion Joe Frazier. Henry drove Frazier around and did other favors; presumably, Frazier helped Henry get his tickets for the Super Fight. When the challenger's camp needed to get Frazier a message from Jamaica, Henry was the obvious envoy. He told Frazier that Durham often took a five-figure cash payment, under the table of course, as a kind of matchmaking fee from promoters. In this case, however, there could be a six-figure bonus going directly to Frazier if he signed on for the Jamaica fight. Henry advised him to push Durham on the Jamaica offer and suggested that if Durham pushed back, it was probably because he wasn't getting the extra cash. Whether Durham's reluctance was due to the nonpayment of secret fees, other terms of the offer, or just a bad feeling about the matchup against Foreman, the situation played out the way Henry said it would. Frazier, spiting Durham, hopped a plane to Kingston. The only thing that kept him from immediately signing the contract was Foreman's inability to catch his flight—twice. When he finally made it to the island, they formally agreed to the terms in a ceremony at the House of Chen.[18]

Not everyone in Jamaica celebrated the news of an impending "Sunshine Showdown"—or the manner in which the island had won it. As Frazier landed in Kingston, Edward Seaga, the opposition party's spokesman on finance, called for an immediate investigation. In an address to parliament, he referred to accusations that "under-the-table payments" had swayed negotiations. He also drew attention to the nearly $2 million that the Jamaican government, via the NSL, had borrowed from the Bank of Nova Scotia and deposited in banks in Pennsylvania, California, and New York. Seaga feared that ticket sales could not cover the fight's expenses; worse, ancillary revenues were still being disputed in American courts, and the paid-television proceeds from Frazier's last two fights generated only 10 percent of the loan amount. Besides the economic risk, Seaga warned, the entire process would "endanger the financial image and reputation of Jamaica abroad at a time when foreign capital" was scarce on the island.[19]

Proponents of the fight did not ignore the risks, but they believed in the payoff, both economically and diplomatically. The NSL retained the services of a Kingston attorney named John Muirhead, an expert on injunction law, and frequently sent him to the United States to keep up with the status of Foreman's lawsuits. For the television contract, National Sports selected Hank Schwartz, the founder of Video Techniques, when he estimated that closed-circuit-television revenue would not only cover the loan amount but also surpass it by a million dollars—even if he had to bring in his own equipment to broadcast in color, since that technology was not yet available in Jamaica. The worldwide broadcast was part of the geopolitical appeal. Fitzritson told the press, "We hope the fight will make people all over the world aware of our aims and objectives. The eyes of the world will be on Jamaica and we hope we can show them the kind of people we are." At a time when the national economy was tens of millions of dollars in the red, oil prices were skyrocketing, and labor strikes and bread shortages plagued the island, a new Jamaican government and a first-term prime minister gambled on hosting a boxing match. A corollary of the "Big Sell Jamaica" campaign, which accompanied the fight—a program that required any commercial advertising of the fight to be "Jamaica oriented"—was the demotion of Valdez to "matchmaker" and Chen to "consultant." In its logistics, financing, and advertisement, the Sunshine Showdown represented the first total government sponsorship of a prizefight since, perhaps, the fall of Rome. The tactic became popular with other nations trying to prove their sovereignty and virility by hosting an international sports mega-event. The extensive and expensive bidding processes for established mega-events like the Olympics prohibited many developing nations from vying for them. Yet in the deregulated world of boxing, even the biggest bouts could be bought, sold, or usurped; in the fight game there was always a chance for an upset.[20]

The Sunshine Showdown looked like proof that "better" had come to Jamaica by the end of 1972. Those whose livelihoods rested in boxing's heavyweight division hoped that "better" would come to them as well. Frazier and Foreman got better purses and better tax rates—even better weather—for their January rendezvous than any of the American suitors offered, and the mid-1970s are still remembered as a "golden era" for the heavyweight division. Better might have come, but it did so at the expense of New York City and Madison Square Garden. Harry Markson saw the future of prizefighting and didn't like it. He retired, and Teddy Brenner assumed his position, one not nearly as enviable as it was when Markson took over in the 1940s as the man responsible for keeping boxing alive at the Garden. In the meantime, he would have to be content beaming in the images of the next heavyweight championship bout while hoping it wasn't too successful. If it worked in Jamaica, after all, every quasi-major city in any old, new, or imagined nation that boasted a venue with a few thousand chairs would start bidding for the next major title fight: the Frazier-Ali rematch. Most of the boxing community believed that Foreman had no more chance of beating Frazier than Terry Daniels or Ron Stander had the year before. Foreman's perfect record and impressive string of knockouts proved only that he had been carefully managed up to this point, that his handlers exclusively paired him against, in the vernacular of the sport, "palookas." In fact, for many the real competition in Frazier versus Foreman was between the venues, promoters, and lawyers. The contest inside the ring, wherever it was fought, was a foregone conclusion—a placeholder for the Super Sequel.[21]

★ 7 ★
I Ain't No Dog

When Frazier and Foreman set up their training camps in Jamaica, *Billboard*'s number-one song was "You're So Vain," by Carly Simon. Stevie Wonder's "Superstition," which held first place on the "Soul Singles" chart, had risen to the second spot on the Top 100 by the week of the fight. It made for a fitting soundtrack to the Sunshine Showdown. Dave Wolf noted in Frazier's camp that the champion sometimes rebuffed directions from his trainer, Eddie Futch, staring at his fists and saying, "I lay my hands on and they fall." George Plimpton surveyed Foreman's camp for *Sports Illustrated* and described it as a "gypsy atmosphere" rife with "soothsayers, dreamers, tea-leaf readers." Vanity versus superstition.[1]

To some, it looked as though Foreman had flown in Doc Broadus for a good luck charm and hired the ex-champion Archie Moore to be something between a pugilistic philosopher and a camp mystic. Moore and Sadler burying their decade-old grudge was just one of many strange phenomena surrounding the challenger. The camp seemed to revolve around an even stranger blend of exercise and ceremony. Nearly every day, Moore overtaped Foreman's fists to a cartoonish degree underneath his huge gloves. As Sadler clung to a heavy bag, Foreman stepped up and rhythmically pounded away with punches reminiscent of the "shovel hook" that Jack Dempsey threw. Sadler hung on "like a sailor clutching the mainmast in a hurricane." The loud, dull thuds, combined with images of Sadler popping backward and Foreman's fist imprinting itself on the bag, made an intimidating scene. But it did not look like much more than intimidation. Bundini Brown surfaced in Jamaica, looked at the tape job, and wondered aloud whether Foreman's hands were broken. After watching the heavy-bag ritual Bundini asked, "What good is that? He's hitting something that doesn't move. . . . Frazier's not going to stand still for him." It did not seem to intimidate Frazier either. His preparations for the title defense included fraternizing with Playboy bunnies, competing in a televised "Mini-Olympics," and, of course, arranging appearances with the Knockouts. Plenty of the attention in his camp was directed at the impending rematch with Ali, not the upcoming match with Foreman.[2]

Gene Courtney of the *Philadelphia Inquirer* did not so much look past the Foreman fight as right through it. Foreman, he wrote, "winds up his right hand like he is cranking an old Model-T" and stood no chance of landing one on their champion. Dan Daniel of *Ring* and the *Jamaica Daily Gleaner*'s Baz Freckleton were not as influenced by hometown bias, but reached similar conclusions. Not only would Frazier seal it up quickly, but each writer intimated that Foreman's camp knew it, too. His team had been stubborn in negotiations simply because it intended to get the most money possible for his first and possibly last significant payday. *Boxing Illustrated* recognized that there were multiple iterations of the challenger to consider—a cover story titled "The Two Faces of George Foreman" described a handful of "Foreman's" that might show up in the Jamaican ring—but stopped short of suggesting that any of them could dethrone Frazier.[3]

Some Jamaican fans held out hope that Foreman might win, but only those who disliked the "establishment" Joe Frazier. Their sentiment affected the betting line. Lucien Chen set 3–1 odds for Frazier in his parlors. Off the books, at least one Jamaican cab driver took Foreman at 7–10. Vic Ziegel in the *New York Post* bet that Frazier's biggest obstacle would be the traffic jam delaying his victory party. "In parts of the world where men's hearts do not affect their betting styles," even Chen acknowledged that one might find 10-1 for Frazier—although Las Vegas sportsbooks did not crest much past 3 1/2–1 on the champ. Boxing's intelligentsia produced myriad obituaries for Foreman in the weeks leading up to the fight. Whether unnamed sports reporters or syndicated columnists, in African American weekly newspapers, mainstream dailies, major wire services, foreign outlets, or boxing periodicals, no one dared to give Foreman anything more than a puncher's chance. Some writers hedged their bets, suggesting that if Frazier had been seriously hurt in the Super Fight, then Foreman might get to enjoy the spoils of Ali's labor. Boxers were rarely conservative in their predictions, however. The ex-champion Jersey Joe Walcott said, "Frazier would eat him alive." The surging heavyweight contender Ken Norton stated his view of Foreman plainly: "He stinks. He's going to need a bunch of luck. . . . He'll last five rounds." In fact, the only member of the boxing fraternity to openly support Foreman, outside those on his payroll, was Joe Louis. But Louis, mired in back taxes and substance abuse, regularly took prompts from Las Vegas oddsmakers to back an underdog in order to stimulate more betting. The Brown Bomber's sudden belief in Foreman—whom he had never seen fight in person—just as the odds were piling up in Frazier's favor suggests that he truly meant it when he told Will Grimsley, "I *got* to give the kid a shot."[4]

For a fighter in the 1970s, having Louis pick you to win was tantamount to receiving the kiss of death. In a manner perhaps not as witty but no less effective than Mark Twain's response to a premature obituary, Foreman tried to clarify that he was not yet dead.

He began to spar with reporters who parroted the familiar story line of him as a decided underdog. "Take it back," he demanded of one interviewer; "I ain't no dog," he snarled at another. Most of the questions lobbed at Frazier circulated around how he stayed motivated for any bout except the rematch with Ali. He spoke about the purse money, recalled his "plantation" in South Carolina, and said he wanted to buy some land in Philadelphia as well. "The kids are always in need of something like new shoes. I always need something like a new home, new car or something." Foreman, on the other hand, reminded the press that he did not even have shoes growing up: "We were po'—not poor—but po' . . . We used to jump on a rich boy in a minute." The simmering memories of his troubled youth boiled over, and Foreman exclaimed, "I'll whip his head until it ropes like okra."[5]

One observer thought the Foreman training regimen looked so bad that it had to be a ruse. "Are you doing your real training in secret?" he asked Sadler. There was a kernel of truth to the question, but the "gypsy" camp was much more serious than it appeared. The "Ageless Warrior" Archie Moore provided a stream of eccentricities for reporters, but behind closed doors, his role was not just "spiritual" or "mystic"; according to Foreman, "he was the key trainer." Moore wrapped his hands before sessions, rubbed him down afterward, shared stories from decades of experience fighting some of the greatest champions—including Joe Louis and Rocky Marciano—and ultimately treated Foreman like a champion. The focus was so singular that Foreman skipped his own birthday and missed the birth of his daughter Michi, though he got photos sent to Jamaica and managed to negotiate naming rights remotely. Adrienne wanted to name her Georgianna, after a friend they called "Georgie," but Foreman vetoed a namesake. He hadn't built much of a name yet.[6]

Camp became almost too serious. Sparring partners got injured, and sand poured out of heavy bags. "All I knew was training," Foreman said. It remained undecided whether that increasing ferocity both in training and with the press was necessary to keep him in contention with Frazier, or whether it would simply propel him into Frazier's "smokin'" attack. "Don't you know smokin' is hazardous to your health?" Foreman retorted. Most believed the challenger to be the one facing a hazard. The only way he could avoid being knocked out, one writer suggested, would be through "the merciful intervention of Mr. Mercante." Perhaps the most respected boxing referee at the time, Arthur Mercante had officiated Foreman's two biggest fights to date, against Kirkman and Chuvalo, as well as Frazier's title defenses versus Quarry and Ali. While National Sports Limited, the Jamaica Boxing Board of Control, and representatives for Frazier and Foreman continued to bicker and barter over which judges would score the fight and what rules would be enforced, Mercante already had his bags packed.[7]

Mercante typically enforced the rules of whichever state athletic commission had jurisdiction over a fight. In Jamaica, everything could be ordered à la carte. After he arrived, he was apprised of the customized rules for this fight. First, one Jamaican and one American judge would score the bout with him, on the traditional ten-point must system. Not many believed the scores would come into play. In fact, to make the Sunshine Showdown last longer, all parties agreed to waive the three-knockdown rule, which otherwise automatically would have stopped the bout if one boxer fell three times within the same round. This was not just a boxing match; it was a sports spectacle. Jamaica could not afford to have it cut short by a technicality. Around ten at night, Jamaica time, on Monday, January 22, Mercante reminded the fighters of these rules one last time. Later he recalled, "As Frazier, Foreman and I stood out there in the ring, it never occurred to me that the fact that the three knockdown rule had been waived would be of prime importance."[8]

The ring they occupied was also a custom job, with a bright "China-blue" mat chosen specifically by Schwartz to make a vivid picture on television. In fact, Jerry Perenchio's television crew had tried to do the same thing for the Super Fight before Markson shot them down. But the atmosphere in Kingston lacked some of the seriousness one might have found at the edge of the Garden's traditional white canvas. Clear-voiced Don Dunphy prepared to call the blow-by-blow for the closed-circuit broadcast. But just as Perenchio had paired Dunphy with Burt Lancaster, a celebrity "expert," for the Super Fight, Schwartz's team gave up even the pretense of expertise in the name of celebrity. It added the singer and actress Pearl Bailey—President Nixon's "Ambassador of Love"—as a color commentator. She arrived decked out in a fur coat over a shimmering, sheer ball gown, but Dunphy remained unimpressed. He gave Bailey the same instruction he had given to Lancaster nearly two years before: "Talk between rounds."[9]

Howard Cosell, on the other hand, was accompanied only by his magniloquence. Cosell's bright pink face suggested that from the Errol Flynn suite of the Stony Hill Hotel, which he shared with his wife, he had conducted more research on the Jamaican coastline than the upcoming fight. Calling the action live for an ABC broadcast that would not air until Saturday, Cosell seemed unusually lax as the stadium readied for the main event. Even more lax than Cosell, however, was the ring announcer, Dwight "Nightingale" Whylie. He had never worked a boxing match—and some suggested he had never even seen a boxing match—before introducing the fighters at the Sunshine Showdown. They stared each other down while Whylie gazed into the crowd, resting against the top rope and waving to friends and fans, completely unaware of the bell sounding to start the fight. As Frazier and Foreman bored in, Whylie made a rodeo-clown-like escape out of the ring. And through it all, Plimpton, in the vanguard of new sports journalists, stared at a moth sitting on the shoulder blade of Red Smith, the standard bearer for a previous generation of sportswriters. Plimpton did not believe that the bout would be a very good fight. But he was pretty sure he could write something about that moth.[10]

Plimpton knew boxing well enough to gasp when Foreman started the bout with a long wide right that soared over Frazier's head, leaving him exposed to a left counterpunch. "Frazier's ... best weapon," Cosell reminded his audience, "the left hook. Foreman is vul-ner-a-ble to the hook." But Frazier did not capitalize on his first great opportunity. Instead, he bobbed, weaved, and feinted to keep Foreman off balance. Less skillfully, Foreman tried to affect Frazier's balance by pushing and pulling him. Both Dunphy and Cosell noted that Frazier usually did not "smoke" so much in the first round while also pointing out that he had entered this fight at least ten pounds heavier than when he fought Ali. Just as they were making excuses for Frazier, however, he landed the feared left hook flush on Foreman's right jaw. It took forty seconds to confirm the suspicions of many. "Foreman has been nailed and nailed good," Dunphy crooned. The only question remaining was how many hacks would it take to fell him.[11]

Foreman seemed unfazed by the first power punch that Frazier landed. In fact, whereas Dunphy had noted earlier that Foreman appeared "tense," he now observed that the challenger looked "a little looser." They stood face-to-face and traded blows, most of which glanced off shoulders and elbows, until a "smart, snappy jab" pierced Frazier's defense and opened a hole just big enough for the underside of Foreman's glove. Overexcited by the successful combination, Foreman launched a torrent of haymakers. Most of them sailed above a crouching Frazier—but not all. Suddenly a voice, maybe the only one in the stadium as nasal and high pitched as Cosell's, rose above the din: "Frash-uh's hurt!" It belonged to Angelo Dundee, Ali's trainer, who had carefully studied Frazier for years and witnessed fifteen rounds of Smokin' Joe firsthand. He had seen Frazier on film, he had seen him in person, and something in Frazier's body language tipped off Dundee, who sat so close to Cosell that the microphone easily picked up "Frash-uh's hurt!" Seconds later, Foreman reined in his unfettered onslaught and revisited the left-jab-right-uppercut combo. It landed even cleaner than the first time, sending Frazier onto the canvas and Cosell into hysterics: "Down goes Frazier! Down goes Frazier! Down goes Frazier!" Dundee's cry may have temporarily overpowered Cosell, but the now-famous call "Down goes Frazier" drowned out the memories of Dunphy's live broadcast, playing on a nascent cable channel called Home Box Office, and forever associated the Sunshine Showdown with ABC's replay.[12]

Sitting just five seats away from Cosell, twelve-year-old Marvis Frazier could hear his commentary and probably Dundee's addendum as well, but he was not as concerned as they were. "Daddy, stop playin', man. Why you playin'? Stop playin'!" he laughed as his father jumped back to his feet. Foreman was absolutely not playing. As soon as Mercante restarted the fight, Foreman pounced, again swinging wildly with both fists in all directions. That tactic wouldn't necessarily work for him this time. His opponent was no "Scrap Iron" Johnson or "Hobo" Wiler. Frazier embodied the gritty and aggressive spirit of boxing in Philadelphia. He pressed forward, working his way to the inside, where he could erase Foreman's height advantage. Foreman composed himself and settled back into a rhythm of jabbing, pushing Frazier, jabbing, and pushing him again, eventually herding the champion into a corner like a stubborn cow into its pen—or an abattoir.[13]

With thirty seconds remaining, Dunphy prepared to score the first round, proclaiming, "Foreman in complete charge of the fight."

While Dunphy scaled down, however, Cosell ratcheted up his call: "Frazier is dazed! He is getting hit again and again and a-gain!" Cosell's voice cracked on the last syllable just as another right uppercut from Foreman crashed against Frazier's face, sending him through the ropes as unceremoniously as "Nightingale" Whylie had flown just a few minutes earlier. "Foreman is all over Joe Fraz-ier!" Cosell's voice cracked again at the end of the sentence, punctuating the left-jab-right-uppercut combo that knocked Frazier down a second time. Mercante later recalled the blow: "[It was] the most devastating punch I have seen, maybe the most demolishing in heavyweight history." Bob Arum and Herbert Muhammad, with millions of dollars riding on a Frazier-Ali championship rematch, for the first time in their lives openly encouraged Frazier to get up. Marvis was still not dismayed, but he was not laughing anymore. He yelled, "Daddy stop playin', man! Why you playin'? Why you playin'?!" It may have looked like Frazier was playing when he bounced up immediately, tried to forgo the standing eight count, and chose to reengage Foreman only seconds before the break, but it was a serious mistake. Foreman kept firing while Frazier lost his ability to bob or weave. The force of Foreman's punches rocked Frazier until he toppled over again, just before the bell signaled the end of the first round.[14]

Frazier barely made it to his feet, and needed Durham's support to stay there. As his cornermen helped him onto a stool and placed a pack of ice on the back of his neck to "restore the senses," ABC replayed in slow motion a sequence showing one of Foreman's uppercuts landing squarely on Frazier's chin, sending waves of skin ripples from his jowls to his brow. Even Marvis lost hope after the third knockdown: "The reality hit me, daddy's not playin', and that was the first time that I realized my dad was human." Interestingly, Muhammad Ali's analysis between rounds focused more on Foreman's weaknesses than Frazier's. "He's just throwing hard, wild punches

and Frazier stands right there and allows himself to be hit by them."
Ali counseled: "If he could get off the ropes and stop trying to slug it
out, he could win this fight, because right now George is very, very
tired."[15]

At the onset of the second stanza, Frazier reflected Ali's optimism
more than Marvis's disillusion. He came out in his usual smokin'
style, pressing headfirst and swinging away at Foreman as if the previous three knockdowns had already been forgotten. "You'll not find
a gamer man than Joe Frazier," Cosell remarked. Foreman was less
impressed. He leaned over Frazier and alternated, like a pendulum,
waist-high power punches that landed on Frazier's head because of
the height disparity and clash of styles. Even Mercante might have
been stunned by the turn of events when he decided to break the
fighters and issue a nondescript warning to Foreman for some un-
specific infraction. "Foreman is being warned . . . Frazier is being
battered," Dunphy announced as the challenger once more backed
the champion into a corner with his body, promptly dislodged him
with a hard right, and with an even harder right hand sent him back
to the canvas. Dunphy was clearly disoriented by the dizzying pace
of knockdowns. He called the fourth knockdown with "45 seconds
to go" in the round, when in fact it was only forty-five seconds *into*
round two. Cosell was no better. In a desperate attempt to fill airtime during a standing eight count, he made a comparison between
the present scene and Foreman's Olympic victory in Mexico City
nearly five years earlier. Cosell barely caught the fifth knockdown,
caused by a short, compact left hook, and also missed the chance to
enunciate its resemblance to the signature punch on which Frazier
had made his now-fading championship run.[16]

Again, Frazier's legs moved faster than his head, propelling him
upright before he could catch his balance. Yet on the restart, Frazier managed to parry Foreman's left jab for the first time in the
match; unfortunately, he did not even see the straight right that

followed until it slammed into his nose. Foreman composed himself and reverted back to what he knew best. Planting his feet as solidly as if quick-drying cement lathered the canvas, he repeated the heavy-bag exercise that Bundini had mocked earlier. Frazier could not have been stiller if Sadler were wrapped around him. The only damage he inflicted was to puncture Foreman's glove with an errant tooth. As Foreman landed each and every concussive blow, Cosell reached the fever pitch that caused him to repeat sentences, emphasizing every syllable. "It's target practice for George Foreman! It-is-tah-get-prac-tice!!" he bawled into the microphone. The last shot lifted Frazier off of the canvas and dropped him back to earth an ex-champion.[17]

"It's ov-ah! It-is-ov-ah!!" Cosell's hysterical pronouncement, underneath the supernova of lights emanating from Jamaica's National Stadium, pierced the tranquility of midnight in the Caribbean. When he regained some composure, he informed viewers who would not hear him for several days, "I am going into that ring to talk to Joe Frazier, the loser, and George Foreman, the winner." He was already late. The most competitive contest of the night was a race to Foreman that started the moment Mercante waved his arms over a prostrate Frazier. From their ringside seats, the veteran broadcaster Don Dunphy and a neophyte second-tier manager from Ohio named Don King ran a furious steeplechase to the center of the mat. Dunphy, a former Manhattan College track star, ducked, dodged, and hustled around throngs of security personnel and the flood of fans they were desperately trying to keep out of the ring. King, a different kind of hustler, had recently graduated from the Marion Correctional Institution after serving time for a manslaughter conviction. He got to Foreman, too. Despite Dunphy's and King's disparate approaches, the heat ended in a draw. Dunphy grasped his microphone and asked questions. King, who arrived at the fight in a limo with Frazier, had been inching closer to Foreman after each knockdown until he at last stood behind him, rubbing the new champ's shoulders and repeating: "My man! You got it! My man!"[18]

The rush for his attention caught Foreman off guard—and knocked him out of character. His sculpted image began to crack under the pressure of the heavyweight crown. Before he left Jamaica, Foreman expressed several aspirations for his reign, some of which were dramatic departures from soul-brother cool and others patently contradictory. The new champ said he wanted to take on all challengers, yet he would also consider retiring from the ring to pursue business ventures or become a preacher. He labeled himself the "baddest man in the world," but he wanted to tear down gyms and build libraries for "juveniles." Foreman called himself "just a country boxer" who wanted to buy a camper and go fishing in the backcountry, yet he bellowed from the center of the China blue canvas in Kingston: "The world is my ring!"[19]

As the stadium lights went down and the sun rose over Foreman's championship era, he and much of the boxing world experienced an evanescent euphoria. The hangover would set in soon. Moore had trained him like a champion before the bout, and Foreman started living like one afterward. In Jamaica, they "treated [him] like a king," and in his postvictory delirium, Foreman imbibed in women and ice cream. When he returned stateside, it was to a "hero's welcome." He accepted an invitation from Bob Hope—extended before he left the island—to appear on his weekly television show. Hope tutored him in their short time together and instilled in the boxer an interest in delivering jokes directly to the camera. Foreman lamented that no one corrected his double negatives, however, which kept him tethered to memories of skipping school during the day and stealing wallets at night in Houston's Bloody Fifth.[20]

His first visit to Houston after winning the title looked a lot different from his return after the Olympics. The city proclaimed "George

Foreman Day." He received a plaque from the Houston Chamber of Commerce, and Mayor Louie Welch presented him with a medal. Back in California, he took his place on the "banquet circuit," shaking hands and affixing a strained but nearly permanent smile on his face. A piece he contributed to the magazine *Nation's Business*, entitled "Don't Knock the American System to Me," affirmed his faith in capitalism and Christianity, and Congresswoman Yvonne Brathwaite Burke of Los Angeles entered it into the *Congressional Record*. These celebrations and accolades, however, masked a deepening dissatisfaction in his personal and professional relationships. The sordid characters that became intertwined with the new champion laid an unstable foundation for his future.[21]

When Cosell announced, "It's over," he called the end of more than just a fight; it may well have marked the end of the long 1960s too. Before Frazier, Foreman, and Mercante met in the ring, the Supreme Court handed down its landmark decision in favor of "Jane Roe" over Dallas district attorney Henry Wade. LBJ died at his ranch in Stonewall, Texas, on the same day. National newspapers such as the *Los Angeles Times* and *Philadelphia Inquirer* ambitiously tried to cram all three stories—*Roe v. Wade*, LBJ, and Foreman's dramatic upset—onto their front pages for January 23. The establishment of a lightning rod for the burgeoning Religious Right and the loss of a bulwark of New Deal liberalism furthered the reorientation of political influence in the United States from the Northeast to the Sunbelt. Prizefighting was not immune to the changes: the new champion chose to live in California, and cities like Houston and Las Vegas outbid Philadelphia or New York for the biggest events of the year. Yet even the fastest-growing region in the country had lost out to a declining stadium in a developing nation. After ABC Sports replayed Frazier versus Foreman, ABC News reported the signing of the Paris Peace Accords, which promised the withdrawal of American troops from Vietnam and called into question the superiority of superpowers. With a champion willing to take his title around the world, any nation ready to commit sufficient resources could offer to put on a heavyweight megamatch and gain the attendant financial and political capital. This new era set the tempo for a period of relative popularity and prosperity, at least in the highest echelons of the fight game. And just as prizefighting became a tool of Cold War diplomacy, Foreman became a transnational commodity.[22]

★ 8 ★
Superman's Evil Twin

He wears his title like a kid wears his first pair of long pants—proud as a peacock—yet still not completely used to the adulation and attention that has come with it.

SHIRLEY NORMAN, "With Foreman, It's U.S.A. All the Way," *Ring*, October 1973, 6

For the powerbrokers of boxing, the sport functioned at its best when its heavyweight stars were aligned. In the chaotic days of early 1973, everything was up in the air. A series of confounding upsets, beginning with the Sunshine Showdown in January, kept the division's outlook murky. Its next up-and-coming contender was Ron Lyle, an ex-convict with a compelling redemption story and a perfect record. Putting him opposite Frazier or the new champ, Foreman, promised a fight with a lot of punches thrown and plenty of excitement if any of them landed. Then he lost to an all-but-forgotten Jerry Quarry in February, undermining his championship aspirations. Muhammad Ali had been lobbying for the first shot at Foreman by taking partial credit for his victory. "I didn't realize I whupped Joe Frazier so bad," he said after the title changed hands. But in March he lost a decision to Ken Norton and suffered a broken jaw in the process. It kept Ali more restrained for the time being, but left Foreman alone at the top in a deafening silence.[1]

From his new perch above Madison Square Garden boxing, Teddy Brenner fumed: "An intolerable situation has developed among the worthwhile heavyweights. Something has to be done about it." For him, "intolerable" really meant "unprofitable." Although made hopeful by the turnover of three judges on the New York state appellate court, which reopened the tax debate, Brenner and the Garden did not have a big-money prizefight on the horizon with which to test the waters. Given the lack of marketable contenders, *Ring* beat the drum for a Foreman-Frazier rematch. Frazier had barely been lifted off the blue canvas with which he had become intimately acquainted when his entitlement to a second chance infused the new editor in chief Nat Loubet's editorials as well as Dan Daniel's features. Daniel noted: "Time was when the publicity engendered by George's feat at Kingston, Jamaica, would have been followed by a rematch. . . . But there is little respect now for tradition, for custom, and whatever was admirable in the ring in days gone by." One letter to the editor suggested that there was really no need for another Foreman-Frazier match anyway, since Foreman should be retroactively disqualified for the "uncouth maneuvers" he used to wrest the title. "They'll give us a return," Frazier's manager told him. "I'm pretty sure they will." Foreman did not weigh in on the prospect, and his silence fanned the flames. Loubet accused the champion of being a "hermit" and declared: "Boxing is no place for hermits."[2]

Even if absent from the prize ring, Foreman was not exactly hiding. After his TV spot with Bob Hope, celebration in Houston, and appearances in California, he went on the road again. An easier road, however, than any before. He booked multiple charity benefits and boxing exhibitions from Las Vegas to Quebec in order to earn a little cash and some good publicity. The photos with prominent figures including Nevada lieutenant governor Harry Reid, New York City mayor John Lindsay, and the sitting governor of California, Ronald Reagan, may have been worth thousands of words, but that was about it. The exhibitions were so disastrous that Canadian authorities barred Foreman from holding any more of them after promoters lost money in Windsor, just over the border from Detroit, and in Verdun, outside Montreal. The financial strains took their toll on Foreman and Sadler as well. Disagreements over Foreman's purses, Sadler's percentages, and the lawsuits still lingering above them rose to the surface as their initial contract expired. At a press conference in Las Vegas, Sadler very deliberately sidestepped any talks of Foreman's next bout. "Words pour from him like bullets from a machine gun," one reporter noted, yet he was unusually guarded at the moment. The safety was released when someone suggested that since Quarry was fresh off his victory over Lyle, Foreman should finally meet him. Sadler unloaded, "Let him fight some of those people that put him on his back first!" It wasn't Sadler's call anymore. Foreman would keep him as a trainer, though not for a 33 percent obligation, let alone the 50 percent or so that he had been drawing. All the stories that Sadler had told Foreman of boxing's underworld in their years of barnstorming together intensified Foreman's suspicion. He was determined to bring in only the people he could trust—family and friends—while becoming a self-managed champion in an unmanageable sport.[3]

As spring bloomed, Foreman withered, and the fickle sports world focused on a younger, bigger, and faster heavyweight. Standing just five-six but weighing nearly 1,200 pounds—including more than twenty pounds of heart—a three-year-old chestnut-colored colt named Secretariat took the nation by storm. At the Kentucky Derby, he upset the popular favorite Sham, breaking last but finishing first in a dramatic two-length victory. Two weeks later, Secretariat made another last-to-first push at the Preakness Stakes and, for the second straight race, beat Sham by just over two lengths. On the last leg of the Triple Crown, at Belmont Park in New York, only three other horses dared to compete against Secretariat. Sham was the lone horse in the field believed to have a chance of upsetting "Big Red." Pushing harder than before, earlier than normal, Sham merely exhausted himself faster. He finished last while Secretariat clocked the fastest time in the race's history and broke its record for biggest lead as well, crossing the line no less than thirty-one lengths ahead of the runner-up. "You couldn't find the other horses with two pairs of binoculars," one columnist wrote. Many of those who bet on Secretariat never even bothered to cash their tickets, since the souvenir from horse racing's first Triple Crown winner in a quarter century might be more valuable than the payout on a small bet. Foreman, only a few months removed from the bright lights of Jamaica and *The Bob Hope Show*, felt as far back and dust-bitten as Sham.[4]

The sport pages turned their attention away from Foreman, but he didn't exactly fight for the press. Secretariat continued to race that season, even after winning the Triple Crown. Frazier, sensing an opportunity after Ali's loss to Norton, stayed busy by outpointing Joe Bugner in London. Those within listening range of Foreman's ringside seat heard him dismiss the effort and state unequivocally that Bugner should have won the decision. Regardless, Frazier went down as the victor and declared that he would beat Foreman in a rematch or quit the sport altogether. The pressure to schedule a title defense mounted, and it fell squarely on Foreman. Though determined to call his own shots, he enlisted an adviser for relief. Leroy Jackson had no experience in the fight game, but he had history with Foreman. They were friends from Parks, and Foreman saw Jackson as the "golden boy" there, an enterprising and likable personality who "always had a little hustle" and was "always trying to sell [him] something." He even had a car—until Foreman wrecked it. "Don't worry," he told him, "when I'm heavyweight champion I'll let you be my manager." Years later, he was ready to repay the damage. "I got this other job," Jackson told him, working for an oil and gas company. "Quit it. I'll make you rich," Foreman replied.

Jackson dropped everything and joined Foreman's team. But the only path to riches was to fight.[5]

To everyone's surprise, Foreman suddenly announced not one but *two* upcoming title matches. When the shock wore off, however, his detractors were far from satisfied. Both of Foreman's proposed bouts were against questionably ranked foreign opponents and set for international arenas. In September, he planned to take on the heavyweight champion of Puerto Rico, Jose "King" Roman, in Tokyo. Perhaps undercutting the competitive value of his first title defense, Foreman preemptively scheduled a second one with the European heavyweight champion (and Spanish rock-lifting champion), Jose Urtain, in Panama for the following January. It appeared that despite the negative reaction to an international title fight, the Sunshine Showdown in Jamaica would be the closest venue to the United States to host a heavyweight championship contest for the foreseeable future. Nobody should have been surprised by the decision to keep Foreman fighting outside the country. He added another member to his entourage, Loren Cassina, a Canadian promoter and political strategist with global connections. Cassina had worked on TV deals with Dick Sadler and Sonny Liston, and during the Canadian stretch of Foreman's exhibition circuit, some wondered whether he would take Sadler's place as manager of the champion. Foreman did not relinquish control, but he did not ignore all of Sadler's connections either. They still needed the international expertise of someone like Cassina, whom Foreman called "the Henry Kissinger of boxing," because more trouble was brewing at home.[6]

The first shot in another volley of litigation against Foreman came from his hometown. Sadler had previously brokered a deal with Houston-based Texas Boxing Enterprises, headed by Ludene Gilliam, for exclusive promotional rights to Foreman—without, of course, consulting the boxer. Although that contract was in-validated, TBE claimed to have another one guaranteeing that a Foreman-Frazier rematch would take place in the Astrodome. It filed for an injunction against the proposed Foreman-Roman bout. The two sides reached a compromise by agreeing that the local hero would take on Frazier at the Astrodome sometime after his engagement with Roman in Japan. Durham knew that such prom-ises meant little in prizefighting. Nevertheless, he tried to stay op-timistic that Frazier would get his rematch, telling reporters, "It's just a matter of how cute Forman's people want to be." Durham died before the promise could be fulfilled, and things got uglier still for Foreman's "people."[7]

"The itinerant life the champion has been living certainly is not conducive to domestic felicity," one writer suggested. It was an understatement. Foreman told another reporter that during his two-year relationship with Adrienne, "We've practically lived by telephone." Now word leaked out of their impending divorce. Even if they had not occupied the same space very often, Foreman could expect to lose 50 percent of his assets in the settlement. Excluding, perhaps, any money owed that had not yet found its way into an American bank account. Under these circumstances, his itinerancy behooved him—and the Japanese fans waiting to catch a glimpse of the champ at the Nippon Budokan, a martial arts hall built for the 1964 Olympics.[8]

This was not Dick Sadler's first glimpse of Japan. He and Charlie Shipes had lived and worked there as the nation experienced a post-war boom that extended from the automobile industry to the prize ring. A major factor contributing to the growth of boxing in Japan, just as in the United States, was the support of television interests that could broadcast to viewers across the country and pay fighters and promoters handsomely. In the early 1970s, however, the ma-jor television companies in Japan began to sever their relationships with prizefighting. Perhaps they foresaw the end of Japan's boom time—oil prices were creeping up, which was a significant problem for an industrial nation that imported 80 percent of its petroleum. The anticipated "oil shock" was exacerbated by the Kuwaiti and Saudi Arabian governments classifying Japan as "nonfriendly" when tensions rose between Israel and its Arab neighbors. Japan witnessed its first industrial decline since World War II, and national anxieties manifested in many ways, including an unforeseen run on toilet paper.[9]

Japan's boxing community had to act fast in order to avoid being flushed down the drain. First it attracted Muhammad Ali for a showdown with Mac Foster in the first meeting between top-ten heavyweight boxers in Asia. Fifteen thousand ticket holders watched them go the distance, though without any knockdowns, in a fight that Ali dominated. The size of the audience emboldened promoters and television interests, which came together to stage the continent's first heavyweight championship title fight. Nippon Educational Television partnered with the Budokan and offered Foreman the same purse for a defense against the barely known Roman as Brenner put up for a fight at the Garden with the persistent "white hope" Quarry: $1 million. It would take a significant investment to keep sumo's competitor in the ring, but NET believed that Foreman was the kind of *yokozuna* (highest-ranked wrestler) that could draw a crowd.[10]

Roman, however, represented the kind of mismatch rarely seen in sumo—but too often arranged in prizefighting. The WBA, which did not have Roman ranked among its top ten heavyweights, initially demurred at sanctioning the fight. When the WBC agreed to approve the title defense, both bodies quickly ranked Roman as the ninth-best heavyweight in the world. But in Japan, the kind of *ozeki* who could rise to challenge a *yokozuna* would be more akin to a top-three contender. Foreman, perhaps unintentionally, widened the gap between them before the fighters even got to Tokyo. He deflected criticism of his choice to defend against Roman by saying, "In other sports they give rookies a chance." Rookies don't get chances against champions in sumo. He verbally demoted Roman from the top tier down to the lowest division, *jonokuchi*. Fans took notice. Japanese media did as well, and reporters pressed him when he arrived in Tokyo. "Roman is unknown. . . . Why was he selected to be your first challenger?" they asked him. "I don't know and I don't care," Foreman shot back. They asked whether he had ever seen Roman fight, and Foreman confirmed that he had not, adding, "I don't intend to." Someone even asked, "What round will you knock him out?" and Foreman quickly answered, "I want to knock him out before the first round ends." A motorcade with Foreman leading, and Roman in the car right behind, attracted plenty of fans to Ginza Street, but that show was free. When the doors opened for paying customers at the Budokan a couple of weeks later, the returns did not look good. Attendance was half of that for the Ali-Foster fight, and the performance resembled the Beatles' visit to the Budokan in 1966—a short, disappointing twenty-five-minute set.[11]

Tickets to Foreman and Roman's duet cost up to 50,000 yen—close to $200—which was nearly double the top price for Ali versus Foster. Seeing this, some American writers believed the event "proved that [the] Japanese economy had flown sky high." But Joe Koizumi's view from ringside was not so rose-colored as that. "Roman opened with a few jabs and closed without even that formality," he wrote. Foreman drove toward Roman, deflecting or absorbing the blows of a challenger he outweighed by at least twenty pounds. He fired powerful hooks and uppercuts that seemed to originate at the floor and extend all the way to the ceiling, but Roman still could not escape them. Less than one minute into the fight, "a right hand . . . exploded on the left rib cage of the challenger," and thereafter, "if Roman had ever harbored any strong desire to stand in with the champ—which seems dubious—it deserted him." Earlier, the American referee, Jay Edson, had arranged a meeting with both parties, and they agreed to waive the three-knockdown rule, similar to arrangement for the Sunshine Showdown, but in retrospect it was a waste of time. Roman fell to the mat once, got back up, and Foreman knocked him down again twenty seconds later. At exactly the two-minute mark of the first round, another impressive uppercut connected with Roman's jaw. On that third fall, Edson counted him out. Some spectators had not yet found their seats; others had seen quite enough by then. Koizumi concluded on behalf of the nation that "if there are any more Foreman-Roman fights on tap, Japan requests that they be kept across the Pacific."[12]

The more significant story line for heavyweight prizefighting did take place across the Pacific, nine days later—and Foreman was there. At the Forum in Inglewood, Ken Norton looked to repeat his victory over Ali. If Norton beat Ali for the second consecutive time, he would look as close to a consensus number-one contender as the sport had seen since the Super Fight. A Foreman-Norton matchup had all the traits of another superlative-studded multimillion-dollar event, right down to the contrast in styles and personalities: an undefeated champion against a challenger who had not lost in three years. The champ was part of a celebrity parade that included Frank Sinatra and Jim Brown, who offered their commentary on this prelude to the next megamatch. Brown's manager, Hayward Moore, who had dismissed Foreman as completely, even if more politely, as Brown had done before he became champion, now tracked him down and befriended him. But in the flash of a scorecard, Norton's path toward the title was diverted to an almost certain rubber match against Ali—without championship implications. Dan Daniel, exasperated with the carousel of challengers, said the premier division only got "curiouser and curiouser" as 1973, the year of upsets, drew to a close. It was a terribly upsetting year for Foreman, too. A few hundred days after the glow of the Sunshine Showdown, the championship did not shine very bright. He had not, as he promised, taken on all challengers, nor had he retired from boxing. He had neither built any libraries nor demolished any gyms. The "country boxer" who was "not interested in buying a lot of clothes that stand out" did, however, earn a nod from the American Fashion Foundation as one of its top-ten best-dressed men. He bought a brand-new burgundy Rolls-Royce to match a stylish suit and handcrafted boots of the same color. Presumably, he could not find a camper or fishing rod in that hue. Only one of the declarations he made in Kingston proved true during Foreman's championship reign: as he took the title from Jamaica to Japan, nobody could deny that the entire world was indeed Foreman's ring.[13]

Ring magazine, however, tried to keep the focus on the home front. In response to Foreman's agreements to fight Roman and Urtain, rather than higher-ranked American fighters, the bible of boxing, which had made its mark by ranking prizefighters the way Walter Camp picked all-American teams in the early days of college football, produced a second hierarchy. Its "U.S. Rankings" took aim at the national or regional titles liberally bestowed on foreign fighters—like the Puerto Rican championship that Roman held or the European title granted to Urtain—which allowed promoters to elevate them over more deserving Americans for title fights. The magazine believed its domestic rankings would be a long-term fix, improving not only the prospects for American boxers but also the quality of championship prizefights generally.[14]

Foreman took it personally. He chose his opponents and the fight locations. He tried to take care of everything, including scheduling and finances. The heavyweight champion of the world answered his own phones—though sometimes disguising his voice to give the impression of being an assistant. He even did his own bookkeeping, carefully recording everything, including the cash payments he received, so that he could avoid the kind of tax troubles that befell Joe Louis and that Foreman could see firsthand affecting Sadler. He could not, however, control the rest of the field. The champion could not resuscitate a declining Joe Frazier or influence how judges scored Ali and Norton. As the chorus of criticism rose over his lackluster matchmaking and failure to fight a real contender, Foreman grew visibly discontented. Escalating divorce proceedings and protracted lawsuits made it worse. And there was no escape. He had to fulfill an agreement to present the winner's trophy after the second "Battle of the Sexes," in September, but that required him to appear at the Astrodome, despite his contentious relationship with Texas Boxing Enterprises, and to sit near Jim Brown, who apparently forgot how he had dismissed Foreman in Harlem a few years earlier as he held out a hand in Houston. Foreman could not disguise his face the way he could change his voice over the phone. Fashionable coolness declined into angry sullenness. Envisioning an image akin to "Superman's Evil Twin," he recognized that "the public began thinking of [him] as a thug."[15]

Some tried to justify the perceptible change in Foreman's demeanor. Statistically, he was the best knockout-punching champion in history. At the end of 1973, his 0.923 knockout percentage surpassed Rocky Marciano's 0.878. But that calculation did not take into account the level of competition. Fans grew tired of paying to see Foreman bludgeon palookas. Joe Louis, interviewed from the floor of Caesars Palace, where he was enjoying his new role as greeter, schmoozer, and semiprofessional gambler, declared, "Foreman is the best and after him everyone else is the same," but added, "he disgraced himself by fighting Roman." Keeping the date with Urtain, who had lost to Roman nine months earlier, would be worse. A rematch against Frazier, after the pummeling in Jamaica and only a questionable win over Bugner, might not be much better. Bugner turned down the offer for a title fight; he had already taken six bouts in 1973, including losses to Frazier and Ali, and felt no desire to stand in as Foreman's punching bag for the going rate of about $100,000. Proposals to resurrect the Oscar Bonavena fight that Foreman had sidestepped a year earlier were shouted down as soon as they hit the press. Offers to match him against Quarry in Atlanta or New York fizzled, too. Daniel opined that "Foreman is worse off than any other top echelon heavyweight since Jack Johnson." The similarities between the current champion and the champion-in-exile during the 1910s were not lost on the current generation of fight fans, who had met Jack Johnson through the filmic portrayal by James Earl Jones in *The Great White Hope* (1970). Foreman needed money but did not want to get paid in the United States before settling his divorce. At the start of the holiday season, he told *Jet*, "I'm about broke." He reassured readers, "I'm not starving," but emphasized, "I don't have any money."[16]

Similarly, Madison Square Garden was feeling a pinch. It wasn't as if the doors were about to close, but it was getting more and more expensive to open them—about $40,000 each time. Although the Madison Square Garden Corporation made most of its earnings from the racetracks it owned, and not from the almost five hundred events that occurred inside the Garden, ticket sales went down with the economy, and the Garden's stock followed. A program from a circus performance cost more than a share of the Garden. "To make the stock more accepted by the financial community," Chairman Irving Mitchell Felt confirmed that the corporation would initiate a reverse stock split to raise the price. It might not have affected the real value of the company, but things looked better on paper. Brenner followed suit; lacking the prospect of a big-money title fight, he settled for the appearance of one. He bought low on Frazier and Ali, both of whom had lost value in 1973, and finally brought the Super Sequel to the Garden. The purses were equally split again, though they had plummeted from $2,500,000 down to $850,000 apiece.

The only title on the line was the one for the NABF—the belt that couldn't seem to keep a champion. But it looked good.[17]

The mounting enmity that Frazier felt for Ali was not an illusion. Ali jabbed him with barbs about his intelligence, his appearance, and everything else; as with his ring strategy, Frazier did not prepare much of a defense. He kept coming at the same speed—calling Ali "Clay"—until he got smacked with a shot that cut him: "ignorant." Ali may have enjoyed their verbal sparring and the way it drove interest in a nontitle fight between two ex-champs who seemed to be reaching the end of their careers. Frazier did not. He wanted to fight back. When Ali called him "ignorant" again, yelling it this time over Howard Cosell's hairpiece and directly to Frazier's face, he tried. On the *Wide World of Sports* set, the two principals gave a brief preview of the upcoming match until cooler heads intervened. Rising ratings and ticket sales in the aftermath of the televised scrum did not diffuse Frazier's anger.[18]

Foreman stayed angry, too—and he was not the only one. The Frazier-Ali rematch may have upstaged him, but it pushed Ken Norton into the wings. After he split two exciting, hard-fought contests with Ali, a third matchup would have generated Norton's biggest purse to date. Yet the dramatic conclusion to their trilogy got sidetracked when Ali signed to meet Frazier instead, and there was no guarantee it would ever get back on course. If Ali won in January, he would have a strong claim for a title shot with Foreman; if he lost again, it would devalue a bout with Norton—if Ali did not just retire in defeat. Either way, Norton's biggest payday rested in limbo while Foreman simply rested.

Even if Norton's cash cow had left for greener pastures, he was still a stud. While Foreman became harder to find and more difficult to like, Norton seemed ready for the spotlight and impossible to hate. He was a clean-living, clear-speaking former marine with a movie star's physique. Although the Super Sequel closed his window on a rubber match with Ali, it opened the door to a title shot. Whispers and inquiries turned into rumors and questions, eventually giving way to a press conference that, not coincidentally, came off just days before the Super Sequel. Norton's and Foreman's representatives affirmed, definitively, that the two would face off in a sanctioned match for the heavyweight title. Yet that was all the information available. It sounded as hollow as the recent announcements of Foreman preparing to defend the title against Quarry or Bonavena. Neither a date nor a venue had been set. The statement engendered more questions, and it became clear that no one had any solid answers. To combat new rumors undermining Foreman versus Norton, the two prospective opponents met at the Super Sequel's weigh-in. Ironically, because of the melee on *Wide World of Sports*, Frazier and Ali did not. They arrived, took the scale, and left separately. That gave Foreman and Norton an opportunity to steal some thunder.[19]

Foreman's weight, approximately 250 pounds, became the story. He appeared to be at least twenty pounds heavier than normal and closer to thirty pounds above his usual fighting weight. Conversely, Norton looked as fit as ever. Foreman acknowledged that there had been "some motivation missing without an opponent to key on," and *Boxing Illustrated* confirmed that inactivity, as it did for virtually every mammal on earth, had caused "the 6-4 champion to put on weight in abundance." Sadler said: "George doesn't drink or smoke but he really loves ice cream. That's his only vice." Although everyone else in the heavyweight foursome at the Garden that night was at least five years older than Foreman, he was the only one who showed up out of shape. Frazier and Ali tipped the scales at 209 and 212, respectively, and fought with the verve of their first match, three years earlier. Closed-circuit-TV proceeds, which once again accounted for significantly more than the purse, fell beyond the jurisdiction of the New York state taxing authorities. Debunking fears their "long-awaited bout" would be "anticlimactic," Frazier and Ali put on another thrilling show. The only differences this time were that the nontitle fight ended after twelve rounds, rather than fifteen, and that Ali won the decision instead of Frazier. Foreman did not go the distance. He left the Garden after the fourth round, he said, because he was "bored." The sweet tooth that Sadler mentioned could not overpower the sour disposition everyone saw.[20]

Basking in the glow of the Super Sequel, a Garden spokesperson rebuffed questions about the return of a heavyweight championship card to the venue: "It is my personal belief that Foreman will not defend the title in the United States." For Frazier and Ali, television revenue compensated for the smaller purses and high taxes. None of Foreman's earnings were safe from the legal challenges facing him, and the announced agreement with Norton, which lacked specifics, seemed to be going nowhere fast. While the heavyweight championship was becalmed, Alex Valdez, promoter of Frazier's group the Knockouts and early facilitator of the Sunshine Showdown, sailed in again. He navigated the trade winds of boxing in the 1970s, which went through stadiums, governments, and television operations as much as they did through fighters, managers, and promoters. He called at some familiar ports while searching for a place to dock Foreman's next fight and shelter his purse. Valdez had arranged performances in Venezuela for Maurice Chevalier and Sammy Davis Jr., and became acquainted with a local promoter, Aldemaro Romero, who controlled a brand-new indoor arena in Caracas called El Poliedro. If a closed-circuit TV outfit could handle the broadcast, as Video Techniques had done in Jamaica, it didn't matter where they fought. Romero met with Hank Schwartz and presented an impressive letter of credit. Romero not only enjoyed the "heavy involvement" of the Venezuelan government, but also brought a promise from the president that all Venezuelan taxes would be waived for the American champion and his challenger, Ken Norton. Foreman took a deal that guaranteed him $700,000—$300,000 less than his offer from the Garden. Besides being tax free, the money would come after his divorce and therefore avoid garnishment. Norton's offer for $200,000 was as large as he had ever earned, and he probably would have taken less for the title shot. Foreman scheduled his third heavyweight championship bout on his third continent—the first one ever held in South America. But given the changes in his body weight and demeanor, serious questions arose about whether he would have the chance to go for a fourth after meeting Norton at El Poliedro on March 26.[21]

★ 9 ★
Man without a Country

Ken Norton began preparing for Foreman right after his upset of Ali in 1973. He and his team, including managers Bob Biron and Art Rivkin, as well as the notable trainer Eddie Futch, vowed not to consider any fights with opponents ranked outside of the top ten so as not to jeopardize their claim to a title shot. Foreman, as evinced by his defense against Roman, was not so particular. Norton became so fixated on Foreman and the title that he, Biron, and Rivkin fired Futch for staying with Joe Frazier in preparation for the Super Sequel. Instead, they brought on an up-and-coming trainer, Bill Slayton, who promised undivided attention to Norton's camp as they hunkered down at the Main St. Gym in Los Angeles.[1]

Conversely, Foreman retained the three-ring circus of Sadler, Saddler, and Moore while officially adding Jackson and unofficially bringing on Hayward Moore as advisers; he started working with Schwartz on the paid-television deal, leaving Cassina to seek his own legal recourse. As the distractions multiplied, the champ took his show on the road. Rather than establishing a home base, Foreman moved his camps around the country. Short-term training occurred in Houston, Philadelphia, and Alameda, California. Sessions were generally open to the public, but this was not a goodwill tour.

"At that point, being heavyweight champion became stressful," he said. "Everything piling on. Divorce, children, another domestic disagreement. He said, she said, he sues . . . attorneys." Norton purposefully minimized external influences; Foreman allowed the outside world to dictate his preparation. Though he preferred to stay close to home in California, he contested lawsuits with George Foreman Associates in Philadelphia and filed for divorce in Houston, where the settlement would likely be more favorable than anywhere in California.[2]

The training sessions, like the camps, looked short and haphazard. Sparring partners told sportswriters that Foreman was distracted, maybe even worried. A noticeably heavy Foreman, who had been expending his energies in courtrooms, tried to make light of the situation: "I boxed four rounds with the electric bill, shadow boxed two rounds with a lawsuit and finished up with two more on alimony!" In reality, he probably broke a bigger sweat during his guest appearance on *Soul Train* than he did in some of his workouts. At the Alameda County Fairgrounds, a score of preteen cheerleaders jumping and chanting around him outpaced the champ in his thirty minutes of chopping wood and another half hour on the heavy bag. Although Foreman still hovered around 250 pounds, Sadler declared, "I'm satisfied. . . . He's damn near ready." Foreman sent mixed messages. "I'm tired of all this training," he said before qualifying. "I want to get it on with Norton."[3]

If Foreman really wanted to get it on, he would not have to look far for Norton, who remained cloistered at the Main St. Gym. Reporters said he appeared lean, fast, and utterly fearless. His estimation of Foreman had not changed in the year since he told reporters, "He stinks." Headlines read, "Norton Confident, Calls Foreman Slow." He studied Foreman on film and concluded, "If you've seen him once, you've seen him a hundred times. His style is basically the same and he doesn't alter it at all." Norton's bouts with Ali were "chess matches," but Foreman had only "one thing in mind." The challenger explained, "We'll have a battle plan formulated to offset Foreman's brute strength." He went on to say, "I'm a combination boxer-puncher," and declared with confidence, "I'm going to look him over in the first round, and then out-smart him." Foreman responded: "Norton can have all the plans and moves in the world but the second I hit him on the chin, it's all over." He likened the upcoming fight to a "duck shoot": he would just sit back, wait, and fire. As the fighters set off for Venezuela, Eddie Futch must have been reading the reports and recalling Frazier's attitude in Jamaica the year before. Now both the underdog who had upset Futch's champion, and the challenger he had guided into a position to succeed him, left for the next international megamatch.[4]

In *Ring*'s "Roundup" of 1972, a dark year for heavyweight boxing in between the Super Fight and the Sunshine Showdown, the magazine identified only one region in the world where heavyweight boxing was on the uptick: Latin America. Unlike much of the developed world, which had weathered an oil shock and experienced "generalized malaise" in the early 1970s, parts of Latin America enjoyed growth—or at least the increased availability of credit—which enabled them to reenter the global economy. Venezuela in particular benefited from the manipulation of the oil supply by the Organization of Petroleum Exporting Countries (OPEC), of which it was a member, and cashed in on the spiking price of petroleum. Though it had an abundance of resources at the turn of the 1970s, the nation felt a desperate need for political capital and international legitimacy. In 1969, Rafael Caldera assumed the head of the government in Caracas. Initially, the strong conservative leader pacified the war-torn nation by negotiating a cease-fire with armed left-wing dissidents, recognizing the Communist Party in Venezuela as a legitimate political group, and granting amnesty to the guerrillas who had threatened political stability in years past. Below the surface, however, the Caldera regime employed coercive and oppressive means. He dramatically raised government "rents," as well as taxes on the booming oil industry, and then funneled those revenues into national (and personal) "security"—the scaffolding of a new Venezuelan defense culture. When students began to protest, Caldera immediately closed the Central University of Venezuela and initiated police raids to root out and execute the leaders. At the same time, he prohibited news outlets from reporting on the school closures or raids. Instead, the diminutive president, his hair slicked back as if he styled it with the same oil that made his nation suddenly wealthy, disseminated "official" political news from his own television program, *Habla el Presidente*.[5]

Like Jamaica's Michael Manley, Caldera came to believe that hosting a sporting mega-event would be a way to demonstrate Venezuela's growth, stability, and sovereignty in the Cold War world. Unlike Manley, Caldera arrived at the conclusion near the end of his tenure. In December 1973, the Venezuelan people voted Caldera out of office after just one term and elected instead the head of the left-wing Democratic Action Party, Carlos Andrés Pérez. The election drew a 97 percent voter turnout—a rate unmatched in Venezuelan history—influenced in part by the American advertising specialists and political consultants that Pérez hired to combat Caldera's domination of the media. But Caldera went down swinging. As a lame-duck president, he gave Romero the green light to promise a tax-free environment for a heavyweight championship prizefight in Caracas. Yet there were tremors of change underfoot in Venezuela, and the boxing world may have wondered whether the country was about to experience a less-than-peaceful transition of power.[6]

Just weeks before the event dubbed El Gran Boxeo, two millionaire brothers were kidnapped and held for ransom. The "personal representative" of the US president, First Lady Pat Nixon, had extra security when she attended Pérez's inauguration in early March. She left unharmed, and the State Department noted that the new president's remarks "were notable mainly for … moderation." But these were not moderate times, and there were genuine concerns about whether someone like Foreman might be a target for extortion in the new Venezuela. If prospective kidnappers had followed the details of Foreman's divorce, however, they probably lost interest in him. During those proceedings, his lawyers produced documents to show that his assets were limited to $145,000, and Foreman owned only about $27,000 of that personally. In addition, the George Foreman Development Company—an Oakland-based company run by Leroy Jackson and his wife—had incurred debts of $173,000. The documents drew a portrait of a heavyweight champion heavily in the red. Other documents revealed that Jackson and his wife ran another venture called Promotall, which received one $360,000 payment from Tokyo promoters. After the divorce settlement was finalized, Foreman's net worth declined by another $235,000.[7]

Sportswriters marked down his value as well. Some bought into the widely reported training disparities between his camp and Norton's; others still had grievances from the last big title fight. No one wanted to be duped again by a champion's aura of invincibility when it was patently clear that his challenger came better prepared. Oddsmakers still favored Foreman at 3–1, some as high as 4–1, and Joe Louis, almost on cue, put his support behind the underdog challenger again. Subsequently, the smart money moved toward Norton. The *Chicago Defender*'s Norman Unger wrote, "The champion has been taking it a little too easy," and suggested that if it were not a title bout, Norton would have been the outright favorite. Doc Young tentatively backed Norton as well. The *New York Daily World* hedged its bet and projected that "if Foreman doesn't take him out early, [Norton] will take Foreman out late."[8]

Outwardly, it did not bother the champion. He arrived in Caracas before Norton, looking relaxed even if still overweight. "There is nothing wrong with Venezuela," Foreman said. "The people are great to me. Kids follow me. . . . Everybody down here seems to have a boxing frame of mind." His camp was not so relaxed, however. When one of Norton's aides attended a Foreman workout and tried to snap a picture, Sadler snapped. He leapt out of the ring and jumped the would-be photographer, relinquishing only when some of the on-site police officers pulled him off. A large police presence attended every workout in El Poliedro, ostensibly to protect the two fighters, since Foreman and Norton shared use of the arena for two weeks before the fight. Although neither boxer was kidnapped, their stay in Caracas was rife with thievery. Members of both camps, as well as Schwartz's television operation, coughed up bribes at every step, from the airport to the arena. Fees, surcharges, and taxes were levied on nearly every service, and payees watched most of the bolivars they doled out slide into the pockets of Venezuelan officials. Protests ended with the same curt response: this was a new president and a new government, which made new rules. Nothing you could do. Too many people had too much invested in the event to pull out over short money. But when authorities suddenly announced that all the judges and the referee for the fight would be Venezuelan, Foreman refused to cave. It escalated past the boxing people and landed on the desk of the US ambassador to Venezuela, Robert McClintock. His reports to the State Department on these negotiations suggested that the scene between Venezuelan officials and the American boxers "could better have been played by the Marx brothers."[9]

As the lead actor, Foreman could take some creative license. He developed a sudden leg injury and suggested he might not be able to fight anymore. The Venezuelan officials called his bluff. Foreman's trainers took him to a local hospital for X-rays. Suddenly, a Seattle-based referee and commissioner of the Washington Boxing Commission, Jimmy Rondeau, arrived in Caracas. The swelling in

Foreman's knee apparently went down very quickly with the announcement that an American referee had been hired, but the same could not be said for his weight. He worked out on only two of the last five days before the fight and tipped the scales at ten pounds heavier than he had ever fought. The number did not include any clothing, because Foreman, in another stroke of unpreparedness, forgot to bring trunks to the weigh-in. Norton, for the sake of either gamesmanship or hygiene, refused Foreman's request to borrow his, noting, "He's the heavyweight champion. He ought to have a whole factory full of trunks." The spartan-like Norton, in his own shorts, came within a few ounces of his target weight of 213 pounds. "If I fought Jesus Christ tomorrow," he said, "I'd think I was in better shape than him."[10]

Foreman, on the other hand, appeared to commit a heavyweight champion's cardinal sin: he looked past the fight at hand. There were rumors that he and Muhammad Ali had already entered into negotiations for the next major heavyweight championship bout. Now, face-to-face with a perfectly trained and singularly focused challenger, he may have seen the error of his ways. Some read his holdout for a referee like Rondeau as a Hail Mary. Yet Norton's camp, too, resisted the Venezuelan Boxing Commission's plan to put in a local referee. It would agree to a Puerto Rican referee, Waldemar Schmidt, who had officiated the recent Quarry-Lyle fight, but Foreman's team expressed concern over a Spanish-speaking referee's ability to "understand" him (although Schmidt was bilingual). Norton's representatives then insisted on Rondeau. They felt that as a former judge and now a commissioner, Rondeau would stick to the letter of the law. Their primary concern, it seemed, was getting a man in the middle who would keep Foreman from pushing, pulling, or otherwise disrupting their meticulously constructed ring strategy. The challenger brimmed with confidence as he jaunted from the dressing room to the ring. Ambassador McClintock, fatigued by the circuitous negotiations over taxes, fees, and referees, cabled Secretary of State Kissinger to declare: "I hope Norton and Foreman mutually knock each other out."[11]

As McClintock and the US Embassy rested, the Venezuelan government itself took a few shots. Rumors that the fight's tax-free status had been reconsidered and that a duty of around 18 percent might be exacted after the fight raised some concern. Romero doubled down on his promise to Schwartz that he could secure a government bond to cover any taxes, but he must have been concerned about the unpredictable new regime. After all, the president had devastated attendance at El Poliedro when he suddenly announced that El Gran Boxeo would be available for free on home television throughout the nation. More than thirty thousand Venezuelans had already paid over $25,000 just to watch training sessions in a nation crazy about the "three Bs": boxing, baseball, and bullfighting. Fewer than ten thousand bought tickets to the stadium, which could cost 600 bolivars, or about $140, each. At least some of the *bolos* saved by those willing to watch on television instead of in person migrated to the bookies. La Rinconada racetrack hummed to the tune of 6,000,000 *bolos*, a record one-day handle. The atmosphere at ringside was less than charged; fortunately, Muhammad Ali, working the color commentary beside the play-by-play announcer, "Colonel" Bob Sheridan, created some excitement. Ali and Oscar Bonavena traded insults and nearly came to blows before the main event. When he returned to Sheridan's side, a huffing and puffing Ali mumbled about being threatened by Bonavena and then blurted out that he and Foreman were already planning a multimillion-dollar bout in a place he pronounced "Zay-eah-urr," but only if Foreman won this fight. Ali's prediction: "I don't think he will." Sheridan, a folksy Irish American with a cattle-ranching background, was just starting a career in broadcasting that would span

several decades and several more angioplasties. His résumé grew to
include more than ten thousand fights, nearly a thousand of which
were title matches. Tapping into his ranching experience, Sheridan
let the bull about a Foreman-Ali match go, and herded Ali's train
of thought back to the fight in front of them. As the principals met
in the center of the ring for their final instructions, both announcers noted that Foreman's intimidating stare did not seem to faze
Norton, possibly because they were the same height—something
Foreman rarely encountered—and also because Norton was immensely confident about his "battle plan."[12]

The plan dictated that Norton start the action fast and furiously.
By comparison, Foreman looked sluggish. Joe Louis, greeting the
fighters in the ring during their introductions, had told Foreman to
"be cool," and Sheridan described that "coolness" early in the fight
as "patient": "He knows he's got a fight cut out for him." But to anyone else, Foreman—normally the aggressor—was just plain slow.
Those watching one of the 200-plus closed-circuit broadcasts in
North America, or in any of the seventy other nations that enjoyed
live satellite feeds from Caracas, needed to check the graphics on
the bottom of the screen to make sure that Foreman was in the red
trunks and Norton in the blue. The challenger hurled a series of long
punches over Foreman's head while the champ just stayed back,
out of reach, snapping a few controlled jabs. Foreman was "fishing"
with his left hand, Sheridan observed, trying to open up space for
his big right. A minute into the fight, two things seemed like bad
omens: Foreman had yet to land any significant punches, and Ali
had not said a word into the microphone. Strange winds blew over
Caracas.[13]

At the end of the first round, most scores were even, if only because neither boxer had done anything of note. Ali jettisoned his
headset and spent the entire break offering advice in Norton's

corner, despite their recent history. Abandoned by his color commentator, Sheridan had to fill all ninety seconds of airtime on his
own. He first noted that Foreman looked as if he had barely broken
a sweat, but had probably earned the edge on points. At least he
landed some of his jabs, while Norton, the busier puncher, caught
mostly air. Ali returned just in time for the bell to signal the second round, but stayed curiously silent while Sheridan called the
action. Foreman came out for the second stanza with a little more
energy, trying to cut off the ring and corner the speedy Norton. The
San Diego sailor tacked and jibed away. Foreman continued to stalk
his prey, but Norton had clearly prepared for this, deftly circling
around the champion while flicking jabs and firing hooks at will.
"Norton has plenty of boxing experience," Sheridan reminded the
listeners. "24 rounds with Ali is a Master's degree in boxing!" Foreman looked like an eager pupil chasing him around the ring to no
avail. He did not get any slimmer or faster as the first minute passed,
but he was certainly less patient. In his frustration, Foreman started
opening up, abandoning the jab for his familiar long hard haymakers. Norton had the champ where he wanted him: out of shape, out
of position, and soon to be out of a title.[14]

Nowhere in his training or preparation, however, could he have
accurately simulated the effect of Foreman's punches. Just as the
champ predicted, everything changed when he hit Norton. A "good
right hand" elicited an audible grunt and left Norton "a bit stunned,"
according to Sheridan. Eddie Futch, sitting in the press row next to
the *Newark Star-Ledger*'s Jerry Izenberg, leaned over and said, "Uh
oh ... fight's over." That momentary lapse slowed Norton enough to
allow Foreman to catch up. His bombardment of hooks and uppercuts propelled Norton into—and almost right through—the ropes.
Rondeau called it a knockdown and initiated a standing eight count,
but as he enunciated the last consonant of "eight," Foreman cata-

pulted from his neutral corner, as fast as he had moved all night, and sent Norton right back into the ropes. The speed and fury of the suddenly animated Foreman surprised Rondeau as well as Norton. The referee seemed unsure whether it was a knockdown and uncertain how to react. Although Rondeau later said he ruled it a knockdown and administered another standing eight count, it might have been the fastest and quietest eight seconds since the invention of measured time. Norton, losing all pretense of a plan, made the same mistake that Frazier had—he rushed back into the fray. But he didn't have any ammunition left to fire. Izenberg's column the next day summed it up: "You cannot stop an elephant with a .22."[15]

The champion loosed his full arsenal. "A left uppercut, a right jab!" Sheridan bellowed, trying to keep up with the action. "Norton is in queersville! He doesn't know where he is!" When Rondeau's count reached five, Norton desperately tried to lift himself off the mat, stumbling along the ropes. Rondeau kept counting: six . . . seven . . . eight . . . By nine, Norton had made it to his feet, but still relied heavily on the ropes to keep him upright. Bill Slayton, on the other hand, was bouncing in the corner as he tried to get Rondeau's attention. Norton did not see him through the fog of war and continued to marshal all his remaining strength. But it was obvious that if the referee did not count him out or call the fight, Slayton would not let the massacre go on. Sheridan needed a breather, too. "It might be all over right here . . . and they . . . are they going to continue it or are they going to stop it?" If he was asking Ali, he got no response. In fact, the Louisville Lip remained conspicuously quiet. Who could blame him? The man that had stood toe-to-toe with him for twenty-four rounds could not stay on his feet for five minutes against Foreman. Ali regained his voice after Rondeau raised Foreman's arm and the champ glared down at him. Ali spouted some insults probably more offensive to Zaïrois than to Foreman: "If you behave like that, my African friends will put you in the pot!" Foreman ignored it, turned away, and paraded around the ring. Don King followed him: "My man!"[16]

The entire event could have been described as anticlimactic. But *Ring* informed its readership that "the epilogue to the Caracas fight makes the most amazing story." Fears of being held for ransom materialized, in a way, when Foreman, Norton, and Schwartz's parties arrived at the airport—and none were allowed to leave Venezuela. They were informed that they each owed back taxes and could not exit the country until they paid. Schwartz exploded, yelling that he had a promise from the president that there would be no taxes. He heard a familiar refrain: "There was a new President." Adding to the taxes, which bit into what little (if any) profit Schwartz made, he claimed that impounding his television equipment was costing him $50,000 a day. Norton's bill came to more than $70,000, and Foreman was assessed over $300,000 of his $700,000 purse, a tax bite of at least 43 percent. Once again they called on the US Embassy. "We got all those people involved," Foreman said later, but McClintock insisted that his hands were tied. This was the largest oil-producing nation outside the Middle East, after all. The ambassador acknowledged a forlorn truth: "My bosses tell me we can't intercede."[17]

The arrival of the US secretary of the treasury, George Shultz, in Caracas on the same day only compounded this awkward situation. Norton raised the funds, or at least enough of them, and left the country. Schwartz and Foreman stayed. As Foreman versus Ali, the most profitable prizefight in the history of boxing, loomed over the horizon, Video Techniques and George Foreman became ineluctably bound together—and entangled with Don King. On the plane ride to Caracas, King had described his position with VT as the company's "black interface"; on the return trip, he claimed to be its president. The truth, as was often the case with King, lay somewhere in between. But there was no doubt he earned a place in VT after orchestrating Foreman versus Ali, the first eight-figure prize-fight. The self-described "hustler extraordinaire" had a proclivity to dramatize the genesis of the $10 million match with stories of high-level diplomats and midnight meetings in parking lots. Foreman recalled King pleading with him to sign for a fight with Ali, tears rolling down as he said, "They think I'm a crook because [of] the color of my skin." Foreman did not need this kind of "black inter-face"; he needed money that was both guaranteed and deferred until his legal wrinkles could be ironed out. When he told King yes, the crying stopped. King brought in African businessmen who gave Foreman a pitch for making his next defense on yet another continent, but King's offer of $5 million had already sold him. "So long as you can put the money in the bank," Foreman told them. On the verge of crying again, King apologized with the news that he would have to offer Ali the same purse—something that had been a sticking point for Frazier in the Super Fight—but Foreman exclaimed, "I would give him five million myself if I had it!" Of course, King didn't have that money either. Neither did Schwartz, which is why he offered a vice president position and a 4 percent ownership stake in VT for King's partnership. The entire prospect rested on investors, credit, and some good luck. None of that would be realized from a Venezuelan airport. Though unsure how much money exchanged hands to get his passport back and put him on a Pan Am flight back home, Foreman was certain that Don King paid it. Ambassador McClintock ended the scene with a letter to Schwartz: "Better luck in Kinshasa."[18]

"To think that an American world champion has to go to Caracas to defend his title," one boxing fan wrote, "is deplorable." When word spread that the next championship bout would take place even farther away, the reaction was yet more critical. That it would occur in Africa—in a decolonized nation-state entirely governed by indigenous Africans rather than European colonists—only added to the fury. Despite constant references to "Darkest Africa" and the not so subtly racialized questions about Zaire's fitness to host such a monumental sporting event, the boxing community had to acknowledge a new era of the fight game was under way. As estimates and projections for purse money and proceeds bloomed to unprecedented levels, even the big-spending Houston Astrodome conceded, "We're out of it." Foreman, some said, had initiated a "dynasty." In less than twelve total minutes of championship fighting, he had become "boxing's first man without a country."[19]

The expansion of closed-circuit television's potential combined with the absence of a major boxing center in the United States to put the sport on a truly global trajectory. "As indicated by a steady rise in *Ring* circulation and subscriptions, and the increase in major matches," Nat Loubet concluded, "the fight game is flourishing amazingly all over the world." But he set boundaries that fit the Cold War era. "Make exceptions of Russia and China, which are too busy with international power and politics to devote any time to boxing." It would be naïve to think that Jamaica or Venezuela invested in hosting these megamatches without any political motivation. They occupied tenuous places in the geopolitics of the era, struggling to prove their sovereignty and solvency in the Cold War world. Even if a megafight lost money—the Sunshine Showdown wound up with at least a $750,000 deficit—the host still hoped the prestige would pay off. Jamaica's increased tourism supposedly turned a net profit. In Venezuela, despite Ambassador McClintock's frustration with the new administration over their handling of the fight, he and Secretary Shultz initiated new discussions about a special taxation agreement for "artistic and sports events generating revenue," similar to the one already in place between the United States and the Soviet Union. "The problem of taxation of foreigners performing temporarily in Venezuela," McClintock said, "may take on increasing significance as Caracas becomes more and more a world conference and entertainment center." These international mega-matches were expensive to put on and unlikely to be profitable; they were *only* about power and politics. The next chapter in this series of transoceanic title fights would be the most expensive—and most politicized—of them all.[20]

Less than three years after he first put on boxing gloves at a Job Corps center in California, George Foreman won an Olympic gold medal in Mexico. After being declared the victor, Foreman pulled a miniature US flag out of his robe pocket and briefly waved it around—a small motion that made big waves when he returned to the United States. (AP/Kurt Strumpf)

President Lyndon Johnson invited George Foreman to the White House in November 1968 to congratulate him for winning the inaugural Job Corps Award of Achievement. When they met, Foreman, wearing his Olympic medal, presented LBJ with a plaque in recognition of "fathering" the Job Corps program, which had rescued him from urban poverty and provided him a high school equivalency education and vocational training, as well as an introduction to boxing. (LBJ Library/

Before his professional boxing debut at Madison Square Garden in June 1969, George Foreman—at the suggestion of the Garden's public relations agent John F. X. Condon—set up outside the arena and handed out miniature US flags to capitalize on his patriotic image and build publicity for his first prizefight. (AP)

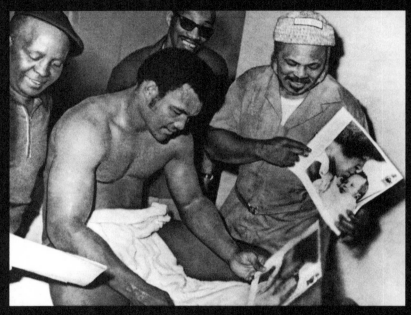

George Foreman's first child, Michi, was born while he trained for a heavyweight title bout against the champion Joe Frazier in January 1973. Foreman got photos of his wife and daughter sent to Jamaica, where he trained with Dick Sadler (left), Sandy Saddler (top), and Archie Moore (right), but did not break camp, instead remaining focused on his shot at the title. (AP)

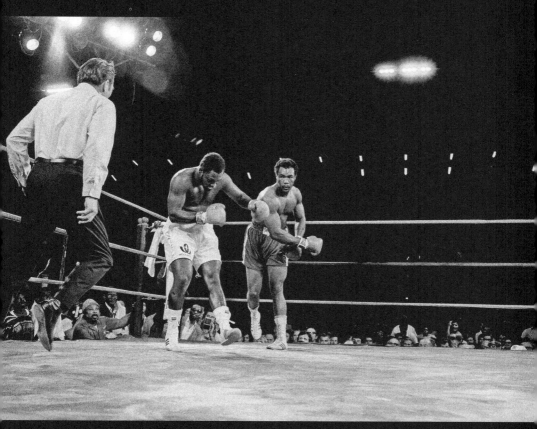

On January 22, 1973, George Foreman won the "Sunshine Showdown" by knocking out Joe Frazier in a stunning upset. Frazier fell six times before referee Arthur Mercante finally counted him out and made the twenty-four-year-old Foreman the new heavyweight champion of the world. (AP)

After winning the championship, George Foreman was celebrated not only in his native Houston but also in his adopted home state of California. Governor Ronald Reagan invited him to the state capitol in February 1973 to congratulate him personally. (AP)

Newly crowned heavyweight king George Foreman aimed for some easy money and publicity by engaging in "exhibitions" and making public appearances at home and abroad. The tours, including trips to Canada and Europe (Foreman is pictured here at Schiphol airport in March 1973), were not profitable, and mounting pressure in the sports media for him to defend the title made his early championship reign a very stressful period. (Wikimedia Commons; Fotocollectie Algemeen Nederlands Fotopersbureau, 1945-1989, access no. 2.24.01.05, pt. no. 926-2854)

George Foreman agreed to defend his title for the first time at the Nippon Budokan in Tokyo. It was the first heavyweight championship boxing match held in Asia, and fans lined Ginza Street to welcome Foreman's motorcade in August 1973. (AP/ Mark Foley)

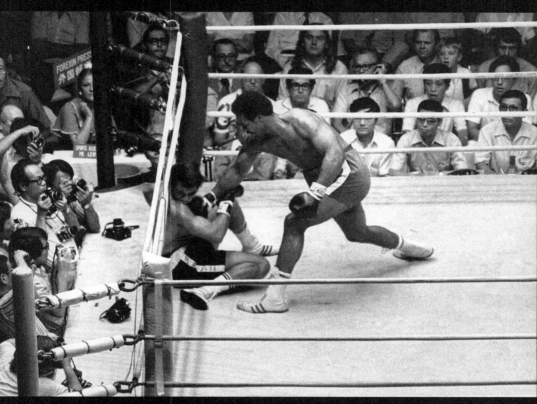

Boxing writers and fans were skeptical of George Foreman's first title challenger, Jose "King" Roman, the Puerto Rican champion who was dubiously ranked as the ninth heavyweight contender in advance of their September 1, 1973, meeting. Many had also been critical of Foreman's increasingly rough popular image, mirrored by his tactics in the ring. Those concerns dovetailed in Japan when Foreman pummeled Roman, even after he appeared to already have fallen, and won by knockout in only two minutes of boxing. (AP)

Despite facing a lawsuit for failing to defend his title at the Houston Astrodome stemming from a deal brokered by his former manager Dick Sadler, Foreman me his obligation to attend the second Battle of the Sexes tennis match at the Astro dome on September 20, 1973, and present the winner, Billie Jean King, with

after Foreman won the heavyweight championship, he and
ery different. Dick Sadler (right) was relieved of his manager
ned only as a trainer, while a friend from Job Corps, Leroy Jacks
l to be the "business manager"; Foreman attempted to manage
fairs. His weight, however, had not been managed effectively, a
that Foreman had ballooned up to 250 pounds by January 19
nced his second title defense would come against a top conter
wo months later. (AP/Dave Pickoff)

Foreman acknowledged that his two years of marriage to Mir
woman Adrienne Calhoun had been conducted largely by tele
he had changed from an aspiring contender to the reigning hea
n, which further strained the relationship. Although they later
ip, the divorce proceedings through the fall of 1973 into early
us. They finally settled at the Houston Domestic Relations Cou
4, just one month before Foreman was scheduled to meet Ken N

The global tour of George Foreman's title went through Caracas, Venezuela, on March 26, 1974. Foreman arranged the first world heavyweight championship fight in South America against a rising challenger and former Marine, Ken Norton. While many viewed Norton as a legitimate threat to Foreman, the champion successfully defended his title with a second-round knockout. (AP)

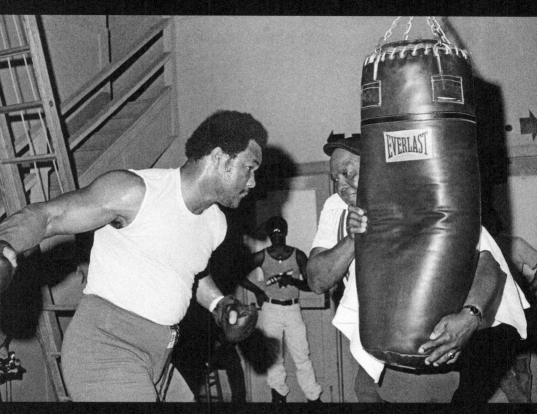

By August 1974, George Foreman was in training for his next prizefight against the ex-champion Muhammad Ali. A regular exercise in his regimen—and an impressive demonstration of his power—included having trainer Dick Sadler hold a heavy bag as still as he could while Foreman rhythmically pounded it until his fist left imprints and, occasionally, sand started to leak out. Members of Ali's camp, however, were quick to point out that one of the fastest competitors in the heavyweight division would not stand still for Foreman. (AP/Robert Houston)

Former light heavyweight champion and heavyweight challenger Archie Moore (right) was an integral part of George Foreman's team in 1973 and 1974 and left with Foreman from O'Hare airport en route to Kinshasa, Zaire, in September 1974. Moore extended his career well into his forties through a variety of tactics, including in some cases resting against the ropes to let his younger opponents exhaust themselves and give "the Old Mongoose" an opportunity to catch them off-guard. (Wikimedia Commons/AP)

The "Rumble in the Jungle" between George Foreman and Muhammad Ali was preceded by a musical festival called "Zaire 74," and both events drew an eclectic mix of people. The Pulitzer Prize–winning photojournalist Horst Faas, better known for his pictures of the Vietnam War, snapped this still of the heavyweight champion sharing a sofa with the music festival's headliner, James Brown, and three of the "promotional girls," including Veronica Porche (next to Brown), who would become Ali's third wife a few years later. (AP/Horst Faas)

After eight rounds of Muhammad Ali predominantly lying against the ropes and George Foreman continuously throwing punches, Ali pounced on an exhausted Foreman. The champion had never been knocked down in a prizefight and did not get up before referee Zach Clayton counted him out. His first loss as a professional also ended his twenty-one-month tenure as champion, which included three title defenses on three different continents. (AP)

Professional boxing was not always a mainstay on the Las Vegas Strip. In an event facilitated by the television promoter Jerry Perenchio, Caesars Palace took a chance by hosting the heavyweight bout between George Foreman and Ron Lyle in its "Sports Pavilion" on January 24, 1976. Foreman-Lyle was one of the most exciting matches of the year, and by the 1980s, many casino-hotels in Vegas bid for

In June 1976, George Foreman took a break from training for a rematch with Joe Frazier in New York to give his oldest child, Michi, a kiss. Foreman also had a son, George Edward Foreman Jr., and was expecting another baby with his third part-ner in October. During 1976 and into 1977, Foreman increasingly indicated that he thought about life after boxing, particularly as his chase for a second shot at the

George Foreman suffered an unexpected loss to Jimmy Young but experienced something even more surprising—a near-death experience and religious conversion—after the fight. He announced his retirement from professional boxing and devoted himself to faith and his four children. By 1981 Foreman was an ordained minister, had split with his church, and participated in or led prayer groups in the

In 1983 George Foreman finally replied to a ten-year-old request from Lady Bird Johnson to donate any of his unwanted boxing memorabilia to the Lyndon Baines Johnson Presidential Library and Museum. Comfortable both in his retirement from the ring and with his minimalist lifestyle, Foreman donated two of his most valuable pieces, a "Fighting Corpsman" warm-up robe and the *Ring Magazine* championship belt from 1973; at the media event to announce the donations, he thanked Lady Bird for keeping the George Foreman name alive. (LBJ Library/Jay Goodwin)

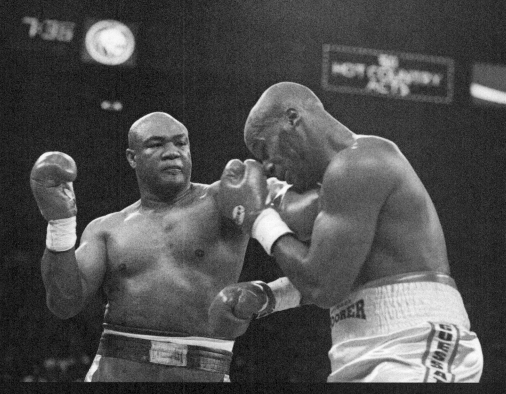

On November 5, 1994, the forty-five-year-old George Foreman challenged heavy-weight champion Michael Moorer, who was nearly twenty years younger. Despite being behind on points late in the fight, Foreman landed one punch that changed boxing history and made him the oldest person to win a heavyweight title. (AP/ Lennox McLendon)

After two years of a royalty-based contract with Salton, Inc., to endorse the "George Foreman Lean Mean Fat Reducing Machine," the steep rise in sales forced Salton to buy Foreman out of the deal by purchasing his name for a reported $137 million. Foreman continued to sell products under Salton's "George Foreman" line, especially in foreign markets, as in this 2012 product-demonstration in London. (AP/Roy Letkey)

George Foreman's television career evolved from game shows and cameos to his own sitcom and then informercials for the Foreman Grill. In 2008, however, he made his foray into reality television with the help of his children, including George Foreman III (right) and George Foreman IV (left), as *Family Foreman* captured the lives of the Foreman family over six episodes. (AP/Matt Sayles)

WILLIAM **SHATNER**   HENRY **WINKLER**   TERRY **BRADSHAW**   GEORGE **FOREMAN**   and Guide JEFF **DYE**

In for the ride of their lives... again.

BETTER LATE THAN NEVER

JAN 1 | MONDAYS 9/8c   NBC

...once a liability in George Foreman's second campaign for the heavyw...
...pionship, became one of his most saleable attributes in a post-boxing c...
...Winkler targeted Foreman, along with other "seasoned citizen" celeb...
...Bradshaw and William Shatner—complemented by a Millennial com...
...ye—to star in *Better Late Than Never* in the fall of 2016. Millions of v...
...Baby Boomers to the iGeneration watched them visit Asia that first s...
...or the first time, a show that featured Foreman was renewed for a s...

★ 10 ★
To the Mountains of the Moon

"What, in Heaven's Name, Is a Zaire?" Sam Taub's provocatively ignorant headline had deep roots. Signature prizefights had been moving farther away from the traditional mecca of the sport in New York City, and now the biggest championship bout in years would take place in a country that no one could find on a map more than three years old. Many, including Taub, still conceived of this part of the world as "Darkest Africa" and latched onto beliefs largely influenced by the Inner Station of Joseph Conrad's *Heart of Darkness*, the 1939 film *Stanley and Livingstone* with Spencer Tracy, or Vachel Linsday's poem "The Congo." Jerry Izenberg, in a special article for *Sport Magazine* about the upcoming match, quoted a short block of Lindsay's poem to set the mood: "Then I saw the Congo, creeping through the black / Cutting through the forest with a golden track." The novelist Norman Mailer, already contracted to write a book about Foreman and Ali's encounter, sent out for a full copy of Lindsay's sixty-year-old work before traveling to Zaire. For those who remained petrified by images of cannibalistic savages and other predators lurking in the untamed jungles through which the Congo swerved, it probably comforted them little to know that Zaire was in fact a more "Western" name than the familiar indigenous word

"Congo." Indeed, *zaire* was the Portuguese corruption of Bantu's *nzere*, meaning "river that swallows all rivers." All that mattered to those criticizing the very premise of a title fight in Africa, however, was the mounting perception that developing countries were swallowing up the stream of heavyweight championship prizefights.[1]

To most, Foreman deserved the blame. His legal imbroglio had sent the Frazier fight offshore, and since then he had not defended his title on the North American continent, let alone in the United States. By the time Foreman escaped from Caracas, his lawsuits and even his divorce had been settled. There were no more impediments to his fighting in the United States, yet he chose to continue defending the title abroad. The former flag-waver suddenly faced accusations of being unpatriotic. Foreman did not take the criticism well, responding, "I would love to cross the street to fight or even fight in my backyard. Then I wouldn't have to pack up any bags or anything." He appeared sullen and angry, and eventually stopped appearing at all. "He is very serious," the boxing media said. "Too serious." Fans wrote to magazines complaining that "he is reticent to a fault." Others commented, "A heavyweight champion who won't talk is a drag on the game." The comparison was only magnified by the sight of seventy-eight-year-old Jack Dempsey entertaining throngs of fans at his restaurant almost daily. In the midst of his reign, Foreman barely entertained anyone. His recalcitrance grew to the point that he did not even attend a press conference to publicize his fight with Ali. When Jim Brown secured an interview, one of the very few granted, the champ was so "bad" that in a complete reversal of their first meeting, Brown wanted to imitate Foreman, saying on camera, "I intend to get it all together like you have someday soon."[2]

Nat Loubet, on the other hand, never wanted to imitate Foreman and rarely even defended him. But he attributed America's "loss" of heavyweight title fights to market forces, a global economy, and taxation: "What hitherto unknown places like Zaire offer most is freedom . . . from taxes." His magazine blamed Governor Malcolm Wilson for vetoing a bill that would have provided tax relief to the Garden and "permitted the big arena to resume its old place as leader in world fistic promotions." Loubet reminded readers that "New York and London, biting off their corporate noses to spite their faces, offer no tax immunity of any kind." By 1974, however, the issue had gone far beyond a few percentage points worth of taxes. American stadia, and the corporations that bought and sold them, could not match the huge investments from national treasuries in countries vying to host the megamatches. When the government of Zaire, through a Swiss-based, Panamanian-chartered puppet firm called Risnelia Investment Inc., offered $10 million for Foreman and Ali's services, even the Garden's Mike Burke had to concede: "It's too big an operation for us."[3]

The "operation" grew too big for Video Techniques as well. Hank Schwartz's outfit had started a paradigm shift with the Sunshine Showdown. It turned prizefights into made-for-television specials that could take place anywhere in the world. That does not mean all of them were successful. VT took a bath on the Foreman-Norton bout in Caracas. Now it had a fight between Foreman and Ali, but needed enough money to put on an *event* in Zaire. Don King traveled to London for a meeting with John Daly of the Hemdale Leisure Corporation. Daly had never stepped into a prize ring, but he came from a boxing family. Both his father and uncle had fought professionally, fitting the stereotype of lower-class and lighter-weight British scrappers. Despite his financial and corporate success, represented by a massive house in St. George's Hill in Weybridge, Surrey, that he purchased from the Beatles, flanked by his neighbors Tom Jones and Engelbert Humperdinck, Daly harbored a little shame for not following in the family's manly business. In offering VT a couple of million dollars for "risk-front money," he found a way to satisfy the "Fighting Dalys." In return, he secured two seats—for him and his father—to that year's Boxing Writers Association of America awards dinner at the luxurious Waldorf Astoria in New York City. "Getting involved with the Foreman-Ali fight was subconsciously my way of atoning to my father and uncle for the fact that I didn't follow the family footsteps," he told VT's public relations man, Murray Goodman. "I feel they have both forgiven me. You should have seen my father on his visit here for the Boxing Writer's Dinner."[4]

Daly and his father enjoyed more than just a place at the table among some of boxing's greats, including the former heavyweight champions Jack Dempsey, "Jersey" Joe Walcott, Floyd Patterson, and Joe Frazier. These turned out to be front-row seats for the opening salvo between Foreman and Ali. The program clearly laid out a night designed as a tribute to Foreman. He would receive the Edward J. Neil Award for Fighter of the Year as well as the *Ring* magazine belt in recognition of his status as the undisputed heavyweight champion of the world. Yet someone saw fit to make Ali a featured speaker of the evening, charged with wrapping up the ceremonies after Foreman collected his awards. It was, to say the least, a combustible situation, and it would detonate before the night was through. As Robert Oppenheimer once said of the Manhattan Project's relation to the atomic bombing of Japan: "The decision was implicit in the project. I don't know whether it could have been stopped."[5]

As he had with nearly every other significant opponent over the past decade, Ali ramped up a personal feud with his adversary. In Foreman's case, the two had a bitter history dating back to 1971. Ali continued stoking those coals after they agreed to fight in Zaire. He started with short quips, long stares, and an ill-advised threat of cannibalism during his color commentary for the Foreman-Norton affair. Ali grew bolder and more offensive during the press conference that Foreman refused to attend. It gave the "People's Champ" an uncontested forum to question Foreman's experience, stamina, legitimacy as a champion, and, ultimately, his authenticity as an African American as well. "When Foreman sees all those brothers in the audience," Ali shouted to the back of the room, despite having a microphone right in front of him, "he'll know he's in Ali country. There ain't no 'Foremans' in Africa." King trafficked in racial tension—inter- or intra—and predicted that Video Techniques would gross more than $30 million from one billion paying viewers. Even though it was hardly necessary to sell a gathering of four hundred boxers and their scribes on a championship prizefight, at the BWAA dinner in late June, Ali's promotion-by-degradation machine ran at full capacity.[6]

Foreman came with a plan. Not to sell the fight—his purse was guaranteed—but to gain the upper hand in the psychological sparring. He knew that not only Ali but also the Nation of Islam members in his corner liked to "psych out" opponents. Ernie Terrell told Foreman that before he took on Ali, a group of men from the Nation came into his house and starting touching things—not breaking or stealing, but just silently handling and moving his stuff. No one ever seemed to hit Ali back in the preamble to a prizefight. So Foreman thought about how he could get inside Ali's head at the BWAA and decided to get inside his jacket. At the proper moment, in front of all the writers and fighters, he was going to rip Ali's suit right off of him. "He had cheap suits anyway," Foreman said. He told Hayward Moore about the plan. His decision, too, was implicit in the project.[7]

After hours of food and awards, an impressive amount of both finding their way to Foreman's table, Ali took the podium for something between a sermon and a roast. Through nearly twenty minutes of extemporaneous promises and invective, Foreman remained silent, staring menacingly at the dais. When Ali said Foreman did not even punch hard, citing the fact that Frazier continued to get up each time Foreman knocked him down with "push punches," the ex-champ wore an angry glower. Finally, Dick Sadler's protective instincts took over. He shimmied over next to Ali and then drowned out the diatribe with an improvised song touting Foreman and predicting his victory in Zaire. The room broke out into laughter. Foreman lightened up and cracked a smile, too. The tension eased, but only for a second.[8]

"You're coming to my country now," Ali yelled before continuing his derogation of the Zaïrois people, saying, "They'll be sticking pins in voodoo dolls of you, George," and finishing with the politics of racial nationalism: "Those Africans are anti-America, they remember how you waved the flags at the Olympics, they don't like that." Sadler's good-natured attempt to divert the flood from Ali's mouth failed, and it became apparent that Foreman was the only one who could dam it. He walked over, nudged Ali off of the mic, and said something to the effect of, "I don't know about you people, but I'm tired of all this talkin' and I want to go home." He took the belt Ali was supposed to present him with, returned to the table to collect his Neil plaque, and waited. Ali wouldn't let him get the last word. He followed Foreman to his table, but he didn't speak. He tapped Foreman's hip, and when the champ instinctively slapped his hand away, Ali reached around with the other one, stole Foreman's plaque, and then spun away. This was the opening Foreman needed. He grabbed the vent of Ali's blue jacket and "ripped it up the back as easily as if it were paper." Everything went according to Foreman's plan—except for Ali's reaction.[9]

Ali aimed for a proportional response, but grabbed only pieces of Foreman's shirt, foiled by a higher-quality tuxedo jacket and the intervention of the Garden's John Condon, accompanied by the writer and cartoonist Bill Gallo, who for some reason found themselves breaking up a fight between two heavyweight boxers in a room full of younger and stronger men. Foreman regained his awards and turned to leave—he "sure wasn't going to fight him for free." Ali, having lost his jacket, turned to projectiles. Screaming wildly over and over again, "You tore my suit! You tore my suit!" he began to throw drinking glasses at Foreman, littering the Starlight Room of the Waldorf with shards of broken glass. A cluster of attendees ushered Foreman into the elevator before he could escalate the situation. It had already gone further than he had envisioned. "I still had to pull that trick," Foreman recalled. "I just didn't know he was going to take it like that. This guy went crazy!"[10]

Even as bystanders herded Ali away from the breakables, he ratcheted up the verbal offensive. In his volley of curses, different people caught different shrapnel. "You Christian blankety-blank" is what stuck to Foreman, who later recalled, "I didn't know what a Christian was. I didn't even know what he was talking about." Raised a Baptist in Houston and still inclined to make references to God and Jesus—particularly in the Houston newspapers that his family might be more likely to read—Foreman did not think of himself as Christian, and if he had heard the term before, it was not a pejorative. Dave Anderson of the *New York Times* focused on the anatomical instead. The "blankety-blank" that some filled in as "tail," Anderson was pretty sure sounded like "ass." But that word was not yet "fit to print" in the "newspaper of record." His transcription in the next day's paper read: "I'll beat your Christian [anatomy deleted], you white flag-waving [expletive deleted]. . . . What hotel's that nigger stayin' at?" Both the physical and metaphysical slurs received careful attention, but no one discussed or redacted the centuries-old racial epithet that hung over the eighteenth floor of the Waldorf.[11]

Ali, reprimanded by both the New York State Athletic Commission and the Nation of Islam, offered a tempered apology the next day: "I apologize to George Foreman and to all those people who were at the dinner. I apologize for getting on him, talking about him, and bringing him down as champion. That probably got him upset. Still, he had no right to grab my jacket and rip it off. I wouldn't be so bold as to do what he did. Not that bold to rip a person's jacket off. . . . That took a lotta nerve." Despite bombarding Foreman with glassware, Ali seemed to be losing his "nerve" as the fight drew closer. At his training camp in Deer Lake, Pennsylvania—virtually always open to anyone with even a semblance of press credentials—some visitors took note of what appeared to be a "sluggish" training regimen. Sometimes the day concluded with Ali resting back against the ropes while his sparring partners, including a former Foreman charge, Eddie "Bossman" Jones, hit him in the midsection until Dundee called, "Time!" When Ali, Foreman, and Frazier traveled to Salt Lake City, Utah, for a series of charity exhibitions in August, Foreman tested those nerves. As Ali walked down the street with a woman, Foreman closed in quietly from behind and barked, "Hey!" and then watched as Ali "almost jumped out of his shoes" and hastily tried to return the pleasantry. The People's Champ regained his cool when he met the "poster girls" for the event, in particular, one named Veronica Porche, before leaving Salt Lake City. But Foreman still had plenty of nerve as they set off for Zaire.[12]

In the five-month buildup just to the *departure*, which was a month before anyone threw a punch, thousands of words were printed about the upcoming fight, but Sam Taub's question—"What, in Heaven's Name, Is a Zaire?"—never really got answered. Misinformation and disinformation crowded out knowledge. Foreman said very little publicly, and Ali seemed to argue with himself. The self-described champion of black rights called Foreman both "Uncle Tom" and "nigger." Despite having visited several African countries in the past, he still suggested that Zaire, which would pay him $5 million, was populated by cannibals and that its people practiced "voodoo." Remnants of Jim Crow America permeated the prelude to Foreman versus Ali, and Norman Mailer got his copy of Lindsay's poem. Izenberg judiciously stopped quoting it in his column, but the poem's images continued winding through American racial references and caricatures of people in Central Africa—where the largest purses in prizefighting history waited for Foreman and Ali. From the first section of the poem, entitled "Their Basic Savagery":

Then along that riverbank
A thousand miles
Tattooed cannibals danced in files;
Then I heard the boom of the blood-lust song
And a thigh-bone beating on a tin-pan gong
And "BLOOD" screamed the whistles and the fifes of the warriors,
"BLOOD" screamed the skull-faced, lean witch doctors ...

Boomlay, boomlay, boomlay, BOOM,"
A roaring, epic, rag-time tune
From the mouth of the Congo
To the Mountains of the Moon.[13]

★

"Black Power is sought everywhere in the world, but it is realized here in Zaire." This message could be seen on large billboards all over the country in preparation for its highly anticipated event. Other giant signs read, "The Zairian people thank their Enlightened Guide, President MOBUTU SESE SEKO, the promoter of this brotherly reunion between the black people who stayed in the land of their ancestors and those [who] were scattered around the world." Dwarfing them all stood a thirty-foot-high, fifteen-foot-wide poster of President Mobutu, decked out in leopard-print hat and scarf, which towered above the Stade du 20 Mai, where the fight would take place. The stadium's name commemorated the *Manifesto de la N'sele*, which Mobutu had signed on May 20, 1967, declaring his Mouvement Populaire de la Révolution (MPR) the only political party in the nation that, ironically, he had renamed the Democratic Republic of Congo a few years earlier.[14]

As the poster suggested, Mobutu dominated the nation. He had done so almost since the first stirrings of decolonization. General Joseph-Désiré Mobutu, as he was known at the time, headed the Armée Nationale Congolaise (ANC) but remained outside formal politics when independence movements erupted in the former Belgian Congo. With help from Belgium and the United States, he arranged for the assassination of the country's first prime minister, Patrice Lumumba. Thereafter, the United States lauded Mobutu as a bulwark against communism in Central Africa and supported his ascension to power. President Kennedy told Mobutu, "General, if it hadn't been for you, the whole thing would have collapsed and the communists would have taken over." The CIA confirmed his place as America's "man in the region" and trained Mobutu's security forces, and the State Department fed him information on other African nations, all as the general tiptoed toward dictatorship. By the time of his *Manifesto de la N'sele*, Mobutu, still leader of the army, had nationalized the police force, created rubber-stamp legislatures to implement his policies without debate, and reorganized the administration of the country into larger units, thereby undermining the many smaller ethnic groups that provided most of his opposition. Mobutu appointed governors and regularly rotated them so that no one spent too much time—or gained too much influence—in any territory. His Second Republic bore a striking resemblance to the Congo of the Belgian era, but he masked the authoritarianism under an anticolonial "authenticity" campaign at the dawn of the

1970s. Mobutu renamed the country "Zaire" and decreed that the capital, Leopoldville, would be called Kinshasa instead. His renaming policy was carried through to personal names. In January 1972, he instructed his people to give up "Christian" names and adopt authentic Congolese ones instead. Mobutu led by example, discarding Joseph-Désiré for the more awesome Mobutu Sese Seko Kuru Ngebendu Wa Za Banga, or "the all powerful warrior who, because of his endurance and will to win, goes from conquest to conquest leaving fire in his wake."[15]

Modesty was not a part of Mobutu's personal authenticity, though he was beneficent enough to cut off the new moniker after "Seko" on all but the most formal occasions. Yet Mobutu had reason for bravado in the early 1970s. Zaire's economy soared on the price of copper, which seemed to be a stable investment in a time of wildly fluctuating oil markets. Attempts to capitalize on the growth by managing the national economy floundered, however, and when the value of copper dropped by 50 percent, it became apparent that the high tide of Mobutu's economy had gone out as quickly as it had come in. In response, the government followed up the policy of authenticity with a new one called "Mobutism"—a general subservience to the teachings, actions, and even thoughts of the president of the republic, president-founder of the party, and commander in chief of the army: the "Enlightened Guide" of Zaire, Mobutu Sese Seko. Recognizing that his political capital, much like oil or copper prices, rested largely on speculation, Mobutu ratcheted up his propaganda apparatus to enhance his cult of personality. State-controlled newspapers portrayed Mobutu as the "Father of the Nation," and television channels began their broadcasts each day with a "surrealistic vision of Mobutu descending from the cloud-filled heavens." The heavyweight championship bout was part of this campaign. Mobutu directed all available resources toward aggrandizing himself further and presenting his nation as a strong, solvent, and "influential country"—to prove the stability and progress of Zaire, the newspaper *Elima* wrote—in order to attract enough investment and tourism to make that image a reality.[16]

In preparation for the prizefight, Mobutu pumped tens of millions of dollars into refurbishing the Stade du 20 Mai and installing the lights necessary to stage a midnight event. He commissioned an airport, new highways leading to the stadium, and a parking lot that would accommodate all the traffic. He convinced the Liberian government to secretly pay millions more in public dollars for a black music festival featuring African, African American, and Afro-Caribbean artists to precede the fight and create a carnival atmosphere. Billboards reminded Zaïrois: "A Fight between two blacks in a black nation organized by blacks and seen by the whole world; *this is the victory of Mobutism*." Finally, to help spread the word, he ordered the placement of more than a hundred telephones with direct links to the satellite station that would beam this scene around the globe, in a way Lindsay never foresaw, from the mouth of the Congo to the Mountains of the Moon.[17]

More outlets did not mean freer speech, however. Public relations specialists in Kinshasa and New York sent a deluge of press releases specifically targeting American journalists, and the US Embassy in Kinshasa kept tabs on what domestic newspapers said about Zaire. It monitored the articles from Tom Johnson of the *New York Times* in June, and not coincidentally, he, along with *Newsweek*'s Andrew Jaffe, had uncommon difficulty in getting visas to enter Zaire. Stories emanating from Kinshasa emphasized the "modern" accommodations in the capital and the similarity of Zaïrois food to southern cuisine in the United States, yet also fetishized African art, music, and people. News accounts promised that in "friendly pygmy villages," hunters would be "delighted to show off their magnificent hunting spears and to pose for photographs in exchange for a few dollars and cigarettes." Everything appeared to promote the country as much as the fight, if not more. Mailer received one such delivery that declared Zaire "a new dateline in the ever-growing almanac of sport."[18]

When Foreman crossed that "new dateline," he met Zaïrois "begging me to beat Ali." Jokes about cannibalism and voodoo drew laughs in America but not in Zaire. High-level diplomats contacted Ali's people to make that point clear. The same government that was carefully monitoring journalists' impressions before they went to print did not give the fighters any more leeway to undermine Mobutu's Zaire. In his previous trip to Africa, Ali had visited predominantly Muslim countries, where his faith automatically won him fans. On his flight to Kinshasa, however, Ali looked for a new strategy to win some hearts and minds in a nation where 75 percent of the population identified as Christian. "Who do they hate?" he asked aloud to an airplane occupied by not just his boxing team but also his de facto public relations team—American sportswriters. Gene Kilroy offered up Belgium. With a colonial past not far in the rearview mirror, many Zaïrois still harbored ill will toward Belgians. That was all Ali needed. When he deplaned in Kinshasa, he did not apologize for past transgressions, he simply changed the narrative altogether. "George Foreman is a *Belgium*!" Chants of "Ali, Ali, Ali" morphed into "Ali *bomaye*!" which loosely translates as "kill him" in Lingala, one of the dominant indigenous Bantu languages in a region that housed more than two hundred apart from the lingua franca, French. In one emphatic yet baseless statement, Ali turned thousands of people against George Foreman—and his dog.[19]

"Afraid of dogs? They've got lions and hyenas!" Foreman laughed off accusations of Belgian ancestry, and since he had a complexion darker than Ali's, let alone most Belgians', the story did not stick. But his "sole companion" Daggo, a beautiful German shepherd, looked the part. The people who created or propelled connections between Foreman and Belgium specifically, or colonialism generally, were quick to point out the similarities between Daggo and the police dogs used by Belgian authorities. Before anyone called Foreman "a Belgium," his choice of pet would likely have been overlooked, particularly by American media, which was confronted with "pet" leopards in gold-plated cages at Mobutu's palace in N'sele, where Foreman and Ali set up their training camps. In this new narrative, however, of Foreman as the colonial oppressor meeting Ali the resistance leader and, ultimately, liberator, even Daggo became newsworthy, particularly stateside. Railing against stories that "made the people seem like they were still in the woods," Foreman simply retreated. Like the unattended press conference, it gave Ali an unopposed campaign. He made the most of it. While Foreman stayed cloistered in N'sele, Ali toured the country—at least as far as the government would allow, in keeping with the stipulations on movement included in his contract—shadowboxing and rapping about how he would beat Foreman and his dog. "We didn't know who George Foreman was," one fan in Kinshasa told *Jet*. "It's not that we thought he was white, but we thought maybe he worked for the white man." Ali, not unlike Mobutu, masked deficiencies with a cloud of authenticity. In his excitement to celebrate Zaire's independence and identify it as a city on the hill for the global black freedom struggle, Ali failed to notice or flatly ignored Mobutu's oppressive, dictatorial regime. The athletic icon quickest to critique fallacies and hypocrisy in the American democratic system, he remained silent about the complete absence of democracy in Mobutism.[20]

That was only one of the similarities between Muhammad Ali and Mobutu Sese Seko. Although his glory-laden name had been given to him by Elijah Muhammad, rather than self-selected, Ali did freely call himself the "Greatest." Like Zaire's economy, he looked to be on the decline, and he, too, relied on a cult of personality and friendly media to keep him afloat. His two recent victories over Norton and Frazier looked unspectacular. Neither close decision could erase the memory of brutal defeats he suffered against both of them. Many pointed out that Ali sometimes seemed to rest during rounds and then finish with a burst before the bell, to convince judges that he was the dominant fighter. The most redeeming characteristic Ali had shown in his last two bouts was not speed, agility, or power but perseverance, an ability and willingness to take a lot of punishment and outlast his opponent. It was not the most desirable attribute in prizefighting, and one that was patently dangerous against someone like Foreman. It had been three years since the champion needed a judge to tell him he won a fight. Ali needed all the good publicity he could accrue in order to justify his place in Foreman's ring.[21]

The ring itself was a compromise. Ali's team wanted a twenty-foot version that would offer more room to maneuver; Foreman's folks insisted on eighteen feet to keep the action close. In the end, Everlast made a custom nineteen-foot ring and sent it direct from Missouri to Zaire. It was one of many compromises made in the execution of an event nicknamed the "Rumble in the Jungle"—a tagline contested by Zaïrois officials as quickly as they jettisoned "Slave ship to Championship." Video Techniques negotiated the date and time of the fight, settling on September 25, before the World Series could split the sporting world's attention, and the starting time for three in the morning local time so that the television broadcast would not begin too late on the East Coast or too early on the West Coast. The best interests of the fighters or the local fans were less important. But the interests of Mobutu's government remained paramount. Only positive messages about Zaire would make their way out of the country as throngs of travelers sought to come in. "No one," a VT executive confirmed, "will have to sleep in the jungle."[22]

The journalists' swelling camp in downtown Kinshasa, however, did start to resemble a jungle of sorts—a hobo jungle from the Depression era. They moved in huddled masses between the press centers at N'Sele, the Hotel Memling, and the Stade du 20 Mai. Hot, bothered, and often cranky, they swapped any information they may have gleaned, culled, or invented for a new lead, a different angle, or just a fresh drink. In this horde of writers—seasoned veterans of boxing reportage and others new to the sport—sentimentality began to shape logic. Ali was *their* man in the region. And he fed them claims that he was already in better shape, weeks before the fight, than he had been at the first bell when he defeated Frazier. "Whenever I feel I want to stop," he told anyone in earshot, "I look around and see George Foreman." The chances of his seeing Foreman were pretty high, of course, because they stayed in the same area and had to share a practice ring. Anticipating visits from Ali and his staff, Sadler spent much time in his familiar position, grasping the heavy bag and putting all his weight behind it while Foreman literally beat the stuffing out of it. The sight of his massive fistprints impressed into the bag while sand poured out gave quote-starved reporters something to devour. "George worked 14 minutes on the heavy bag," Izenberg wrote. "George said nothing. Neither did the bag." But Ali, as usual, had a retort. "When Sadler holds the heavy bag, George can punch a hole in it," he reminded the photographer Howard Bingham, but "ain't nobody gonna be holding me!" After caricaturing Foreman as a European colonist, he began to describe him as an Egyptian "mummy," stumbling forward with outstretched arms that would never reach Ali.[23]

In fact, his sparring partners could barely touch him—unless he let them. Ali brought in promising young heavyweights of Foreman's stature, including Roy "Tiger" Williams and Larry Holmes. When Dundee started the action, Ali smoothly ducked their hooks and slipped their straights. As he had done in Deer Lake, he leaned back against the ropes, almost inviting them to get some shots in. Instead of staying there until Dundee broke it up, however, he waited only a few moments and then sprang off the ropes in a flurry of punches that made Williams and Holmes look like heavy bags with headgear. Ali appeared to be in peak condition about a week before fight night. Foreman looked closer to base camp. His sherpas, Sadler, Saddler, and Moore, brought in a pack of sparring partners that included a light heavyweight, Terry Lee; one former light heavyweight, Elmo Henderson; and a moonlighting trucker three years removed from his last prizefight (and five from his last win), Bill McMurray. Even against this motley crew, Foreman did not exactly impress onlookers, although he was not looking for adulation. He was looking for rhythm—not just power or endurance, but pace and timing. Despite still carrying some extra weight, which the mounting skepticism of the pundits of prizefighting magnified, Foreman believed he was on the right track: "I was a boxing machine. The rhythm I coveted all these years I finally achieved." It was harder to observe, let alone measure, Foreman's "rhythm," given his tightly controlled camp and personal reticence. Gauging Ali's physical fitness and undeniable confidence was much easier. Even the pseudoscience of "biorhythms" reinforced the belief in Ali by "proving" he would be in a better physical and emotional state than his opponent in the predawn hours of September 26, local time. Then, in a heartbeat, the collective biorhythms in Kinshasa plummeted. During a sparring session with the champ, McMurray got overwhelmed and covered up with his elbows out. One of them caught Foreman in the face, and he quickly turned to Sadler to tell him he was cut. "No you're not!" Sadler yelled back. A current of crimson poured from its delicate source, just between Foreman's right eyelid and eyebrow. "You're not bleeding!" cried Sadler against the undeniable evidence of an inch-long gash. The rhythm broke. The cut could be stitched shut for now, but stitches wouldn't hold up against a heavyweight punch. They would have to come out before Foreman could get back in the ring—a process that could take weeks. Foreman's eye would heal, but the damage to the event—not just the fight but also the Zaire 74 festival and the anticipated tourism associated with all of it—looked irreparable.[24]

★ 11 ★
I Don't Run 'Cause I Don't Have To

"I feel as if somebody close to me just died," Ali told the television reporter Bill Brannigan after hearing the news about Foreman's cut. It was, he said, in a rare moment of complete candor, "the worst thing that could have happened." Not that he was particularly concerned about Foreman's health or wellness, but Ali claimed to have trained longer and harder than normal for his chance to regain the title. He weighed just a little over two hundred pounds and looked in the best shape one could expect for a thirty-two-year-old with more than a decade of fights behind him. Everything had gone according to plan in the months since signing the contract. Now he had to maintain that indefinitely. Norman Mailer arrived in Kinshasa the day the news broke and immediately visited N'sele. Battling a stomach flu, Mailer perceived some inner turmoil in Ali as well. With rumors of at least a monthlong postponement—which meant several more weeks of strict training and rigid diets—it seemed to Mailer that "every cell in [Ali's] body could be ready to mutiny."[1]

Conversely, the hiatus forced Foreman to cool off. During the first ten days, he was instructed not to sweat for fear of compromising the stitches. Mobutu's people would not allow him to leave the country for a second medical opinion, but they granted him permission to move out of N'sele and take an air-conditioned room at the Hotel InterContinental in Kinshasa—a newer and much nicer hotel than the Memling, where most journalists stayed. Mailer didn't have a room at either hotel; his reservation got lost, leaving him desperately searching for both a bedroom and a bathroom. He bought a plane ticket instead and caught the first flight back to New York. Mailer did not believe that he would miss anything significant while Foreman rested in the air-conditioning and Ali festered in N'sele. The Zaïrois government, on the other hand, worked itself into a frenzy. Officials who strenuously blue-penciled every report leaving the country, editing, revising, or deleting anything they felt might inhibit tourists from coming, were unable to quash the reports of Foreman's injury. Now they rushed to debunk suggestions that the Rumble in the Jungle would be canceled or relocated.[2]

Exposés of big bugs or bad service that did escape the blue pencils and reach their intended audiences probably had little if any effect on tourism for the fight. In fact, suggesting that the cockroaches roaming Kinshasa were big enough to play for the Green Bay Packers might have attracted readers from Wisconsin. But without a Rumble, they were not coming to the Jungle. As communiqués from the few telex machines that had not yet been rendered inoperable confirmed suspicions of the postponement, prospective tourists had to reconsider their options. For those who were already in Kinshasa, however, the decision about what to do was even harder. Leaving the country carried some risks. The *New York Post*'s Larry Merchant followed Mailer out of town, eager to enjoy some comfortable accommodations and watch the baseball playoffs at home. From New York, he learned that Mobutu's government would not renew his visa to return. One of his reports, representative of his background as a "Depression-era Brooklynite [with] a built-in bullshit detector," detailed how a government-approved travel agent scammed one American woman, selling her a $3,000 tour package before revealing, after she landed, that it covered only her travel to Zaire. When Mobutu's people saw the article, they immediately barred Merchant's reentry, and a future Hall of Fame boxing broadcaster missed his opportunity to report on the biggest fight of the era. These machinations were hardly a secret. Officials in the US Embassy in Kinshasa made notes of a 62 percent increase in hotel costs since May, and inquired about a new governmental policy that required tourists to spend at least $40 in the country each day. The embassy, however, chose not to leak such information back to the American press.[3]

Marghuerite Mays, ex-wife of the baseball star Willie Mays, had no problem spending the compulsory amount. She and her daughter were two of many who came to Kinshasa for a holiday that was to be punctuated by a significant sporting event. After hearing of the fight's postponement, they decided to stick to their original itinerary, enjoying the sights, safaris, and shopping, without extending their stay for a bout that might never come off. At least they got to see the Zaire 74 music festival, which, given the difficulty in coordinating more than thirty groups and artists, half of which came from overseas, could not be rescheduled. For many of the tourists, as well as the huge cadre of writers and photographers that remained in Kinshasa at the end of September, the festival was about all they had left. Leon Gast and his film crew, shooting for a documentary about the fight, captured enough footage to produce a full-length feature on the concert. Conceived as a means to "document the history of the beat" and its transference from Africa to the larger Atlantic world, Zaire 74 highlighted the disparity of experiences between continents as well. While African American artists such as B. B. King and the Spinners gave voice to an evolving black freedom struggle in the United States, the South African Miriam Makeba's "Click Song" played the refrain of invisibility that persisted in the era of decolonization. The unquestioned headliner of the festival,

James Brown, brought his nouveau-big-band style and mass appeal to the stage. "You can't get liberated broke!" Brown beamed through his ever-present cackling laugh. But the punch line was that tickets for the festival, even after word that it would not directly precede the fight, cost about 25 percent of the annual salary for most Zaïrois. With tourists wavering and locals priced out, the low attendance at Zaire 74 seemed a bad omen for the Rumble in the Jungle.[4]

Of all the American newspapers and magazines represented in Zaire during the fall of 1974, *Rolling Stone* should have been the most interested in providing equal coverage for the concert and the fight. Yet its correspondent had little interest in either. The famed "gonzo" journalist Hunter S. Thompson told George Plimpton how much he hated this assignment, but was nonetheless eager to be abroad after recently being run out of a speaking engagement at Duke University. Although immensely popular with the student body, Thompson said that he raised the ire of the administration when he answered a question about the university president's political aspirations by calling him a "worthless pig fucker" while spilling the half-full glass of Wild Turkey he kept with him onstage. It seemed like a good time to get out of the country. In Kinshasa, the vials, bottles, and pill cases filling his *Rolling Stone*–embossed duffel bag audibly clinked with each short nervous movement, but no one seemed to mind. At least it was movement on the media savannah, where an information-starved press scoured the horizon for something to write about.[5]

Right in front of them, Foreman was, as he said later, running "like a deer" around Kinshasa. Since he was unable to spar and unwilling to talk, however, the pack of journalists hunted elsewhere for a morsel of news. Back in N'sele, Ali feasted. His decrease in energy concerned the Nation of Islam, and Herbert Muhammad's doctor, Charles Williams, determined that it was caused by hypoglycemia.

Dr. Ferdie Pacheco, who had been associated with Ali for nearly a decade, was as shocked as anyone by the sudden diagnosis and pre-scription—eat more sweets to raise the blood sugar. The change in diet did not exactly reinvigorate Ali. While Foreman's training be-came reduced to roadwork, Ali ran less. Some days he only shadow-boxed or hit the heavy bag before concluding the session. He expe-rienced a predictable side effect, weight gain, while Foreman kept running, dropping pounds until his clothes practically fell off him. Ali reallocated time from training to talking, while Foreman almost stopped conversing altogether. He didn't even shake hands. He kept his fists in his pockets most of the time, occasionally taking them out to play a silent game of table tennis with Moore or Bill Caplan, the jack-of-all-trades for Henry C. Winston who now functioned as Foreman's press agent. When the champ spoke, it was purposeful. To those reaching for a handshake, he said, in a drawl sweet enough to boost Ali's glucose levels, "Excuse me for not shaking hands with you, but you see I'm keeping my hands in my pockets." To reporters still sniffing around for a story, he made clear: "I don't want to be part of a sideshow."[6]

Plimpton immersed himself in the whole circus. Again on as-signment for *Sports Illustrated* as a stand-in at these international megamatches for the magazine's lead boxing writer, Mark Kram, who disliked flying, he also landed on the day McMurray cut Fore-man. Unlike Mailer, Plimpton stayed during the postponement, hoping to capture something that would give the book he planned to write more detail, maybe even more gravitas, than the one for which Mailer already secured an advance. Plimpton navigated not only the boxers and musicians but all the literati as well: sports-writers like Dick Young of the *New York Daily News*, Thompson, and even the photographers and war correspondents, who, Plimp-ton confirmed, were just as bored as the rest of them but took smug satisfaction in how much better they handled it. Young poured over days-old baseball box scores and sometimes popped his head up to complain about the food or accommodations, although Mobutu warned journalists against spreading such "lies." The Pulitzer Prize winner Horst Faas shared the gruesome details behind his gory pictures of war-torn lands just as matter-of-factly as Young rhymed off Johnny Bench's stats from secondhand newspapers. Thompson and Bill Cardoza developed their own fictive language to trade theories of African coups and Nazi war criminals hiding across the border in Brazzaville. Representatives for *National Geographic* and *Newsday* crossed into neighboring countries such as Niger and were promptly thrown out. The US Embassy there made it clear that the only story lines journalists should pursue were located between Kinshasa and N'sele. The cameraman for *Sports Illustrated*, Howard Bingham, befriended Ali and stayed in his camp. Plimpton and the magazine's first boxing editor, Budd Schulberg, continued to ride the bus between both venues.[7]

They grew so starved for stories that one day they probed Angelo Dundee about the contents of a little black bag he carried. Dundee called it a "kit bag," but it more closely resembled a surgeon's. The question yielded a surprisingly long and detailed discussion of all the tools and tinctures that Dundee kept with him. He had a vast array of pills and powders to treat bleeding, swelling, or anything else he feared would disrupt his fighter. Somewhere between fifteen and twenty containers of smelling salts, which Dundee bought in bulk from a local funeral parlor, lined the inside of an apparently bottomless bag. Scores of homemade cleansers and coagulants, lightened or darkened so that they would not make an easy target regardless of his boxer's complexion, rested on the bottom. Then Dundee expanded into a careful recounting of exactly which substances and applicators he kept in his right and left shirt pockets, as well as in his right and left pants pockets, so that the moment his charge came to their corner, he could go to work. It was amazingly long and woe-

fully insignificant. Schulberg, with his soft stutter, and Plimpton, in
his patrician accent, forgot about the bag as they left N'sele, negotiating instead over who would use a brief aside from Dundee about
a boxer turned pimp who fell in love with his charge and then mur-
dered her clients. They were glad to have had something that helped
pass the time.[8]

Scores of reporters wandered around, bleary-eyed from their
search for something worth writing down. They hounded one another for nuggets of information and traded whatever they heard for
new info from another colleague. Some, in their desperation, simply made up stories and tossed them out like boomerangs, waiting
to see how long it would take for the rumors to return. One writer
insisted that Foreman had told him, very discreetly, about a recent
dream in which he was trying to teach one of his dogs to ice-skate.
A tornado of Freudian psychoanalysis touched down in Kinshasa.
The relationship between boredom and ridiculousness strength-
ened as the media awaited the fight. It had been rescheduled for the
end of October, but only after a secret meeting in the bowels of the
Hotel InterContinental. Mobutu's representative, Mandungu Bula;
Don King, who took the lead for Video Techniques, since Schwartz
had been arrested earlier that month in London for fraud and extortion; and Dick Sadler negotiated the scheduling without input
from either fighter or any doctors. Unless Foreman's eye healed,
however, the fight would be no more a reality than a skating dog.[9]

After the announcement of the revised date, the Zaïrois government finally agreed to let American agents start selling tour pack-
ages for the rescheduled fight—at much lower rates. Travel *and* accommodations could now be had for less than $2,000. Of course,
no amount of money could guarantee that Foreman's stitches or
the Central African monsoon season would hold up until the end
of October. When Foreman first climbed back in the ring, he let
Henry Clark, who had lost to McMurray in 1967, repeatedly punch

him in the eye. Clark landed shots with increasing force dead on the cut while the firm of Sadler, Saddler, and Moore anxiously watched the twitches, not the stitches. They were confident enough in their man's eye, but not yet certain that he trusted it. Instead, they found this lighter version of Foreman to be looser as well. He took Clark's shots with confidence, and as soon as his corner gave the green light, Foreman bounced up and unloaded. "Everything was messed up. But I had this confidence," Foreman believed. "I didn't need to spar. I didn't need anything." The fight was on.[10]

Mailer returned to Kinshasa and, like Foreman, tried to make up for lost time. He watched the champion's workout and did not just observe the exercises: he counted the punches. On the heavy bag, Mailer calculated a steady rhythm of 50 shots a minute in a series of simulated three-minute rounds. Foreman took thirty seconds to dance around the bag after each round and then went back for another 150 consecutive blows to a Sadler-strapped heavy bag. According to Mailer, he never lost any power, even after 500 shots. Reifying the narrative of Foreman's fists versus Ali's feet, Mailer personally tested the challenger's fitness. After a night of rich food, cheap booze, and a series of other gambles, the out-of-shape writer arrived at Ali's camp in time for his scheduled run at five in the morning. Mailer insisted that he kept up with Ali for half of the three-mile course. Later, he measured their route and found it a half mile short. If speed had been Ali's primary advantage over an otherwise bigger, stronger, and younger opponent, the monthlong break during which Foreman ran more and Ali apparently ran less closed the gap. It did not bode well. "Having seen my gentle friend Foreman hit," Ambassador McClintock wrote to the embassy in Kinshasa, "if Muhammaed [sic] gets in the way of such a fist, he will rapidly be translated to his Muslim masters."[11]

Ali conducted diplomacy of his own. He sent a communiqué from the embassy to the White House, offering to pay for a direct link from the mouth of the Congo to President Ford's television. Ford replied indirectly, through official channels, with a congratulatory message to Mobutu for his "outstanding contribution to a sporting event of world significance." Ali exchanged official diplomacy for the personal and gave Mobutu a kiss. At a joint press conference in the Stade du 20 Mai, Foreman greeted the Enlightened Leader and accepted some applause. Ali planted one on Mobutu's cheek and sparked thunderous cheers. But Foreman refused to accept defeat in any ring, even the ring of public opinion. He slipped off his jacket and flexed the muscles that had become more visible as Foreman focused on roadwork and shed superfluous pounds. Ali desperately tried to take back the spotlight, but was foiled by a stubborn button on his wrist. It may have been a blessing, since the contrast in physiques, especially in the midst of the hypoglycemia diet, did not look good for Ali. Yet on the bus ride back to N'sele, he fumed about the button while trying to convince everyone aboard, including Plimpton and Bundini—perhaps even himself—that "the people are still for Ali."[12]

Regardless of whom "the people" were for, the money changed directions. Risky gamblers' flirtations with Ali in September slowly tapered off through October. The weigh-in, three days before fight night, showed that Foreman had dropped to 220 pounds—even lighter than he had been against Norton—while Ali seemed to gain weight right in front of people's eyes. Initially announced at 206, his weight, after correcting the metric conversions, officially came in at 216. It was only a few pounds below what he carried on the night Norton broke his jaw. That tipped the scales for oddsmakers, who had Foreman a 3–1 favorite less than seventy-two hours before the bell. The press corps in Kinshasa, on the other hand, was the diametric opposite. Murray Goodman conducted an informal poll of sportswriters, as did Kitemona N'Silu, who wrote for *Elima* in Zaire, and both got the same results: writers were 3–1 for Ali. The

New York Daily News' Phil Pepe explained the phenomenon in his headline "Logic: Foreman; Sentiment: Ali."[13]

Plimpton's sentiments always resided with Ali. He tried to arrange a meeting with one of the many *féticheurs*, or "witch doctors," who were reportedly willing to influence the outcome of the fight for the right price. Not that Plimpton wanted to solicit their services—he wanted Ali to regain the title on his own merit—but he intended to write "against the background of mumbo jumbo" in Central Africa. It would be much more interesting than a requiem for boxing's greatest showman. Mailer's notes suggest he expected the same outcome but strained for something deeper to write about. He flew through notepads from the Hilton at Logan International Airport in an attempt to link the struggles among and between black and Jewish Americans; his strained attempts to find connections between Bundini, Ali, and Mobutu covered stationery from Pan-American Airlines. Finally, in his own notebooks, the scribbles, research material, and scheduled meetings storyboard a narrative of Ali as a tragic protagonist: "Defeat was in the air Ali alone seemed to refuse to breathe."[14]

Zach Clayton was responsible for keeping the air of defeat in a neutral corner. Not quite as well known as Arthur Mercante, perhaps, Clayton was an obvious choice in this context. In 1952 he became the first African American to officiate a heavyweight championship; he refereed Foreman's pro debut in 1969; and he stood in the middle during Frazier's last successful title defense, against Ron Stander. His neutrality would be tested in Kinshasa, however. Almost twenty years later, Herbert Muhammad told the journalist Thomas Hauser that the Nation of Islam authorized a payment of $5,000 for Clayton just to keep Ali safe, even if that meant stopping the fight before Foreman could beat on him too badly. But a decade earlier, in a huddle with Gene Kilroy and George Foreman at an award presentation in Houston, Muhammad acknowledged sending $35,000 to Clayton so that he would look away from Ali's elbows if they found their way to Foreman's neck—or higher. That would have slightly outbid Foreman's camp. Sadler asked the champ for $25,000 in cash that he could take to Clayton in exchange for leniency against Foreman's propensity for low, late, or otherwise illegal blows. Although Foreman fully expected Sadler to pocket some of that money, it is possible that more than $50,000 came at Clayton from both sides. More might have been spent on *féticheurs* to perform intricate ceremonies in advance or to craft hex pouches to leave under the ring that would curse one of the fighters. Jim Brown, recently added to VT's broadcast team, gave voice to the mounting suspicions about everything from hexes to bribes: "If Ali wins the fight, it's been fixed."[15]

The "hard, implacable, and humorless" Brown bore a strong resemblance to Foreman, whom Mailer described as a "catatonic menace" in Zaire. One day before the fight, however, Foreman took on a new role. He had refused almost every request for an interview, and sometimes even disavowed his press agent. In fact, Foreman did not speak to Caplan for much of their stay, and the two communicated via handwritten notes or silent gestures in and around the Ping-Pong table. Some of those notes, perhaps indicating a scheduled press conference, were crumpled up and discarded without being read. But the champ suddenly loosened up. He not only attended a press conference, but also parried reporter's lunges with humor. They asked how he would counter Ali's verbal jabs, and Foreman told them he looked forward to doing it: "I never do get a chance to talk much in the ring. By the time I begin to know a fellow, it's all over." Probed about the odd hour of the fight, Foreman said, "When I was growing up in Houston I had a lot of fights at three and four in the morning." When they pressed him on Ali's speed advantage, Foreman nearly kept a straight face as he retorted: "I don't run 'cause I don't have to. I can hit a man on the jaw fast enough."[16]

Dick Schaap observed that everyone in Ali's camp appeared to fear for his safety as the fight approached. No one told Dundee about the bribe, so he took it upon himself to protect his fighter. On fight day, he reportedly grabbed a wrench out of his kit bag, perhaps the only tool in there he did not show Plimpton and Schulberg during their visit to N'sele, and meticulously tightened every ring post to firm up the canvas before throwing more resin on the mat. These actions made the surface faster, benefiting a fighter who wanted to move around a lot. As the huge Central African sun began to set that night, a throng of ticket holders and hangers-on moved incessantly to form and re-form the queue outside of the Stade du 20 Mai. They were undismayed by an afternoon drizzle because, in the heart of monsoon season, it seemed miraculous that heavy rains had not yet flooded the stadium. Even weather cycles apparently waited for the fight. In a much less orderly fashion, the press flocked to the back of the Hotel Memling and grabbed impatiently for their media passes. That is, all but Hunter S. Thompson. Rather than watch the fight in the stadium like everyone else, he intended to break into the presidential compound and watch the bout on a television with Mobutu himself, who surely had a closed-circuit hookup waiting. An especially good idea, he thought, because he had lost his press credentials. Thompson did not make it into the palace; he did not even make it out of the InterContinental. Instead, he spent the night floating naked in the hotel pool, surrounded by a green algae-like slick of soaked marijuana, which likely went unnoticed because apart from him, the entire hotel, the city, the nation, and much of the world was focused on the fight.[17]

Ali had to be especially focused. In his dressing room, he could feel the concern that rippled through his entourage. After refusing a robe that Bundini handpicked for this occasion, and an ensuing slap-studded argument, even his most stalwart supporter emanated sadness and despair. The mood had never been like this before an Ali fight. It resembled the final moments before a funeral procession. The People's Champ made a last plea to break the somberness, reminding everyone that he feared only Allah, thunderstorms, and choppy plane rides. He had spent the whole day watching bad horror movies such as *Baron Blood* and still was not afraid. Grasping for a way to light a spark in the room, he first tried to rekindle Bundini by playing to his ego, reminding him how important he was to the performance. As Bundini rejuvenated, the rest of the dressing room started to come alive, just as it granted entrance to Doc Broadus. Foreman, out of appreciation for his mentoring in the amateur ranks, and maybe guilt for choosing Sadler to manage him professionally, had brought Broadus along to perform a variety of tasks—in this case, monitoring the challenger's hand taping. With Broadus standing beside him, Ali brazenly divulged his team's strategy. "Are we gonna dance?" he called. "All night long!" Bundini responded. "Are we gonna dance?! All-Night-Long!!" they yelled back and forth, over and over again until they reached a crescendo and Ali ordered Broadus, "Tell your man he better get ready to dance!" Broadus murmured, "I'm not telling him nothing"—as big a lie as anyone uttered that night. Then a hysterical Pacheco came in, fuming that he had not yet been allowed into Foreman's dressing room, and promptly ushered Broadus out as shouts of "All-Night-Long!" echoed through the tunnels.[18]

Foreman's room stayed quiet as he sat, draped in so many towels that he did look like an Egyptian mummy. He and Sadler performed their ceremonial rehydration. In fact, Foreman had abstained from water even longer for this match, which should have made the short sips before the bell taste sweeter. Instead, he thought they tasted like "medicine." When he told Sadler, his trainer's response—"Same

water as always!"—came with the same certainty with which he
had yelled, "You're not bleeding!" after McMurray's elbow. The
champ was increasingly skeptical of his circumstances, but the inner circle—Foreman, Sadler, Saddler, and Moore—reaffirmed their
faith. As they joined hands to pray, Moore simply asked that Ali
would live through the fight. Uncomfortable as the dressing might
have been, however, Foreman's team still took its time before starting out toward the ring. Stalling like this, leaving the challenger
alone in the ring for a prolonged period, was a common tactic.
Some fighters become unnerved by the wait. Not Ali. He reveled in
sole possession of the stage, dancing, shuffling, and shadowboxing
for more than sixty thousand fans. They had sat through the last
hour without a preliminary bout to keep them occupied—the result
of a scheduling mishap that left one of the fighters in N'sele—and
now unloaded their pent-up excitement. "Ali Boom-a-ye!" rose up
fortissimo. It did not come with the "blood-lust" that Vachel Lindsay had imagined; rather, it was infused with the giddiness of thousands upon thousands of Ali supporters hoping for a miracle. In the
midst of it all, Mailer thought he saw Dundee take out a wrench. It
is debatable whether he did, and if so to what end: tightening the
ring posts further to make the ring even faster for Ali, or suddenly
changing his mind, as Mailer believed, and loosening the ropes so
as to slow down the fight. No one else saw Plimpton dive under the
ring, though it is generally accepted that he did, and he came back
without any evidence of "hex pouches" that might have unduly influenced the outcome.[19]

Only the slow procession of Foreman and his entourage toward
the ring disrupted the "Ali Boom-a-ye!" chorus. In the moments before the fight, the noise trailed off. As the two men stood toe to toe,
Ali employed one more tactic to psych out his opponent, reminding
Foreman, "When I won the heavyweight championship you were
still in high school!" But Ali hadn't done his homework; Foreman

never spent a day in high school. After the bell rang, it was too loud for trash talk anyway. Contrary to popular expectations, Ali did not dance around or avoid Foreman; rather, he came out swinging, and Foreman clumsily retreated. The Rumble in the Jungle did not have a measured prelude, so spectators had to adjust their tempi accordingly. Even the athletic Clayton struggled to keep up with a pace that was much faster than anticipated. In the broadcast booth, David Frost, the British journalist and television host, maintained a similarly allegro play-by-play between Joe Frazier and Jim Brown's duet of color commentary. By the end of the round, Foreman, attuned to the frenetic cadence, used hard jabs to keep Ali at bay as the first movement concluded.

Just as the pace speeded up all around, even in his corner, Ali prepared to slow everything down. At the break, Bundini rushed to tighten the ropes to help keep his man moving fast, but Ali shouted, "No, don't! Leave 'em alone!" Dundee shooed a perplexed Bundini away from the buckles. When the bell rang to start the next movement, the maestro conducted an adagio. Instead of engaging, he slowly backed into the ropes and guarded his head. "Oh Christ, it's a fix!" Plimpton shouted to an awestruck Mailer as they watched Ali recline, waiting for Foreman to strike. The champion cautiously approached, closer and closer, until his long jabs became short hooks and tight uppercuts. Dundee screeched, "Get off the ropes!" but Ali did not move until the waning seconds of the round, when he suddenly bounced up and landed stinging straights and crosses until Clayton intervened. This was the dance that would go on all night long.[20]

Mailer recognized Ali's ploy from the first Frazier fight. He recalled Ali coasting through the meat of the round and then coming on strong at the end in order to sway the judges. Now a few years older and a few steps slower, he seemed only more committed to the strategy as he lay back on the ropes, not even pretending to mount an attack for long stretches, before pitching a torrent of physical and verbal jabs inside the last minute. Whether the tactic influenced the judges would not be known until—or unless—they were called for a decision. But to anyone watching the broadcast, it became clear that the ringside announcers bought it. Jim Brown went against his earlier prediction and admitted that Ali was winning the fight, calling him "unreal." Mailer rightly pointed out that it was one of the highest accolades a person could get from the taciturn Brown. Although Frazier tried to argue on Foreman's behalf, John Daly quickly joined the booth and sided with Brown. It is possible that Daly harbored some ill will toward Foreman, since speculation arose that Foreman's representatives had threatened that day to call off the fight if Foreman did not receive an extra half-million dollars. Moore and the rest of Foreman's corner kept encouraging him—"Get him! Get him!!"—apparently unconcerned that throwing countless punches in the thick humidity of Zaire's pending monsoon season was exhausting the poorly hydrated champion.[21]

This refrain played on through the rest of the fight. Only once did Ali open up his guard again, as he had in the first round, and Foreman immediately caught him with a shot that spun his head around—his body trailing shortly thereafter—and sent aftershocks rippling all the way to Dundee. He shrieked, "Don't play with that sucker!" and Ali obediently scrambled to the ropes again, returned to his laid-back position, and covered his head. He did not come to life until the final moments of the round, when, once more, he unfurled a flurry of punches until time was up. Despite the repetition, Foreman never adjusted his strategy in principle, only in force. He threw more punches with more vigor as the fight wore on, but most only found their way to Ali's gloves or elbows. As his stamina became depleted, the champion put his hope in landing the one concussive punch that would end the fight, but he was losing his ability to throw it. He began resting on top of Ali at times until Clayton broke them, and then he slowly lurched toward Ali, looking as slow and stupefied as the mummy caricature Ali had drawn of him.[22]

Without any discernible breeze in the stadium, Foreman began to sway like a tree in the wind. He was losing his balance as well as his energy. Yet that did not stop him from hammering away at Ali, whose grimace became more pronounced with every blow. The absorption of so much punishment took its toll, and he sat on the ropes with his mouth agape during each interval Clayton created. Approaching the halfway point, it seemed as if neither fighter would be able to maintain his strategy and last the full fifteen rounds. Ali briefly stood up to engage Foreman, who leapt at the opportunity, but launched such an errant "godawful" haymaker that the momentum nearly carried him all the way to the floor. After almost taking himself out, he pivoted and popped Ali with an uppercut so strong that it reminded everyone he could still end the fight at any moment. When the bell rang, both fighters lumbered back to their corners and began to plot the second half of this grueling bout.[23]

As the signal sounded to begin the eighth round, however, Ali noticed Foreman struggling even to stand up from his stool. Feeding off the fatigue of his opponent, he found a new energy, eschewed the ropes, and bounded toward his mark. Like a matador, he circled the ring, using his fists and his words to manipulate Foreman into a position for the *estocada*. Foreman looked to gore him, but he had been weakened by seven rounds of Ali's physical and verbal banderillas. He later recalled what was going through his mind: "The most frightening thing is when Ali whispers, 'That all you got,' and you think, '*Yup.*'" Foreman propelled everything he had into one last knockout punch, but Ali countered and sent him plummeting to the canvas for the first time in his career. With Clayton counting in one ear and his corner yelling incomprehensible, contradictory instructions to the other, he staggered to one knee but stopped there. Foreman failed to meet the oldest rule in the sport: he was not up to scratch.[24]

The Stade du 20 Mai, much of Zaire, and almost the entire sporting world exploded as Clayton waved his arms and the timekeeper rang in Ali's second reign as heavyweight champion. The Central African skies echoed their cries as thunder, lightning, and a driving rain introduced the year's monsoon. Foreman slunk out of the ring and only briefly occupied his dressing room before exiting the stadium. It was for the best, since more than a foot of water began to fill it as the storm washed out the stands, soaked the ring, and flooded the tunnels. The writer Pete Bonventre and the photographer Ken Regan tried to beat a hasty retreat back to N'sele with hopes of getting early access to Ali. But when the rain became so heavy that they could no longer see the road in front of them, they had to pull off and wait for the storm to pass. It took hours for them to reach the twice-crowned champ, who, in the afterglow of boxing's greatest upset, sat on a stoop and did some magic for Zaïrois children—a series of rope tricks.[25]

★ 12 ★
You Got to Have a Boss

Staring up into a wet African sky, though,
Foreman knew he'd have to get up.

JACK B. BEDELL, "George Foreman in Zaire,"
Hudson Review 62, no. 2 (2009): 259

"In the idiom of Brooklyn," Archie Moore said, "[Foreman] blew his cool." The veritable professor of pugilism, who had a view from the corner of the ring, reduced the ex-champ's fall to pithy slang. Foreman was not going to regain any coolness in Kinshasa. He got out of Zaire as fast as he could—without any of the impediments he faced in Venezuela—but he couldn't go home yet. There were too many unanswered questions, and questions he did not want to answer at all. The Rumble in the Jungle left him searching, as the Louisiana poet Jack Bedell wrote, "for some succubus to blame." The water in the dressing room, the ropes before the fight, the advice from his corner during the action, his team's mixed signals after his knockdown, and the referee's count all replayed over and over in his head. To explain his first professional defeat, Foreman thought about outside interests like gangsters and gamblers, and about an inside job by Sadler, Saddler, or Moore. "I felt as if my core had evaporated," he recalled, so Hayward Moore whisked him away to rebuild it through weeks of intensive retail therapy. Over the next two years, Foreman crafted a new core, one more in line with that of a large percentage of Americans as he doggedly chased a chance to regain the heavyweight title.[1]

The process started in Paris, where Moore arranged for daily massages and brought food to Foreman's hotel room so that he could heal physically as well as mentally. From there they flew to Los Angeles, but only to hop a plane bound for Hawaii. Alternately feeding the birds and feasting on macadamia pancakes aided his recovery. When Moore asked what Foreman needed before he could go home, he had an answer: a convertible Rolls-Royce. Again taking care of the details, Moore had a Chicago dealer send one to Houston, where they picked it up and drove back into reality—a lost title, a new paternity suit, and an identity crisis.[2]

It took time to resolve the paternity case with a short-term girlfriend from Pleasanton, Pamela Clay, but that delay paled in comparison with the quarter century it took for Foreman to realize that his old nickname Mo'head was more than a dig at his big cranium. It was a reference to his biological father, Leroy Moorehead. Confirming enough details with siblings and aunts, he eventually confronted his mother and heard the truth. Foreman arranged a meeting in Texarkana, not too far from the ranch that he had purchased in his birthplace, Marshall. Foreman's and Moorehead's relationship lasted only a few years, until Moorehead's death in 1978, but the experience left an indelible impression on Foreman. When test results proved he was the father of Clay's son, he insisted the baby take his full name: George Edward Foreman. If he had any more sons, he intended to do the same. His kids would know for certain where they came from.[3]

As Foreman tried to figure out where he was going in his post-championship life, one thing he knew for sure was that he was not going back to Dick Sadler. The general cynicism cultivated by Sadler over their years together fed a strong suspicion of him in Foreman, particularly after losing the title. When Herbert Muhammad asked Foreman to sign a new contract with Sadler so that he could arrange a championship rematch, Foreman demurred. He intended to fight Ali again, but not under the same circumstances. He refused to appear below Ali, backing out of a bout with Oscar Bonavena because it would have been the undercard of Ali's title defense against the "Bayonne Bleeder," Chuck Wepner, in March 1975. Always an offensive brawler who openly admitted, "I've never been one of the Marquis of Queensbury's [*sic*] biggest supporters," Wepner went on the defensive when boxing writers questioned the way he had leapfrogged Foreman for a shot at the championship: "I saw the movies of Foreman and Ali. . . . Foreman looked like an AAU novice." Wepner may have forgotten that in 1969, only a year removed from the AAU tournament, Foreman pummeled him into a third-round TKO. Despite living up to his nickname, the crimson-covered Wepner gave Ali a much better fight than Foreman did in Zaire. He scored a knockdown and inspired Sylvester Stallone's *Rocky*, which would open in theaters the following year. But Ali's lackluster showing had more immediate consequences. Heavyweight sharks began circling as they sensed the champion's vulnerability. Ken Norton, who replaced Foreman on the undercard, made overtures for another shot at Ali. Joe Frazier, the only other fighter to beat Ali, also called for a decisive tiebreaker in their drawn-out saga. Heavyweights who had previously lost to Ali, such as Joe Bugner, angled for second chances. Ron Lyle looked for his break, but an upset loss to Jimmy Young in February seemed to tank his claim to Ali while simultaneously propelling Young into the conversation. Joe Louis once again backed Foreman, as he had in Jamaica, giving public voice to the popular belief that Foreman deserved a rematch as soon as possible. It became readily apparent, however, that Ali's camp did not share the same opinion.[4]

Four months. By the end of 1975. Within one year. After Wepner, then Lyle or Bugner and perhaps Frazier. Promises and time lines for the rematch streamed from Ali, his management, and the press that flocked to them. It was set to take place in Houston, in New

204 ★ NO WAY BUT TO FIGHT

Orleans, back at the National Stadium in Kingston, in a new arena in Cairo, or in a rebuilt Colosseum in Rome. "I was going to enter the ring in a chariot—seriously—one of those Ben Hur things," Ali told reporters. "Four big, white horses and trumpets blowing and me coming in and that fella putting his thumb down. We had it going.... I can't say no more." But it never got going, and Foreman grew impatient. Red Smith referred to 1974 as "the year the golden egg cracked" for what he deemed an unsustainable inflation of prizefight purses stimulated by Foreman's series of international megamatches. In reality there was still more money to be made, particularly by exciting heavyweights, from American television networks as well as political leaders in the developing world. None of these available riches seemed destined for Foreman, so he initiated a "campaign" to get Ali in the ring.[5]

Like countless other California transplants, Foreman found himself hanging out in Hollywood "for the sole purpose of promoting" himself. When he was the champ, he felt as though he didn't need to seek out publicity. Now he was a regular on talk shows and game shows such as *Hollywood Squares* and *Bowling for Dollars,* as well as a guest star on *The Six Million Dollar Man,* and even had a cameo in the Sidney Poitier–Bill Cosby comedy *Let's Do It Again,* a movie about rigging boxing matches. He accepted almost every invitation for publicity, and was prepared to do some "strange stuff" in order to put pressure on Ali for the rematch. He convinced a photographer from *People* magazine to visit his ranch, and orchestrated a photo op that left him holding a seven-hundred-pound calf across his shoulders. The picture made the magazine—and newspapers as well—but when asked whom he was training for, he could not answer definitively.[6]

It turns out he was training for five opponents—on the same night. Strange stuff indeed. To prove his stamina after Zaire, Foreman wanted to take on a handful of heavyweights in one event.

The idea was not unprecedented; Jack Dempsey had organized several similar events during his comeback in 1931–1932. Ali, too, had floated the notion before. Foreman was serious. He partnered with Henry C. Winston to make it happen. But Winston struggled to find the right venue and get the necessary financial backing. The Mephistophelian Don King suddenly appeared, promising network-television money from ABC and a major sports arena, Toronto's Maple Leaf Gardens. Foreman could not reject King's offer, although he asked him to keep Winston involved. Not surprisingly, Winston disappeared from the promotion well before the event, which was scheduled for April.[7]

King delivered on his promises. He found five veteran heavyweights with some name recognition, including a couple of Foreman's former victims (Boone Kirkman and Charley Polite), and a onetime championship challenger, Terry Daniels. Against a backdrop of accusations that the entire event was a farce, a carnival, or a circus, King reminded everyone that even if it was technically an exhibition, the fallout from a loss to any one of these fighters would be severe. "The money is on the line for a return bout with Muhammad Ali," he bellowed. "George is literally $5 million on the line in taking a chance against these men." ABC Sports went all in too, agreeing to broadcast the event live on its flagship *Wide World of Sports* program, complete with ringside commentary from Howard Cosell and Muhammad Ali. The arena sold more than 10,000 tickets for $5–$20 each. Everything fell into place, and all Foreman had to do was to produce results—five times in a row.[8]

Forty-year-old Alonzo Johnson, then Jerry Judges, and then Daniels came out fighting, and all three suffered multiple knockdowns before the referee, Harry Davis, waved them off. Judges landed the only significant punch of the night, snapping Foreman's head back with a crisp right hand, but even with his weight topping 230 pounds, Foreman controlled the ring. In the fourth contest,

Charley Polite landed the evening's only kiss, planting his lips on Foreman's chin during the prefight instructions, but he connected with little else. Coincidentally, he was the only fighter to avoid being knocked down by Foreman—something he could not say about their first meeting, in 1970. Kirkman ran the anchor leg, with aspirations of avenging his loss to Foreman and resurrecting his career without the help of his late manager, Jack Hurley. He failed in both respects. Foreman battered him around the ring, sending him to the floor in the first and opening a sizable gash on his head in the third. Kirkman perhaps took some solace in the fact that he remained on his feet after three rounds, considerably better than he had done in their initial engagement.[9]

Foreman's toughest battle throughout the night was an ongoing verbal feud with Ali. The champion drowned out Cosell's commentary, which sounded like a nasal refrain of words such as "travesty," "disgrace," and "discredit," to berate Foreman and coach his challengers. When Foreman tried to respond between opponents, it came off somewhere between sour and salty. Cosell bit on it. "Have pity on poor George Foreman," he implored ABC's viewers. "The scene you're seeing here today is sad. It's pathetic. This is not the same man who carried the American flag around the ring in Mexico City nearly seven years ago and in no way is this the same man who utterly destroyed Joe Frazier a little over two years ago. What has happened to George Foreman?" Nat Loubet of *Ring* indicated that the only redeeming quality of the show was financial, since the "Burlesquers" received $7,500 each, far more than any of them would have commanded in a genuine prizefight. Foreman, for his efforts, earned between $100,000 and $200,000, although King indicated that the money was only an advance against the big payday of a Foreman-Ali rematch. But the *Chicago Defender*'s sports editor, Norman Unger, compared the spectacle to "the disaster movie craze," and the *New York Times* television critic John

Leonard, writing as "Cyclops," took the gloves off: "I wouldn't have looked out a window to watch George Foreman sodomizing Pattycake." Of course, disaster movies filled theaters, and Cyclops had to admit that he did in fact watch the Foreman fiasco. It drew better ratings than the tennis match between Jimmy Connors and John Newcombe that ran at the same time on CBS, and buried the Major League Baseball games airing on NBC. The allure of Foreman's knockout punch still attracted spectators and home viewers to a sport that, outside its heavyweight champion, seriously lacked star power.[10]

Foreman made no bones about the fact that he was campaigning for another title shot, and he was decidedly unhappy about having to do it: "Now that I've whipped five, I want to whip three—Joe Frazier, Ken Norton and Muhammad Ali, that low-down god-for-nothing [sic] powderpuff." Emboldened by his five-in-one, Foreman offered to take on all three in the same day. Unimpressed, Ali gave his preferred schedule: rematches with Bugner and Frazier before meeting Foreman again. Dundee chimed in to add that Ron Lyle was still an option, despite his recent loss. When Ali and Lyle signed a contract for the next title fight, Teddy Brenner offered Foreman $300,000 to face Norton. Brenner knew that with Ali scheduled to meet Lyle and then Bugner, hardly the summer blockbusters that the Garden had envisioned at the start of the year, a Foreman-Norton bout might be the biggest ticket of the season. When Ali suddenly announced he would retire after the Bugner fight, there were no more maybes about it. Yet King shut it down immediately: "We might take $300,000 but not from Brenner—we don't do business with him."[11]

Still functioning as his own manager and trainer—John Gray worked the corner at the Maple Leaf Gardens—Foreman could not yet promote his own fights. King stayed closest, and even without an explicit agreement, he clearly influenced Foreman's options. So the bitter feud between King and Brenner over the future of boxing in New York City kept Foreman out of the Garden. He watched Ali dismantle Lyle in the Las Vegas Convention Center and then head out to another set of big paydays from international hosts. *Boxing Illustrated*'s editor, Jack Welsh, speculated that only the "oil-rich" countries of the Middle East could afford Ali's services now. But they did not need such an event to attract more attention; their manipulation of petroleum production achieved that regularly. Instead, the next two heavyweight championship fights landed in the archipelagos of Southeast Asia. In the weeks and months following the fall of Saigon to North Vietnam, its neighbors in the South China Sea desperately looked to prove their value and keep their place in the mounting complexity of the Cold War world. Malaysia paid Ali $2 million to defend against Bugner, and the Philippines would offer him considerably more to come out of a retirement that never started for his rubber match with Frazier.[12]

As a nation caught between the superpowers, trying desperately to sustain its economy while deflecting attention from its political instability and corruption, the Philippines relished the opportunity to host a signature international sporting event. The Filipino government relied primarily on debt-driven growth during the Ferdinand Marcos regime, borrowing funds that were then promptly pumped into social welfare programs, infrastructure improvements, agribusiness investment, and a burgeoning tourism industry. Although backlashes against some of these policies caused significant and sometimes violent reactions from students and political dissidents, President Marcos maintained control by issuing Proclamation No. 1081 in 1972, which declared martial law. Theoretically a temporary measure, it was still in effect three years later, when Frazier and Ali signed contracts to hold their third and final fight there. One target of Marcos's proclamation included the Moro National Liberation Front, an Islamic separatist organization that battled for political and religious independence from the Christian Filipino majority. Ali made no mention of Marcos's repression of his religious brethren, focusing instead on what Richard Hoffer described as the "iambic denigration" of Frazier: "It will be a killer and a chiller and a thrilla when I get the gorilla in Manila." Frazier, incensed by the comparison to a gorilla, likewise ignored the brutal dictatorship in his host country, couching the boxing match as an existential threat: "I'm gonna eat this half-breed's heart right out of his chest. I mean it, this is the end of him or me." It nearly was. After fourteen rounds that perfectly reflected the growing hatred between Ali and Frazier as well as their declining reflexes, Ali could barely move and Frazier couldn't see. Eddie Futch signaled the referee, Carlos Padilla, to stop the fight. Frazier did not regain the title, but he could still walk out of the ring, with about $5 million to help ease the pain. Ali made almost double that, some of which came directly from the same Marcos family that imprisoned Muslims and, given their proclivity to siphon off American aid money for their personal use, part of the champion's purse may have been unintentionally donated by the US government, which he criticized effusively. In total, one year after Red Smith thought the "golden egg" had cracked, a nation that used to be an American territory put up more money than any US sponsor to host an international megamatch in the "era of fantastic millions" that Teddy Brenner lamented from his office at Madison Square Garden.[13]

George Foreman did not earn one dollar, let alone any "fantastic millions," from a sanctioned prizefight in 1975. But his fortunes for 1976 looked promising. *Ring* ran a cover with him posing on a classic car and wearing a pink jacket and a half smile, with "I'M NO BAD GUY" in all-caps along the bottom. Another image transition seemed to be taking place as a funnier and friendlier version of the former champion spread through local and national media. Foreman recalled, "[I] did everything I could . . . to build a following so

I could demand a title shot. Hollywood, and speaking around the country . . . any group that would hear me." Just as he had befriended Jim Brown's manager, Hayward Moore, Foreman started a relationship with Tom Collins, who worked as a manager for Kareem Abdul-Jabbar. Given his client, Collins understood the connections between sport, race, and religion in 1970s America. He noted the opportunity afforded a Christian challenger in the shadow of a Muslim champion. Foreman began speaking to church groups—including a growing congregation in Garden Grove, California, for the Reverend Robert Schuller. "What to say?" he asked. "Ali's always talking about Allah. Why don't you say something about Jesus?" The loosely Baptist boxer who occasionally referred to but never really discussed faith took a leap. "Jesus, do this! I'm gonna rely on Jesus! Jesus is gonna help me!" He admitted it was the first time he had ever said such things, but Schuller's congregation accepted it as the gospel truth. "They liked that," he noted. "I didn't believe in that stuff." But many Americans did, and they would believe in Foreman, too.[14]

His plan to build demand for a championship rematch worked, and the alliance with Don King added leverage on the supply side. Since King had secured promotional rights to the "Thrilla in Manila" as well as the closed-circuit broadcast through his own television outfit, Don King Productions, he enjoyed a virtual monopoly on Frazier and Ali's third fight. King even got Bob Arum and Hank Schwartz to work with him on the project from the sixty-seventh floor of 30 Rockefeller Plaza. He felt certain that regardless of the outcome in the Araneta Coliseum, he could control the next heavyweight championship event as well—and if it included Foreman, perhaps the next one after that. With such formidable leverage in the heavyweight division, New York granted King a promotional license, and Brenner agreed to "rent out" the Garden on the understanding that King would bring a major title fight back to the mecca of boxing in time for the bicentennial celebrations the next summer.[15]

In addition to his speaking engagements, both secular and religious, Foreman donated proceeds from some exhibition fights to the US Olympic team in preparation for the Montreal Games. He cultivated a broad cross section of Americans to support his campaign for a championship bout. Even when he traveled abroad, Foreman sought to curry favor back home. Before a trip to South Africa, he followed the lead of Arthur Ashe, who, contrary to Ali, consulted with prominent black leaders in the United States about the best ways to counter apartheid while being hosted by its protectors. Unlike Ashe, however, Foreman listened to them and tried to achieve a delicate balance of refusing racial segregation without offending the South African government. His exhibitions would be open to integrated audiences—a subtle jab against state-sponsored segregation that scored points with his American fan base.[16]

Without a real fight, however, it was all moot. More than a year since his last bona fide bout, Foreman needed to get back in the ring. He agreed to meet the Argentinian knockout artist Pedro Lovell, whose string of quick KOs made for an impressive record similar to Foreman's early in his career, for a guarantee of $250,000. But the fight had to take place in the Las Vegas Convention Center because the Garden could not afford it. Two weeks after the Thrilla in Manila, it took a last-minute investment from the United Federation of Teachers to save New York City from bankruptcy. Two weeks after that, President Ford vowed that no federal money would be used to bail out the Big Apple, prompting the *New York Daily News* to paraphrase him on its front page: "Ford to City: Drop Dead." For the Garden, it amounted to the same thing. Even though CBS, desperately trying to bring boxing back to network television and dislodge ABC from its dominant position in televised sports, committed more than $200,000 to the Foreman-Lovell fight, and Argentinian television put up another $150,000, such an operation would require at least a half-million-dollar investment. The Garden, standing tall in the middle of a crumbling city, did not have the cash to promote bouts that it would not even have accepted years earlier. Brenner had to entertain notions of selling the arena, renting it to promoters like King, or sending fights it promoted to other cities such as Las Vegas.[17]

Once again, Ken Norton picked up a fight that Foreman left behind and soundly beat a "hapless" Lovell, who retired from the ring shortly after. Foreman looked ahead to a proven, even if imperfect, opponent and settled on Ron Lyle. He then sought out a similarly vetted trainer to get him ready. Attempting to reinvent his fighting style as much as his image, Foreman wanted to be sure that the next time he met Ali, the crowd would be on his side and he would keep them there for all fifteen rounds if necessary. But he needed a trainer. Not long after Foreman's break with Sadler, reports connected him with Gil Clancy. In truth, he was only one of the trainers Foreman contacted in 1975. Other highly regarded trainers were disinclined to "interview" with anyone, even a top heavyweight contender, and some may have balked at Foreman's insistence that he wanted only a trainer while continuing to manage himself. Clancy was not above any of it. He answered Foreman's questions and "gave great ideas"—after all, he had trained Quarry before his shocking upset over Lyle and had spent years working for Emile Griffith, who made a long career out of winning decisively on judges' scorecards. But Quarry had all but quit the ring, and Griffith was reaching the end of his career. Clancy needed a project, preferably one involving a title contender. In a stark turn from the twenty-one-year-old who wanted to "show 'em who's boss," the twenty-six-year-old Foreman said: "You got to have a boss."[18]

In fact, he hired two. Perhaps hedging his bets, Foreman also reached out to "Kid" Rapidez. Once the trainer for the welterweight champion Jose Nápoles, who used his power to dethrone and defend against Curtis Cokes in 1969, Rapidez prepared him to win a unanimous decision over the Clancy-trained Griffith. It was the kind of change in style that Foreman hoped to achieve. Rapidez and Clancy stifled their animosity toward each other and coexisted in Foreman's ecosystem—for a while. Their work paid dividends, since Foreman looked not only lighter on his feet but much quicker with the jab as he warmed up on Jody Ballard at a Thanksgiving fund-raiser in the Catskills. Still not satisfied, they threw him into an exhibition in San Francisco a few weeks later to finish crafting Foreman as a boxer before he stood face-to-face with the slugger Lyle.[19]

The "short and snappy" jabs from his exhibition bouts lasted only until Lyle drew him into the kind of brawl that Foreman used to instigate. Even though the ex-champ came out on top, it toppled the new "boxing family" he had described to *Ebony*. He cut Rapidez loose to keep Clancy happy, and he reconsidered his working relationship with Jim Brown, who got his feet wet in promotion by partnering with Perenchio on the Foreman-Lyle event. Afterward he thought, "I wished I had never met Jim Brown.... Fighting Ron Lyle almost killed me!" It may not have been exactly what Foreman had envisioned, but the timing could not have been better. Televised boxing reached new heights of profitability in the mid-1970s. Although boxing dominated sports programming in the 1950s, the networks in that decade competed for an estimated total revenue of around $5 million a year. Now that revenue potential had jumped to $25 million annually, notwithstanding the stiff competition posed by football, baseball, and professional basketball. With this new valuation, ABC and CBS once again vied to make prizefighting a mainstay of home television viewing. Foreman's combination of

name recognition and knockout ability remained the ideal product with which to sell nontitle bouts on network television; closed-
circuit proceeds drove the financing for multimillion-dollar purses
in the sport's biggest events.[20]

Immediately after Foreman's knockout of Lyle, Don King looked
to capitalize on the interest it created by talking about his vision for
a seven-figure rematch with Ali. Potential venues included Macau,
Istanbul, Kuwait, and Sudan. The next day, however, he hypoth-
esized about Ali settling his score with Norton on Independence
Day at Shea Stadium in New York, Pontiac Stadium in Michigan, or
some other "patriotic" site such as Philadelphia. Either fight would
have to wait for at least one more stop on Ali's transnational Bum-
of-the-Month-Club tour. The next installment was scheduled for
the recently completed Coliseo Roberto Clemente in San Juan,
Puerto Rico, which had been built to lure such major events as a
heavyweight championship fight. Ali's title bout against the Belgian heavyweight Jean-Pierre Coopman proved to be the venue's
first and last. Mark Kram called it "the worst mismatch in heavyweight championship history," and the local press blasted the impending charade, for which good tickets still cost more than $200.
Ali deflected criticism of his lackluster opponent: "I got Ken Norton and George Foreman ahead of me. Let me have a little rest in
between." Later he suggested, "It's not fair that I do all the fightin'.
Let Norton and Foreman clean up their business and I'll meet the
winner."[21]

Neither of these top-two contenders, Foreman or Norton, would
risk their status against the other. But on the eve of the Coopman
farce, Ali announced another opponent of questionable pedigree,
Jimmy Young, whose upset of Lyle remained the only notable win
on his record. The challengers-in-waiting could not afford to remain
idle. Norton opted to stay warm against Ron Stander. Foreman tried

to hold out. Yet when Perenchio and Caesars Palace offered to put up $1 million for a Foreman-Frazier rematch, it warranted strong consideration. "The most thing is, I love to fight," Frazier said in defiance of suggestions he should have retired after the Thrilla in Manila. Besides, he confirmed: "I watched films of my first fight with him. . . . I didn't see one thing wrong except that I got hit." So the two ex-champions agreed on financial terms and an early-summer date, even though the venue for what writers dubbed "the homeless fight" remained in question. In the nation's bicentennial year, a site with patriotic associations would be nice. And not only was Vegas not exactly the cradle of American democracy, but the re-match between two former champions also merited more than the five thousand seats in the casino's Sports Pavilion. Caesars backed Perenchio while he looked for a place to hold a bicentennial brawl. The nexus of American patriotism and boxing nostalgia could have been the center of Yankee Stadium, but the baseball people did not want to risk their grass in the middle of a regular season by adding the requisite fifteen thousand seats for a big-time prizefight. Instead the Nassau Coliseum—one of the early suitors for the first meeting between Frazier and Foreman—came through with a deal amenable to all stakeholders. Perenchio, whom Foreman described as "a man of vision" and "the most creative guy who had ever stepped foot into a boxing arena," billed this fight as the "Battle of the Gladia-tors," since it would come off at the Coliseum, and distributed pro-motional photos of the fighters in gladiator costumes. Exploiting all available angles, he also emphasized the context of the bicenten-nial summer by producing short television spots showing Foreman and Frazier dressed up as significant figures in American history, including Betsy Ross. Frazier did seven characters, and Foreman nineteen, all of which aired on ABC as well as one hundred inde-pendent stations across the United States and Canada. Finally, both battlers put on open-air, free-to-the-public training sessions right in the heart of New York City. Foreman's camp even offered ringside tickets to the "best heckler."[22]

The winner of Foreman's contest had plenty of fodder on fight night. When Frazier came into the ring, he removed his hooded robe to display a freshly shaved head. And below the shining cranium, he looked noticeably fleshier than normal. Though half a foot shorter than Foreman, they weighed the same when they met in the center of the ring. As the bell rang, however, Frazier did not come out in his signature smokin' style; rather, he focused on defense, moving his head furiously to make Foreman miss, only occasionally resting his neck to snap a punch. In the fourth round, he landed a series of left hooks that caused a mist of sweat to jump off Foreman's head. Despite the extra weight, he evidently did not pack the same punch. Foreman responded in the next round with "murderous" blows that jarred the mouthpiece from Frazier's face—along with six of his teeth. He got up from the first knockdown, but just as he did in Jamaica, Foreman attacked and dropped him right back to the canvas. Struggling mightily to beat the count, Frazier scrambled to his feet one more time. Eddie Futch beat him to the canvas. He was already up on the apron, and for a second consecutive time he told the referee his man was through. After the fight, with a swollen face hiding the stitches that kept it together, Frazier admitted, "It's time to hang the gloves on the wall." Foreman complimented Frazier and aimed most of his comments at Ali: "I have beaten every heavyweight anybody knows about except the champ. I'll fight anybody in the world, but I should be fighting the champion." He exuded a renewed confidence as well: "It'll be like a country boy pickin' peas."[23]

"We took the [Frazier] fight for two reasons," Clancy told Jerry Izenberg. "The money and the fact that it is the shortest route to the title match we want." Both rationales looked questionable in the aftermath. Frazier's appearance and lackluster performance undermined the significance of Foreman's victory, and the damn Yankees overshadowed the entire event. Shortly before Frazier and Foreman squared off, Ali and Norton signed on for their tiebreaker—an open-air bout at Yankee Stadium in September. News of the title match in late summer did not help sell tickets to the Coliseum. It was only half full for the main event, which meant it was blacked out for the New York television audience. All told, the operation had lost somewhere around $2 million before the opening bell.[24]

Like Frazier, Perenchio withdrew from the fight game after this disaster. His promotional ventures had begun with the Super Fight in 1971, and he attached himself to Foreman in 1975 for the sole purpose of engineering something else on a similar scale. He even used his clout as a producer to get Foreman on an episode of *Sanford and Son*. But as it became clear that he could not strong-arm Ali into giving Foreman a role in the ring, Perenchio washed his hands of the fight game. Others perceived that even without an Ali rematch in sight, Foreman was still a valuable commodity. Recently frozen out of his special relationship with Ali, Don King believed Foreman was his ticket to at least a portion of the next multimillion-dollar megamatch. He also convinced Barry Frank, vice president of CBS Sports, that the former champion would be the network's conduit to unseating ABC as the leader in boxing on home television. As CBS and ABC began ramping up their production of "free" televised fights, they noticed that double-digit Nielsen ratings followed. Foreman, a household name with a made-for-TV knockout punch, would give CBS a significant advantage. Clancy and Foreman, still focused on Ali, merely wanted to stay active and prevent any more "rust" from accumulating. Their plan to fight frequently meshed with King's interest in staying close to Foreman and CBS's desire to showcase him on the flagship program *Sports Spectacular*—the rival of ABC's *Wide World of Sports*. They soldered an agreement for King to promote and CBS to broadcast Foreman's whistle-stops as he campaigned for a rematch with Ali.[25]

★ 13 ★
A Gangster's Game

Foreman's television tour in pursuit of Ali was not all that different from the barnstorming that Sadler had employed to get him a title shot with Frazier years earlier. It still relied on mismatches with unknown entities in out-of-the-way places in front of a few thousand spectators. The only difference was that this time around, big crowds watched on the small screen. Charlie Shipes, a Sadler protégé who worked with Foreman on many of those "eatin' money" bouts, replaced Rapidez beside Clancy in Foreman's corner. Shipes was down on his luck and needed some cash. Unlike Foreman's earlier excursion through the has-been circuit, this round paid pretty well. Profiting from what amounted to glossy televised versions of club fights, CBS supplemented gate receipts, and Foreman's purses crested into the hundreds of thousands; even some of his challengers received six-figure deals. All Foreman had to do was to win, but preferably not before several commercial breaks.

The first leg of Foreman's campaign started right where he had left off, in New York, but a little farther upstate. He took on Minnesota's "Fighting Frenchman," Scott LeDoux, at the Utica Memorial Auditorium. In advance of Foreman's visit, the mayor of Utica declared "George Foreman Week" and gave him a key to the city.

Soon thereafter, 4,200 fans watched him bludgeon LeDoux into a third-round TKO. Then he turned south for a similar affair at the Hollywood Sportatorium in Pembroke Pines, Florida, against John "Dino" Dennis. In this cofeature with the reigning lightweight champion, Roberto Duran, about 5,000 ticket holders, including more than 100 of Dennis's friends and family from New England, essentially formed the live studio audience for a TV program. "Hands of Stone" Duran deviated from the script, scoring a knockout just two minutes into his bout, well before sponsors could air their ad spots. Foreman, on the other hand, gave the advertisers and Dennis four solid rounds of battery before earning another TKO. Television revenue from this doubleheader featuring two of the sport's best punchers, tagged as the "Kayofest in the Sun," beat expectations. Playing live to home viewers during the "family hour" at seven thirty, in order to clear room for some sparring between vice presidential candidates Walter Mondale and Bob Dole at a more traditional boxing time slot of nine thirty, the high ratings inflated Foreman's take to more than $500,000.[1]

"I have two goals," Foreman announced, in an attempt to answer everyone's queries at once. "One is to get revenge on the only defeat I have suffered, and the other is to become champion of the world again." Those aspirations converged on Muhammad Ali. He punctuated his statement with the assertion, "I'm on the express to the heavyweight championship!" Reporters peppered Foreman with questions largely because of recent developments at the top of boxing's biggest division. Not only had Ali versus Norton been a financial disappointment—in part because a police strike, which opened the door for wanton crime and violence around Yankee Stadium, strongly discouraged "window sales"—but those who saw the fight felt robbed, too. Ali looked slow and sluggish; Norton took an early lead and then stopped fighting. In the end, a very narrow split decision awarded Ali a highly contestable victory. Shortly after, at a stop in Istanbul, he told reporters, "[I] will leave boxing after my upcoming bout with George Foreman." Before he left Turkey, however, he announced his immediate retirement. Although by no means the first time he had claimed to quit the prize ring, this time his words reflected real pressure from the Nation of Islam to direct his full attention to "the struggle" while he still enjoyed widespread popularity.[2]

Some thought it might be another publicity stunt. Others suggested it was a calculated maneuver to get around growing demands from boxing's sanctioning bodies for Ali to defend against the top-ranked challenger, Foreman, within three months. The now–champion emeritus also acknowledged Foreman as the top contender for a soon-to-be-vacant title. "None of them niggers want Foreman," Ali said, before adopting the epithet he used against Foreman at the Waldorf a couple of years earlier. "Only this nigger, me, can take him." Don King would not even acknowledge Ali's retirement. He sidestepped a $1 million offer for a Foreman-Norton rematch and declared that Syria's government had agreed to put up $15 million for the only pairing that would be sure to attract a huge international audience in 1977—assuming that Ali "un-retired" again. King had a few reasons to believe Ali would take the fight. In the summer, Ali dedicated a Filipino shopping mall named after him and announced that he would like Manila to host his rematch with Foreman. In September, Ali told reporters that he would not fight a fourth match with Norton, because their score had been settled, but he wanted to beat Foreman again before leaving the sport for good. He bragged, "I'll be ready in nine months. People are bidding as high as $14 million." A month later, while in Houston to film his biopic *The Greatest*, he said: "I want Foreman. I will destroy Foreman." When Foreman crashed the set to speed up the process, however, Ali demurred, and a police escort ushered the challenger out. Behind the scenes, King disclosed that Herbert Muhammad gave him a ninety-day ultimatum to secure the funds. Officially, the champion remained in retirement but an Ali-Foreman title fight was definitely on the market.[3]

Roone Arledge bid for the hottest commodity in the fight game, too. *Ring* anointed Foreman "Fighter of the Year" for 1976, and *Boxing Illustrated* called him "The Man Who Will Be King," so the czar of ABC Sports pried him away from his rivals at CBS. To do so required a deal sweeter than just a huge pot of money: a "talent contract" that covered his home-TV bouts as well as work at the broadcaster's table when he was not inside the ropes. Foreman had done some color commentary for ABC at the 1976 Olympics, and after the "Kayofest in the Sun," Arledge wanted to secure Foreman in the ring and on the mic. Foreman was scheduled to meet the Puerto Rican heavyweight champion, Pedro Agosto, next. But having him alongside Cosell for an amateur tournament between American and Soviet boxers, as well as on the twenty hours of live coverage that ABC bought for Don King's proposed United States Boxing Championship tournament, was also lucrative. Cosell worked with Foreman in the booth just as Bob Hope had tried to coach him on stage—"patient and leading and guiding" a raw Foreman in what amounted to on-the-job training for a neophyte commentator. Despite Foreman taking umbrage at Cosell's negativity during the "Foreman versus Five" event, they had a good relationship dating back to 1968, when they traded some trash talk off camera in Mexico City. "He was a tough guy," Foreman said of the diminutive Cosell, "but he babied me along." It was an appropriate analogy, since Foreman fathered his second daughter, Freeda George, in October 1976 with a St. Lucian–born girlfriend named Andrea Skeete. Broadcasting offered a measure of security in an uncertain sport in which one punch could, theoretically, end his career—or worse. Foreman was now responsible for three children, and the supplemental work for ABC promised not only short-term publicity but perhaps also a long-term retirement plan. He admitted to taking some lumps, but added, "If you got instincts you'll fight your way out." And he did, almost literally, when he called the United States Boxing Championship and all hell broke loose—along with Cosell's toupee.[4]

Ali remained the only American wearing a championship belt when King's USBC tournament began. Three rounds of single-elimination bouts would determine a new "American champion" in every weight class, "revitalize boxing in all divisions," and usher in its "grand renaissance." Riding high on the huge revenues from closed-circuit broadcasts of major prizefights, as well as the mounting investments by network television for lesser events, the sport hardly needed a renaissance. But King certainly needed some revitalization. Excommunicated from the cult of Ali, he not only lost his percentage of the champion's huge purses, but also could not profit off a challenger, because neither Bob Arum nor Herbert Muhammad would deal with King's fighters. According to contemporaries, this was the closest to depression King ever came. He went so far as to cut his hair, "which only made him look more pathetic." Apparently, the coiffure was not the source of his promotional strength. King was among several insiders who saw that the recent success of American boxers at the Summer Olympics in Montreal provided a template: tournament-style matches with patriotic significance drew Americans to their televisions. Kram, surprisingly sanguine about the USBC, called it "nationalism in an international arena, a professional Olympiad." Hank Schwartz, Teddy Brenner, and Paddy Flood—a trainer for journeymen like Chuck Wepner—all claimed to have had the idea first. But King turned it into a reality. He took on Flood and Al Braverman (Wepner's manager) as "consultants" to work out the details in his penthouse office.[5]

Braverman once said, "Just gimme a pay phone in a candy store. All the rest is garbage." The USBC, then, became a symbiosis of

King's penthouse grandiosity and the pay phone practicality of Braverman and Flood. They brought on James A. Farley, the New York state athletic commissioner, to be the tournament's "supervisor," but none of the bouts would take place in the only state where he had regulatory powers. In fact, the unique and spectacular venues—the aircraft carrier USS *Lexington*, anchored off Pensacola, the US Naval Academy in Annapolis, and the Marion Correctional Facility, where King had formerly resided—were all federal properties that fell outside the jurisdiction of any state athletic commission. All decisions, including the appointment of officials, remained completely at the discretion of King, Flood, and Braverman. They also chose the fighters and the matchups, but made it clear that only professionals ranked in the top ten of their divisions by the "Bible of Boxing," *Ring* magazine, would receive invitations. Those rankings rested in the hands of one senior writer, John Ort. Adding legitimacy, ABC Sports had already committed more than $1 million to the enterprise, as well as its new favorite broadcasting tandem, Cosell and Foreman. On January 16, 1977, the first round of quarterfinals came off on the deck of the *Lexington* like a traditional "navy smoker"—just a few thousand sailors watching two pugs beat each other up inside an impromptu ring. The only difference was a contingent of eleven television cameras reminding the fighters and sailors alike that millions of civilians were watching, too. Thirty million, in fact. It drew a Nielsen rating of 14.6, representing more than 30 percent of that day's television audience, a number impressive enough to stifle most concerns about the tournament.[6]

One month later, the second set of quarterfinals took place in Annapolis. Again, a modest crowd of about 7,500 spectators, almost entirely navy men, functioned as props on the set of this television special. Even if the fighters were not much better than those in the first round, they were more aggressive. Three of the first five bouts ended in TKOs, creating a charged atmosphere for the heavyweight finale between Scott LeDoux and Johnny Boudreaux. It turned out to be one of the less interesting bouts, but it generated plenty of excitement after the bell. LeDoux knocked Boudreaux down in the third, and the latter "appeared converted to pacifism by that experience." After five more uneventful rounds, in which LeDoux tried to start a fight that Boudreaux did not care to participate in, the judges, handpicked by King, Braverman, and Flood, turned in their scorecards. Foreman, who had knocked LeDoux around just six months earlier, agreed with Cosell that in this contest the "Fighting Frenchman" was clearly the more aggressive boxer and scored the only knockdown, which made it a relatively easy fight to score. They were shocked when the judges ruled unanimously in Boudreaux's favor. Paddy Flood, working in Boudreaux's corner despite his position as a consultant for the whole tournament, celebrated. Cosell screamed, Foreman groaned, and LeDoux went berserk. He charged Boudreaux and tried to kick him in the face during a postfight interview. Foreman deftly slipped the attack, but the less agile Cosell lost his hairpiece in the melee. He scooped it up immediately and slapped it on backward. But the consummate professional regained his microphone, turned his toupee around, and interviewed LeDoux instead. The fighter blurted out that someone had told him to stay away from this tournament because it smelled fishy: all the boxers, despite being invited to the tournament, had to pay a booking fee directly to Braverman, and rumor had it that only fighters connected with him, Flood, or King were going to win. Cosell took the issue to King, who flatly denied the allegations, but now the tournament's commercial success became its Achilles' heel. Too many people had watched the same fight and come to the same conclusion—even if LeDoux was not right, something was very wrong with this picture.[7]

ABC Sports, to protect its investment as well as its reputation, began to investigate. Many of the answers to its questions had been available in print since before the tournament's first fight, but only through a cheap boxing rag innocuously titled *Tonight's Boxing Program*, mimeographed out of a bathtub in Queens by Malcolm "Flash" Gordon. The major newspapers and sport magazines wrote highly positive pieces about the USBC, including the usually acerbic Kram in *Sports Illustrated*. Only the handful of Gordon's subscribers or the boxing fans who bought one of the copies that he and his friends hocked outside fights in New York and sometimes Philadelphia—either because they wanted the inside juice or because they thought they were purchasing a legitimate program for that night's event—knew it. For now.[8]

As more people started digging, more boxers, managers, and writers shoveled dirt. Many admitted to paying booking fees, which were common in the fight game but clearly unethical in an invitational tournament in which a fighter's ranking supposedly determined his admission. Some boxers left out of the tournament charged that they had been "blackballed" for refusing to pay the fees or meet the conditions demanded by tournament organizers. Most of the fighters selected were already tied to King, Braverman, or Flood. If they were not involved with one of these men beforehand, the standard contract bound their future fights to DKP through a "right of first refusal" that essentially guaranteed King could promote any or all of their matches over the next two years. Those not attached to one of the triumvirate were probably represented by Chris Cline. He was a good friend of Ort, and suddenly some of Cline's charges appeared in the *Ring* rankings just before they received an invitation to the USBC. But Gordon and others who compared the *Ring Record Book* for 1975 or 1976 with the freshly issued 1977 edition discovered that Ort had changed the records of some fighters and falsified others. He invented recent victories for those who had not competed in years, which allowed him to alter the rankings to include them in his top ten. Investigators found checks for thousands of dollars written by King to Ort. Likewise, Kram admitted to taking money from King for providing him with good publicity, and lost his job at *Sports Illustrated* because of it. Farley, the supervisor, accepted travel reimbursement, expenses, and gifts from King, a lapse of judgment that cost him his leadership of New York's athletic commission. The third phase of the tournament fittingly took place at the Marion Correctional Facility, where more than a thousand convicted criminals watched a crooked operation's last gasp. Mark Jacobson of the *Village Voice* and the *New York Times*' Red Smith both reported that one inmate, frustrated by "smelly mismatches and slow waltzes," cried out: "Hurry up, I only got 20 years!"[9]

Ali was feeling a time crunch, too. As expected, he announced his return. He did so in a manner that only he could pull off, by simply denying that he had ever retired in the first place. He did not, however, speak of the fantastic millions awaiting him and Foreman—at least not yet. Ali's first target of 1977 was Duane Bobick, the best white hope at the time. While Bobick undeniably wanted the big check that a date with Ali commanded, one major obstacle impeded their negotiations: Bobick had already signed to meet Norton at Madison Square Garden. This posed no problem for Ali, who simply wanted Norton to step aside, fight someone else, and even join in on a cofeature if necessary. Norton demanded a quid pro quo for such a transaction. He would comply only if Ali guaranteed him another title shot. The champion made it clear that he would not entertain a fourth bout against Norton, certainly not before the much more lucrative rematch with Foreman. Teddy Brenner and Mike Burke of the Garden, which recently had agreed to promote fights in other venues or even other states, suddenly found themselves with interest from the heavyweight champion, a top contender, and the best white challenger. They scrambled to hold on to this embarrassment of riches. Brenner offered Norton his choice of stand-in in exchange for relinquishing Bobick from their contract, but the deal still hinged on his title rematch. "Ali won't fight Norton," Brenner complained. "He won't even take phone calls from Norton."[10]

As the stalemate wore on, Foreman grew more frustrated. Agosto, whose arms measured nine inches shorter than his, could not hit Foreman with the breeze from his punches much less the leather. Foreman pummeled him at will, causing two knockdowns in the third round and three in the fourth that triggered an automatic TKO. It was the best television that a terrible boxing match could have produced. But it did nothing to solve the Ali-Norton deadlock. To stick to Foreman and Clancy's timetable and keep him fighting every two months, King moved fast for another bout. They chose the quick-moving but light-punching Jimmy Young as the next—and, they hoped, last—stepping-stone on the way to Ali. Although most believed it would be a mismatch comparable to Ali versus Coopman, the consensus remained that it was nearly impossible to put on a worse show than that one. The Coliseo Roberto Clemente in San Juan happily fronted the money for another chance at a major heavyweight fight, even if it wasn't a championship bout.[11]

In his mind, Young, too, saw the upcoming bout as the gateway to a rematch with Ali. His defensive, counterpunching style had pushed the champion through fifteen rounds in their first meeting, and some even suggested that Young should have won the decision that ringside judges unanimously gave to Ali. But when Ali gave up his chase for Bobick, choosing instead to remain in retirement a little longer, he flatly denied any talk of Young, whom he described as "nothing." Though Young was a native Philadelphian, his style ran contrary to that city's century-old fistic expectation of fast-paced, hard-punching offensive attacks. Young elicited "more yawns than cheers" and drew little revenue at the gate or on television—even in his hometown. For Ali, the money was in a Foreman fight, particularly since boxing writers had started identifying another "new," much more likable Foreman persona. Some thought Clancy had fashioned him into a better boxer, instilling the finer points of the sweet science into a natural brawler. Others found him simply more engaging and accessible than ever before, largely because of his foray into broadcasting. Undoubtedly, Foreman's stock had risen on the open market of boxing consumerism. When news broke that Ali and Bobick could not make a deal, leaving Bobick to fight Norton in May, an editorial in *Ring* suggested that Don King might be wise to pull Foreman out of the Young fight just to keep his calendar open for the champion's return to action. After all, Ali steadfastly maintained that Foreman was the number-one contender, and that any potential successors to his title "would have to fight George Foreman before a true champion could be crowned."[12]

Nat Loubet followed up his strategic advice for King with a caveat: "It is possible that Foreman might want an easy opponent so as to maintain his fighting edge prior to meeting Ali." Young, in his opinion, fit the bill. *Boxing Illustrated* agreed. Its preview of 1977 called Young "a cutie" who "lacked the punch to be championship caliber." To highlight the contrast between him and Young, Foreman told reporters, "I'm not cute or fancy," and disclosed his strategy weeks before their St. Patrick's Day rendezvous: "I'm going to go out there and knock his head off." King reminded him not to knock anything off too soon—they expected good television ratings, and sponsors wanted their ads to run while people were still watching. Young counted on Foreman's aggression, however. "I guarantee," he said during the prefight buildup, "before the third round, you're going to hear some boos because George Foreman is going to get frustrated and do something dirty."[13]

The prediction became a self-fulfilling prophecy. Seconds into the fight, after the first of many breaks called by Waldemar Schmidt, Young began yelling through his thick mouth guard and gesticulating with ten-ounce gloves that he had been fouled. His corner reinforced the point by yelling at Schmidt, who seemed to listen. "The referee doesn't have an ear," Foreman later reflected. "He has a pocket." Whatever opening Young's camp may have exploited, it got the fight it wanted—slow action and fast breaks. Perhaps Norton's folks in Caracas should have campaigned harder for Schmidt. To make matters worse, Young bounced around an extra-large, twenty-one-foot ring, and Foreman had to chase him through the same kind of heat and humidity he had encountered on the precipice of monsoon season in Kinshasa. When Foreman could cut off Young, Schmidt was there to intervene. Foreman turned to the tactics that Young said he would, pawing at his face or holding his head down after clinches while menacingly glaring at Schmidt.[14]

In the third round, after less than ten minutes of fighting, Young's plan to "make points for himself from George's bad habits" came to fruition. Schmidt instructed the two ringside judges to deduct a point from Foreman. Cosell, calling the fight for ABC's telecast, claimed, "Young and his people have the official leaning very heavily in his favor." In response, Foreman became angrier and fought dirtier, Schmidt broke the boxers even quicker, and Young circled around the huge ring faster. "You could see from the takeoff," Foreman later contended, "they had already stacked the deck against me." Maybe Young had an inkling of what was coming when he guaranteed that the fans would jeer Foreman. Midway through the fight, the crowd, which the *San Juan Star* suggested would back an underdog in the absence of a local boxer, whistled their derision at Foreman and then burst into a chant of "Jim-my Young! Jim-my Young!!"[15]

It had taken two years to construct the new George Foreman image—in the ring, in the boxing magazines, and on television—but only seconds to tear it down in San Juan. *Sports Illustrated*'s correspondent wrote that Foreman "pushed, laced, elbowed, hit on the break and once, in a clinch, almost broke Young's left arm." Two readers subsequently fired off a letter arguing that "he should be charged with assault for his behavior in the ring." The stark contrast between the two men outran a David-and-Goliath comparison. Pat Putnam observed, "The crowd reacted as though it were witnessing Godzilla mug Peter Pan." Foreman dwarfed the shorter, narrow-shouldered Young, and when the fighters moved into the right position, he completely eclipsed him. During the intermission between rounds six and seven, Young's corner hollered at Cosell that it was "no contest"—they were ready to call the fight, either because they knew it was a foregone conclusion or because they were afraid one punch from Foreman could prove them wrong.[16]

Young's strategy against Foreman mirrored Ali's template from Zaire: remain on the defensive; entice Foreman to throw numerous unnecessary punches and tire himself out in a hot, humid environment; influence the referee to call fast and frequent breaks; and finish rounds with flurries of punches to persuade the judges. Ironically, before the fight Foreman had chastised Young for "imitating" others and suggested, "It means he has no growth." Halfway through the bout, however, Foreman appeared to have learned nothing. Losing stamina and points, he once again altered his intensity rather than his strategy. He opened the seventh round by swinging viciously, as if to make his last stand on his own terms, rather than simply running out of gas in the eighth round again. But this time Foreman landed the punch, a booming left hook that staggered Young. "He's hurt!" Cosell shouted. The right uppercut that followed did more damage, and Young stumbled away on trembling legs as Cosell's voice confirmed, "Now he's got him! Jimmy Young in trouble. In des-per-ate trouble!" He evaded the incessant and unpredictable free swings of a predatory Foreman. The Coliseo crowd forgot its recent affinity for Young and grew lively as Foreman's kill shot seemed imminent—something they did not get to see in the Ali-Coopman bout. When the round ended with both fighters on their feet, however, they remembered their former allegiance: "Jimmy Young! Jim-my Young! JIM-MY YOUNG!"[17]

Foreman belied his growing fatigue by laboriously bouncing on his toes before unleashing occasional bursts of long, heavy punches. "He's fought a lot of empty air tonight," Cosell noted, crediting Young's "Philadelphia smarts" for negating Foreman's advantages, even if Young lacked the "Philadelphia punch" to finish him off. Although Foreman made it past the eighth round and remained on his feet into the twelfth, it looked like he needed a knockout to salvage a victory. In this crucial moment, it was the "unarmed and almost childlike Young" who floored the bigger, stronger Foreman. He popped up quickly, but the damage had been done as time expired. Even though the entire ABC booth agreed that Young won more rounds than Foreman, they stopped short of predicting his victory. Throughout the broadcast, Cosell reminded his audience that it was difficult to score a bout involving Young because his "cleverness" did not always resonate with officials.[18]

As they awaited the judges' decision, Cosell hopped into the ring. Foreman, struggling to stand, gave him a curt "no comment." Don King looked as defeated as Foreman, standing bleary-eyed and nervously waiting for the announcement in a very rare moment of silence for him. The only one talking was Young, who admitted that he had been "hurt real bad" in "the fifth." Cosell had to remind him it was in the seventh round when Foreman landed the biggest punch of the night. Young later divulged, "While I may have been standing, I was out cold. He could have pushed me over with his little finger." During his confession to Cosell, the public-address system pierced through the cheering and jeering: "Ramos . . . ciento y dieciseis, ciento y doce . . . Jeemy Young; Schmeet . . . ciento y dieciocho, ciento once. . . . Jeeeeemmmmmyy YOUNG!" Unsurprisingly, the referee's score was the most lopsided, awarding Young ten of the twelve rounds compared to eight on Ramos's card and seven by

Ismael Fernandez. But few people even heard the announcement of Fernandez's 115–114 score, because the verdict had already been rendered. Even if Foreman heard it, he didn't have the energy to contest it. Barely able to walk away under his own power, the exhausted and dehydrated Foreman had been ushered out of the ring and down into the dressing room.[19]

"I told George that if Jimmy Young beat him, he would get a return shot," Don King confirmed. "But I must go where the wild goose goes." He was clearly not in control of Young at this moment, and he was giving up influence over Foreman to a higher power. With his championship aspirations dying, Foreman started to come alive again. Or, as he later said, he was reborn. Alternately sweating, shaking, and vomiting, he suddenly leapt from the table and called out loud affirmations of Christian faith. Clancy acted more secularly and called an ambulance. At Presbyterian Hospital in San Juan, they called it "heat prostration." The chief of neuroscience, Dr. Jorge Davila, said it was a concussion. These diagnoses sent Foreman to the intensive care unit for a prescribed twenty-four hours of hydration and observation. Instead, he left after breakfast. Young's stunning upset "traumatized the heavyweight boxing scene," in the words of one boxing writer. Foreman said it made everything clearer for him. His near-death experience after the fight prompted him to give up boxing. On Mother's Day 1977, he announced his retirement on a local radio station in Houston.[20]

Foreman's sudden retirement, at age twenty-eight, came as a surprise, but most in the boxing community did not take it seriously. After all, Ali had repeatedly cried wolf. "Will it stick?" *Ring* wondered, printing a retrospective photographic essay of Foreman's truncated career. Yet it included him in projections of the heavyweight division in 1978. Mounting evidence, however, seemed to confirm that Foreman had indeed fought his last match. Even before meeting Young, he talked about retiring, "not at what age, but at what income." The fight drew an impressive Nielsen rating of 36—in the late afternoon and early evening of St. Patrick's Day, more than half of the televisions that were turned on in the United States were tuned in to ABC's broadcast of the bout, mainly to watch Foreman. But he felt the outcome proved that Young's people had more power than a reeling Don King. It became obvious that Foreman was immobilized by the tangled webbing that enveloped an unregulated sport's highest honor. Ali held his ground, at odds with competing organizing bodies, which issued "edicts" and ultimatums to defend against Foreman within ninety days. "I'm the champion and I'll fight him in 91," he countered. At the same time, the deepening rift between King and Herbert Muhammad stonewalled any King fighter's chance of getting a title bout. King revealed that even if Foreman had beaten Young, the best he could have done was to match him with a former Ali sparring partner, Larry Holmes. Foreman was looking for something more.[21]

Although Foreman fired Clancy and talked to Dick Sadler, he reached out again to Tom Collins too. No one, including his own family, believed his story. He took up residence in his mother's house, afraid that at "any minute" he was "gonna die." He asked Collins to get Robert Schuller for him, and he recounted his experience for the televangelist. "George, I'm a reverend, psychologist, and theologian," he affirmed, "and I believe you." He persuaded Foreman to visit his church again and tell his story to his whole congregation. At the same time, Foreman began looking for a church in Houston as well. After some experimenting, he joined a transdenominational one with Baptist and Pentecostal influences: the First Church of the Lord Jesus Christ, in the northeastern part of the city. The church encouraged the kind of emotion he had felt in San Juan. Services blended familiar messages with less familiar practices such as speaking in tongues. It was comforting. He was all in. Foreman even convinced a former beauty queen who he had known since she was a teenager, Cynthia Lewis, to join the church as well. She agreed to go with him, then to become a born-again Christian like him, and eventually to marry him. The *New York Times* reported that "peace has broken out in George Foreman's bosom removing him from the raffish environs of the prize ring."[22]

Nat Loubet assured his readers that prizefighting would go on without Foreman, because "there is sufficient talent in the bushes and there is sufficient money to be made to insure that the heavyweights will prosper and so will boxing." But problems extended beyond the murky succession plan for the heavyweight championship. In August, *Sport* magazine ran a cover photo of an unidentifiable boxer covered by a large sheet with the United States Boxing Championship logo underneath a bright red block-letter headline: "DEATH OF THE DON KING TOURNAMENT." ABC had canceled its broadcast of the USBC four months earlier, announcing that "the very basis of the tournament has been severely compromised." Without television coverage, the tournament became a nonevent: the matches ceased, and no titles were ever bestowed. But the vicious infighting among those involved carried on. In this multidimensional version of the prisoner's dilemma, it seemed all the accused pointed their fingers at somebody else, eventually bringing to light more dirty secrets from the USBC.[23]

Foreman did not have any inside knowledge of the machinations behind the USBC, but he was not terribly surprised by them either, noting, "It figured." So while the scandal did not play a role in his decision to retire, all the negative attention on the sport and the swift reaction by television networks to reduce their boxing programming certainly did not entice him to fight again. His contract with ABC, ostensibly but not exclusively as a broadcaster, looked like more evidence that television networks had ventured into boxing promotion. Arledge let him out of the agreement after his retirement, but it was likely that if he suddenly returned to the ring,

ABC would claim the same right of first refusal that King had foisted on USBC invitees. The 1976 light-heavyweight gold medalist, Leon Spinks, was already under contract with CBS. The increasing power of television networks drew easy parallels to boxing in the 1950s, when a coalition of gangsters and promoters controlled the participants and proceeds in more than 80 percent of all championship matches. In that case, it took a government-ordered dissolution of the IBC under antitrust laws, as well as criminal charges for conspiracy and extortion against Frankie Carbo and his right-hand man, Francis "Blinky" Palermo, to unseat the monopoly and return a measure of fairness to the fight game. As if the comparisons to boxing's notorious IBC era were not clear enough, Palermo reappeared in the 1970s and applied for a boxing manager's license in Pennsylvania even as the *New York Times* drew lines connecting him with Jimmy Young. Although Young's camp vehemently denied it, Palermo withdrew his application, in order to avoid "embarrassment." He turned his attention to New Jersey, where he became one of the focal points in a state investigation of organized crime in boxing while Atlantic City was vying to host more prizefights in the 1980s. "If the same mob presence we have found in boxing existed, for example, in professional baseball or football, it would constitute a massive public scandal," the New Jersey Commission of Investigation wrote in its report. It was all too normal in the fight game. "Boxing, it's an outlaw. You can't corral it," Foreman reflected after his premature exit from the prize ring. "It's truly a gangster's game."[24]

★ 14 ★
Jesus Rode on a Jackass

"George, I just had this vision!" Don King called to say, out of the blue and out of breath. "What did you see, Don?" he asked. "It was like a dreaaaam, George. You were back in boxing, entering the ring with a cross on your robe and trunks—." The Reverend George Foreman interrupted him. "Don, you don't put the cross on your robe. You put it on your heart."[1]

King tried to coax Foreman back into the ring for years after his sudden retirement, but Foreman approached his faith with the same singular focus he had given boxing a decade earlier. He became more active in the First Church of the Lord Jesus Christ, and the church was happy to have not only his enthusiasm but also his checkbook. He poured over $100,000 into the physical building on Rosemary Lane, which was essentially equidistant from his old addresses in the Fifth Ward and his new place in Humble—a suburban home that cost about half the amount he gave to his church. Yet his work extended well beyond the walls he paid for. Foreman spoke to groups large and small, giving his testimony as often as folks would listen. When some teenagers invited him to preach in the street, he took them up on their offer. "If you can't think of anything to say," they coached him, "just say, 'Thank you Jesus!'" The onetime heavyweight champion of the world regularly stood in front of the Houston courthouse, thumping on a Bible and thanking Jesus. He continued to give impromptu sermons in public, but it was not for publicity. In fact, when he saw a transcript of his speech to Schuller's congregation published in newspapers, he was furious. He declined to confirm its accuracy for the *Los Angeles Times* and refused to talk to Schuller. "I didn't speak to that man for years," he said later.[2]

Much as in his former career, Foreman had to be pushed out of the amateur ranks of the ministry. He was happy to preach informally, but when one family asked him to talk to their son who was serving time in prison in Huntsville, he discovered that only ordained ministers were allowed to provide spiritual guidance there. With the help of the Reverend L. C. Masters of the First Church of the Lord Jesus Christ, Foreman became a bona fide evangelist so that he could visit the prison. Now that he was official, Foreman got more requests. "I would've never thought I was a minister," he said, but when he found himself standing next to a coffin and delivering words of consolation at a funeral, he had a realization: "I had no doubt I was." Like the Apostle Paul not long after this Damascene conversion, Foreman found himself in trouble with the law. Inspired by a dream, he drove up to Tomball and started preaching at a school there. When the authorities told him to shut it down, he told them, "I can't stop." They became more insistent as they drove him to the police station. After a visit from one of the Kleins, a notable Tomball family, he posted bail but did not lose faith. "The police have a job to do," he said, "but I had a job and I have a boss, too." He asked the Houston City Council for permission to preach in the streets. "The best way to save someone," he told them, "is to go down on the streets." They punted his case to the mayor's office and the police department. "Just a few can become world champions," Foreman insisted, "but anyone can be saved."[3]

Foreman's parish extended out of town from Tomball to Tyler, out of state to places such as Shreveport, and even internationally: he returned to Zaire to preach instead of punch. Likewise, Foreman's reverence for authority rose above the leadership of the First Church of the Lord Jesus Christ. He discovered that the Reverend Masters intended to leave his wife in order to pursue a parishioner— and that he had counseled her to terminate a pregnancy with her husband in order to facilitate his plan. The revelation touched on many sensitive points for Foreman. Another child, Georgetta, had been born to Charlotte Gross shortly after his retirement from the ring and just before he married Lewis. Foreman and Lewis divorced after less than two tumultuous years, and by 1980 he was fully devoted to his new calling. By the time he heard about Brother Masters's indiscretions, the thrice-divorced single preacher with four children by different mothers had prioritized his relationships with the church and his kids over any romantic ones; he had developed a strong resistance to abortion, also. The scandal offended each of these sensibilities. Foreman did not question his own faith, but he called out Masters. He left the church as a member but came back with another minister, once to literally pull the plug on a service and expose Masters to the congregation. The ensuing dustup among four preachers, only one of whom had previously held a world heavyweight championship, landed in court. Each was declared not guilty, at least in the eyes of the law. To Foreman's dismay, much of the congregation sided with Masters.[4]

Foreman flew back to California, where he still had some family and friends, but not a church—or a house. Leroy Jackson had tried to sell the ranch in Livermore secretly and pocket the proceeds, and a caretaker had set up an "estate sale" and sold off everything in the place. Foreman caught wind before the closing date and sued Jackson to get the profits from the sale back. It may have been for the best. Although he purchased a radio spot and spread the gospel on the airwaves around the Greater Los Angeles area, it did not have the same effect as preaching at home. Foreman returned to Texas, bought a short weekly time slot on Houston radio, and spent most of his time at the ranch in Marshall rather than at his house in Humble. When he came in for his radio show, however, he began receiving invitations to informal worship gatherings like Bible studies and prayer groups. The radio exposure as well as his appearances on the Praise the Lord network with Jim and Tammy Faye Bakker and *The 700 Club,* in addition to mainstream morning shows such as *Good Morning America* and *The Today Show,* helped spread his image and the "doctrine of love" he promoted. The gatherings grew larger— too big for some of the homes where they met, including Foreman's. He could throw a tent up on his ranch, but not everyone would be able to make the drive. When he went to sell a tractor, however, the shop informed him that they had previously sold another one of his and he had never picked up the cash—$25,000. With the proceeds, Foreman bought a small plot on Lone Oak Road, just two miles from First Church of the Lord Jesus Christ on Rosemary Lane, and established the Church of the Lord Jesus Christ. Services were held under a tent, like old-time revival meetings, until he could afford to erect a "tiny metal pre-fab" structure that might hold a couple of hundred people if needed. The church didn't exactly fill up, but it kept busy as Foreman delivered sermons on Wednesday, Saturday, and twice on Sunday. He spoke for hours each week from the pulpit, and hours more before, after, and between services; but the champ almost never talked about boxing. He insisted he would not fight again, and even turned down an invitation for a charity bout as part of a born-again Christian fund-raiser in Orange County, California. He told Gary Smith of *Sports Illustrated,* "Sure, I could get in shape and box now. I could be champ, isn't that what you're supposed to say? And nine months later you'd be embarrassed for me. I've got nothing against boxing, but you should make your million, then run and hide."[5]

The fight game clung to its only measure of stability, Muhammad Ali. But he needed more help. Ali noticeably slowed both in and out of the ring as Ken Norton ratcheted up his claim for a title shot. Like Don King, Ali called Foreman and tried to lure him back into the ring. "I can't beat him. George, you can. He's afraid of you," Foreman recalled Ali saying. "Please come back and beat him for me." Presumably, Ali at this stage of his career felt more confident of his chances in a second slow waltz with Foreman than a fourth dance-off against Norton. Foreman turned Ali down, as he had King, and anyone else who wanted him to fight again. Ali ignored Norton's challenge and took on a Foreman-esque Earnie Shavers instead, returning to Madison Square Garden for the first time in four years, but with a new gimmick from NBC to enhance the experience. Between rounds, television cameras zoomed in on the judges' scorecards, broadcasting live results to everyone watching outside the stadium. The ploy was meant to give the television audience an insider's view that even those who had paid for a ticket could not enjoy, while also providing transparency in order to dispel any allegations of "fixed" results. Instead, it only added to the mounting perceptions of unfairness in the ring. Dundee had a runner who watched the broadcast on television and then relayed the scores round by round to Ali's corner. By the twelfth round, they knew that Shavers could win only by knockout, and Ali stopped fighting. Shavers's corner had not been privy to such information. The equal access to scores would not have made Shavers a better fighter, and probably would not have affected the outcome, but in a climate already odorous with scandal, this added another whiff.[6]

Perhaps the notion that he had profited from NBC's broadcast of the scorecards added extra pressure, either to Ali or to the judges, before his next defense, against Leon Spinks. Or maybe an aging heavyweight champion simply could not keep up with a natural light heavyweight. In any case, he finally lost one of the many close decisions he had received since his knockout of Foreman. The fallout shook boxing's uneasy foundation. When Spinks opted for more money in a rematch with Ali, rather than defend against the World Boxing Council's number-one challenger, Norton, the organization stripped him of his recently earned title and proclaimed Norton heavyweight champion. The World Boxing Association disagreed. Then Norton lost in his first defense, against Larry Holmes, making him "the only heavyweight champion in history never to have won a heavyweight championship bout." Spinks subsequently lost the decision in his return bout with Ali. Now a three-time champ, the Greatest retired again, leaving his title vacant and dramatically increasing the size and suction of a new power vacuum. This set a precedent for competing governing bodies to determine their own champions, splitting titles and thereby devaluing them. The formation of two new boxing organizations in the 1980s, the International Boxing Federation and the World Boxing Organization, exacerbated the problem; the title of heavyweight champion became more complicated and less prestigious than ever before just as another scandal came to light.[7]

An enterprising newcomer in the world of boxing, Harold J. Smith, conjured a plan to usurp Arum's and King's roles as the country's dominant boxing promoters. The twofold strategy relied on gaining the loyalty of boxers through name recognition and cold, hard cash. Smith paid Ali a "leasing fee" for the right to call his company Muhammad Ali Professional Sports (MAPS), even though the ex-champion played no role other than renting out the use of his name. Then MAPS offered fighters huge purses, well above the going rate, to lure them and their managers away from more established promoters. The process engendered questions about where all the money was coming from, however, since the promotions that Smith and MAPS put on could not cover the high prices they paid the talent; profitability was out of the question. Asking the same questions, law enforcement groups in the Los Angeles area found their answers in a branch of the Wells Fargo bank from which Smith and MAPS's president, Sam Marshall, had embezzled more than $20 million. MAPS disintegrated, Smith went to jail, and fight purses deflated once again.[8]

Foreman resisted the temptation to reenter the prize ring. The same could not be said for his old colleagues Frazier and Ali. Each came back for another fight in the early 1980s. Ali went directly for the title. When negotiations to take on WBA champions John Tate and, subsequently, Mike Weaver fell through, he challenged his former sparring partner, Holmes. The Easton, Pennsylvania, native had unintentionally become one of the least popular heavyweight champions in recent memory. He was not malicious, just whiny. Not a villain, just a grouch—albeit a grouch with a magnificent jab. That single punch from his long arms functioned successfully as both Holmes's offense and his defense, but it made for uninteresting fights. Against Ali, he stood to make considerably less money than the challenger. "I shouldn't have to be here telling you who's the best heavyweight in the world today," he scolded the crowd around a sparring session. "If you don't see it, you should wear glasses, because I'm telling you like it is." It was symptomatic of the public attitude toward an unlikable champion in a decaying sport. Holmes frequently was mistaken for the Pittsburgh Steelers' linebacker Ernie Holmes. An assistant on *Good Morning America* introduced him as "George Foreman," and even in his home state, an Allentown fair promoter announced him as "the next heavyweight champion," fully two years into Holmes's reign. Ali took up the quest not only to give the boxing community a "people's champion" again, but also to dispel rumors that he suffered from an advancing neurological disorder. The fight was a disaster. Holmes looked like a big teenager picking on a senior citizen. Ali, unable to move as fast as he used to, absorbed jabs with his sagging face until his corner stopped the bout. Frazier returned to action in December 1981 and looked just as bad, squeaking out a draw against an ex-con club fighter named Floyd Cummings. He promptly re-retired after the debacle, but Ali, as usual, got the last word. He fought again one week after Frazier did, lost a unanimous decision to Trevor Berbick, and admitted: "I think I'm too old." Foreman appeared all the wiser for avoiding such pain and humiliation.[9]

William Nack wrote, "The quality of heavyweight fighters, like the length of skirts and the price of cabbage, is given to periodic fluctuations," but the boxing-film historian Jimmy Jacobs looked at its biggest battlers in the early 1980s and deemed them the worst crop since the dark ages of the early 1930s. As boxing lost supporters, another series of deleterious events stirred more critics. When Holmes, scrounging for challengers, took on a vastly overmatched Randall "Tex" Cobb in 1982, the one-sided drubbing so incensed Howard Cosell that he swore off boxing entirely. Cobb claimed that as his greatest contribution to the prize ring. Two weeks later, the Korean lightweight Duk Koo Kim died in Desert Springs Hospital from injuries suffered during a fight at Caesars Palace. A groundswell of opposition reintroduced calls for the abolition of professional boxing, and the American Medical Association published a scientific opinion that boxing constituted a serious risk to brain health. Ferdie Pacheco, now Ali's former doctor, emphatically defended the position that trauma from absorbing punches had caused a neurological disorder in the ex-champ. He, along with the AMA and others, called for increased safety measures, including age limits. A headline in the *Journal of the American Medical Association* read: "Boxing Should Be Banned in Civilized Countries." Since Las Vegas lay outside that category, it had a chance to become the new "Boxing Capital of the World" in the 1980s.[10]

Foreman could not deny the sad state of boxing. Speaking in Nebraska at a celebration for Colonel Barney Oldfield, which included Oldfield's announcement of a scholarship in Foreman's name for an outstanding "minority" student in journalism, the ex-champ KO'd suggestions that government regulations could save the fight game. "How are you going to organize a fist fight?" he asked. "The more you try to organize it, you'll run it into a hole or out into a back alley." He became so disenchanted with boxing that he finally responded to a ten-year-old offer from Lady Bird Johnson. He sent a handwritten letter from Humble across the state to her ranch in Stonewall, asking whether she was still interested in some of the memorabilia he hadn't lost to Jackson's fast one in Livermore or the slow march of time. He offered his two most valuable pieces, in fact—the 1973 heavyweight championship belt and his "Fighting Corpsman" robe. On behalf of the LBJ Presidential Library, Lady Bird happily accepted them. At the media event in the fall of 1983 to announce the donation, Foreman admitted, "I used to love them, and when I first had the invitation I said, 'I can't depart [*sic*] with these things. I fought too hard for them.'" But now, he just expressed his gratitude for the opportunity "to keep on making the George Foreman name, keeping it alive." Foreman's appetite for fame might not have been much smaller than Ali's or Frazier's. But he had managed to satisfy the craving without fighting—yet.[11]

Don King miraculously survived not only the doldrums of a lackluster heavyweight division and a deteriorating sport, but also the financial threat of Harold Smith and MAPS, an ass kicking from the Nation of Islam in the Bahamas—when King tried to insert himself in the Ali-Berbick fight, a group from the NOI went to his hotel room in Nassau and beat him up badly enough that he went to the hospital (not, however, to the police)—and federal charges of tax evasion. Associates, acquaintances, and employees got caught, but nothing stuck to "Teflon Don"—though he did suffer a broken nose in Nassau. In 1983, the governor of Ohio, James Rhodes, gave King

a full pardon for his manslaughter conviction, too. Even past transgressions slid off King as he navigated the new dark ages by supply-
ing quantity rather than quality. He promoted the first-ever dual
heavyweight championship card, as the WBC and WBA champs,
Holmes and Michael Dokes, defended their titles on the same night
in what he dubbed the "Crown Affair." Don King Productions had
promotional rights to both heavyweight champions, and King's son
Carl managed the two heavyweight challengers on the card, Tim
Witherspoon and Mike Weaver. Moreover, the new medium of pay-
per-view television fused closed-circuit principles and pricing with
the convenience of home television and drove up ancillary revenues
from the major boxing events once again. Naturally, King started up
his own pay-per-view outfit, the Don King Sports and Entertainment Network, to rival Arum's Home Box Office and ABC's RSVP
channel. King controlled so many boxers in the early 1980s that it
didn't matter that none of them were as popular as any of the champions of the 1970s: Frazier, Foreman, or Ali.[12]

By mid-decade, however, Foreman was arguably the last man
standing of the championship triumvirate from the golden age. He
appeared happy, wealthy, and at least mentally healthy—they had
all gained weight, but only Foreman tipped the scales at more than
300. By contrast, Frazier and Ali lost money, spoke slowly, and
tripped over some of the words they got out. Foreman still preached
multiple sermons a week behind a grin that stretched with his waistline. Throughout his retirement, rumors swirled that he had secured
a contract to record a gospel album and that Jim Brown had signed
on to play him in an upcoming biopic. Frank Deford suggested that
the "Clubber" Lang character in the third part of Sylvester Stallone's
Rocky saga was a reprisal of a past George Foreman. Readers wrote
to the editors of *Sports Illustrated* and *Jet* to affirm their support
for this new Foreman, especially when stories of his religious conversion and good deeds gained prominence. As the sports-media

complex prepared for ten-year retrospectives of the Rumble in the Jungle, Foreman gave plenty of interviews and otherwise stayed in the public eye. He officiated a wedding during the halftime of a United States Football League game in the Astrodome, gave an opening prayer before a boxing card at The Summit in Houston, and accepted an invitation to be flag bearer at the Olympic boxing tournament in Los Angeles. Although he admitted that he could no longer make a fist, much less use one, the fighter turned preacher with a protruding gut and a bald head evoked an American Every-man and remained popular across multiple demographics.[13]

Despite the smiles and speeches, however, Foreman wasn't much better off than his former rivals; he just wore a more convincing mask. Like Ali, Foreman struck up a relationship with one of the "poster girls" for the Rumble in the Jungle, Sharon Goodson, although it did not become as public or contentious as Ali's marriage to Veronica Porche. Foreman and Goodson reconnected in 1981 and quickly married, but split up in less than a year. Days after the divorce became final, Foreman hastily married another past girlfriend, Andrea Skeete. They already had a daughter together, Freeda, and Andrea gave birth to a son, George III, in 1983. It did not salvage their troubled relationship, which ended, for all intents and purposes, when Foreman traveled to Germany for a speaking engagement and Skeete absconded with the kids to her native St. Lucia. After Foreman returned home and learned what had happened, he had to formulate a plan and keep his mask on, too—he was expected to preach the next day: "I had to make [the congregation] feel better. . . . It's like a doctor, you've got to do a correct surgery whether your hand hurts or not." He plastered on his minister's smile and gave a sermon, then turned around, got hold of a contact in St. Lucia, pulled cash from a trust fund, and hopped a plane. Relying on a mixture of bribery, chicanery, and threats, Foreman managed to get his kids and evade the authorities, who were waiting for him at the airport, by slipping onto a boat headed off the island. The scene ended with the devout minister tending to a seasick toddler and wailing infant alongside two naked Rastafarians who were drying their ample supply of marijuana on deck. Fortunately, he did not have to endure such episodes with all four of his ex-wives, or the two other women with whom he had children, but Foreman's series of failed relationships were increasingly tense and terribly expensive.[14]

The negative experiences did not dissuade Foreman from pursuing another wife—and another St. Lucian—a year later. Mary Martelly cared for Foreman and Skeete's two children and also for Foreman's other children when they came to visit. She continued to work for Foreman after the divorce, which included a joint-custody agreement for Freeda and George III. As Foreman and Martelly's relationship evolved from professional to personal, he sprang for a ring that, he recalled, cost less than $100, and she accepted the impromptu proposal. Subsequently, more of Foreman's children came to visit more often, stay longer, or make his suburban Houston residence their permanent address. His life revolved around children, and his work moved in that direction as well. Across the street from the Church of the Lord Jesus Christ on Lone Oak, Foreman built a similar structure as a "youth center" where local kids could work out, play basketball, or try their hand at boxing. It was a noble enterprise, but that didn't make it an inexpensive one. Foreman drew from his savings and the trust he had set up for his retirement to fund the project and maintain the building. He estimated the amount at around $300,000—almost half the total of the annuity he had built up by contributing about 25 percent of his earnings since his first year as a prizefighter. "Once you touch it wrong, it never does get straight," he realized. Its value already eroded by alimony and child support payments, the nest egg was not big enough to support the mission. "Next thing you know," he said, "I was behind the eight ball. I just couldn't catch up."[15]

Over a game of basketball at the freshly christened George Foreman Youth and Community Center, a lawyer friend told him plainly: "You don't want to end up a Joe Louis story." Louis had been dead for several years, but his story was very much alive in the boxing world. The most dominant heavyweight champion of the modern era had lived the second half of his life broke, buried under tax bills, and sunk in a financial abyss by bad investments. Foreman at midlife was headed in the same direction. He had cut his spending significantly in the early 1980s. After almost losing the Livermore property, he willingly sold the house in Bel Air. He exchanged the exotic animals that required special food to be shipped in from the St. Louis Zoo for the meager flock of his congregation. And his stable of cars, like the custom-painted Rolls-Royce, dwindled to a pickup truck for the ranch and a car for town—domestic, sometimes compact, but always in stock colors. The Reverend Foreman became adept at deflecting questions about his Chevette or Fiesta with a blend of scripture and humor. "Jesus Christ rode on a jackass!"[16]

Considering the expenses of the church and youth center, however, Foreman wouldn't be able to afford much more than a donkey unless he started bringing in some revenue. He leveraged his name recognition and began speaking, predominantly in churches, for money: "Sometimes they would donate $900 or something and that would be enough for the note on the building." But Foreman was only treading water. He accepted an extended invitation for a three-day engagement in Georgia, believing that it would result in a nice check. But it, too, was tantamount to spiritual panhandling. The church's pastor called for donations from the congregation at the end of Foreman's visit. Then he called some more. "I know we can do better than this," he pleaded, but Foreman could tell that "these people [didn't] have any money." He felt ashamed for asking and left determined not to do it again. After nearly a decade of retirement, and twenty years since his first foray into the ring, boxing was still the fastest way for him to make some money. That same day, Foreman "made [his] mind up" to stage a comeback. But when he tried to go running, he didn't get very far before asking himself, "Man, how am I going to do this?"[17]

Foreman's first call went to his last trainer, Gil Clancy. It did not get the response he wanted. "Let me take a look at you first," Clancy told him before committing to anything. "I never called him back again," Foreman said. Maybe he could train himself. He knew that what mattered was the television coverage, so he called old contacts at the major networks. They were worse than Clancy. People who had once fought for his services were uniformly uninterested now. "Why are you calling us, George?" they asked. But at least they answered. Don King wouldn't even come to the phone. Foreman recalled: "His assistant would say 'he's busy now,'" and he never got around to returning the call. Feeling that the skepticism was due to his age and maybe his weight, Foreman tried calling doctors instead. Dan Rios, working at the MD Anderson Cancer Center in Houston, agreed to bring Foreman in for tests—brain scans, MRIs, stress tests on stationary bikes and treadmills. The results looked good. Rios said Foreman had "the heart of an Olympian" even though he didn't exactly look like one anymore. Confident in his ability to move forward, Foreman recognized that he would have to delve deeper into his past for help. He could not step back into the late 1970s with Clancy, King, and network TV. Instead he turned to the early '70s by calling Charlie Shipes to get him ready, and his former press agent Bill Caplan to spread the word. Shipes was eager to help out, just as soon as he was released from prison. Foreman waited for him, though he started serious training on his own at the ranch. When Shipes joined him, they increased his stamina to the point that the preacher who could run only a few steps in Georgia was now covering six miles at a time in Marshall. Caplan was a little more reluctant. He wanted to help, but suggested they arrange to hold his first comeback fight in early 1987 and stage it somewhere in Europe, possibly Cannes—"like opening a play in Hartford." In case it was a bad show, it would play before a limited audience.[18]

Instead, Foreman went to Vegas. As news of his impending return spread, he wanted to "get back on the scene," so he made an appearance at the next heavyweight title fight. Trevor Berbick was set to defend his WBC version of the championship against a contender who had just turned twenty years old, Mike Tyson. Foreman spoke to Berbick before the fight, waved to Don King from his seat—at least King returned the wave, though he quickly turned his head—and then, like everyone else in the place or paying to watch it on HBO, settled in to see whether this "Kid Dynamite" was for real. He had failed to make the Olympic team that competed in Los Angeles, so Foreman hadn't met him or watched him fight. But in less than two years as a pro, Tyson had won all twenty-seven of his bouts, and only two had gone to a decision. "I got the spirit," Berbick told Foreman, who thought he was "evidently one of the religious types." It did not appear to be the fighting spirit, however. Jim Jacobs said that Berbick "fought as if he was in slow motion," and Tyson dominated from the opening bell until the second round, when the referee, Mills Lane, waved it off and Tyson became the youngest person to hold a heavyweight championship. "He was throwing pineapples," exclaimed Angelo Dundee, working Berbick's corner for the first time. "He looked as awesome as George Foreman did when he took Joe Frazier out." Foreman felt it too as he watched the next star of the sport. He thought, "There is truly excitement back in boxing" at the end of 1986.[19]

As the New Year rang in, Foreman's comeback still lacked a date or an opponent. After he lost the title, Don King arranged most of those details. But Foreman had been telling himself for years that he gave King a lifeline after Ali's people kicked him out. If that was true, he reasoned, then he didn't need King to get his own second wind. "I wanted people, but I didn't need anyone," he thought. His first ten years in the fight game, particularly while on the road listening to and learning from Sadler or Moore, had given him everything he needed: "From Doc Kearns to Archie Moore to Dick Sadler, I knew how to train, how to work out, how to put up posters, do exhibitions, talk to media. . . . I was Doc Kearns re-created." He arranged a date in West Texas with a Kearns contemporary who, unfortunately, died before the deal could be executed. He tried another in Tucson, but it also fell through, as did Caplan's preference for a European venue when a proposal for Cannes was canceled. Nearing the one-year anniversary of the space shuttle *Challenger* disaster, news programs saturated American television with memorials and reminded viewers that the shuttle was supposed to symbolize the democratization of American space travel. The seven-person crew had included one Asian American, one African American, and two women, one of whom was not a trained astronaut but the first person selected for NASA's "Teacher in Space" program. Likewise, the return to professional sports of a middle-aged and overweight Foreman represented the democratization of boxing—yet few people expected him to take off.[20]

"Why do you want to come back to boxing?" A member of the medical board of the California Athletic Commission did not beat around the bush when the organization called Foreman in for a full and public hearing to determine whether it would grant him a license to fight in the state. Foreman wasn't messing around, either. He chose California specifically because "it was the most difficult state" in which to obtain licensure. "Pick on the giant first," he thought. If he got a license in California, every other state would follow suit. So Foreman trimmed down to about 270 pounds, provided all the test results from Dr. Rios, allowed observers to watch his workouts, and faced down the board in San Diego. They remarked that from the X-rays that his "skull was thicker than they'd seen," and Foreman quipped, "My wife could've told you that." He was still "articulate," they deemed. There was no physical reason they could find to deny the request, and as Richard Hoffer wrote for the *Los Angeles Times*, "the commission is prohibited from using common sense as one of its criteria." But why return to boxing? "Life, liberty, and the pursuit of happiness," Foreman replied. Although he may have meant it in a more Lockean sense—the pursuit of property—and a boxing license for a forty-year-old was not exactly an unalienable right, he knew that "they didn't want to mess with that." He took his license, used his network to dredge up a West Coast promoter who had worked with Henry C. Winston, Don Chargin, and set a date for March at the ARCO Arena. The athletic commission still exercised its influence by rejecting the first proposed opponent, and Foreman shot back by refusing theirs. Finally Foreman, Chargin, and the commission agreed on Steve Zouski, but they all knew that only one heavyweight really mattered. By the time Foreman climbed back in the ring, Tyson had added the WBA title to his WBC belt, and he was on track to "reunify" the heavyweight championship. Tyson had knocked out Zouski in three rounds the year before. Foreman "pummeled" him for three, and in the fourth he told the referee, "I'm going to hurt him." Henry Elespuru took the cue and stopped the fight. It was getting harder for anyone to say no to Foreman. "I'm not trying to rain on Tyson's parade," he said. "He's the youngest champion, I just want to be the oldest."[21]

★ 15 ★
Man of
La Mancha

"I was going right back," Foreman recalled as he charted a course to regaining his title in early 1987. Not just back to the top of the sport, however, but back to the methods that had gotten him there in the first place: roadwork and road trips. "Minor leagues," he said. "Back of the bus." By the end of the year, he weighed less than 250 pounds and had fought almost once a month, wherever he could get work and for whatever it would pay. He found old promoters who wanted back in the game, new promoters trying to stay in, and prospective ones who wanted to get their feet wet. He agreed to deals that paid little to nothing upfront, and he relied on percentages of relatively small gates. Foreman fought anywhere from the Hitchin' Post in Springfield, Missouri, to Anchorage, Alaska—"Armories, clubs, bars," he recalled—not just to fight but also for the "meet and greets, [to] shake hands." Foreman became a self-promoter in every way. The media, which he once considered as adversarial as anyone he met in the ring, now became his greatest allies—even the critical ones. "Guys would sit, have long conversations, then write a full column about why Foreman shouldn't box," he noted. "Didn't matter to me. I got a full column!" He briefly considered buying his own column as a space for rebuttal, and asked his brother to look into it. When he saw how much it cost, he said, "Let 'em talk." Still functioning as his own manager and promoter, Foreman closely followed the press he got, calling it "franchise journalism": "They'd hear something and instead of talking to me they would just print what they heard." So he used that to his advantage, too. He repeated some of the great lines he read in the sport pages to other journalists, who credited him. Foreman made or repurposed jokes about his age and weight as well as his training and eating habits. The California Athletic Commission did not find it funny and threatened to revoke his license unless he lost more weight, but Chargin came to his defense. "George is a huge man," he said. "If people expect him to be the body beautiful he was years ago, forget about it."[1]

Others saw potential in this softer incarnation. One Nevada doctor claimed that after reviewing films from the 1970s, he thought the musculature of a young, fit Foreman suggested that he was too tense, locked in "an energy draining state." Now he appeared "very relaxed," to put it politely, and the doctor thought his stamina might actually have improved. The antithesis of this lovably "relaxed" Baby Boomer was the now "undisputed" heavyweight champion, Tyson. Fortunately, he didn't need to test the stamina of his chiseled yet potentially "energy-draining" physique. He collected seven-figure checks for one-sided matchups—two of his last three fights ended after ninety-one and ninety-three seconds—and people not only paid for tickets but also shelled out to watch them at home on pay-per-view. Percentages of the PPV revenue surpassed his purses in some cases, and Tyson became the first boxer to sign exclusive deals with PPV providers, which paid him hundreds of thousands of dollars more just for the right to broadcast what might be only a minute or two of fighting. Foreman's matches were not much more competitive. Asked about his string of "tomato can" opponents, he snapped back: "They're only saying that because it's true!" Although not yet worthy of PPV, Foreman's fights drew enough interest to creep onto cable TV channels such as ESPN, the USA Network, and the Financial News Network's weekend service, "Score." Arum insisted that Foreman meet reputable opponents, and the *New York Times* threatened to stop publishing reports of his monthly fights against unknown ones, but Foreman did not budge. "You've got to work your plan and plan your work," he told the *Las Vegas Sun*. His tilt with Carlos Hernandez generated the USA Network's highest ratings to date. "I was having fun," he said. "And fun sells." After his eighteenth consecutive win, against an opponent too high on cocaine to get off his stool for the third round, Foreman proclaimed, "Tyson's next," and although some interpreted that as a joke, plans to match the odd couple of prizefighting became serious.[2]

Not only were Tyson and Foreman physical opposites, but they started to represent contrasting images as well. After the death of Tyson's trainer, Cus D'Amato, and later his manager, Jimmy Jacobs, he underwent a transition as stark as any of Foreman's alterations over the years. Tyson grew closer to King, fell further away from the team that he had worked with since his amateur days, and reconnected with old friends from his rough Bronx neighborhood. "Iron Mike" proudly wore the moniker "Baddest Man on the Planet," and did his best to live up to that title on and off camera. He reflected the growing—and to many, threatening—subgenre of gangsta rap and did more fighting in courtrooms or in parking lots than in a prize ring. "Madison Avenue," Phil Berger wrote, "ceased doing business with him," although Tyson closed out the decade with two decisive victories. Foreman, on the other hand, took five bouts in 1989 and, for the first time in almost fifteen years, graced the cover of *Sports Illustrated*. Tyson had not been on the cover in more than a year. Foreman kicked off the 1990s with a $1 million guarantee to fight thirty-three-year-old Gerry Cooney. One writer labeled it "Geezers at Caesars (Atlantic City)," and Foreman, predictably, played along with the joke. He helped bring in a sellout crowd for a card that didn't have much else to offer except a WBO middleweight title bout and a couple of young heavyweights as counterbalance to the middle-aged headliners. Boxing titles and derisive labels notwithstanding, Foreman was a one-man headline. Ironically, Tyson, at about the same age as a young Foreman was when he fashioned a blaxploitation-style image in the early 1970s, constructed a rapsploitation persona for the end of the 1980s that divided his fan base just as sharply. The new incarnation of Foreman, however, embodied all the conservative, crossover appeal of the *Cosby Show*. In fact, even though he didn't watch the show, Foreman asked Bill Cosby for advice about taking on more commercials as the buildup to Cooney generated phone calls from advertising departments. "Don't come here with that," Cosby shot back. "You should be proud that someone would ask you." Then he told Foreman, "If you don't want 'em, I'll take 'em!"[3]

Foreman took all the calls himself, and answered the bell for Cooney too. In the second round, he knocked him down twice and sent his mouth guard across the ring before the "firm but fair" referee, Joe Cortez, ended the bout. Gil Clancy, working Cooney's corner, had picked the wrong geezer. Even Arum joined the chorus of hype calling for Tyson versus Foreman. At the bare minimum, as Al Albert noted in his "top-ten list" for reasons why Tyson should fight Foreman, "it would take Tyson at least 93 seconds to circle Foreman." The hullabaloo rose to such a fever pitch that some believed the two fighters could resurrect the "era of fantastic millions" with another international megamatch. But the financial losses incurred by such host nations in the 1970s and the thawing of the Cold War in the 1980s deterred many potential sites from entertaining the idea. One nation, however, did have the resources and a need for some good publicity after a pesky student protest in the spring had carried on through the summer of 1989. Bill Wheeler, a Seattle lawyer younger than Foreman who dreamt of promoting the biggest prizefight of the decade, announced that the Chinese government had offered him $25 million. Tyson's embattled manager, Bill Cayton, confirmed the rumor, adding, "Foreman is the only opponent the Chinese are interested in." Days after the plans came out in print, soldiers and tanks from the People's Liberation Army flooded into Tiananmen Square to quell the protests. Over the next few days, images of the violent suppression of democratic endeavors inundated American print and television news. Wheeler reversed course. "To put a fight there would be tacit support of the Chinese government," he acknowledged. "If freedom and democracy are crushed in China, that diminishes democracy here. If we don't support the Chinese seeking democracy, do we deserve to be the light of freedom?" No one had asked those questions when negotiating transnational megamatches in the 1970s. Foreman did not hear about the proposal from China but, steadfast in his fistic realpolitik, said he would have met Tyson "anywhere for $5 million."[4]

Wheeler offered an alternative. If "the American people" raised at least $5 million, he promised to find a venue, negotiate the television rights, and create enough revenue to pay Tyson and Foreman something like the same stratospheric sums they expected from the Beijing deal. Then he pledged to donate 80 percent of the net proceeds to Chinese students in America, who would filter the anticipated millions of dollars to victims of the now-infamous Tiananmen Square incident. Despite this generous offer, professional boxing remained a decidedly for-profit industry. Generations removed from Mrs. William Randolph Hearst's Milk Fund fights of the 1920s, which aided poor children, the championship was not a charity, and the next major title bout would not be a fund-raiser; nor would it be transnational, particularly if it featured two American fighters. As Las Vegas pulled prizefighting into its orbit, international boxing promotions returned to being merely alternatives for uncompetitive tune-up matches that the stars of the sport took between major events. Audiences with undiscriminating pugilistic palates—or simply fewer options to choose from—still paid for the privilege of watching the champion, no matter whom he faced. Promoters of these fights expected low pay-per-view numbers and hoped that ticket sales to a boxing-starved populace somewhere across the world would at least cover their investment. Solidifying the dramatic transformation of the sport from its international era in the 1970s, the title fights that did occur overseas were no longer megamatches, but nonevents.[5]

Tyson's February 1990 title defense against James "Buster" Douglas, staged at the Tokyo Dome in Japan, had all the markings of one of these nonevents. Chosen primarily to keep Tyson warm during the negotiations for a blockbuster bout with Foreman, Douglas entered the ring as a 42–1 underdog on the sportsbooks at the Mirage in Las Vegas. Most bookies, however, would not even take a bet on the "gross mismatch." The pairing resembled professional wrestling's weekly Saturday programming, in which its biggest star played opposite an unknown character, to a certain verdict. It was fitting, then, that two weeks before the fight, Tyson and King held meetings with Vince McMahon, president and CEO of the World Wrestling Federation, about a boxing-wrestling crossover event. Perhaps inspired by Ali's spectacle with a Japanese wrestler, Antonio "Pelican" Inoki, in 1976, or the introduction to *Rocky III* in 1982, they speculated about a "matchup of superheroes" between Tyson and the professional-wrestling champion Terry "Hulk" Hogan. This would make them some real money. The charade in the Tokyo Dome would not earn Tyson more than $6 million, and generate only $2 million for King. Douglas signed for a purse of slightly over $1 million, but as a King-controlled fighter, he could expect liberal garnishments for "expenses"—he did not even receive any free tickets.[6]

No one in Japan expected much revenue from Tyson versus Douglas either. But since an economic bubble thirty years in the making now looked poised to burst, any event that could divert attention from the collapse of the yen would be welcome. As with the last heavyweight championship held in Tokyo, Foreman versus Roman, the nation's capital hosted a bad fight in order to gain some good publicity. In 1973, Foreman predictably dismembered Roman in a matter of minutes. In 1990, Douglas refused to play his role. He dominated the champion in every way, throwing more punches and landing a higher percentage of them as well. Even when Tyson finally connected with his renowned right uppercut, knocking his mark off his feet, Douglas refused to stay down. He went back on the offensive and knocked Tyson out in the tenth. When the Japanese stock market crashed within the next six months, dropping the value of many shares to less than half their worth before the fight, it ushered in the country's "Lost Decade." Had boxing been publicly traded, its shares might have fallen even further after the dethroning of Tyson.[7]

A figure somewhere between Moses and Methuselah, Foreman suddenly looked like a viable candidate to lead prizefighting back into the light. The burden grew so great that he finally agreed to step into the ring against a top-ten contender, Adilson Rodrigues. The Brazilian journeyman was only two years younger than Cooney and had a split record—one and one—in his two American bouts. But on the strength of more than thirty wins in Brazil, the WBA elevated him to its tenth-ranked heavyweight. Foreman was not too concerned about Rodrigues, but he didn't like what he saw behind him: "Only thing that worried me about the fight was Angelo Dundee was in his corner." He did not mess around with Dundee's newest charge, relying predominantly on his jab in the first round before turning to uppercuts and hooks in the second, ultimately scoring a knockout after only about five minutes of fighting. That was when the pursuit began. Catching up with Dundee in the airport, Foreman made a play for Ali's former cornerman. Dundee gave him permission to call, but Foreman had to get his number from Arum. "He's a good guy for you," Arum said, "in case you have to go 12 rounds." Foreman hadn't fought that long since the Jimmy Young match, and had come close only once in his comeback campaign, but if anyone could prepare him, it was Dundee. Foreman, still a self-described "free agent" who ran all aspects of his career without any contractual obligations to promoters or television networks, made the pitch directly. He offered Dundee $50,000 a fight. Dundee asked for $75,000. About to refuse the steep price, Foreman stopped. "What's wrong with you?" he asked himself. He needed all the help he could get as his shot at taking back the title came into view. Buster Douglas was already looking past a date with Evander Holyfield to a big payday with the fan favorite Foreman. "If I don't get to him soon, he'll be too good for me," Douglas said. Holyfield's manager, Lou Duva, dismissed Foreman as a "con man" but couldn't deny the fans he brought with him. "Duva's gotta say that because Holyfield means nothing to anybody," Foreman replied. "I'm not conning anyone. The will of the people is mighty, and the people have decided to adopt me and follow me to the championship."[8]

Ultimately, Douglas should have followed his gut, which was starting to look like Foreman's. Instead, he agreed to meet Holyfield at the relatively new Mirage hotel and casino in Las Vegas. The champ showed up to his first title defense fifteen pounds heavier than when he won the belt, and decidedly less motivated. Holyfield peppered him for the first two rounds, and when Douglas went down one minute into the third, he looked disinclined to rise. Despite the earlier criticism of Foreman from Holyfield's camp, it quickly offered him an eight-figure gift in time for the holidays. Holyfield could likely earn $20 million against Foreman, not much less than he might get for finally settling the score with Tyson. Now the reigning champ, he was also essentially a house fighter in Atlantic City—since turning pro, he had taken more bouts in Atlantic City than anywhere else, including Las Vegas. Plus, in the Convention Center, he enjoyed a firm twenty-foot ring that accentuated his foot speed. Holyfield just needed to show up and look good snapping some jabs while circling Mount Foreman.[9]

They called it the "Battle of the Ages." The slogan was plastered on billboards and in print ads as large as a full page; it was repeated on radio and television. And not just the week before fight night. It was a protracted advertising blitz through April, in anticipation of the heavyweight championship bout coming up on the 19th. The long campaign reflected changes in the way major prizefights were consumed at the start of the 1990s, and the intensity was due to unprecedented financial expectations. It was all about numbers. A twenty-eight-year-old champion facing a forty-two-year-old challenger; a converted cruiserweight barely over 200 pounds and one of the heaviest contenders ever, slipping in at just under 260. After winning his first twenty-five professional bouts, Evander "Real Deal" Holyfield would defend his three heavyweight titles, awarded by competing sanctioning bodies, for the first time against "Big" George Foreman, who would be vying for his seventieth win and second championship reign. It was a study in contrasts, with opponents so disparate that it might have required a tale of two tapes. Yet it was already measured a success, projected to generate $100 million—the highest gross revenue in the sport's history and the first time a ninth digit would be needed to account for a boxing-match's revenue. If only 10 percent of the television viewers in America with pay-per-view access paid $35 each to watch, let alone the $5 surcharge if they ordered on the day of the fight, this copromotion by Arum's Top Rank and Dan Duva's Main Event, Inc.

would be more than halfway to the nine-figure goal. Add in another $10 million to $20 million for closed-circuit rights and foreign markets, and at least $10 million more for selling out the Atlantic City Convention Center, and the target would be in sight, even before any T-shirts were sold. "Surely," Duva said, "$85–90 million is practical."[10]

Whether it was practical, the revenue projections led some, including one grandson of immigrants who inherited thirdhand real estate wealth, Donald Trump, to believe that Holyfield versus Foreman could wrest control of championship boxing from Las Vegas and install it in Atlantic City in the 1990s. A decade earlier, it had looked as if the sport was simply following the trajectory of its favorite champion, Joe Louis, who pocketed cash and chips from casino owners in exchange for shaking hands and mingling with guests. Investing a small amount of money in Louis could return a profit if tourists chose to gamble where Louis gambled. It was not too different from paying the water bill for a lavish fountain or keeping bright, shining, ever-blinking lights on all day and all night. As new hotels and casinos crowded the Strip, whatever got more people through the door and onto the floor was probably worth the cost. After the USBC and MAPS scandals, the defeat and retirement of Ali, and the negative publicity from Howard Cosell and the AMA, prizefighting looked like an aging Louis; some Vegas moguls would put a little money into hosting a fight if it might get a few more people to the slots. Sin City became not the mecca of boxing, but at least its Taj Mahal—a beautiful mausoleum that still attracted visitors. But the convergence of the most popular heavyweight champion since Ali and the rise of a more extensive broadcasting platform initiated a revolution in the prize ring. Pay-per-view sales paid for the promotions and made fighters, especially Tyson, rich. Casinos paid ballooning "site fees" for the right to host a big fight because increased action from the sportsbooks and at the tables more than covered the cost while filling hotel rooms, too. Comps for high rollers became a blue-chip investment, since all the money fronted for tickets or rooms could come back to the house after a few rolls, spins, or flips. In this new era, everyone got a bigger take while selling fewer tickets. Prizefighters took three of the first five spots in *Sport* magazine's "top 100" salary survey for 1987, and accounted for the four highest-earning athletes from 1988 to 1990. In 1989, Jeff Ryan looked into the future of boxing in the 1990s and echoed Mike Jacobs's decades-old prophecy that soon the biggest matches might take place in television studios. Closed-circuit broadcasts had devalued the live gate for at least twenty years, but now the pay-per-view blockbusters from Las Vegas put ticket sales on par with merchandising receipts. Holyfield versus Foreman had the most popular underdog challenger in recent memory, and that was worth selling.[11]

The Battle of the Ages was expected to be the most lucrative prizefight in history, but it wasn't the bout everyone wanted. The next megamatch was supposed to be a mismatch in style, not substance: Holyfield versus Tyson. Against Foreman, the champion was a prohibitive favorite, in the betting odds at least, even if not in public sentiment. Holyfield carried a chiseled physique under a quiet demeanor, and he was similarly reserved in the ring, too. Sportswriters compared him to the partially human protagonist of *Robocop*, which was already a few years out of the theaters and not exactly getting better with age. During a comeback campaign that had been around as long as *Robocop*, however, Foreman accrued a huge following in small rings around the country and in the big offices on Madison Avenue. He was very funny and broadly relatable. Although he did not dazzle in all his fights, and the competition at times was questionable, Foreman remained undefeated after twenty-four bouts, ten of which occurred after his fortieth birthday. Many Americans wanted to know how far this comeback could go, and Foreman became one of the biggest draws in box-ing. The outcome seemed a foregone conclusion, but the intrigue was valuable. So Trump shelled out an exorbitant site fee to get Holyfield versus Foreman in the Atlantic City Convention Center in exchange for the live gate, and with expectations of hotel and gambling revenues. Unfortunately, Atlantic City did not have the weather or the infrastructure of Vegas, so the number of visitors in mid-April did not meet projections—many interested fans refused to pay the steep ticket prices, and some of those willing to pay could not get hotel rooms on the boardwalk. Trump cited the country's military engagement in the Persian Gulf as part of the "act of God or war" clause in his contract when he tried to renegotiate his terms with Arum and Duva. They cut him a deal but cut him out of the ticket sales, turning an investment opportunity into an ad buy, since Trump retained little more than the right to purchase prime tickets, which he could then hand out to celebrities, giving the veneer of an A-list screening to what sportswriters were already panning as a B movie at best.[12]

When the boxers met in the ring for the prefight ceremonies, after the R&B stars En Vogue performed the national anthem, Fore-man did the dancing. He bounced around the ring, playfully tapped on Holyfield, performed an intricate bow for special guests Frazier and Ali, and looked years younger than his former foes. Having a couple of seventy-somethings, Moore and Dundee, in his corner didn't hurt the perception of his age either. In fact, he had been the more energetic of the two principals since they got to Jersey, drop-ping in on the pressroom regularly and hosting visitors in his suite at virtually any hour. The endless "ballyhoo" he conducted in concert with Dundee's training had Foreman in fighting shape, even if his contours stayed much more rounded than his opponent's. Holyfield came out as he did against Douglas, looking to land a lot of jabs from all angles. Foreman used Moore's old cross-armed defense to negate most of them while sending back some shots of his own. At the end of the first round, Holyfield took to his stool while a quartet of cornermen covered him in Vaseline, ice, and advice. Foreman stood in his corner, as had been his habit during the comeback campaign, nonchalantly chatting with two old friends. "Do what you do. Keep poppin,'" Dundee said. And he did. Halfway through the round, Foreman interrupted Holyfield's rhythm and stunned him with lefts and rights. One jab snapped Holyfield's head so far back that it saved him from the subsequent cross, which came up a half inch too short, and lessened the blow of the uppercut that completed Foreman's two-hand, three-punch combination. The bout would not be a few minutes of glorified sparring. "It was," as Frederick Klein wrote, "12 rounds of heavy leather and hard breathing, and, in the end, they counted up points instead of counting over a body. There have been better fights over the years, but few that deviated farther from form."[13]

A smoke bomb went off near the $1,000-ticket section and only added to the confusion—this supposed mismatch looked dead even. At the seventh, Foreman still refused the stool during breaks and was surprised that they had already fought for more than twenty minutes. "I never could have done those things without Angelo Dundee," he said. His trainer not only had prepared him for a long bout but also took on the referee, Rudy Battle, who nagged and warned Foreman repeatedly about everything from low blows to elbows all night long. Some of the warnings might have been jus- tifiable, but Dundee kept scrapping as long as Foreman did. Battle outdueled Dundee, finally deducting a point from Foreman in the eleventh round, but it likely did not make a difference. Foreman knew he "played too much jazz" as he went the distance with the champ. He had become a much better boxer with age, maturity, and Dundee—Foreman agreed to pay him $100,000 for every fight afterward—but he was still a puncher, and he never landed the knockout blow. Holyfield held onto Foreman like Sadler on a heavy bag during the final round to make sure that one punch wouldn't change the outcome. Judges ringside and at the press tables varied in how many rounds they gave to Holyfield, but virtually everyone agreed he won the majority. Even Foreman, who embraced the champ and whispered, "You won" as they awaited Michael Buffer's official announcement. Holyfield took the decision but, like the receipts, didn't meet expectations.[14]

A grand total of $75 million, $55 million of which came from the 11 million paying viewers in 1.45 million homes, still set new records for gross revenue and pay-per-view buys, even if it came up well short of the $100 million dream. Promoters kept their sights set on that nine-figure target, just as Foreman did not let the loss deter him from his goal of regaining the title. "If you can live you can dream," he told reporters after the loss. Some writers began to reconsider the meaning of victory as they sent in headlines such as "Foreman as Big a Winner as Holyfield" and "Foreman Wins Fight by KO with Sponsors." The challenger gained credibility; the champion lost some cachet. Holyfield's lackluster performance and Mike Tyson's subsequent arrest for rape derailed the megamatch that the Battle of the Ages was supposed to set up, not upstage. Holyfield lost his titles the next year, while Foreman signed a lucrative "promotional contract" with HBO, similar to his talent contract with ABC in the 1970s, which bundled rights to Foreman fights with broadcasting gigs for HBO/TVKO and promised an entertainment special as well. He did commercials for McDonald's, Kentucky Fried Chicken, and Frito-Lay's Doritos, despite the fact he had not even sampled some of the products until he showed up for filming. Nike signed Foreman to an endorsement deal, and he appeared alongside Bo Jackson in an installment of the famous "Bo Knows" campaign, in which he delivered a confident: "George knows." More importantly, Foreman was *known*—and not only by the generation that

grew up with him in the 1960s and 1970s, but also by a new generation of Americans who could scarcely flip a channel without seeing
one of his commercials. "If I wasn't known beforehand," Foreman
said, "I was a household name now."[15]

Big George might have been the only household name in the
pool of active boxers during what Budd Schulberg called the "Nox-
ious 90s." The sport's biggest star, Tyson, morphed from hero to
heel from the late 1980s to the early 1990s, and in early 1992 he was
reduced to a convicted rapist with a six-year prison sentence. Since
Tyson's defeat by Douglas, an "alphabet soup" of titles went around
a carousel of champions. Three of the "resplendent (and redundant)
heavyweight belts," the WBC, WBA, and IBF, followed Holyfield,
who lost to Riddick Bowe. Two of them came back to Holyfield
when he won the rematch, but the WBC bestowed its belt on Lennox Lewis. Immediately, Holyfield surrendered the WBA and IBF
titles to the undefeated left-hander Michael Moorer, who became
the heavyweight division's first southpaw champion. Pursuing
Holyfield's titles required Moorer to vacate his WBO championship, probably the least prestigious of the four, but a title nonetheless, and Foreman acknowledged that he wanted to just win *a* championship before retiring: "I can't stay around forever. I want to go
out right. Going out right means getting a title belt around my waist.
Make that a belt around my neck. It doesn't matter what alphabet
it is—W.B.A., W.B.C., A.B.C.—it's all the same to me." Even if it
was unable to secure the highest-rated boxers, the WBO could still
make a play for the highest ratings. It rushed to fill its title vacancy
by matching a recent movie actor with Hollywood bloodlines—
Tommy "the Duke" Morrison, great-nephew of John Wayne—with
the sport's biggest presence on television. "All of my kids born in
the 80's call me George," Foreman noted, "no one calls me dad,"
because he popped up on numerous commercials. ABC created a
sitcom for him, *George*, in which Foreman played the boxer turned

counselor George Foster, and scheduled filming to start the month after what most expected to be his *final*, final fight.[16]

Morrison, on the other hand, had a less impressive record in the ring, although his performance opposite Sylvester Stallone in *Rocky V* put him in the public eye. The notoriety helped get him a shot at the WBO title, but Morrison took a beating from Ray Mercer. Now the film was a few years old, and he badly needed something else to sustain his career. He made it his mission, or at least his talking point, to "retire Foreman," although he could accomplish that feat by winning or losing. Betting odds vacillated from 3–2 Foreman to 7–5 Morrison, but the purse was squarely in Foreman's favor, with a guaranteed $7 million to Morrison's $1.25 million. Despite uncertainty at the sportsbooks, a writer's poll by the *Las Vegas Sun* was decisive, returning 2–1 for Foreman, with one abstention from Mike Katz: "Don't know, Don't care." Morrison, the underdog earning a fraction of the purse guaranteed to Foreman, cared deeply. His team claimed to have watched more than two hundred hours of film from Foreman's comeback, and they scored an early victory when Mills Lane, over the loud objections of Arum, who believed he had unfairly officiated Foreman's last bout, with Pierre Coetzer, was appointed referee. From the bell, Morrison was busier, but Foreman looked more efficient. Morrison won most of the rounds, but not without enduring some punishment. As the bout wore on, it seemed clear Foreman would need a knockout to win, especially after Lane deducted a point for a low blow, but Morrison kept his head moving to avoid that concussive conclusion. Just as in his last chance at the title, Foreman knew the outcome before the judges' cards came back. "I didn't have it," he said softly, winking at Arum. If he had played too much jazz against Holyfield, his performance versus Morrison was more like the blues. Even after the official announcement, he earned most of the applause, waving with both hands to a live and television audience that soaked in what almost everyone believed to be Foreman's curtain call.[17]

A chorus often heard during Foreman's swan song was that middle age is not a "death sentence." He lived and worked even harder after losing his title bid to Morrison. He not only showed up for all the meetings and filming of *George*, but also tried to memorize every script, despite learning that most of it would be cut before the tape rolled. The formulaic sitcom, produced by the star of another such show, Tony Danza, did not win over critics, and ABC canceled it after only eight episodes. "It didn't get the ratings they wanted," Foreman said, "but it got the ratings I needed" to stay relevant. More sponsors added him to their payrolls, including Oscar Mayer, for its all-beef line of hot dogs, and Houston-based Meineke Car Care Centers. He stayed close to the fight game without going inside the ropes—HBO kept Foreman on with the likes of Jim Lampley and Larry Merchant for its biggest pay-per-view events. He was ringside when Moorer upset Holyfield, and he didn't pull any punches from the microphone. Foreman suggested the Duvas influenced the outcome, adding controversial commentary to a debatable decision, and even though his statement was edited out of the rebroadcast, it stuck with the Duvas. They said Moorer would not defend his new titles on HBO if Foreman called the fight. In one sense, they got their wish, since Foreman did not have a seat at the broadcasting table for Moorer's first championship defense. But the Duvas, Moorer, and the rest of the boxing world had to reckon with the fact that George Foreman was still the best face that prizefighting could put on. Just as ABC had used a proven recipe for sitcoms when it aired *George*, heavyweight champions acknowledged the Foreman mystique when it came to selling pay-per-view buys. Until Tyson got out of prison, perhaps, Moorer's only shot at an eight-figure purse was to take on the oldest (known) challenger for a heavyweight championship—the Everyman of the prize ring. The match was promoted as "One for the Ages."[18]

The WBA threw the first shot, threatening not to sanction the bout, because Moorer bypassed higher-ranked contenders when he agreed to defend against Foreman. The challenger didn't back down—along with his lawyer, Henry Holmes, and the former attorney Arum, who still promoted Foreman for specific fights—he counterpunched with a lawsuit that focused on age discrimination. Since the WBA had historically exercised latitude in sanctioning title defenses, the only difference in this case, Foreman's team argued, was that it centered on a forty-five-year-old. The judge agreed, noting that Foreman had already demonstrated his stamina by enduring hours of argument and testimony. Holmes and Arum lauded the decision, but in chambers with Foreman, they voiced a dissent on the question of his stamina. Both asked Foreman, perhaps more than once, whether he really wanted the fight and would be able to get in shape. They, like most of the boxing world, thought they had seen Foreman's last stand a year earlier. The challenger proved his commitment by moving to California for serious training. Moorer set up camp in Palm Springs, closer to the desert conditions where the fight would take place. Foreman went to the coast and ran Malibu beaches between workouts at the original Gold's Gym, where tortured screams surprised him almost as much as the sight of men with bodies fit for magazine covers curling the same weight he had been bench pressing. He had always believed that he could adapt to any environment, and hoped that his fitness and figure would fit the mold of the Muscle Beach area, but to finish preparations for his last run at the title, he went back to the rough die that first cut him, in Houston.[19]

There, in less prestigious settings than Gold's—such as the modest workout facilities of his youth and community center—Foreman jumped rope until exhaustion and then popped in a cassette of Sam Cooke singing "If I Had a Hammer" and jumped some more in order to build the stamina he would need to not just last twelve rounds but also win the majority of them. The weather imposed an intermission, however, when a mid-October flood brought more than two feet of rain to some parts of the Houston area, which created record stream flows from its surrounding rivers and creeks. The water displaced thousands of Houstonians, including family and friends of Foreman, whom he helped relocate. But water also became an integral part of his private training regimen. Taking a cue from Mike Tyson's routine in the 1980s, Foreman gave up his public displays of knocking sand out of heavy bags and instead hung a water-filled punching bag in his loft, where no one could watch. The problem, he discovered, was that it didn't retain the imprint of his fists, so he couldn't gauge his accuracy. Foreman carefully drew his spots on a liquid-filled effigy of Moorer and practiced hitting it hard and strategically. He did everything Dundee asked of him in the gym, but at home he was honing a new strategy—"taking the steam off" a lighter jab to make sure he could follow up with the hardest straight right he could throw. By the time the principals returned to Vegas, six months after Moorer won the title whose legitimacy and longevity Foreman questioned, things had changed. Foreman was down to 250 pounds and not quite his former jovial self. He produced an artistic interpretation of the Rumble in the Jungle—albeit an abstract one—that finished with him jabbing the pencil until he broke its lead tip. After explaining that the rage he had felt up until that fight with Ali had subsided during his comeback, prompting him to let up on opponents and influence referees to stop bouts before he hurt anyone, Foreman confirmed that he had regained the old urge: "I've got nothing against Michael Moorer but I'm out to kill him." When one of Moorer's sparring partners suggested that sentiment was not very preacher-like, Foreman yelled back, "Shut up, boy!"[20]

Moorer, a former light heavyweight who had bulked up to 220 pounds for the first time in his career, started to think of himself as a heavy puncher, too. He insisted they wear Cleto Reyes gloves—

"the puncher's glove"—rather than more thickly cushioned Everlast mitts. But he remained a lightweight in the pressroom. "I don't like to talk," Moorer told reporters. "You don't win the fight by talking." He was content to let Foreman and Lou Duva dominate the conversation while his trainer, the Cus D'Amato protégé and former Tyson cornerman Teddy Atlas, whispered in his ear. Duva repeated the party line that Foreman had talked his way into this fight, an undeserving self-promoter. He emphasized that Foreman had lost the title twenty years ago by "quitting" in the eighth round, and then noted the irony of sportsbooks pegging the over-under for Foreman versus Moorer at eight rounds. Atlas suppressed his animus toward Foreman, which had surfaced regularly since Moorer got the decision over Holyfield, and while echoing Duva's assessment of Foreman in Zaire, he recognized how dangerous a long memory and deep regrets could make this particular challenger. Atlas told Richard Hoffer, "20 years later, he knows he could have taken that punch. He knows he quit. And he knows that if he had taken the punch, it wouldn't have hurt as much as what he's lived with." Foreman continued to press Moorer in the pressroom, insisting that his handlers "let him speak for himself" and suggesting that the champion couldn't look him in the eye. Moorer explained to reporters in a private workout that Foreman, who "had his era in the 1960s or '70s," was "only here because he promotes himself real good." Foreman may not have disagreed. Before they met in the ring, Foreman had cracked the top-ten list of sports celebrity endorsers for 1994 and secured a book deal for his autobiography, to be published in 1995—the contract stipulated a bonus if he won the title. Regaining the heavyweight championship, any of the extant championships, was more than a bonus for Foreman though. It was his calling.[21]

★

The events of November 5, 1994, exemplified the unpredictability of an unregulated sport. All the information accrued in the months of buildup to the fight, let alone the years of video evidence from the past or ten rounds of action in the present, was completely obliterated in one fraction of a second. HBO's broadcast of Foreman versus Moorer started with a montage of the challenger training—roadwork in a hooded sweater, chopping wood in overalls—interspersed with clips of his megamatches from the 1970s and the not-so-mega matches from his comeback. The video cut back or split the screen to show Foreman in a tuxedo, under the spotlight, giving a spoken-word rendition of "The Impossible Dream" from *Man of La Mancha*. Even if Foreman did not cover the song as well as Andy Williams, Frank Sinatra, or Luther Vandross, he was a perfect representation of a quixotic quest for the end of the millennium. Like Don Quixote's old armor, Foreman chose a set of trunks from his championship reign in the 1970s (adjusted to his 1990s waistline)—a relic from his farthest and fastest conquest, Roman in Tokyo—as he prepared to tilt at the heavyweight windmill one more time.[22]

This prelude to the fight probably marked the first time that HBO had asked a heavyweight challenger to perform a show tune; it was also the first time Foreman could remember somebody asking what song he wanted played when he walked out of the dressing room toward the ring. Foreman chose Cooke's "If I Had a Hammer." It had become the "tired song" that he used "to get [his] bounce back" in training. The heavy bass on the hip-hop track that Moorer used for his ring walk resounded in the arena, but the Foreman faithful easily drowned out the acoustic Cooke. Moorer had "It Takes Two" by Rob Base and DJ EZ Rock. It was a dis, but it was not a lie. Moorer had to defend against someone while the sport waited for Tyson's release, and Foreman's fame had launched him into a middle ground between tune-up quality and marquee financing. It took the two of them, Moorer with his championship belts and Foreman with his "sheer likeability," to sell this event as a viable contest for the title. "George is a star," Larry Merchant acknowledged, and boxing had more champions than stars at present. Of course, Merchant didn't believe the star would shine that night. Even Gil Clancy, Foreman's former trainer, who took his place between Merchant and Lampley, gave the challenger "very little chance," although he could not recall the champion's name. Those who wanted to believe in the 3–1 underdog, which sentimental bettors had brought down to 2–1 in some sportsbooks that day, had to reevaluate after Joe Cortez called for the opening bell.

The first round foreshadowed the entire fight. They stayed close and traded jabs. Moorer, in defiance of any conventional wisdom, circled clockwise, left, into the line of Foreman's big right hand. Foreman tossed a lot of lefts—some fastballs and some change-ups— trying to paint the corner before he heaved one over the plate. After three minutes, they had thrown an equal number of punches, but Moorer landed twice as many. Foreman opened the door once with his jab and slipped the straight right past Moorer's guard. The accumulation of punches he took, however, left a noticeable "mouse" of swelling under Foreman's left eye. At the break, Teddy Atlas, the son of a doctor, diagnosed the case and prescribed a course of action for Moorer. "The hardest part of the fight is over," he told his patient before warning, "He's trying to set you up for one shot." The cure was to keep moving to the *right*, counterclockwise, away from danger. Dundee, on the other side of the ring, said about five audible words: "Stay close. You're better off." Subsequent rounds followed the same script. Despite Atlas's recommendation, Moorer continued to veer left, testing Foreman, but cutting him off with faster punches. Foreman tried to pry Moorer open with jabs so that he could find room to land the right. After four rounds, HBO's contingent shared their unofficial scorecards: Lederman gave all four rounds to Moorer (a judgment echoed by the Associated Press), and Clancy and Merchant had it 3–1 for the champ. A third of the way through the show, it looked as if Foreman would need a hammer to achieve his impossible dream.[23]

By the fifth, Foreman was slowing down, moving less and throwing fewer punches, while Moorer was taking his corner's advice and speeding up. The champion hit more often and more accurately, emboldened to turn his single jabs into combinations. Foreman, conversely, gave up on combos. Several times he scored with the left and cocked his right, but refused to unleash it. In the sixth, he fell back into old habits—not just from his early pro career but also from as far back as Lyons Ave. He flailed at Moorer with haymakers, and a handful hit pay dirt. Even on the tough scorecards of Lederman or the AP, Foreman probably won the round. Merchant called it "a good round at any age," but it was a pyrrhic victory. As Foreman opened up his arsenal, Moorer's jab nearly closed his eye. Atlas kept yelling at Moorer to move, and move in the correct direction—counterclockwise—while Dundee silently worked on Foreman's eye and Shipes repeated: "More than one, George . . . more than one," knowing it would take more than a single shot to save this fight.[24]

As the seconds ticked away to close out the ninth round, Foreman and his fans lost steam. He threw thirty punches in the round, half the average he pumped out in the first eight. Two of the official judges had Moorer with a five-point advantage, an almost impossible deficit for a challenger to make up that late in the fight. The pro-Foreman crowd fell silent, reconciling themselves with the likely result and the fact that they would have to watch nine more minutes of fighting before it was official. Atlas, by comparison, barked loudly at Moorer to make sure he stayed vigilant and kept moving. "He's lookin' to set you up with one shot," he said, again. Dundee echoed it: "You gotta put this guy down," he said. "You're behind, baby." Foreman took it to heart and came out for round ten, it seemed, determined to finish the fight one way or another. He fired long hooks that sailed over and around Moorer, although they corralled him back into a counterclockwise circle. Lampley was impressed, but Foreman grew tired, and the hard haymakers turned into soft jabs. Clancy started delivering Foreman's eulogy midway through the round, "a 45-year-old man in a young man's game." Then the middle-aged, overweight Foreman did something that the young, chiseled version never could. Late in the bout and way down on the scorecards, he landed the punch that ended it all. At the thirty-minute mark, he caught Moorer with one more left, and this time the straight right came behind it—the punch that had taken him from Lyons Ave. to Litton Industries; from Mexico City to Madison Square Garden; around the world and back into the Gomorrah of the Desert. The right sliced through Moorer's gloves and connected on the point of his chin. Its force drove the heavyweight champion onto his back, staring up at the "dark lights" while blood trickled out of his mouth. Foreman kneeled in a neutral corner to pray. Cortez counted as Moorer tried to sit but barely managed a roll. Foreman had trouble getting up as well. When Cortez hit ten, Lampley screamed, "It happened! It happened!" which he later admitted was a reflection of his own disbelief. The ring announcer, Michael Buffer, remained calm and circled back to HBO's opening scene: "The impossible dream has happened. Heavyweight history has happened."[25]

Others joined Buffer to historicize the moment. Bob Arum said it was "the greatest night" he had had in almost thirty years of the fight game. Clancy called the decisive blow "the greatest punch ever landed in the history of heavyweight boxing." Foreman led off the

postfight interview with a jab of self-deprecating humor, acknowl-
edging "all [his] old buddies in the nursing home," before hitting a
note from "When You Wish Upon a Star" and then plugging sponsors and partners like Wendy's and HBO. Foreman did not break
character as he did in his first moment of championship euphoria, in
1973—probably because this one fit better, not only on him but also
in the new era. From the center of the sports universe at the end of
the twentieth century, Foreman looked back on the troubled 1970s
and said: "[I] exorcised the ghost once and forever."[26]

Epilogue

After solidifying his place in the record books, Foreman sat down to write his own book. A journalist that Henry Holmes knew, Joel Engel, came to help him put the memories "in English" for an autobiography under contract to Random House. There was no shortage of interest in writing or selling a Foreman story, especially now that he was a reigning heavyweight champion, but Holmes and Foreman selected Engel because he promised to produce a color-blind, apolitical narrative. They agreed that there were "only two races of people, decent and indecent," echoing visions of postracialism at the end of the twentieth century that the Rodney King riots and O. J. Simpson trial belied—visions that, in part, fueled a Republican resurgence in the 1994 midterm elections. Many of the victors in those contentious congressional races, particularly ones that mounted strong comebacks after early polling cast them as underdogs, were quick to invoke Foreman's name when the votes were tallied, just days after he shocked the sports world. Although he consciously stayed out of politics after his mixed emotions in the late 1960s, Foreman subtly endorsed the incumbent Democratic governor of Texas, Ann Richards, who ultimately got caught in the conservative wave and lost to George W. Bush. In the era of culture wars, it became harder to forge mass appeal across the widening fault lines about government involvement in creating economic opportunity or protecting personal choice. Navigating those national divisions, however, was essential to the branding of George Foreman.[1]

Holmes boasted that they received hundreds of phone calls and millions of dollars in new endorsement deals and speaking fees over the coming year. Foreman appeared on everything from *The Today Show* to *The Tonight Show*; sat down with all kinds of television hosts, including David Letterman, Charlie Rose, and Larry King; let *60 Minutes* do a piece about him; and even hosted *Saturday Night Live*. The scripts from *SNL* writers were much shorter than the ones he had tried to memorize for episodes of *George*, but Foreman found *SNL* harder to digest. He once said he would do anything on television—from Bob Hope to game shows, from ABC to HBO—as long as he didn't have to say anything offensive. *SNL* had made its mark in television comedy by pushing the relaxed boundaries of a late-night time slot. The musical guest, Courtney Love, seemed much more comfortable in this atmosphere than Foreman, who smiled through his monologue and slogged through his sketches, but confided to the sportswriter Mort Sharnik in his dressing room, "I just never shoulda done this." He won limitless opportunities when he regained the title, but he had also reached a point where he could be selective.[2]

After more than twenty-five years as an amateur and a professional, with over one hundred boxing matches behind him, Foreman found a lucrative source of income that did not require him to get punched in the face. But maintaining his championship, at least one of them, would remain critical until *By George* hit bookstores and Mike Tyson returned to the ring. Prospectors of prizefighting speculated that the matchup would command a $50 million purse and perhaps $200 million in total revenue, since interest in Foreman versus Tyson only grew as the new champion looked like a better boxer and the ex-champ appeared to be a worse person. Merchant summed it up as "good guy vs. evil; old guy vs. rapist." Before Tyson's release, pressure mounted on Foreman to defend his titles. He agreed, but on his terms. Although it would mark another "first" during this second dynasty—his first title defense in the United States—the choice of a German national with credentials as questionable as his English sparked something of an international incident.[3]

Axel Schulz had the record of a contender, twenty-one wins with one loss and one draw (both against Henry Akinwande), but had not worked his way into the top-ten rankings of either the WBA or IBF, which sanctioned Foreman's titles. The WBA refused to consider Schulz a legitimate contender, stripped Foreman of its championship, and hastily set a decisive bout between two Don King–controlled fighters, Tony Tucker and Bruce Seldon. The IBF quietly maneuvered Schulz into the ninth-ranked heavyweight position and officially endorsed the Foreman-Schulz bout, which promised not only a good domestic pay-per-view audience because of the Foreman factor, but also millions of buys from Germany. The foreign market buoyed the figure of an estimated thirty million viewers, just as the more than a hundred German journalists added to a crowd of over eleven thousand at ringside. The malleability of the rankings matched the subjectivity of the scorecards when Buffer announced a majority decision—two judges had it 115–113, and one called it a draw—for the champion. Foreman landed more punches, but the ones he took left their mark in the swelling around his eyes or on top of his head. Schulz scored on a higher percentage of punches and moved more than Foreman may have expected. While some fans and writers openly questioned the decision and called it a "gift" to the popular American champion, Foreman challenged the score as well: "I was shocked beyond all reason that someone would score that thing even when that boy was running from a grandpappy."[4]

The only decisive winner, it appeared, was the IBF, which suddenly looked more prophetic than pathetic after a better-than-expected fight. It immediately called for a rematch. "I would never fight that kid again," Foreman said. "Wherever he came from, let him go right back." The IBF revoked its title in response, leaving only the brand-new World Boxing Union to recognize Foreman as a heavyweight champion. Arum, resurrecting a line from his years with Ali, affirmed that Foreman was the people's champion, regardless of what the spectrum of sanctioning bodies said. Yet Arum also discussed the possibility of a heavyweight tournament to, presumably, fill Foreman's place if he retired. Foreman joked about the clandestine agreements between sanctioning bodies, promoters, and pay-per-view providers with Jerry Izenberg, who wrote that "top 10 ratings go not to the best but rather to the best connected." Izenberg singled out King as one who manipulated rankings through "sanctioning fees" as well as bribes and kickbacks, and then shortchanged fighters but paid "the boxing politicians who made it possible" very well indeed. Foreman reminded him, "The reason I got to fight for the title wasn't ratings. It was that people came around and bought tickets to my fights." Then Foreman suggested a heavyweight tournament as well, one to determine who might be his final opponent, but added that he could function as the "commissioner": "I'll take under-the-table money and everything." He caught himself and told Izenberg, "No, no. Take that last part out. I was only kidding." It was a serious issue in the oversanctioned yet underregulated sport. Arum testified years later, during an investigation into the IBF, that he had agreed to pay the organization hundreds of thousands of dollars above the sanctioning fee to alter its rankings in order to make the Foreman-Schulz title fight possible; he later refused to cough up some of what he "owed," because he heard that the IBF had shaken Foreman down for about $250,000 as well. Henry Holmes was less concerned about the seedy machinations behind the scenes than the product he saw in front of the camera. Holmes agreed that the Schulz fight brought into question whether the champ should quit while he was ahead. And Holmes had a good idea just how far ahead he might be as the autobiography was set to be released and a deal with Salton, Inc. took root.[5]

By the summer of 1995, even without the imprimatur of most boxing organizations, Foreman's name recognition drove *By George* to near the top ten of the *New York Times*' and *Wall Street Journal*'s lists of best-selling nonfiction books. Some members of his informal brain trust—now made up almost exclusively of friends and family, who "didn't have fees, all they had was a heart"—suggested he use that power to do more than appear in commercials and endorse other products or companies. They looked out for a chance to sell the George Foreman name at the height of its popularity. Ironically, the rise of the overweight champion coincided with a healthy-food movement that the designer-retailer Michael Boehm hoped to exploit with a new kitchen appliance. Boehm's "steam grill" was picked up by Hamilton Beach in the early 1990s but did not make an imprint in the marketplace. He began pushing prototypes of a "fat reducing" grill to manufacturers over the next few years. More than anything, however, it needed a name. The "Great Hamburger Maker" evolved into the "Great Hamburger-Steak Maker" and then the "Short Order Grill," emphasizing speed rather than health, but all without getting any bites. At least nine companies, including Salton, passed on Boehm's pitch before Salton's CEO, Leon Dreimann, came back to it. Dreimann thought the small, sloped grill that pressed and drained fat did have a place—with a different name. Boehm says Dreimann, a big believer in the power of celebrity endorsement, challenged him to find a suitable pitchman. Then Salton purchased the product outright, and Dreimann renamed it himself: "The Lean Mean Fat Grilling Machine," an homage to 1974's *The Longest Yard* that most of his target demographic likely didn't recognize. They would probably never recognize its inventor, either. Boehm would not receive royalties if the grill did take off under its new moniker, and even the patent reverted back to the Chinese company he was working for when he invented it.[6]

The rebranded grill's launch, at the 1994 Gourmet Products Show, had about as inauspicious a start as its antecedent's. Everyone passed; only one came back. A veteran marketer of home products such as the Veg-O-Matic, Mike Srednick took a second look. Srednick knew through an attorney named Sam Perlmutter, another Holmes connection, that Foreman was interested in opportunities that offered a bigger stake than just taping commercials. Holmes also represented Hulk Hogan, who may have reflected the "lean" and "mean" title more closely than Foreman. But Foreman's connection with hamburgers and a personal weight-loss story fit together as neatly as Boehm's combination of a declining plate for draining liquids counterbalanced by reverse angle grooves to keep solids in place. It was all about fit. Srednick talked Dreimann into essentially giving away the grill and connected him directly with the manufacturer. Then Srednick charged Perlmutter with getting the appliance in front of Foreman. Shipping the product to his house was easy, but getting a response proved harder. Perlmutter and Holmes pressed him, but Foreman admitted, "So many things came to my house, if it didn't have a check in it I wouldn't look at it." His wife overheard the discussion and quickly added her perspective: "I use it!" Her endorsement was enough, sealed with a hot-off-the-nonstick-surface burger, and he signed a seemingly insignificant contract that did not offer much above a bunch of free grills up front. The money was in the royalties, because Salton did not have much else to invest in it. Foreman got his opportunity to have his name on a product, "The George Foreman Lean Mean Fat Reducing Machine," and secured a deal that promised him a plurality of the net profits—45 percent, compared with 40 percent for Salton and a 15 percent nod to Srednick and Perlmutter.[7]

Less than a week after inking the contract, Foreman became a headliner at the next Gourmet Products Show, conveniently held in Las Vegas, where he was training for Schulz. Foreman had more success with a hundred retail executives at a cocktail party orchestrated by Salton and on the floor of the trade show in March then he did in the ring in April. The boxing world grappled with what to do about Foreman, but Salton only wanted more of him. They filmed a half-hour infomercial, "The George Foreman Grilling Show," while Foreman alternated between appearances at book signings and product demos. The first cut of the infomercial, however, opened with a sweaty clip of Foreman throwing punches and spliced in too much boxing footage to resonate with the home-shopping demographic. It became clear that Foreman's appeal in the mid-1990s did not rely on boxing alone. The marketing team replaced most of the punching with family shots, and in the revised cut viewers saw the king of the ring bantering with the "Queen of Infomercials," Nancy Nelson, about cooking quick and healthy meals for a big family. He landed his key line—"Knocks Out the Fat!"—repeatedly, with more force than finesse, but the grill was not exactly an overnight success. Hundreds of thousands of grills sold in the first year after Foreman's association, yet that was not far off the pace of Boehm's original Steam Grill, which Hamilton Beach had discontinued. Foreman's live demos in department stores and taped infomercials gave the product some fame, but that hadn't yet translated into sales, and without a major prizefight on the horizon, his place as a household name seemed transitory.[8]

The closest he came to some action happened at the broadcaster's table after Riddick Bowe escaped Andrew Golota via disqualification for low blows, and a riot broke out. Foreman leapt up to protect his HBO colleagues. "Don't do it, son," he repeated in his preacher's voice to enraged fans. "You don't want to go in there. It's going to be all right." It was a real and spontaneous reaction that generated positive feedback not just from his terrified fellow commentators, Merchant and Lampley, who managed to keep their equipment functional behind the one-man barricade so that viewers could at least hear him in action. Dreimann directed Foreman's spontaneity toward the biggest stage for small household appliances: QVC, aka "Quality Value Convenience," the quintessential home-shopping network. He thrust Foreman on television, live, to hock grills while watching the telephones in the studio carefully as barometers of new sales. Foreman looked remarkably comfortable in this contrived setting. He didn't just banter with the QVC presenters or wait for them to set up his cues to demonstrate how much fat slid off the grill and, therefore, not into one's arteries; rather, Foreman engaged with the product and the audience while puttering around the stage and using the appliance. Dreimann watched intently until flashing red lights signaled an emergency—at least, a QVC emergency. All the manned phone lines were occupied. New callers might get the dreaded busy signal. The lights were an all-hands-on-deck warning that sent every available QVC employee to the closest phone. After reviewing the tape, Dreimann found the tipping point. In the middle of the demo, Foreman grabbed a bun off a table, stole a burger from the grill, and took a huge bite. "It was so spontaneous," Dreimann said. "It was a real reaction. People saw that he eats what he sells."[9]

Royalties from the boxer's namesake appliance, generally known as the "Foreman Grill," rose as the purses for a nominal heavyweight champion's defenses against lesser-known challengers plateaued. Salton reportedly grossed $5 million from the grill in 1996, a positive marker even if more than half of the profits were redirected to Foreman, Srednick, and Perlmutter. Foreman matched Salton's grill sales in his only fight of 1996, earning $5 million for a unanimous decision over Crawford Grimsley. The next year, he collected $4 million for winning a split decision against Lou Savarese and another $5 million in a loss by majority decision to Shannon Briggs.

Salton achieved a record $183 million in total sales for 1997—a significant chunk coming from the grill. In 1998, the company claimed more than $500 million and attributed over $200 million of that to grill sales. Foreman's royalties escalated to millions of dollars a *month*. The Briggs bout, in particular, brought into sharp relief the cost-benefit analysis of continuing to box. Despite Foreman landing more punches, with higher accuracy, and breaking Briggs's nose in the process, two judges gave Briggs the win, and one scored it a draw. Foreman's promoters, Irving Azoff and the television producer Jeff Wald, feverishly challenged the decision and accused the New Jersey Athletic Control Board's commissioner, Larry Hazzard, of fixing the results. Foreman was more sanguine: "How can a guy say 'I was robbed' when he walks away with a million bucks in his pocket?" No longer a heavyweight champion—lineal or titular—he was clearly losing interest in the politics of prizefighting. He confirmed that "it would take a lot of money to get [him] back in the ring," but he knew that it would also take a lot to get him ranked and sanctioned for another major bout. On the other hand, Foreman already occupied the fourteenth spot on *Forbes*'s list of wealthiest athletes. He retired from the prize ring for the second time, twenty years after his first retirement, following his loss to Briggs in 1997. Fittingly, in his postfight interview, he gave HBO's Merchant a plug for the Foreman Grill: "No home should be without this thing. God bless you. Go get one."[10]

The astounding success of the Foreman Grill was due as much to its spokesperson's commitment to word-of-mouth sales, like his pitch to Merchant after the fight, as it was to Salton's investment in print and television advertising or to QVC partnerships. It caught everyone, especially Dreimann, by surprise. Only four years into their contract, the grill sold so many units—more than ten million, a forty-fold increase from 1995—that the agreement with Foreman became untenable. Salton needed to exchange the unpredictability of royalties for a fixed payment in order to responsibly invest and grow. Its solution was to buy George Foreman's name. Salton offered $137.5 million to keep the name and quit the kickbacks. Foreman accepted what was then the largest athlete endorsement in history and instantly became the third highest-paid sports pitchman, behind only Michael Jordan and Tiger Woods. The new deal included language obligating—or, more accurately, allowing—Foreman to continue doing sales for the grill, and the company could place his name on other products under its umbrella.[11]

Retiring from the prize ring and selling his name to Salton was bittersweet. "I was really scared," Foreman admitted. "I didn't want to lose my job." But the arrival of reality television at the turn of the millennium ensured that a broadly popular celebrity who preferred to take the stage unscripted would not remain idle. Jeff Wald lost his appeal of Foreman's decision against Briggs, but he remained friends with the ex-champ and always had a close hand in network television. When reality shows like *Big Brother* and *Survivor* took over prime-time slots, Wald stumped for a boxing-centric version with the intrigue of the former and more direct, violent confrontations—boxing matches—than the latter. As a champion boxer with celebrity status, Foreman seemed like an obvious choice for such a concept. He demurred while producers and networks batted around the idea that eventually manifested in 2005 as NBC's *The Contender*—hosted by Sylvester Stallone. Foreman, who knew that Stallone had been working with television writers, soon discovered that he had another movie project in the works as well: *Rocky Balboa*. The sixth installment of Stallone's boxing saga featured a long-retired former heavyweight champion who stages a comeback, despite concerns about his age and health, and defies the odds by making a competitive fight against the current, much younger champion. After receiving the script before the film was released in late 2006, Foreman cracked, "I already knew that."[12]

The convergence of unpolished boxing and underdog stories in film and on TV at the height of the reality era created a new opportunity. According to Foreman, his older sons constructed the idea of a reality show based on their own large family, and he agreed: "When you do something with your family, it's a joy." Not having to memorize scripts or spots made it all the better. The TV Land network put up an offer to film the household and air the episodes during 2008's summer lull. It projected, in essence, an attempt to capture a real-life *Cosby Show* in the window between the end of that series and the downfall of its namesake, all during the historic campaign of America's first black presidential nominee. The show stayed fixated on the family through profiles of the participating Foreman children and behind-the-scenes footage of a famous baby boomer. But just like *George*, the scripted sitcom from a previous decade, *Family Foreman* generated only a handful of episodes over its single season. Yet a demographic of viewers who had grown up with Foreman, were about his age, shared some of his experiences, and suffered from some of his afflictions might follow him into another show.[13]

In early 2015, Henry Winkler bought into an Americanized version of the South Korean hit *Grandpas over Flowers*, which followed well-known, aging actors as they traveled to other countries. Winkler attracted Foreman, William Shatner, and Terry Bradshaw to make up the diverse cast of the show, renamed *Better Late Than Never*. Foreman knew Bradshaw informally as a fellow sports celebrity from the 1970s who occasionally crossed paths with him at the Shreveport Regional Airport when Bradshaw headed to his native Louisiana and Foreman flew in or out of the closest airport to Marshall. Foreman had been a fan of Winkler and Shatner from *Happy Days* and *Star Trek*. Yet the similarities between these notable "seasoned citizens" became clear to Foreman: "Guys who had done a lot of things but missed out on a lot of things" as they rose to fame.

Tapping into the roots of the show, perhaps in hopes of pitching it to foreign markets, the first season produced four episodes of the cast traveling around Asia under the comically dubious guidance of Jeff Dye. Foreman noted, "We're just ourselves[;] we didn't have to do any acting," although the man who had traveled to Japan at least once in both of his professional boxing stints played as oblivious a tourist as his cast mates when the show aired in the summer of 2016. A steady audience of seven million viewers approved, and Foreman, shortly before his sixty-eighth birthday, finally got to film a second season of a TV show.[14]

In the spring of 2017, Foreman said he would be unavailable for interviews for a while—he was getting on a plane with Winkler, Shatner, Bradshaw, and Dye to shoot another season of *Better Late Than Never*. Details were not much more specific than that. But eventually NBC started teasing their next adventure, which centered on Europe, with a quick jaunt to North Africa, during prime time's winter interludes. The show used the same recipe, but with twice as many episodes to fill, it magnified the caricatures and ratcheted up the humor. Comparisons to the Griswold family in *National Lampoon's European Vacation* were prominent in trailers, with that film series' theme song, "Holiday Road," foreshadowing this international lampoon of aging icons. Winkler's and Shatner's yin and yang of the exuberant versus the esoteric was threaded through the episodes, and Bradshaw's phobias were juxtaposed with his surprising comfort with public nudity. Quick pans to a sleeping Foreman continued to be a mainstay across both seasons, with Winkler referring to the "Slumber in the Jungle" as the youngest of the four co-stars appeared to snooze through some of the action that attracted about two million fewer viewers than their maiden voyage to Asia.

Some of this might have looked like a rerun to Foreman anyway. He had traveled to Germany multiple times since his first trip as a teenage Olympic hopeful. But the second season also incorporated dramatic asides for personal and familial histories: Shatner's Lithuanian heritage, Winkler's homage to an uncle that did not make it out of Nazi Germany with his parents, and one carefully orchestrated reunion—under the auspices of a beauty pageant for goats—with the family of Ionas Chepulis, whose (bleeding) face launched Foreman into nearly a hundred prizefights and a much more rewarding post-boxing career. Later, in Barcelona, he almost instinctively pitched the George Foreman Grill, and when they arrived at the Bonfires of St. John, he resolutely refused to throw anything onto the flames because, he said, "I've got nothing to give up." The circumnavigation of his memory concluded with his one wish in Morocco: to visit a youth boxing center. When he got there, Foreman drew out the similarities not only between this gym and the youth and community center he had built on Lone Oak Road, but also the hunger he saw in front of him. A lifetime away from food scarcity, Foreman extolled the main virtue of an otherwise unvirtuous sport. In Houston, his mom could sometimes provide him with only one meal a day; prizefighting did not just put food on his table but also afforded him the chance to give her three squares for the rest of her life. Left on the cutting-room floor, perhaps, was any mention of the mental strength and agility required to persevere through the business of boxing, make something salable outside the prize ring, and build the kind of empire that ensured his descendants wouldn't have to fight in the same way.[15]

The fighter who had to overcome his age in the late twentieth century capitalized on it in the twenty-first. On the *Fruits of the Fifth Ward* mural's third panel, next to the one with Foreman's picture, the caption reads: "They will still bear fruit in old age." Foreman proved it. While he returned to television, two of his sons co-produced a documentary film centered on his unprecedented return to the heavyweight championship. Decades after his last stand in the ring, then, he remained visible on the big and small screens; a full half century after he first boxed on television, George Foreman was firmly entrenched in American pop-cultural history. His journey from the working poor to the 1 percent required, besides an ability to fight, a willingness to adapt and a proclivity to sell. As a keynote speaker at the Sage Summit in 2017, he told crowds of aspiring entrepreneurs, "If you learn to sell, you will never starve"—a fact shown by his own road from a hungry child to a highly coveted pitchman in the food industry.[16]

"Preaching really helped me, because I learned to sell," Foreman explained, although he did not traffic in his fame to increase the size of his congregation or proselytize the impressionable visitors to his youth center. Religion might have been his least successful sales venture; his own mother didn't buy his pitch. Yet from his earliest days in Houston, Foreman sold his toughness for cultural cachet in the rough edges of the Fifth Ward. He traded on the patriotism ascribed to him in the late 1960s as he moved into professional boxing, and then borrowed soul style to become more marketable for the early 1970s. Only after winning the championship did he quit trying to sell himself, yet when the title was gone, he went back to work changing, refining, and promoting a more broadly appealing image to campaign for another shot—not knowing how long it would take to get it or how much it would depend on his self-promotion. "I'm a salesperson. That's what I do. I even sold boxing to convince the world that I could be heavyweight champ," Foreman affirmed. "That was selling." Old-guard sportswriters like Dave Anderson looked back on the 1970s, particularly after rewatching ad nauseam the image of Mike Tyson spitting a piece of Evander Holyfield's ear across the ring, which became a metaphor for boxing at the end of the twentieth century, and pined for the days when strong characters like Ali, Frazier, and Foreman established compelling narratives and competed for one undisputed championship. Fighters and writers alike began to remember the first half of the 1970s as one of boxing's golden eras, though it was only gilded for Foreman. He helped create that environment but was not always comfortable in it. Fortunately, as he has insisted, "anyone can be shaped and re-shaped, because environments always change." With new technology in a different cultural context at the turn of the millennium, Foreman realized his era of fantastic millions and left boxing to its own business.[17]

Acknowledgments

No one gave more to this book than Erika Cornelius Smith. She is my team teacher, peer editor, coparent, best friend, and love of my life. Erika made many sacrifices and gave immeasurable support from the moment I pitched the idea of writing a dissertation about George Foreman. That project had its own list of people to thank, and I will try not to repeat too many, but Erika deserves another shout-out and, without question, the first acknowledgment. You rock.

Some time ago, Tommy Hunt made a very compelling argument for why this work belonged in the Todd Series. Everything he said about the staff and resources at the University of Texas Press was absolutely true. Robert Devens is a tremendous editor who listened, advised, and helped the book take shape. Sarah McGavick's impact, particularly with regard to the images that enhance the finished product, cannot be overstated. The excellent copyediting from Kip Keller (a freelancer), as well as the publicity work by Joel Pinckney and Cameron Ludwick, was essential. The entire UT Press team has my deepest gratitude.

Two sport historians that I greatly admire, David Wiggins and Ryan Swanson, read the manuscript carefully and provided thoughtful insights that undoubtedly made this a much better book. Many others aided in the research process. Special acknowledgment goes to Allen Fisher and Ruth Goerger at the LBJ Presidential Library for their exceptional help with documents and photographs and for unforgettable opportunities to interact with artifacts that make history come alive. For this specific topic, the Joyce Sports Research Collection at the University of Notre Dame was the most important resource, and its curator, the incomparable George Rugg, one of the most valuable contributors.

Turning a dissertation into a book required a great deal of support, and much of it came from Nichols College's Office of Academic Affairs, led first by Alan Reinhardt and then Mauri Pelto. They allowed me to teach in the History and Sport Management programs, the foundation for a work on "the business of boxing," funded multiple research trips, and coordinated with the Faculty Development Committee on a course release. That extra time allowed me to conduct interviews and—with the help of the excellent staffs in the Newspaper Reading Room at the Library of Congress and the Houston Public Library—verify as many of the memories as possible with print sources. The many conversations with George Foreman were the most rewarding aspect of this process. His willingness to answer the phone every time, and often stay on the line longer than the time allotted, is truly appreciated.

Finally, I have benefited from a huge community of friends and family. After graduate school, Nate Corzine, Eric Hall, Andrew McGregor, Jamal Ratchford, and Johnny Smith dispersed around the country but have always been very supportive from afar. In the Northeast, many colleagues at Nichols showed interest and enthusiasm, including those who participate in our "Research Collaborative," which aims to incubate more scholarship on The Hill. The North Brookfield–based "Book/Fight Club" has been a catalyst for reading for fun again, and the books and great conversation with friends helped me write for a broader audience. The broadest audience is my family—an extended network across North America. Everyone on both sides of the border has been incredibly encouraging. I am particularly fortunate to have such trusting parents, given my admittedly odd career trajectory; the best in-laws anyone could ask for; and Simon Smith, who went beyond the call of duty as a big brother to teach me many things—some of which are best forgotten—but perhaps most importantly a passion for reading and writing. I hope to have the same effect on Sophie and Phoebe, my amazing daughters, who have been a part of this book every day of their lives—the best part of it.

Notes

The following abbreviations are used in the notes:

ABC	Avery Brundage Collection, University of Illinois at Urbana-Champaign
AEC	American Embassy Caracas
AEK	American Embassy Kinshasa
CFPF	Central Foreign Policy Files
GFBF, HPL	George Foreman Biographical File, Houston Public Library
JSRC	Joyce Sports Research Collection, University of Notre Dame, South Bend, IN
LBJL	Lyndon Baines Johnson Library, Austin, TX
MAC	Muhammad Ali Center, Louisville, KY
NARA-AAD	National Archives and Records Administration—Access to Archival Database
NMC	Norman Mailer Collection, Harry Ransom Center, University of Texas at Austin
NUAC	Northwestern University Africana Collection, Evanston, IL
NUSC	Northwestern University Special Collections, Evanston, IL
OCG 19	Organizing Committee of the Games of the XIX Olympiad
OTOHP	1968 Olympic Team Oral History Project, H. J. Lutcher Stark Center for Physical Culture and Sports, University of Texas at Austin
RG	Record Group
SSDC	Secretary of State, Washington, DC
USIS	United States Information Service
WPA	Works Progress Administration

PROLOGUE

1. Interviews with George Foreman, in possession of the author, cited as Foreman interview; Richard O. Davies, *The Main Event: Boxing in Nevada from Mining Camps to the Las Vegas Strip* (Reno: University of Nevada Press, 2014), 204.

2. Red Smith, "Ambush Among the Slots," *New York Times*, January 25, 1976; George Foreman and Joel Engel, *By George: The Autobiography of George Foreman* (New York: Villard, 1995), 133–134; Leonard Koppett, "Foreman, Down Twice, Knocks Out Lyle in 5th," *New York Times*, January 25, 1976.

3. "Foreman Struggles to K.O. of Lyle in 5th," *Baltimore Sun*, January 25, 1976; "Foreman's Off-the-Canvas Win over Lyle Spurs Talk of Frazier Rematch," *Boxing Illustrated*, May 1976, 14; Koppett, "Foreman, Down Twice"; *Foreman*, dir. Chris Perkel (Triple Threat Television, 2017).

4. Jim Cour, "George Foreman Gets Fourth [*sic*] Round Knock Out Over Lyle," *Atlanta Daily World*, January 29, 1976; "Foreman Struggles to K.O."; Pat Putnam, "Sweet Science, Indeed," *Sports Illustrated*, February 2, 1976, 19; "Foreman's Off-the-Canvas Win," 15.

5. "Foreman Shakes Rust; Aims for Title," *Baltimore Sun*, January 26, 1976; Putnam, "Sweet Science," 18; "Foreman's Off-the-Canvas Win," 12–14; John Ort, "Foreman KO's Lyle," *Ring*, April 1976, 8; Red Smith, "The Fighters Took a Little Longer," *New York Times*, January 26, 1976; Lester Bromberg, "Does Television Need Boxing," *Ring*, June 1977, 6–7, 46; "Lyle-Foreman Fourth Nearly Changed Course of Heavyweight History," *Boxing Illustrated*, March 1977, 36.

6. Richard Hoffer, "Ko'd," *Sports Illustrated*, November 14, 1994, 21–22.

7. Andrew R. M. Smith, "Sculpting George Foreman: A Soul Era Champion in the Golden Age of Black Heavyweights," *Journal of Sport History* 40, no. 3 (2013): 455–473.

8. Richard Hoffer, "Born Again and Again," *Sports Illustrated*, December 1, 2003, 70.

9. Randy Roberts and Andrew R. M. Smith, "The Report of My Death Was an Exaggeration: The Many Sordid Lives of America's Bloodiest 'Pastime,'" *International Journal of the History of Sport* 31, nos. 1–2 (2014): 72–90.

CHAPTER 1: FRUITS OF THE FIFTH WARD

1. Interviews with George Foreman, in possession of the author, cited as Foreman interview; *CNBC Titans: George Foreman* (NBC, 2010).

2. Laurie Johnson, "Fifth Ward Mural," *Houston Public Media*, October 20, 2006, houstonpublicmedia.org/articles/news/2006/10/20/5408/fifth-ward-mural.

3. Robert S. Maxwell, *Whistle in the Piney Woods: Paul Bremond and the Houston, East and West Texas Railway* (1963; repr., Denton: East Texas Historical Association and University of North Texas Press, 1998), 91–98; Archie P. McDonald, "Tenaha, Timpson, Bobo, and Blair," *Texas Escapes*, January 2001, texasescapes.com/DEPARTMENTS/Guest_Columnists/East_Texas_all_things_historical/TenahaTimpsonBoboBlairTx1AMD101.htm.

4. Maxwell, *Whistle in the Piney Woods*, 91–98; McDonald, Tenaha, Timpson, Bobo"; Foreman interview.

5. Barry J. Kaplan, "Houston: The Golden Buckle of the Sunbelt," in *Sunbelt Cities: Politics and Growth Since World War II*, ed. Richard M. Bernard and Bradley R. Rice (Austin: University of Texas Press, 1983), 196–212; Robert Fisher, "Organizing in the Private City: The Case of Houston, Texas," in *Black Dixie: Afro-Texan History and Culture in Houston*, ed. Howard Beeth and Cary D. Wintz (College Station: Texas A&M University Press, 1992), 260; Foreman interview.

6. Foreman interview; George Foreman and Joel Engel, *By George: The Autobiography of George Foreman* (New York: Villard, 1995), 4.

7. Foreman and Engel, *By George*, 4; Darlene Clark Hine, "Black Migration in the Urban Midwest," in *The Great Migration in Historical Perspective: New Dimensions of Race, Class, and Gender*, ed. Joe William Trotter Jr. (Bloomington: Indiana University Press, 1991), 130.

8. Patricia Kelly Hall and Steven Ruggles, "'Restless in the Midst of their Prosperity': New Evidence on the Internal Migration of Americans, 1850–2000," *Journal of American History* 91, no. 3 (2004): 829–846; Barbara J. Rozek, *Come to Texas: Enticing Immigrants, 1865–1915* (College Station: Texas A&M University Press, 2003), 61.

9. James N. Gregory, *The Southern Diaspora: How the Great Migrations of Black and White Southerners Transformed America* (Chapel Hill: University of North Carolina Press, 2005), 23–38; Randy Roberts, *Joe Louis: Hard Times Man* (New

Haven, CT: Yale University Press, 2010), 10–15; Andrew R. M. Smith, "Blood Stirs the Fight Crowd: Making and Marking Joe Frazier's Philadelphia," in *Philly Sports: Teams, Games, and Athletes from Rocky's Town*, ed. Ryan A. Swanson and David K. Wiggins (Fayetteville: University of Arkansas Press, 2016), 139–141.

10. Bernadette Pruitt, *The Other Great Migration: The Movement of Rural African Americans to Houston, 1900–1941* (College Station: Texas A&M University Press, 2013), 3–6; WPA, *Houston: A History and Guide* (Houston: Anson Jones Press, 1941), 96; George Fuermann, *Houston: Land of the Big Rich* (New York: Doubleday, 1951), 14.

11. WPA, *Houston*, 127; David McComb, *The Bayou City* (Austin: University of Texas Press, 1961), 187–190, and *Texas: A Modern History* (Austin: University of Texas Press, 1989), 145–147; Pruitt, *Other Great Migration*, 9; *Time* quoted in Fuermann, *Houston*, 112.

12. David McComb, *Houston: A History* (Austin: University of Texas Press, 1981), 162, and *Texas*, 159, 170–171; Foreman interview; Foreman and Engel, *By George*, 15.

13. Fuermann, *Houston*, 215; McComb, *Houston*, 138–139; Beth Anne Shelton et al., *Houston: Growth and Decline in a Sunbelt Town* (Philadelphia: Temple University Press, 1989), 46, 73–75; A. R. Hirsch quoted in Komozi Woodard, *A Nation within a Nation: Amiri Baraka (LeRoi Jones) and Black Power Politics* (Chapel Hill: University of North Carolina Press, 1999), 31; Robert D. Bullard, *Invisible Houston: The Black Experience in Boom and Bust* (College Station: Texas A&M University Press, 1987), 30–36.

14. Pruitt, *Other Great Migration*, 30, 41–42; WPA, *Houston*, 172–173; Bullard, *Invisible Houston*, 23–27, 82; Fuermann, *Houston*, 12–13.

15. Foreman interview; Foreman and Engel, *By George*, 3–4.

16. Foreman and Engel, *By George*, 6–7; Foreman interview.

17. US Census Bureau, "Weighted Average Poverty Thresholds for Families of Specified Size: 1959–2015," under "Historical Poverty Tables: People and Families—1959 to 2015," https://www.census.gov/data/tables/time-series/demo/income-poverty/historical-poverty-people.html; Foreman interview; see also, David Shipler, *The Working Poor: Invisible in America* (New York: Vintage, 2004).

18. Foreman interview.

19. Foreman and Engel, *By George*, 3, 11, 15; Foreman interview; McComb, *Houston*, 232–233.

20. Foreman interview; see also David H. Russell, Doris Gates, and Constance M. McCullough, *Roads to Everywhere* (New York: Ginn, 1948).

21. Foreman interview.

22. Foreman interview; "Democratic Ticket Is Backed By Negro Group," *Houston Post*, October 2, 1960; "Religious Issue in the Presidential Campaign Harms the Country," *Houston Post*, October 9, 1960; "Political Fervor at Highest in 1960," *Houston Post*, November 1, 1960; "Democrats Deny Role in Controversial Ad," *Houston Post*, November 4, 1960; "Each Side Asks Apology for 'Unsavory' Tactics," *Houston Post*, November 6, 1960.

23. John M. Logsdon, *John F. Kennedy and the Race to the Moon* (New York: Palgrave Macmillan, 2011), 1–4, 111–113. A transcript of the Rice University speech is available at http://explore.rice.edu/explore/kennedy_address.asp.

24. Foreman and Engel, *By George*, 15.

25. "George Foreman," OTOHP, transcript of interview, January 16, 2013; Ralph Cooper, "George Foreman: Trouble in Camp," *Black Sports*, November 1973, 28, 46; Paul Zimmerman, "Violent and Eloquent," *Sports Illustrated*, October 5, 1981, 41–49.

26. Cooper, "George Foreman," 46; Foreman and Engel, *By George*, 14–15.

27. Foreman and Engel, *By George*, 12–13; Foreman interview.

28. Foreman interview.

29. Charles Wolf and Kip Lornell, *The Life and Legend of Lead Belly* (New York: HarperCollins, 1992), 70–87.

30. Foreman interview.

CHAPTER 2: CORPSMAN'S CALL

1. Interviews with George Foreman, in possession of the author, cited as Foreman interview; George Foreman and Joel Engel, *By George: The Autobiography of George Foreman* (New York: Villard, 1995), 12–13.

2. Foreman interview; "George Foreman," OTOHP, transcript of interview, January 16, 2013.

3. "Will Clay Still Talk on His Way Down?," *Houston Post*, February 24, 1964; Gene War, "A Preview of the Third Round: Liston's Hook Blazes . . . And Clay Starts Slow-Motion Fall," *Houston Post*, February 24, 1964; "Liston 7–1 Favorite to Button Lip," *Houston Post*, February 25, 1964; Foreman interview.

4. Foreman and Engel, *By George*, 12–13; Foreman interview.

5. William Clayson, *Freedom Is Not Enough: The War on Poverty and the Civil Rights Movement in Texas* (Austin: University of Texas Press, 2010), 13–18.

6. Steinbeck quoted in David G. McComb, *Texas: A Modern History* (Austin: University of Texas Press, 1989), 1; Sean P. Cunningham, *Cowboy Conservatism: Texas and the Rise of the Modern Right* (Lexington: University Press of Kentucky, 2010), 65–67.

7. Lyndon B. Johnson, "The Great Society," *Saturday Evening Post*, October 31, 1964, 30–31, and "Toward the Great Society," *Saturday Evening Post*, November 11, 1964, 84; Gary Smith, "After the Fall," *Sports Illustrated*, October 8, 1984, 67; Foreman and Engel, *By George*, 25–26.

8. Michael L. Gillette, *Launching the War on Poverty: An Oral History* (New York: Oxford University Press, 2010), xi–xiv, 212–234; Clayson, *Freedom Is Not Enough*, 44–45, 59–62.

9. Foreman interview; Clayson, *Freedom Is Not Enough*, 80–97; Foreman and Engel, *By George*, 26–27.

10. Foreman interview.

11. Foreman and Engel, *By George*, 29; Foreman interview.

12. Foreman and Engel, *By George*, 29–32; Foreman interview.

13. Foreman and Engel, *By George*, 31; John D. Fair, *Mr. America: The Tragic History of a Bodybuilding Icon* (Austin: University of Texas Press, 2015), 71–72; Foreman interview.

14. Foreman interview; Othello Harris, "Muhammad Ali and the Revolt of the Black Athlete," in *Muhammad Ali: The People's Champ*, ed. Elliott J. Gorn (Urbana: University of Illinois Press, 1995), 58; Randy Roberts and Johnny Smith, *Blood Brothers: The Fatal Friendship Between Muhammad Ali and Malcolm X* (New York: Basic Books, 2016), 227; George Pasero, "Pasero Says," *Oregon Journal*, November 11, 1965; "Surprise in Store for Floyd," *Oregon Journal*, November 20, 1965; "Clay Rules as 3–1 Choice," *Oregon Journal*, November 22, 1965.

15. Foreman interview; Foreman and Engel, *By George*, 33; *Corpsman*, October 15, 1965, 8; December 25, 1965, 7; February 1, 1966, 2, 9; George Girsch, "Foreman a Gentle Giant," *Ring*, May 1973, 8. The Job Corps changed the title of its newsletter from the *Corpsman* to *Job Corps Happenings* in 1974, and some individual centers published their own regular letters, such as the *Corpsman's Call*, published by the Parks Job Corps Center; see *Job Corps Happenings*, July 1974, 1, for the change of title and the *Corpsman*, May 15, 1966, 7, for a reference to the *Corpsman's Call*.

16. Foreman interview; Foreman and Engel, *By George*, 34.

17. Foreman and Engel, *By George*, 34–35.

18. Foremann interview; Foreman and Engel, *By George*, 35.

19. Foreman and Engel, *By George*, 37–39.

20. *Corpsman*, May 15, 1966, 7; Foreman and Engel, *By George*, 40; Girsch, "Foreman a Gentle Giant," 8; Foreman interview.

21. "Curry Kayoes Fred Hackman," *San Francisco Chronicle*, February 18, 1967.

22. "Raves for Golden Gloves," *Las Vegas Sun*, February 25, 1967; "Boxers Arrive on Schedule," and Ray Grody, "National Gloves Meet Opens Here Tonight," both in *Milwaukee Sentinel*, February 25, 1967; Frank Mastro, "2 Chicagoans Draw Byes in Glove Opener," and "Golden Gloves Results," both in *Milwaukee Sentinel*, February 28, 1967; Foreman and Engel, *By George*, 43.

23. Frank Mastro, "Hodges Heavyweight Champ" and "Wisconsin Blanked in Gloves Tourney," *Milwaukee Sentinel*, March 1, 1967; Foreman and Engel, *By George*, 43.

24. Foreman interview; "Raves for Golden Gloves."

25. Foreman interview; Foreman and Engel, *By George*, 44.

26. Foreman and Engel, *By George*, 44; Foreman interview.

27. "Clay: I'm a Texan," *San Francisco Chronicle*, February 3, 1967; "Clay Refuses to Step Forward" and "U.S. Boxing Authorities Strip Clay of title," *Houston Post*, April 29, 1967; David Remnick, *King of the World: Muhammad Ali and the Rise of an American Hero* (New York: Vintage, 1998), 286–290; Mike Marqusee, *Redemption Song: Muhammad Ali and the Spirit of the Sixties* (New York: Verso, 2005), 218–225; Andrew McGregor, "Ali at Purdue: Reconsidering the Impact and Legacy of his Campus Speeches," *Sport in American History*, February 16, 2017, https://ussporthistory.com/2017/02/16/ali-at-purdue-reconsidering-the-impact-and-legacy-of-his-campus-speeches.

28. Girsch, "Foreman a Gentle Giant," 42; Allen J. Matusow, *The Unravelling of America: A History of Liberalism in the 1960s* (Athens: University of Georgia Press, 2009), 238; Hal Wimberly, "Job Seekers Outnumber Summer Positions Available Here," *Houston Post*, May 7, 1967; Bill Helmer, "A Context for Tragedy," *Texas Observer*, June 9–23, 1967.

29. Foreman interview; Foreman and Engel, *By George*, 45; Marqusee, *Redemption Song*, 225–227.

30. Foreman and Engel, *By George*, 45–47.

31. Robert Self, *American Babylon: Race and the Struggle for Postwar Oakland* (Princeton, NJ: Princeton University Press, 203), 206, 220–223; Peniel Joseph, *Waiting 'Til the Midnight Hour: A Narrative History of Black Power in America* (New York: Holt, 2006), 121–122; Jeffrey O. G. Ogbar, *Black Power: Radical Politics and*

African American Identity (Baltimore: Johns Hopkins University Press, 2004), 118; Yusef Jah and Sister Shah'Keyah, *Uprising: Crips and Bloods Tell the Story of America's Youth in the Crossfire* (New York: Touchstone, 1995), 151–162.

32. Foreman interview.

CHAPTER 3: GOD BLESS THE PUNCHER

1. Yvonne Brathwaite Burke, "Philosophy of George Foreman, Heavyweight Boxing Champion of the World—How the Federal Government Helped Him Get a New Start," *Congressional Record*, April 12, 1973; interviews with George Foreman, in possession of the author, cited as Foreman interview.

2. Foreman interview; George Foreman and Joel Engel, *By George: The Autobiography of George Foreman* (New York: Villard, 1995), 46–47; Burke, "Philosophy of George Foreman."

3. Foreman interview; Foreman and Engel, *By George*, 47–48; Jack Fiske, "The Tube to the Rescue," *San Francisco Chronicle*, February 23, 1968.

4. Foreman interview.

5. Foreman and Engel, *By George*, 48; Foreman interview; "McCoy Fight Part of Shipes Ticket," *Hayward (CA) Daily Review*, January 21, 1968.

6. Dave Taylor, "Mexicali Sub Named Star of Golden Gloves Tourney," *Long Beach Independent Press-Telegram*, February 23, 1964; "Hodges Upsets in Olympic Go," *San Mateo (CA) Times*, May 14, 1964; John Simmonds, "One Oakland Boxer Wins Western Title," *Oakland Tribune*, May 14, 1964; "Slugger, Giant to Battle for Olympic Ring Birth," *Pasadena Star-News*, May 20, 1964; "Hodges Cops Glove Title," *Pasadena Star-News*, March 2, 1967.

7. Larry Whiteside, "Boxer Clay (Hodges) Seeks Crown—And Law Career," *Milwaukee Journal*, March 1, 1967; "RH Dads Club to Present Boxing," *Palos Verdes (CA) Peninsula News*, November 8, 1967; Foreman interview; "The State," *Los Angeles Times*, January 26, 1968.

8. "Shipes KO's Serrano in 1st," *Fremont (CA) Argus*, January 25, 1968; "Clay Hodges Picks Ali," *Palm Springs Desert Sun*, October 25, 1974; Foreman and Engel, *By George*, 49; Foreman interview.

9. "Everybody's Talking about George Foreman in Mexico," *Baltimore Afro-American*, October 15, 1968; Foreman and Engel, *By George*, 50–51; "Akins Up-

sets Hodges in Gloves Semifinals," *Los Angeles Times*, February 26, 1968; "Golden Gloves Goes Wednesday," *Las Vegas Sun*, March 12, 1968; Tom Diskin, "Golden Gloves Action at Center Tonight," *Las Vegas Sun*, March 13, 1968.

10. "Clay Hodges Picks Ali"; Pete Ehrmann, "Heavyweight Clay Hodges: The Man Who Beat George Foreman ... But Lost to Dempsey," *Ring*, April 1995, 64; "Marine Here Wins Gloves Heavy Title," *Honolulu Advertiser*, March 30, 1968.

11. "Kickoff Dinner Slates Promoting AAU Boxing," *Toledo Blade*, March 17, 1968; Foreman interview; Foreman and Engel, *By George*, 51.

12. "Esquibel Advances in Amateur Boxing," *New York Times*, April 11, 1964; "Datelines in Sports," *Los Angeles Times*, April 11, 1964; Paul O'Boynick, "Short Bouts Are Few," *Kansas City Times*, March 24, 1966; Frank Mastro, "Milwaukee's 1st 175-lb. Gloves King," *Chicago Tribune*, March 26, 1966; "Hodges Surprised in Golden Gloves," *Oakland Tribune*, March 26, 1966; "Forest Ward AAU Champ," *Arizona Republic*, April 9, 1967.

13. Jim Taylor, "Nesenson After Fistic Fame," *Toledo Blade*, April 6, 1968; "AAU Ring Champions Move Up," *Oakland Tribune*, April 6, 1968; Jim Taylor, "No Bells, Just Bows for Beeler," *Toledo Blade*, April 7, 1968; "Harris in 3rd AAU Fight Title," *Hayward (CA) Daily Review*, April 7, 1968; Ehrmann, "Heavyweight Clay Hodges," 64; J. J. Pickle, "George Foreman—The Heavyweight Champion, Job Corps Graduate," *Congressional Record*, April 12, 1973.

14. Geoffrey Ciani, "The History of Boxing with Emmanuel Steward, Part IV: Amateur Boxing," *East Side Boxing*, September 2012, eastsideboxing.com/2012/the-history-of-boxing-with-emanuel-steward-part-iv-.

15. Taylor, "No Bells, Just Bows"; "Mike Quarry, Hodges Head Amateur Card," *Los Angeles Times*, April 15, 1968; "Liston Back in Ring," *San Francisco Chronicle*, March 16, 1968; "U.S. Boxing Team to Face Germans," *Fort Myers (FL) News-Press*, August 12, 1968; John Hall, "The Police Olympics," *Los Angeles Times*, September 13, 1968.

16. "Boxers Defeat Yankee Squad," *Fresno Bee*, August 17, 1968; Foreman and Engel, *By George*, 51; Foreman interview.

17. "Marine Boxer Nears Olympic Team Berth," *Newport (RI) Daily News*, September 6, 1968; "Olympic Boxing Self Supporting," *Albuquerque Journal*, September 20, 1968.

18. "Marine Here Wins Gloves Heavy Title"; "George Foreman," OTOHP, transcript of interview, January 16, 2013; "Area Boxers' Bids Fail," *Pittsburgh Post-*

Gazette, September 7, 1968; Girsch, 8; "Job Corps Heavy Step from Games," *Oakland Tribune*, September 6, 1968; "Local Heavy Trials King," *Oakland Tribune*, September 8, 1968.

19. "Boxers Follow Tough Conditioning Period," *Santa Fe New Mexican*, September 10, 1968; Judy Jones, "Sweatshop Hours for Olympic Boxers," *Albuquerque Journal*, September 15, 1968; "Boxing Team Members Are Unofficial," *Santa Fe New Mexican*, September 23, 1968; Ben Moffett, "Boxers Repeat Wins," *Albuquerque Journal*, September 22, 1968; Foreman and Engel, *By George*, 52.

20. Foreman interview; Gilbert Rogin, "George Has the Rhyme, Pappy Has the Reason," *Sports Illustrated*, October 7, 1968, 74–75; Jones, "Sweatshop Hours for Olympic Boxers"; "Al Jones," OTOHP, transcript of interview, November 2, 2007; Sam Lacy, "Ring Coach Undismayed by Low Regard for Team," *Baltimore Afro-American*, October 22, 1968.

21. Foreman interview.

22. Rogin, "George Has the Rhyme," 74–75; Foreman interview; Andrew R. M. Smith, "Sculpting George Foreman: A Soul Era Champion in the Golden Age of Black Heavyweights," *Journal of Sport History* 40, no. 3 (2013): 456–457.

23. A. Smith, "Sculpting George Foreman," 457; Rogin, "George Has the Rhyme," 74–75; Harry Edwards, *Revolt of the Black Athlete* (New York: Free Press, 1969), 80–89; Andrew McGregor, "Ali at Purdue: Reconsidering the Impact and Legacy of his Campus Speeches," *Sport in American History*, February 16, 2017, https://ussporthistory.com/2017/02/16/ali-at-purdue-reconsidering-the-impact -and-legacy-of-his-campus-speeches; Othello Harris, "Muhammad Ali and the Revolt of the Black Athlete," in *Muhammad Ali: The People's Champ*, ed. Elliott J. Gorn (Urbana: University of Illinois Press, 1995), 54–69.

24. "Addresses of President Avery Brundage at Solemn Openings of I.O.C. Sessions Between 1952 and 1968," *Collected Speeches of President Avery Brundage, 1952–1968* (International Olympic Committee, 1969); Avery Brundage to Dr. George G. Tan, September 24, 1968; Brundage to Patricia Rylane, April 11, 1968; Brundage to IOC Members, memo, April 24, 1968; Brundage to A. de Las Alas, March 28, 1966; Brundage to Jozef Rutkowski, March 27, 1968; Brundage to M. Obeidullah, August 19, 1965, all correspondence in ABC; Allen Guttmann, *The Games Must Go On: Avery Brundage and the Olympic Movement* (New York: Columbia University Press, 1984), 234–235; John Matthew Smith, "It's Not Really My Country: Lew Alcindor and the Revolt of the Black Athlete," *Journal of Sport History* 36, no. 2 (2009): 223–244; Dexter Blackman, "African Americans, Pan-Africanism, and the Anti-Apartheid Campaign to Expel South Africa from

the 1968 Olympics," *Journal of Pan African Studies* 5, no. 3 (2012): 1–25; Edwards, *Revolt of the Black Athlete*, 98–100; Tommie Smith and David Steele, *Silent Gesture: The Autobiography of Tommie Smith* (Philadelphia: Temple University Press, 2007), 166–167; Frank Murphy, *The Last Protest: Lee Evans in Mexico City* (Kansas City, MO: Windsprint, 2006), 139–141.

25. Foreman and Engel, *By George*, 55; Rogin, "George Has the Rhyme," 74–75; "George Foreman" and "Al Jones," OTOHP.

26. Foreman interview; "Al Jones," OTOHP; "Yugoslavia Upsets Russia in Olympics," *Santa Fe New Mexican*, October 23, 1968; "Amateur Athletics to Be Studied," *Santa Fe New Mexican*, October 24, 1968.

27. "Al Jones," OTOHP; Foreman interview.

28. Foreman interview; "Foreman, Hall, Davenport Winners," *Chicago Defender*, October 17, 1968; Foreman and Engel, *By George*, 56.

29. "Clay Hodges Loses," *Long Beach Press Telegram*, October 24, 1967; Foreman and Engel, *By George*, 57.

30. "Everybody's Talking about George Foreman"; Austin Murphy, "Where Are They Now: John Carlos," *Sports Illustrated*, July 14, 2008, 84–86; Smith and Steele, *Silent Gesture*, 164–165; "George Foreman," OTOHP.

31. Alan Hubbard, "Finnegan's Rainbow," in *Official Report of the Olympic Games 1968*, ed. Bob Phillips (London: World Sports, 1968), 43–45, ABC; Foreman and Engel, *By George*, 59.

32. "Mexico 68 News Bulletin 74," OCG 19, August 19, 1968, 74 (Mexico City); "Mexico 68 News Bulletin 75," OCG 19, August 27, 1968; *The Story of the Olympics and Mexico; Souvenir of the Nineteenth Olympiad, Mexico 1968*, Woolworths National Olympic Foundation (Australia: Evan-Keegan, 1968), 53, all in ABC.

33. "Gold Medal Boxer Joins 'Anthem' Sing in Mexico," *Baltimore Afro-American*, October 29, 1968; Bob Ottum, "Fresh, Fair and Golden," *Sports Illustrated*, November 4, 1968, 27; Foreman interview; A. Smith, "Sculpting George Foreman," 457.

CHAPTER 4: EATIN' MONEY

1. Howard Cosell, *Cosell* (Chicago: Playboy, 1973), 64; "Mexico: The Problem Olympics," *Sports Illustrated*, September 30, 1968, cover; "Olympians Wave Farewell; U.S. Captures Team Title," *Chicago Defender*, October 28, 1968; Avery Brundage to Erie Jones, February 22, 1965, and "Here's A Way for the Olympics

to 'Go Dutch,'" unidentified newspaper clipping, April 14, 1959, both in ABC; interviews with George Foreman, in possession of the author, cited as Foreman interview.

2. Harry Edwards, *Revolt of the Black Athlete* (New York: Free Press, 1969), 4; A. S. Young, "The Week's Wash," *Chicago Defender*, November 13, 1968; Ralph Ray, "Black Power Unleashed on the Sports Front," *Sporting News*, October 4, 1969, 22; Brad Pye, "Olympics No Platform for Problems," *Los Angeles Sentinel*, October 24, 1968; Booker Griffin, "Some Untold Tales of Mexico City," *Los Angeles Sentinel*, October 24, 1968; John Hall, "Foreman's Fan Club," *Los Angeles Times*, November 6, 1968.

3. George Foreman and Joel Engel, *By George: The Autobiography of George Foreman* (New York: Villard, 1995), 60; "Says Flag-Waving Wasn't Against Black Power," *Jet*, December 19, 1968; "Gold Medal Boxer Joins 'Anthem' Sing in Mexico," *Baltimore Afro-American*, October 29, 1968; "For the Presidents Night Reading," October 28, 1968, LBJL; Foreman interview.

4. Foreman interview; George Christian to Jim Jones, memo, October 29, 1968, and "Job Corps' First Award of Achievement Goes to Olympic Champ Foreman," October 31, 1968, both in LBJL.

5. Transcript of the Nixon rally at Madison Square Garden, October 31, 1968, available at "Protests, Rallies, Demonstrations," Pacifica Radio Archives, https://www.pacificaradioarchives.org/sites/default/files/images/nixon_rally.pdf; Bob McElwaine to Juanita Roberts, October 23, 1968; Juanita Roberts to Lyndon Johnson, memo, October 24, 1968; Jim Jones to Bob McElwaine, October 25, 1968; Christian to Jones, memo, October 29, 1968; Jim Jones to Lyndon Johnson, memo, October 30, 1968; and photograph with attachments, "Inscribed 'To George Foreman, with best wishes,'" December 18, 1968, all in LBJL; Foreman and Engel, *By George*, 61.

6. Foreman interview; Foreman and Engel, *By George*, 60–61; Gary Cartwright, "How Foreman Finally Beat Ali," *Texas Monthly*, September 1989, 172.

7. Foreman interview; Foreman and Engel, *By George*, 61–63.

8. Foreman interview; Foreman and Engel, *By George*, 63–64; Gay Talese, "Floyd Patterson," Pete Hamill, "Up the Stairs with Cus D'Amato," and David Remnick, "Kid Dynamite Blows Up: Mike Tyson," all in *At The Fights: American Writers on Boxing*, ed. George Kimball and John Schulian (New York: Library of America, 2012), 159, 313, 439.

9. Nat Loubet, "Foreman, 19, Aspires to Success as Pro Champ," *Ring*, February 1969, 10–12, 36; Foreman interview; Paul Delaney, "Job Corps, Its Funds Reduced,

Is Facing an Uncertain Future," *New York Times*, December 25, 1971; Carl Lieberman, "Legislative Success and Failure: The Social Welfare Policies of the Nixon Administration," in *Richard M. Nixon: Politician, President, Administrator*, ed. Leon Friedman and William F. Levantrosser (New York: Greenwood, 1991), 107–110; Judith Sealander, *The Failed Century of the Child: Governing America's Young in the Twentieth Century* (New York: Cambridge University Press, 2003), 168.

10. Foreman interview; Foreman and Engel, *By George*, 65.

11. Foreman interview; Randy Roberts, *Jack Dempsey: The Manassa Mauler* (1979; repr., Urbana: University of Illinois Press, 2003), 36–41; Foreman and Engel, *By George*, 66.

12. Foreman interview; Foreman and Engel, *By George*, 66–71.

13. Dave Newhouse, "Sadler, Famed Ring Trainer, Dies at 88," *Oakland Tribune*, June 5, 2003; "Dick Sadler: The Amazing Man behind Foreman," *Boxing Illustrated*, June 1973, 17–19.

14. Foreman interview; Foreman and Engel, *By George*, 71–72.

15. "Foreman to Make Pro Debut on Frazier-Quarry Program," *Chicago Defender*, June 10, 1969; "Foreman Turns Pro," *Chicago Defender*, June 12, 1969; "Frazier, Quarry Taper Off for Monday Battle," *Chicago Defender*, June 17, 1969; "Will George Foreman Steal NY Title Show," *Los Angeles Sentinel*, June 19, 1969; "Quarry Outclassed, Frazier Top Contender," *Ring*, September 1969, 41; Andrew R. M. Smith, "Sculpting George Foreman: A Soul Era Champion in the Golden Age of Black Heavyweights," *Journal of Sport History* 40, no. 3 (2013): 458. For a photograph, see *Chicago Defender*, June 18, 1969, 32.

16. Foreman interview; Nick Tosches, *The Devil and Sonny Liston* (New York: Little, Brown, 2000), 132–133.

17. Foreman interview; Richard Hoffer, *Bouts of Mania: Ali, Frazier, Foreman, and an America on the Ropes* (Boston: Da Capo, 2014), 25.

18. "Foreman Finishes Vernon Clay in 2D," *New York Times*, October 8, 1969; Deane McGowen, "Foreman Beats Davila for No. 8," *New York Times*, November 1, 1969; Harlan Haas, "Liston Fat at 226, but Moore Goes Out in Third," *Ring*, January 1970, 54.

19. Nat Loubet, "Foreman-Davila Goes Eight," *Ring*, February 1970, 28, 57; "Foreman Connects," *Pittsburgh Courier*, November 8, 1969; William Verigan, "Even Ref Went to Sleep says Ali of All-Stars," *Baltimore Afro-American*, November 4, 1969; A. Smith, "Sculpting George Foreman," 459.

20. Shaun Assael, *The Murder of Sonny Liston: Las Vegas, Heroin, and Heavyweights* (New York: Penguin, 2016), 83–85.

21. Foreman and Engel, *By George*, 70; Assael, *Murder of Sonny Liston*, 21–22, 85–87; Foreman interview.

22. Foreman interview; "Powell Stopper in 10th Battle," *Reno Gazette-Journal*, September 3, 1954.

23. Foreman interview; Michael Ezra, *Muhammad Ali: The Making of an Icon* (Philadelphia: Temple University Press, 2009), 45; George Main, "Anonymous Bets $5000 on Moore Win," *Los Angeles Herald-Examiner*, November 9, 1962, and "Grim Archie Set Now," *Los Angeles Herald-Examiner*, November 11, 1962; Melvin Durslag, "$75,000 Worth of Insults," *Los Angeles Herald-Examiner*, November 12, 1962; Sam Balter, "Clay in Four? Don't Ever Sell Amazing Archie Short," *Los Angeles Herald-Examiner*, November 13, 1962; George Main, "Clay Holds at 2–1 to Overpower Foe," *Los Angeles Herald-Examiner*, November 14, 1962; Melvin Durslag, "Too Many Conned By Cassius," *Los Angeles Herald-Examiner*, November 15, 1962.

24. Foreman interview. For the IBC era in boxing, see Steven A. Riess, "Only the Ring Was Square: Frankie Carbo and the Underworld Control of Boxing," *International Journal of the History of Sport* 5, no. 1 (1988): 29–52; Jeffrey T. Sammons, *Beyond the Ring: The Role of Boxing in American Society* (Urbana: University of Illinois Press, 1990), 137–175; and Barney Nagler, *James Norris and the Decline of Boxing* (New York: Bobbs-Merrill, 1964).

25. Anthony Marenghi, "Frazier 4–1 Choice to Beat Ellis," *Newark Star-Ledger*, February 3, 1970, and "Frazier, Ellis Meet Tonight," *Newark Star-Ledger*, February 16, 1970; Jerry Izenberg, "Night of Nights," *Newark Star-Ledger*, February 16, 1970.

26. Bob Decker, "Foreman Still Unbeaten on Unpopular Decision," *Newark Star-Ledger*, February 17, 1970; Deane McGowen, "Foreman Takes 16th in Row, Beating Peralta; Verdict Booed," *New York Times*, February 17, 1970; "They Booed," *New York Amsterdam News*, February 21, 1970; "Foreman Still Undefeated," *Chicago Defender*, February 21, 1970; Wilfrid Sheed, "TV Talk," *Sports Illustrated*, March 9, 1970, 7; Howard Cosell, "Cosellisms," *Sports Illustrated*, March 30, 1970, 83–84.

27. Anthony Marenghi, "Who's Left for Frazier," *Newark Star-Ledger*, February 18, 1970; Jerry Izenberg, "The Other Fight," *Newark Star-Ledger*, February 19, 1970; Deane McGowen, "Woody Is Stopped by Foreman in 3D," *New York Times*, April 18, 1970; "George Foreman Whips Woody for 18th Victory," *Atlanta Daily World*, April 29, 1970; "Foreman Wins with Quick KO," *Oakland Tribune*, July 21, 1970; Hank Hollingsworth, "Foreman KO's Scrap; Cruz Thrashes Rose," *Long Beach Press-Telegram*, May 17, 1970; "Scrap Iron Halted," *Los Angeles Senti-*

nel, May 21, 1970; Sheed, "TV Talk," 7; "Boxing's Young Lions—Who Are They?," *Ring,* April 1970, 23; Jersey Jones, "New York's Month That Was," *Ring,* May 1970, 20; "Fight Strategy," *Hayward (CA) Daily Review,* July 14, 1969; "Foreman Scores KO," *Hayward (CA) Daily Review,* November 6, 1969; "Wednesday's Fights," *Long Beach Press-Telegram,* November 6, 1969; Foreman and Engel, *By George,* 72–75.

28. Thomas Hauser, *The Black Lights: Inside the World of Professional Boxing* (New York: McGraw-Hill, 1986), 83; Mays Andrews, "Does Foreman Compare with Joe?," *Los Angeles Sentinel,* May 28, 1970; "Foreman Rolls On; Joe Frazier a Long Way Off," *Atlanta Daily World,* August 2, 1970; Loubet, "Foreman-Davila Goes Eight," 57; "Frazier Undisputed Champ," *Ring,* May 1970, 9; "How Good is Foreman?," *Boxing Illustrated,* 15, 60–61.

CHAPTER 5: SCULPTING GEORGE FOREMAN

1. Michael Brennan, "Voices From His Past," *Sports Illustrated,* March 25, 1991, 74 (emphasis added).

2. Mark Kram, "Have a Piece of Georgie Boy," *Sports Illustrated,* July 31, 1967, 26; Jerry Glick, "George Chuvalo: 'The Toughest of the Tough,'" SecondsOut, December 1, 2010, secondsout.com/columns/jerry-glick/george-chuvalo-the -toughest-of-the-tough; George Chuvalo, *Chuvalo: A Fighter's Life; The Story of Boxing's Last Gladiator,* with Murray Greig (Toronto: HarperCollins, 2013), 194–195, 225–227; "Foreman Set for Chuvalo in Garden Match," *Newark Star-Ledger,* August 3, 1970.

3. Interviews with George Foreman, in possession of the author, cited as Foreman interview; Chuvalo, *Chuvalo,* 233–235; *The Last Round: Chuvalo vs. Ali,* dir. Joseph Blalioli (National Film Board of Canada, 2003); Anthony Marenghi, "Foreman Beats Chuvalo; Ref Stops it at 1:41 of 3d," *Newark Star-Ledger,* August 5, 1970; George Girsch, "Foreman KO Points Chuvalo to Exit," *Ring,* November 1970, 36.

4. Anthony Marenghi, "Foreman Solid Favorite to Defeat Vet Chuvalo," *Newark Star-Ledger* August 4, 1970, and "Foreman Beats Chuvalo"; John Matthew Smith, "The Resurrection: Atlanta, Racial Politics, and the Return of Muhammad Ali," *Southern Cultures* 21, no. 2 (2015): 18–24.

5. Chuvalo, *Chuvalo,* 236.

6. Chuvalo, *Chuvalo,* 236–237; Andrew R. M. Smith, "Sculpting George Foreman: A Soul Era Champion in the Golden Age of Black Heavyweights," *Journal of Sport History* 40, no. 3 (2013): 459–460; Marenghi, "Foreman Beats Chuvalo"; Dan

Daniel, "Here Comes Foreman," *Ring*, November 1970, 7; Les Mathews, "Foreman Ready for Frazier," *New York Amsterdam News*, August 8, 1970; Martin Kane, "Salute the Grand Old Flag Raiser George F.," *Sports Illustrated*, August 17, 1970, 56–57; Dave Anderson, "Assault to Head Shakes Canadian," *New York Times*, August 5, 1970, 27; Robert Lipsyte, "George," *New York Times*, August 6, 1970.

7. Foreman interview; Anderson, "Assault to Head Shakes Canadian"; Kane, "Salute the Grand Old Flag Raiser," 57; Girsch, "Foreman KO," 36.

8. Kane, "Salute the Grand Old Flag Raiser," 57; Bob Goodman, "Dangerous Duo Elder, Matthews Vie for Shot at Heavy Crown," *Ring*, October 1970, 36.

9. Brad Pye, "Frazier-Foster Fight for Brotherhood," *Los Angeles Sentinel*, November 12, 1970; "Hurley Picks Kirkman to KO Foreman," *Chicago Defender*, October 31, 1970, 29; Jack D. Hopkins, "Jack Hurley—Last of the Old Breed," *Boxing Illustrated*, June 1968, 36–37; Jack D. Hopkins, "Look Out Frazier—Kirkman's Back!," *Boxing Illustrated*, July 1970, 18.

10. A. Smith, "Sculpting George Foreman," 461; "Garden Offers Live, TV Fights Nov. 18," *New York Times*, October 20, 1970; "TNT Slates Boxing's 1st Double Card," *Chicago Defender*, October 20, 1970; "Joe Frazier Set for First Title Defense Tonight," *Chicago Defender*, November 18, 1970; "Foreman Fights Kirkman Tonight," *New York Times*, November 18, 1970; Mike Weber, "Foreman TKO Boosts Record to 24 in Row," *Newark Star-Ledger*, November 19, 1970; Nat Fleischer, "Nat Fleischer Speaks Out," *Ring*, March 1971, 5; "2d Smallest Title Crowd," *Newark Star-Ledger*, November 19, 1970; Pat Putnam, "One Round of Boxing Was More than Enough," *Sports Illustrated*, November 30, 1970, 20–21; Marshall Reed, "Foreman Lowers 'The Boone,'" *Boxing Illustrated*, February 1971, 21, 61.

11. Weber, "Foreman TKO"; Reed, "Foreman Lowers 'The Boone,'" 61; Nat Loubet, "Vaunted Kirkman Reduced to Myth by Foreman in 2," *Ring*, February 1971, 12–13; Dan Daniel, "Jack Hurley, 1897–1972," *Ring*, February 1973, 25; Dan Daniel, "Is Foreman Ready for Frazier?," *Ring*, May 1972, 9.

12. George Foreman and Joel Engel, *By George: The Autobiography of George Foreman* (New York: Villard, 1995), 76; Weber, "Foreman TKO"; Loubet, "Kirkman Reduced to Myth," 12; Fleischer, "Fleischer Speaks Out," March 1971, 5; "Jess Peters, "Jess' Sports Chest," *Pittsburgh Courier*, November 28, 1970; Arthur Daley, "A Destructive Fighter," *New York Times*, November 20, 1970.

13. Foreman and Engel, *By George*, 74; George Blair, "Foreman Scores K.O. But . . . Who Was That Other Guy?," *Boxing Illustrated*, May 1971, 10; "Foreman KO's Mystery Opponent, Crowd Boos," *Chicago Defender*, February 11, 1971; "WBA Picks Foreman," *Pittsburgh Courier*, February 20, 1971.

14. Michael Arkush, *The Fight of the Century: Ali vs. Frazier, March 8, 1971*

(Hoboken, NJ: Wiley, 2008), 118–128; Claude E. Harrison, "Ain't No Fight Worth $250," *Philadelphia Tribune*, December 26, 1970.

15. A. Smith, "Sculpting George Foreman," 462–463; David Remnick, *King of the World: Muhammad Ali and the Rise of an American Hero* (New York: Vintage, 1998), 213, 305; Thomas Hauser, *Muhammad Ali: His Life and Times* (New York: Simon & Schuster, 1991), 102; "Frazier Pays a Bill," *Chicago Defender*, January 15, 1972; Lee Jenkins, "Frazier Choice to Whip Ali," *Chicago Defender*, March 8, 1971. For the complete poem, see Gwendolyn Brooks, "Black Steel: Joe Frazier and Muhammad Ali" (Detroit: Broadside Press, 1971), in NUSC; for the fight program, see "Professional Boxing Programs," JSRC.

16. Brad Pye, "Prying Pye," *Los Angeles Sentinel*, November 12, 1970; Thomas Hauser, *Boxing Is . . . Reflections on the Sweet Science* (Fayetteville: University of Arkansas Press, 2010), 88; Mel Ciociola, "The Story behind the Commercial of the Century," *Boxing Illustrated*, July 1971, 26–27; *Facing Ali*, dir. Pete McCormack (Lions Gate, 2009).

17. A. Smith, "Sculpting George Foreman," 462; Jeffrey O. G. Ogbar, *Black Power: Radical Politics and African American Identity* (Baltimore: Johns Hopkins University Press, 2004), 118–119; Amy Abugo Ongiri, *Spectacular Blackness: The Cultural Politics of the Black Power Movement and the Search for a Black Aesthetic* (Charlottesville: University of Virginia Press, 2010), 52–53; Foreman and Engel, *By George*, 79; Edwin Keister Jr., "The Walt Frazier Style," *Sport*, March 1971, 62–69; Jerry Kirshenbaum, "And Still a Classic of Cool," *Sports Illustrated*, February 10, 1975, 22–25; Harvey Araton, *When the Garden Was Eden: Clyde, the Captain, Dollar Bill, and the Glory Days of the New York Knicks* (New York: HarperCollins, 2011), 223–239; Robin D. G. Kelley, *Yo Mama's Disfunktional! Fighting the Culture Wars in Urban America* (Boston: Beacon, 1997), 25–32.

18. Foreman and Engel, *By George*, 79, 100; Richard Majors, "Cool Pose: Black Masculinity and Sport," in *Critical Perspectives on Sport, Men, and Masculinity*, ed. Michael A. Messner and Donald F. Sabo (Champaign, IL: Human Kinetics, 1990), 120–142; Walt Frazier and Ira Berkow, *Rockin' Steady: A Guide to Basketball and Cool* (Englewood Cliffs, NJ: Prentice Hall, 1974), 11–20.

19. William L. Van Deburg, *Black Camelot: African American Culture Heroes in Their Times, 1960–1980* (Chicago: University of Chicago Press, 1997), 74; "Fight Will Be Uptown," *New York Amsterdam News*, March 6, 1971; "Foreman Pulls Modest Switch: Challenges Ali-Frazier Loser," *New York Times*, March 9, 1971; Foreman interview.

20. Arkush, *Fight of the Century*, 190; Dave Anderson, "Target Date Set for Feb. 15 or 22," *New York Times*, December 9, 1970; Les Matthews, "Champ Joe Frazier

May Hang Up Gloves," *New York Amsterdam News*, March 13, 1971; Bryant Gumbel, "Is Joe Frazier a White Champion in a Black Skin?," *Boxing Illustrated*, October 1972, cover; Phil Pepe, *Come Out Smokin': Joe Frazier, the Champ Nobody Knew* (New York: Coward, McCann & Geoghegan, 1972), 130–134; "No. 1 Contender Downs Ali-Frazier Fight," *Jet*, April 29, 1971, 50; Robert E. Johnson, "World's Biggest Event Brings Mixed Reactions," *Jet*, March 25, 1971, 12–14; George Foreman, "Frazier's Ready to Be Taken," *Boxing Illustrated*, June 1971, 12–13.

21. Ted Carroll, "Take Charge Sadler Tells Foreman," *Ring*, June 1971, 26; A. Smith, "Sculpting George Foreman," 461–463; Arkush, *Fight of the Century*, 118; Thomas Hauser, *Winks and Daggers: An Inside Look at Another Year in Boxing* (Fayetteville: University of Arkansas Press, 2011), 161; "Sadler's Dawn and Dusk; George Foreman, Liston," *Chicago Defender*, October 30, 1969.

22. Foreman interview; "Foreman Stops Harris in Second," *New York Times*, April 4, 1971; "Playboy Czar Hosts Feast and Fisticuffs; Foreman Wins 27th in Row," *Jet*, April 22, 1971, 51.

23. Nolan Zavoral, "Ali a Champion with UWM Students," *Milwaukee Journal*, April 1, 1971; Arlen Boardman, "Ali's Wit as Quick as His Punches," *Appleton (WI) Post-Crescent*, April 2, 1971; "Frazier Has Rock Group," *Palm Springs Desert Sun*, March 26, 1971; "People Are Talking About," *Jet*, April 8, 1971, 42; Ozeil Fryer Woodcock, "Social Swirl," *Atlanta Daily World*, March 21, 1971. Photos of Foreman's training appear in the *New York Amsterdam News*, December 19, 1970, 51, and in *Jet*, January 7, 1971, 36.

24. Leslie Matthews, "The Sports Whirl," *New York Amsterdam News*, April 24, 1971; Nat Fleischer, "Nat Fleischer Speaks Out," *Ring*, August 1971, 5; "Tripleheader was Fistic and Financial Failure," *Ring*, August 1971, 10–11.

25. Foreman interview; "Foreman's Pilot Manager of the Year," *Atlanta Daily World*, June 27, 1971; Dave Anderson, "Boxing Dinner: 3 Get Awards, Foreman Gets Fiscal Offer," *New York Times*, June 27, 1971; Earl Wilson, "Ageless Joan Rivers Still Wondering," *Hartford Courant*, February 9, 1970; "Incentive for Bodell," *Guardian*, November 15, 1971.

26. Foreman and Engel, *By George*, 78–79; Mike Freeman, *Jim Brown: The Fierce Life of an American Hero* (New York: HarperCollins, 2006), 16, 165–169; "Jim Brown Fined $300 for Pushing Deputy," *Los Angeles Sentinel*, January 9, 1969; "Walt Frazier: His Sex Image and His Lifestyle," *Jet*, April 4, 1974, 52; Keister, "Walt Frazier Style," 63–65.

27. Foreman and Engel, *By George*, 79–80; A. Smith, "Sculpting George Foreman," 463; Van Deburg, *Black Camelot*, 153–154; Ed Guerrero, *Framing Blackness:*

The African American Image in Film (Philadelphia: Temple University Press, 1993), 74–79; Keith Harris, *Boys, Boyz, Bois: An Ethics of Black Masculinity in Film and Popular Media* (New York: Routledge, 2006), x, 60; Novotny Lawrence, *Blaxploitation Films of the 1970s: Blackness and Genre* (New York: Routledge, 2008), 18–25, 38; *Baadasssss Cinema—A Bold Look at 70's Blaxploitation Films*, dir. Isaac Julien (Independent Film Channel, 2002); Richard Iton, *In Search of the Black Fantastic: Politics and Popular Culture in the Post-Civil Rights Era* (New York: Oxford University Press, 2008), 104–105.

28. Floyd Patterson, "What Now, Heavyweights?," *Boxing Illustrated*, June 1971, 22; Dan Daniel, "Is George Foreman Next Champ?," *Ring*, July 1971, 6–7; Les Matthews, "Will Ali Befriend Jerry Quarry?," *New York Amsterdam News*, July 31, 1971; "Pires Suffers Broken Elbow," *New York Times*, October 31, 1971; Les Matthews, "Foreman Is Star Material," *New York Amsterdam News*, November 13, 1971; "It Was a Good Workout for Ali," *Boxing Illustrated*, October 1971, 48; Foreman interview.

CHAPTER 6: BETTER MUST COME

1. Dan Daniel, "NY Garden Paralyzed by Intolerable Tax," *Ring*, December 1971, 18–19; "Frazier Tours Europe," *Chicago Defender*, May 3, 1971; Bert Sugar, "Boxing Can Learn from Football," *Boxing Illustrated*, May 1972, 6. On the golden age of heavyweight boxing in this period, see Ira Berkow, "Memorable, Forgettable, and Others," *New York Times*, January 1, 1991; Lennox Lewis quoted in Thomas Hauser, *A Beautiful Sickness: Reflections on the Sweet Science* (Fayetteville: University of Arkansas Press, 2001), 22; Richard Hoffer, *Bouts of Mania: Ali, Frazier, Foreman, and an America on the Ropes* (Boston: Da Capo, 2014); and Jerry Izenberg, *Once There Were Giants: The Golden Age of Heavyweight Boxing* (New York: Skyhorse, 2017).

2. Randy Roberts and Andrew R. M. Smith, "The Report of My Death Was an Exaggeration: The Many Sordid Lives of America's Bloodiest 'Pastime,'" *International Journal of the History of Sport* 31, nos. 1–2 (2014): 80; Michael Arkush, *The Fight of the Century: Ali vs. Frazier, March 8, 1971* (Hoboken, NJ: Wiley, 2008), 175–178; Jeffrey T. Sammons, *Beyond the Ring: The Role of Boxing in American Society* (Urbana: University of Illinois Press, 1990), 96.

3. Nat Fleischer, "Nat Fleischer Says," *Ring*, August 1971, 5; Nat Loubet, "Roundup of the Year," *Ring*, March 1972, 16; Dave Anderson, "State Tax Jeopardizes Garden Boxing," *New York Times*, March 29, 1972.

4. Gilbert Rogin, "Mr. Boxing Himself," *Sports Illustrated*, August 6, 1962, 54–

60; Dan Daniel, "Fate: Appointments With Destiny," *Ring*, March 1972, 38; Steven Riess, "Professional Boxing in New York," in *Sport in America: New Historical Perspectives*, ed. Donald Spivey (Westport, CT: Greenwood, 1985), 124; Nigel Collins, "The History of a Boxing Institution," RingTV.com, November 12, 2008 (article no longer available); Monte Cox, "Nat Fleischer, Mr. Boxing," *Wail!*, July 2006, Cyber Boxing Zone, cyberboxingzone.com/boxing/0001-cox.html.

5. Don Dunphy, "Recalling Johnny Addie," *Boxing Illustrated*, June 1972, 32–33; "Johnny Addie, 69, Announcer at Garden Boxing Bouts, Dead," *New York Times*, December 21, 1971; Nat Fleischer, "Federal Income Bite of 30 Percent on Foreigners Adds to Promoters Woes," *Ring*, February 1972, 17; Dan Daniel, "Frazier-Clay Rancors Peril Second Meeting," *Ring*, April 1972, 38; Nat Fleischer, "NY Economy Drive Hits Dooley Staff," *Ring*, April 1972, 35; Daniel, "Fate," 40; "Nat Fleischer, 84, Dead; Was Sports 'Mr. Boxing,'" *New York Times*, June 26, 1972; "Nat Fleischer Dies at 84," *New York Times*, June 26, 1972.

6. Daniel, "Fate," 50; Andrew R. M. Smith, "Sculpting George Foreman: A Soul Era Champion in the Golden Age of Black Heavyweights," *Journal of Sport History* 40, no. 3 (2013): 456.

7. "Muhammad Ali, Bob Foster Win over Quarry Brothers," *Atlanta Daily World*, June 30, 1972; Brad Pye, "Muhammad Ali Is a Merciful Man," *Los Angeles Sentinel*, June 29, 1972; "Ali Turns LA People On," *Los Angeles Sentinel*, June 29, 1971; "Ali Chants: I Want Frazier," *Las Vegas Sun*, June 29, 1972; Mark Kram and Tex Maule, "Agony and Ecstasy," *Sports Illustrated*, July 10, 1972, 16–17; Matthew Henry, "He Is a 'Bad Mother *$%@!#': 'Shaft' and Contemporary Black Masculinity," *African American History Review* 38, no. 1 (2004): 114–119; Robin D. G. Kelley, *Yo Mama's Disfunktional! Fighting the Culture Wars in Urban America* (Boston: Beacon, 1997), 24-25; A. Smith, "Sculpting George Foreman," 464.

8. "Ali Chants: I Want Frazier"; Lester Bromberg, "Lester Bromberg Sez," *Boxing Illustrated*, December 1971, 18–20; Dan Daniel, "Is Foreman Ready for Frazier," *Ring*, May 1972, 8–9; Jack Gallagher, "Foreman Counts His Blessings," *Houston Post*, August 27, 1972; "Insiders Say," *Sporting News*, May 30, 1970, 4; Sybil Leek, "Frazier-Ali," *Boxing Illustrated*, June 1972, 19; Phil Pepe, *Come Out Smokin': Joe Frazier, the Champ Nobody Knew* (New York: Coward, McCann & Geoghegan, 1972), 130, 215–217; Daniel, "Frazier-Clay Rancors," 11; Nat Fleischer, "Nat Fleischer Speaks Out," *Ring*, May 1972, 5.

9. "Oklahoma Takes Title from Frazier," *New York Times*, July 7, 1972; Red Smith, "Oklahoma? Where's That At?," *New York Times*, July 12, 1972; "Jolts & Jabs," *Boxing Illustrated*, October 1972, 6; Norman Unger, "Smokin' Joe May Lose

His Crown," *Chicago Defender*, July 10, 1972; Martin Kane, "The Tide Turns for Sam," *Sports Illustrated*, August 21, 1972, 9–10.

10. "Frazier vs. Foreman?," *Chicago Defender*, July 11, 1972; "Personalities: Back in Groove," *New York Times*, July 12, 1972; "Frazier Offered $500,000," *Pittsburgh Courier*, July 22, 1972; "Frazier Gets $50,000 [*sic*] Offer from Foreman," *Atlanta Daily World*, July 27, 1972; "Frazier May Fight Foreman," *Palm Springs Desert Sun*, August 17, 1972; "Frazier Mulls $750,000 Offer to Fight Foreman," *Jet*, October 19, 1972, 50; Steve Cady, "Personalities: Frazier May Box Foreman," *New York Times*, August 18, 1972; Claude E. Harrison Jr., "Heavyweight Claims He Is Logical Contender for Frazier's Crown," *Philadelphia Tribune*, September 9, 1972; "Frazier-Foreman . . . Is Bushed," *Baltimore Sun*, September 9, 1972; "750-G's for Joe Frazier?," *Chicago Defender*, October 4, 1972; "Frazier Offer Upped 50-Grand," *Chicago Defender*, October 11, 1972.

11. Daniel, "Frazier-Clay Rancors," 38; Dan Daniel, "Ali-Patterson Fiasco Over, N.Y. Garden Studies Rich Vein of Frazier-Foreman," *Ring*, December 1972, 8–9; David McComb, *Spare Time in Texas: Recreation and History in the Lone Star State* (Austin: University of Texas Press, 2008), 94–95.

12. Interviews with George Foreman, in possession of the author, cited as Foreman interview; Daniel, "Is Foreman Ready for Frazier," 9; "Foreman Files Suit," *Chicago Defender*, October 21, 1972; "The Sports Log," *Boston Globe*, October 26, 1972; "Foreman Sues for $11 million," *New York Times*, October 18, 1972; "Foreman's Stalling on Middleton Fight May Result in Ban," *Houston Post*, October 28, 1972; "Suit Names Foreman," *Chicago Defender*, November 4, 1972; "Frazier Title Bout in Danger," *Baltimore Sun*, November 16, 1972; Will Grimsley, "Selling of a Heavyweight Champion," *Los Angeles Herald-Examiner*, March 10, 1974.

13. Dave Anderson, "The Intrigue of the Jamaica Affair," *New York Times*, November 17, 1972; "January 22nd," *Atlanta Daily World*, December 8, 1972; "Frazier in 'Sunshine Bout,'" *Chicago Defender*, January 20, 1973; Dan Daniel, "Jamaica Chases American Frazier-Foreman Bidders Out of Battle for Title," *Ring*, January 1973, 6–7; Don Majeski, "Yank Durham Raps," *Boxing Illustrated*, January 1973, 10, 12, 63, 69; Rebecca Tortello, "Frazier vs. Foreman," *Jamaica Gleaner*, January 13, 2003; Christopher James Shelton, "Down Goes Frazier! The Sunshine Showdown," Ringside Boxing Show, ringsideboxingshow.com/SheltonBLOGForemanFrazier.html; Red Smith, "A Moveable Feast," *New York Times*, January 22, 1973.

14. Frank Senauth, *The Making of Jamaica* (Bloomington, IN: AuthorHouse, 2011), 8; John D. Forbes, *Jamaica: Managing Political and Economic Change* (Washington, DC: American Enterprise Institute for Public Policy Research, 1985), 6–17;

Richard Moore, *The Bolt Supremacy: Inside Jamaica's Sprint Factory* (New York: Pegasus, 2017), 33; Michael Kaufman, *Jamaica under Manley: Dilemmas of Socialism and Democracy* (Westport, CT: Lawrence Hill, 1985), 50, 71–72; Darrell E. Levi, *Michael Manley: The Making of a Leader* (Athens: University of Georgia Press, 1990), 126; Hans J. Massaquoi, "Interview with Jamaica Prime Minister Michael Manley," *Ebony*, February 1990, 110; "Jamaican Joshua," *Time*, August 21, 1972, 22; see also Michael Manley, *A History of West Indies Cricket* (London: Andre Deutsch, 1988).

15. R. Smith, "Moveable Feast"; "Fifteen Named to National Sports Board," *Jamaica Daily Gleaner*, September 7, 1972; Raymond Sharpe, "Making Better Use of Stadium," *Jamaica Daily Gleaner*, September 11, 1972; "Mullings Calls for Sports Mecca," *Jamaica Daily Gleaner*, September 14, 1972; "Football Punched in Stadium Row," *Jamaica Daily Gleaner*, September 16, 1972; Raymond Sharpe, "Ugly Start to Football Season," *Jamaica Daily Gleaner*, September 16, 1972; "Fitz-Ritson [*sic*] Initiates Quick Action," *Jamaica Daily Gleaner*, September 14, 1972.

16. "Fitz-Ritson Initiates Quick Action"; "WBC Gives Frazier Up to September 20," *Jamaica Daily Gleaner*, September 11, 1972; "Frazier, Foreman Told to Set a Date," *New York Times*, October 20, 1972; "Move to Get World Title Fight Here," *Jamaica Daily Gleaner*, October 20, 1972.

17. "Will Jamaica be the Venue?," *Jamaica Daily Gleaner*, October 23, 1972; "World Title Bout Likely Next Year," *Jamaica Daily Gleaner*, October 28, 1972; Dan Daniel, "Jamaica Chases American Frazier-Foreman Bidders out of Battle for Title," *Ring*, January 1973; Foreman interview.

18. Foreman interview; Stan Hochman, "Too Much Heart For His Own Good," *Philadelphia Daily News*, October 20, 1959; Jack Saunders, "Jack Saunders Says," *Philadelphia Tribune*, August 4, 1973; Claude Harrison Jr., "Frazier Beats Ali in 15 Rounds," *Philadelphia Tribune*, March 9, 1971; "Frazier Here for Signing," *Jamaica Daily Gleaner*, November 11, 1972; Raymond Sharpe, "Frazier In to Sign for Title Fight," *Jamaica Daily Gleaner*, November 9, 1972; "Signing of Contracts Delayed," *Jamaica Daily Gleaner*, November 10, 1972; Raymond Sharpe, "Frazier Fights Foreman Here January 22," *Jamaica Daily Gleaner*, November 11, 1972; "Act 1 of Title Fight Completed," *Jamaica Daily Gleaner*, November 11, 1972.

19. "Seaga Wants Title Fight Arrangements Probed," *Jamaica Daily Gleaner*, November 10, 1972.

20. Pearnel Charles, "Jamaica and the Third World," *Jamaica Daily Gleaner*, December 3, 1972; "Nothing Is Wrong With Me—Frazier," *Jamaica Daily Gleaner*, December 13, 1972; Baz Freckleton, "Inside Sports," *Jamaica Daily Gleaner*, No-

vember 20, 1972; "Promoters Guaranteed $800,000," *Jamaica Daily Gleaner*, November 23, 1972; Raymond Sharpe, "Title Fight Has $3m. Potential," *Jamaica Daily Gleaner*, November 28, 1972; "TV Rights Awarded to Fight," *Baltimore Sun*, November 24, 1972; Forbes, *Jamaica*, 21; "Bread Shortage Worsens as Strike Spreads," *Jamaica Daily Gleaner*, November 9, 1972; "Act 1 of Title Fight"; "Big Sell Jamaica Campaign," *Jamaica Daily Gleaner*, November 11, 1972; R. Smith, "Moveable Feast."

21. Nat Loubet, "As Nat Loubet Sees It," *Ring*, June 1973, 5; Dan Daniel, "New Deal in N.Y. Garden Hopeful with Brenner Directing, Markson Retired," *Ring*, June 1973, 10; Dick Peebles, "George's Turn," *Houston Chronicle*, January 17, 1973; Jack Griffin, "Frazier Losing Recognition Bout," *Chicago Sun-Times*, January 20, 1973, and "Frazier-Foreman Fight Intrudes in Paradise," *Los Angeles Times*, January 21, 1973; Sam Toub, "Foreman Not Spectacular in Stopping Pires in Four," *Ring*, February 1972, 14; Marshall Reed, "Foreman Wins Again . . . with Ease," *Boxing Illustrated*, February 1972, 30, 53; Les Mathews, "The Sports Whirl," *New York Amsterdam News*, March 11, 1972; Lester Bromberg, "Let Us See the Real George Foreman," *Boxing Illustrated*, September 1972, 8, 60.

CHAPTER 7: I AIN'T NO DOG

1. *Billboard*, January 13, 1973, 24, 48; *Billboard*, January 20, 1973, 23, 62; Thomas Hauser, *Boxing Is . . . Reflections on the Sweet Science* (Fayetteville: University of Arkansas Press, 2010), 90; George Plimpton, "You Better Believe It," *Sports Illustrated*, February 5, 1973, 24.

2. Plimpton, "You Better Believe It," 24–27; Jack Dempsey, *Championship Fighting: Explosive Punching and Aggressive Defense*, ed. Jack Cuddy (New York: Prentice Hall, 1950); photo in *Jamaica Daily Gleaner*, December 8, 1972; Robert W. Creamer, "Prelude to Act II," *Sports Illustrated*, December 18, 1972, 18; "Mini Games Add Frazier," *Chicago Defender*, December 18, 1972; "Frazier Slows Down on Workouts," *Newark Star-Ledger*, January 19, 1973; "Unimpressive Frazier Finishes Work, Predicts KO of Foreman," *Houston Chronicle*, January 20, 1973; "Joe Says He'll KO Foreman, Naturally," *Houston Post*, January 20, 1973; advertisement in *Jamaica Daily Gleaner*, January 20, 1973; John Hollis, "Frazier People Not All That Concerned," *Houston Post*, January 21, 1973; "The Joe Frazier Show—A Swinging Affair," *Jamaica Daily Gleaner*, January 30, 1973.

3. Gene Courtney, "Who's Joe Frazier Fighting—A Bush-League Muhammad

Ali?," *Philadelphia Inquirer*, January 20, 1973; Dan Daniel, "Foreman May Lay Career on Line against Frazier," *Ring*, November 1972, 7; Baz Freckleton, "Inside Sports," *Jamaica Daily Gleaner*, November 8, 1972; "Is Foreman Really Ready for Frazier?," *Jamaica Daily Gleaner*, November 19, 1972; Bert Sugar, "The Two Sides of George Foreman: Is He or Is He Ain't?," *Boxing Illustrated*, February 1973, cover, 11–13, 63.

4. "Jamaicans Pulling for Foreman, Their Hearts Belong to Ali," *Los Angeles Times*, January 20, 1973; Shirley Povich, "Frazier a Villain to Most Jamaicans," *Chicago Sun-Times*, January 21, 1973; John Hollis, "Ring Record Book Stowed Away, It's Off to See Joe and George," *Houston Post*, January 20, 1973; Vic Ziegel, "Frazier's Facing That Question," *New York Post*, January 22, 1973; Jack Griffin, "Foreman: What's to Be Nervous About" and "An Island for Love, and a Fist Fight," *Chicago Sun-Times*, January 21 and 19, 1973; "Frazier 3 1/2–1," *New York Post*, January 18, 1973; Dan Daniel, "New Deal in N.Y. Garden Hopeful with Brenner Directing, Markson Retired," *Ring*, June 1973, 11; Baz Freckleton, "Inside Sports," *Jamaica Daily Gleaner*, November 1, 1972; Manley Lumsden, "Running with Smokin' Joe," *Jamaica Daily Gleaner*, November 23, 1972; "Is Joe Frazier Washed Up?," *Los Angeles Times*, January 22, 1973; "Frazier-Foreman," *Ring*, February 1973, 10–11, 40; Arthur Daley, "Forecasts for 1973," *New York Times*, January 7, 1973; "Joe Frazier—An Analysis," *Atlanta Daily World*, January 14, 1973; A. S. "Doc" Young, "Frazier vs. Cass-Mu," *Los Angeles Sentinel*, December 14, 1972; "Foreman: Frazier's Toughest Test since Ali," *Orlando Sentinel*, January 22, 1973; Craig Heath and Tim J. Dee, "Punch Lines," *Ring*, September 1971, 30; Keoui Cassidy, "Punch Lines," *Ring*, May 1972, 28; Jersey Joe Walcott, "Heavyweights," *Boxing Illustrated*, March 1972, 19; Plimpton, "You Better Believe It," 23; Randy Roberts, *Joe Louis: Hard Times Man* (New Haven, CT: Yale University Press, 2010), x; Will Grimsley, "Louis Likes Foreman; Fans Like Ex-Champ," *Miami Herald*, January 20, 1973; "He's Got the Support," *Chicago Defender*, January 22, 1973; Jack Griffin, "Gambling a Way of Life in Jamaica," *Chicago Sun-Times*, January 22, 1973; "Joe Louis Sees Foreman as the Winner," *Jamaica Daily Gleaner*, January 20, 1973.

5. Edwin Shrake, "Set for a Wood Chopper's Bowl," *Sports Illustrated*, January 15, 1973, 35; "Frazier Says He'll Stop Foreman," *New York Times*, January 20, 1973; "Foreman Explodes," *Jamaica Daily Gleaner*, January 18, 1973; "Title Fight Tonight," *Jamaica Daily Gleaner*, January 22, 1973; "Frazier the Betting Favorite," *Jamaica Daily Gleaner*, January 15, 1973; Gene Courtney, "Frazier Says He'll Teach Foreman Some Respect," *Philadelphia Inquirer*, January 21, 1973; Milton Richman, "It's Fantastic, Says George Foreman," *Los Angeles Sentinel*, December 28, 1972.

6. "The Winner and New Champion," *Newsweek*, February 5, 1973, 89; Frank Deford, "The Ageless Warrior," *Sports Illustrated*, May 8, 1989, 102–114; interviews with George Foreman, in possession of the author, cited as Foreman interview; George Foreman and Joel Engel, *By George: The Autobiography of George Foreman* (New York: Villard, 1995), 85, 90; "I Will Send Home Foreman Early—Frazier," *Jamaica Daily Gleaner*, January 11, 1973; "People in Sports," *New York Times*, January 9, 1973; Red Smith, "Conversations with the Challenger," *New York Times*, January 19, 1973; "Frazier Defends Crown against Foreman Monday," *Atlanta Daily World*, January 21, 1973; "Foreman Still at the Heavy Bag," *Jamaica Daily Gleaner*, January 21, 1973; "Heavies Break Camp Friday," *Jamaica Daily Gleaner*, January 17, 1973; "Foreman: From Rags to Riches," *Chicago Defender*, December 23, 1972; "Foreman 'Sees' His Daughter," *Jamaica Daily Gleaner*, January 10, 1973; Milton Gross, "Family Man," *New York Post*, January 19, 1973; C. J., "George Foreman's First Wife Was Very Happy with Her Heavyweight despite Ali's Jabs," *Minneapolis Star Tribune*, January 4, 2019.

7. "Foreman Rough on Spar Mates," *Houston Chronicle*, January 18, 1973; "Foreman Makes Things Hot for Sparmates," *Jamaica Daily Gleaner*, January 9, 1973; "Foreman Gets Rough in Training Session," *Jamaica Daily Gleaner*, January 10, 1973; Vic Ziegel, "Foreman Pours it On," *New York Post*, January 18, 1973; John Hollis, "Smokin' Bad for Frazier," *Houston Post*, January 21, 1973; "Foreman Predicts He'll Knock Out Joe Frazier," *Houston Chronicle*, January 19, 1973; Baz Freckleton, "Inside Sports," *Jamaica Daily Gleaner*, November 12, 1972; Jack Griffin, "Foreman Trainer 'Butt' of Fight Jokes," *Chicago Sun-Times*, January 19, 1973; "Ref Leak Irks Sadler," *New York Post*, January 22, 1973.

8. Raymond Sharpe, "10-Point Must Scoring for Title Fight," *Jamaica Daily Gleaner*, December 19, 1972; "Fight Rules Out Today," *Jamaica Daily Gleaner*, January 18, 1973; "3-Knockdown Clause Not Applicable," *Jamaica Daily Gleaner*, January 19, 1973; Arthur Mercante, "Second Knockdown Was Turning Point Says Ref Mercante," *Ring*, May 1973, 6.

9. John Hollis, "Foreman Smokes Out Joe," *Houston Post*, January 23, 1973; Dave Berman, "Foreman-Ali Promoters Predict Record Viewing of Closed Circuit TV," *Ring*, September 1974, 34; Michael Arkush, *The Fight of the Century: Ali vs. Frazier, March 8, 1971* (Hoboken, NJ: Wiley, 2008), 124–127; Gerald Eskenazi, "Don Dunphy, 90, Distinctive Fight Broadcaster," *New York Times*, July 24, 1998; "Dumphy [sic] Not Dumfield," *Jamaica Daily Gleaner*, January 15, 1973; Showman, "Pearl Bailey: Nixon's Ambassador of Love," *Jamaica Daily Gleaner*, January 21, 1973.

10. "A Glittering Evening for the 'Sunshine Showdown,'" *Jamaica Daily Gleaner*, January 23, 1973; Shirley Povich, "Foreman King; Frazier Down 6 Times," *Los Angeles Times*, January 23, 1973; Gordon Forbes, "Spectrum Fans Abandon Frazier," *Philadelphia Inquirer*, January 23, 1973; Plimpton, "You Better Believe It," 24–27.

11. Plimpton, "You Better Believe It," 27.

12. Anthony Marenghi, "Foreman Champ on TKO in 2d," *Newark Star-Ledger*, January 23, 1973; Christopher James Shelton, "Down Goes Frazier! The Sunshine Showdown," Ringside Boxing Show, ringsideboxingshow.com/SheltonBLOGFore manFrazier.html.

13. Marvis Frazier quoted in *Thrilla in Manila*, dir. John Dower (HBO Documentary Films, 2008); Andrew R. M. Smith, "Blood Stirs the Fight Crowd: Making and Marking Joe Frazier's Philadelphia," in *Philly Sports: Teams, Games, and Athletes from Rocky's Town*, ed. Ryan A. Swanson and David K. Wiggins (Fayetteville: University of Arkansas Press, 2016), 127–145.

14. *Thrilla in Manila*; Mercante, "Second Knockdown," 6; Jerry Izenberg, "Things That Go Bump," *Newark Star-Ledger*, January 25, 1973; Vic Ziegel, "Foreman KOd Doubters Too," *New York Post*, January 23, 1973; John Wilson, "Frazier Wasn't Same Fighter Who Whipped Ali," *Houston Chronicle*, January 23, 1973; "Dethroned Frazier Wants Another Shot at Foreman," *Houston Post*, January 24, 1973.

15. Sheldon, "Down Goes Frazier!"; *Thrilla in Manila*.

16. Mark Kram, *Ghosts of Manila: The Fateful Blood Feud between Muhammad Ali and Joe Frazier* (New York: HarperCollins, 2001), 21; Plimpton, "You Better Believe It," 27.

17. Plimpton, "You Better Believe It," 27–28; Milton Gross, "The Champ," *New York Post*, January 24, 1973; Jack Gallagher, "Foreman Finally Brings Houston a Long Overdue Sports Champion," *Houston Post*, January 24, 1973.

18. Shelton, "Down Goes Frazier!"; Eskenazi, "Don Dunphy"; Jack Newfield, *Only in America: The Life and Crimes of Don King* (New York: Morrow, 1995), 1–20, 34, 46–47.

19. "'It Was Just My Night' Foreman Says of His Win," *Jet*, February 8, 1973, 58–59; "Foreman Was 'Hoping It' Would End," *Philadelphia Inquirer*, January 23, 1973; Ronald E. Kisner, "What's Ahead for New Heavyweight Boxing Champion?," *Jet*, February 15, 1973, 53; Nat Loubet, "Foreman's Kayo of Frazier One of Top Feats in Boxing History," *Ring*, April 1973, 6; Shelton, "Down Goes Frazier!"; Shirley Norman, "With Foreman, It's U.S.A. All the Way," *Ring*, October 1973, 6–7, 35; Newfield, *Only in America*, 34, 46–47.

20. Foreman interview; "Television," *New York Times*, February 8, 1973;

George Girsch, "Foreman a Gentle Giant," *Ring*, May 1973, 13; "Photo Essay: A George Foreman Retrospective," *Ring*, August 1977, 18–23.

21. Foreman interview; Parker Ledbetter to Leonard Patillo, interoffice correspondence, "George Foreman Day," February 19, 1973, GFBF, HPL; Ray Collins, "Foreman Has Triumphant Homecoming," *Houston Post*, February 20, 1973; Jack Gallagher, "Going Back Where the Fish Bite and Dogs Bark," *Houston Post*, February 21, 1973; Louie Robinson, "New Boss of the Heavyweights," *Ebony*, April 1973, 44; "Don't Knock the American System to Me," *Nation's Business*, April 1973, 38–45; Yvonne Brathwaite Burke, "Philosophy of George Foreman," *Congressional Record*, April 12, 1973.

22. David Farber, "The Torch Had Fallen," in *America in the Seventies*, ed. Beth Bailey and David Farber (Lawrence: University Press of Kansas, 2004), 23; Darren Dochuk, *From Bible Belt to Sun Belt: Plain-Folk Religion, Grassroots Politics, and the Rise of Evangelical Conservatism* (New York: Norton, 2011), 345–353; Mark Hamilton Lytle, *America's Uncivil Wars: The Sixties Era from Elvis to the Fall of Richard Nixon* (New York: Oxford University Press, 2006), 163; William H. Chafe, *The Unfinished Journey: America since World War II* (New York: Oxford University Press, 2007), 441–449; Niall Ferguson, "Introduction: Crisis, What Crisis? The 1970s and the Shock of the Global," and Alan M. Taylor, "The Global 1970s and the Echo of the Great Depression," both in *The Shock of the Global: The 1970s in Perspective*, ed. Niall Ferguson et al. (London: Belknap, 2010), 20, 98.

CHAPTER 8: SUPERMAN'S EVIL TWIN

1. "Lyle's Manager Wants Foreman, Nixes Ali Bout," *Newark Star-Ledger*, January 24, 1973; "Lyle Wants Foreman," *New York Post*, January 23, 1973; Dave Anderson, "Quarry Wins by a Decision, Giving Lyle First Ring Loss," *New York Times*, February 10, 1973; "Ali: Frazier Is Finished," *Philadelphia Inquirer*, January 23, 1973; "Frazier Finished," *Houston Post*, January 23, 1973; "Frazier Loss No Surprise to Ali," *Los Angeles Times*, January 23, 1973; "Ali Unaware He 'Whupped Joe So Bad,'" *Houston Chronicle*, January 23, 1973; Sam Boyle, "Ali Takes the Credit," *New York Post*, January 23, 1973; "Ali Takes the Credit for Softening Frazier," *Chicago Sun-Times*, January 23, 1973; "Ali 5–1 Choice Over Strongboy Norton," *Los Angeles Times*, March 31, 1973; "Norton Breaks Ali's Jaw, Wins on Split Decision," *Los Angeles Times*, April 1, 1973; Dan Levin, "Bury His Heart at Wounded Jaw," *Sports Illustrated*, April 9, 1973, 28–29; Tex Maule, "The Mouth That Nearly Roared," *Sports Illustrated*, April 23, 1973, 29–33.

328 ★ NOTES TO PAGES 134–137

2. Nat Loubet, "Putting Heavy Jigsaw Puzzle Pieces Together Problem for Promoters," *Ring*, June 1973, 8–9; James F. Jensen, "Heavyweight Division's New Look," *Boxing Illustrated*, June 1973, 21; Dan Daniel, "New Deal in N.Y. Garden Hopeful with Brenner Directing, Markson Retired," *Ring*, June 1973, 10–11, 34; "Frazier, His Manager Will Start All Over," *Los Angeles Times*, January 24, 1973; Dan Daniel, "Foreman's Exhibitions Not Drawing, Fans Look to Champion to Defend Title," *Ring*, August 1973, 10; "Frazier May Get Rematch in Houston," *Houston Chronicle*, January 24, 1973; Nat Loubet, "As Nat Loubet Sees It," *Ring*, July 1973, 5; Dan Daniel, "Heavyweight Bidding Makes Million Only Starting Point as Foreman Disdains N.Y.," *Ring*, July 1973, 8.

3. "How'd He Do That?," *Chicago Defender*, February 10, 1973; "George Foreman's Success Story," *Los Angeles Herald-Examiner*, March 11, 1973; Robert Moss, "Not Interested in Quarry Says Foreman in Las Vegas," *Ring*, August 1973, 8–9, 32; Daniel, "Foreman's Exhibitions," 10; Tim Tyler, "George Foreman: The Great White Hope," *Sport*, July 1973, 84–86; Frank Allnutt, "Montreal and Ontario Bar Foreman Exhibitions," *Ring*, August 1973, 34; Shirley Norman, "With Foreman, It's U.S.A. All the Way," *Ring*, October 1973, 34; interviews with George Foreman, in possession of the author, cited as Foreman interview.

4. Steve Cady, "They Like Sham in Times Square," *New York Times*, May 4, 1973; "The Derby: Secretariat Wins in Record Time with Sham 2d," *New York Times*, May 6, 1973; Joe Nichlols, "Six Are in Preakness Today, but It's a Two Horse Race," *New York Times*, May 19, 1973; Larry Schwartz, "Secretariat Demolished Belmont Field," ESPN Classic, November 19, 2003, http://espn.go.com/classic/s/secretariatadd.html; James C. Nicholson, *The Kentucky Derby: How the Run for the Roses Became America's Premier Sporting Event* (Lexington: University of Kentucky Press, 2012), 165–166; see also Lawrence Scanlan, *The Horse God Built: The Untold Story of Secretariat, the World's Greatest Racehorse* (New York: Macmillan, 2010).

5. Ron Oliver, "Bugner Down for Nine but Frazier Doesn't Come Out Smoking," *Ring*, September 1973, 10–11; Joe Frazier, "I Will Beat Foreman or Quit!," *Ring*, August 1973, 6; "Foreman Fires Sadler: Will Manage Himself," *Jet*, July 19, 1973, 48; Norman, "With Foreman," 34; Foreman interview.

6. Pat Putnam, "One Little Move, a Giant Step," *Sports Illustrated*, June 18, 1973, 22–29; Norman, "With Foreman," 34; Daniel, "Foreman's Exhibitions," 10; Steve Green, "Cassina a Titan in the Boxing World," *London (ON) Free Press*, February 7, 2012.

7. "Lawyer Seeks to Block Foreman-Roman Contest," *Jet*, August 2, 1973, 53; "Foreman to Defend Next for Houston Promoter," *Japan Times*, August 8, 1973; "Frazier-Foreman Fight Now Set for Houston Astrodome," *Jet*, September 6, 1973, 55; Richard Hoffer, *Bouts of Mania: Ali, Frazier, Foreman, and an America on the Ropes* (Boston: Da Capo, 2014), 135; "Yancey Durham, Fight Manager Who Taught Joe Frazier, Is Dead," *New York Times*, August 31, 1973.

8. Dan Daniel, "Court Orders May Stop Foreman from Defending Title in this Country," *Ring*, January 1974, 6–7; Norman, "With Foreman," 34; Dan Daniel, "Shavers' KO of Ellis in One Interesting, But He's Not Yet in Major League," *Ring*, September 1973, 12–13.

9. Foreman interview; Martin Collick and Richard Storry, "The New Tensions in Japan," *Conflict Studies* 48 (1974): 16; "Oil Crisis Déjà Vu," *Daily Yomiuri*, December 3, 2000.

10. Daniel, "Court Orders," 6–7; Nat Loubet, "Roundup of the Year," *Ring*, February 1973, 17; Leslie Nakashima, "Not Only Foster Got Stung," *Sports Illustrated*, April 10, 1972, 80–85; "$1 Million Guarantee," *Japan Times*, August 1, 1973; "Foreman, Roman Cheered in Tokyo," *Japan Times*, August 20, 1973; Leslie Nakashima, "World Champ Foreman Arrives for Title Bout," *Japan Times*, August 16, 1973.

11. Leslie Nakashima, "Foreman KO's Roman in 1st," *Japan Times*, September 2, 1973; "Foreman Says He's Giving Rookie Boost," *Japan Times*, August 2, 1973; Nakashima, "World Champ Foreman"; Al Ricketts, "On the Town," *Stars and Stripes*, July 2, 1966.

12. Katsundo Mizuno, "Experts Here Pick Foreman to Retain Crown by Knockout," *Japan Times*, August 31, 1973; Joe Y. Koizumi, "Foreman's Two-Minute Kayo of Roman Brings Fruitless Hassle," *Ring*, November 1973, 6–7; "Foreman, Roman Agree to Waive Knockdown Rule," *Japan Times*, August 31, 1973; Nakashima, "Foreman KO's Roman"; Frank Iwama, "It Takes Two to Tangle," *Sports Illustrated*, September 10, 1973, 16–19; Nat Loubet, "As Nat Loubet Sees It," *Ring*, December 1973, 5.

13. Bill Gallo, "But Let Me See Norton Do It Again," *Ring*, September 1973, 17; George Foreman and Joel Engel, *By George: The Autobiography of George Foreman* (New York: Villard, 1995), 83, 95; "Norton Thought He Whipped Ali Again," *Los Angeles Times*, September 11, 1973; Dan Daniel, "Foreman Says, 'Quarry and Frazier'"; "Report Ali-Joe again in N.Y.," *Ring*, December 1973, 7; Norman, "With Foreman," 34.

14. John Ort, "U.S. Champions—Boom to Boxing," *Ring*, November 1975, 20;

Michael Katz, "A Boxing Buff Buys the Ring Magazine," *New York Times*, July 16, 1979.

15. Foreman interview; Foreman and Engel, *By George*, 94; Gerard J. DeGroot, *The Seventies Unplugged: A Kaleidoscopic Look at a Violent Decade* (New York: Macmillan, 2011), 329.

16. George Girsch, "Foreman All-Time Kayo King among Heavy Champions," *Ring*, January 1974, 10; "Joe Louis Ranks Foreman No. 1; Others All the Same," *Jet*, October 4, 1973, 72; Dan Daniel, "Foreman Waits While Joe-Ali Meet Again," *Ring*, February 1974, 6; Jack Welsh, "Heavyweights Offer Sugar Plums for Fight Buffs," *Boxing Illustrated*, December 1973, 6; "Three Key Atlanta Blacks Bid for Foreman Fight," *Jet*, October 18, 1973, 76; Daniel, "Court Orders," 6–7; Melvin Durslag, "Foreman Defends in Pizza Joint," *Los Angeles Herald-Examiner*, December 9, 1973; Deane McGowen, "Quarry Pilot Pressing for Title Match," *New York Times*, December 16, 1973; "'I'm About Broke,' Boxing Champion Reveals," *Jet*, November 29, 1973, 79; "George Foreman Reveals: 'I'm Going Out Knocking,'" *Jet*, December 6, 1973, 77.

17. Gerald Eskenazi, "Garden Scoring with Reverse Stock Split," *New York Times*, May 29, 1973; Nat Loubet, "As Nat Loubet Sees It," *Ring*, September 1973, 5; Hoffer, *Bouts of Mania*, 125–126; Jerry Izenberg, *Once There Were Giants: The Golden Age of Heavyweight Boxing* (New York: Skyhorse, 2017), 89–90.

18. Izenberg, *Once There Were Giants*, 90; Arkush, *Fight of the Century*, 206–207.

19. Dan Daniel, "Norton Looks like Foreman's First Problem as Quarry Waits," *Ring*, March 1974, 20; Michael Arkush, *The Fight of the Century: Ali vs. Frazier, March 8, 1971* (Hoboken, NJ: Wiley, 2008), 207.

20. "'Hefty' Foreman Ready, Bored by Ali-Frazier," *Chicago Defender*, January 31, 1974; Ernest Havemann, "Fighter at the Crossroads," *Sports Illustrated*, December 24, 1973, 89; Jack Welsh, "What Foreman Does When He's Not Fighting," *Boxing Illustrated*, August 1973, 10–15; Mark Kram, "Scenario of Pride—and Decline," *Sports Illustrated*, January 21, 1974, 22–29; "Ali-Frazier Duel Again in $1.7 Million N.Y. Rematch," *Jet*, October 25, 1973, 78; Dan Daniel, "Watch Out for No. 3 in Rich Ali-Frazier Series; No. 2 Decision Justified," *Ring*, April 1974, 6–13; Jack Welsh, "Foreman Wants Three to Five Fights in '74, Rates Lyle as Top Contender," *Boxing Illustrated*, February 1974, 13.

21. Daniel, "Court Orders," 6–7; "Foreman Running Out of Time," *Chicago Defender*, December 3, 1973; Red Smith, "Someone Has to Unconfuse George," *New York Times*, December 17, 1973; Larry Merchant, "Foreman's Mistakes," *New*

York Post, March 25, 1974; "Foreman, Norton Square Off in Heavyweight Bout Tonight," *Atlanta Daily World*, March 26, 1974; "'Hefty' Foreman Ready"; Jack Newfield, *Only in America: The Life and Crimes of Don King* (New York: Morrow, 1995), 34–35; Hoffer, *Bouts of Mania*, 136.

CHAPTER 9: MAN WITHOUT A COUNTRY

1. John Greensmith, "Jaw Buster Norton's Side Opposes Delay if Foreman Is Ready to Defend His Title," *Ring*, July 1973, 6, 60, 81; John Greensmith, "'I Was Fired'—Futch," *Ring*, May 1974, 22–23; Don Page, "Confident Norton Ready for George," *Los Angeles Herald-Examiner*, March 13, 1974.

2. Interviews with George Foreman, in possession of the author, cited as Foreman interview; Will Grimsley, "Selling of a Heavyweight Champion," *Los Angeles Herald-Examiner*, March 10, 1974; "Fed Suit Hits Foreman," *Chicago Defender*, March 26, 1974.

3. "Sparmates Say Champ is Worried," *Chicago Defender*, February 25, 1974; "Sadler Says Champ Is Ready to Fight," *Chicago Defender*, February 21, 1974; "Johnny Mathis Stars on Soul Train Revue," *Chicago Defender*, February 21, 1974; Doug Krikorian, "Foreman: He Looks Unbeatable," *Los Angeles Herald-Examiner*, March 6, 1974.

4. Don Page, "Confident Norton Ready for George," *Los Angeles Herald-Examiner*, March 13, 1974; "Norton Confident, Calls Foreman Slow," *Chicago Defender*, February 16, 1974; "Norton Predicts Win," *New York Post*, March 20, 1974; "Norton Did His Homework," *Chicago Defender*, March 13, 1974; "Foreman: Open Door," *Newark Star-Ledger*, March 22, 1974; "Foreman Puts Title on Line with Norton," *Houston Post*, March 24, 1974; "Foreman Can't Wait!," *Chicago Defender*, March 25, 1974; "Foreman, Norton Square Off in Heavyweight Bout Tonight," *Atlanta Daily World*, March 26, 1974.

5. Nat Loubet, "Roundup of the Year," *Ring*, February 1973, 17; Jeremy Adelman, "International Finance and Political Legitimacy: A Latin American View of the Global Shock," in *The Shock of the Global: The 1970s in Perspective*, ed. Niall Ferguson et al. (London: Belknap, 2010), 115–126; H. Michael Tarver and Julia C. Frederick, *The History of Venezuela* (Westport, CT: Greenwood, 2005), 119–121; Marco Cupolo, "Public Administration, Oil Rent, and Legitimacy Crises in Venezuela," in *Reinventing Legitimacy: Democracy and Political Change in Venezuela*, ed.

Damarys Canache and Michael R. Kulisheck (Westport, CT: Greenwood, 1998), 99–112.

6. Janet Kelly and Carlos A. Romero, *The United States and Venezuela: Rethinking a Relationship* (New York: Routledge, 2002), 19–22; Judith Ewell, *Venezuela: A Century of Change* (Palo Alto, CA: Stanford University Press, 1984), 164–183, 200–211.

7. AEC to SSDC, "Fedecamaras President Attacks Caldera," January 15, 1974, "Mrs. Nixon's Trip to Venezuela," March 7, 1974, "Mrs. Nixon's Attendance of Presidential Inauguration—Venezuela," March 9, 1974, and "Remarks on Petroleum Policy in Inaugural Address of President Carlos Andres Perez," March 14 and 18, 1974, all in CFPF, RG 59, NARA-AAD; "Foremans in Court," *Houston Chronicle*, February 13, 1974; "Lawyers to Negotiate Property Settlement in Foreman Divorce," *Houston Chronicle*, February 17, 1974; "Champion Foreman Floored By $235,000 Divorce Pact," *Jet*, March 14, 1974, 55; Grimsley, "Selling of a Champion."

8. "Louis Picks Norton Speed, Strength," *Newark Star-Ledger*, March 26, 1974; Norman Unger, "History Says Don't Count Norton Out," *Chicago Defender*, March 18, 1974; A. S. "Doc" Young, "Good Morning, Sports!," *Chicago Defender*, March 25, 1974; "Norton Has Chance vs. Foreman," *New York Daily World*, March 26, 1974; Dan Hafner, "Foreman 4–1 Pick, but Norton Has Backers," *Los Angeles Times*, March 24, 1974.

9. Bud Furillo, "Foreman's Still for America," *Los Angeles Herald-Examiner*, March 13, 1974; Richard Hoffer, *Bouts of Mania: Ali, Frazier, Foreman, and an America on the Ropes* (Boston: Da Capo, 2014), 138–139; AEC to SSDC, "Fight Over the Fights," March 26, 1974, CFPF, RG 59, NARA-AAD; Dave Anderson, "The Caracas Caper: Tax and Facts," *New York Times*, March 30, 1974.

10. Vic Ziegel, "Foreman Hurt; Fight in Doubt," *New York Post*, March 26, 1974; Red Smith, "Fair Play and Justice Made Easy," *New York Times*, March 25, 1974; Dick Young, "Foreman Needed Referee, Not Doctor, for Injury," *Miami Herald*, March 27, 1974; "Foreman Camp Creates a Stir," *Newark Star-Ledger*, March 25, 1974; "Norton Unruffled by Preparations for Foreman-Ali Fight," *Houston Post*, March 25, 1974; Dan Daniel, "Foreman Supreme after 2nd Round KO over Norton," *Ring*, June 1974, 6; Leonard Gardner, "Stopover in Caracas," *Esquire*, October 1974, 184–187; "Bulky Foreman's Not Worried, Rejects Overweight Charge," *Miami Herald*, March 26, 1974; "Foreman Brings 224 3/4 Pounds But No Trunks to the Weigh-In," *Los Angeles Times*, March 26, 1974; Vic Ziegel, "Norton Supplies Angle" and "Champ 224, Norton 212," *New York Post*, March 21 and 25, 1974; "Both Fighters at Peak Weight," *Chicago Defender*, March 26, 1974.

11. Red Smith, "The Referee Is a Boy's Best Friend," *New York Times*, March 27, 1974; "Ali, Foreman Will Battle in Africa This September," *Chicago Defender*, March 30, 1974; AEC to SSDC, "Fight Over the Fights."

12. Jerry Izenberg, "El Gran Boxeo," *Newark Star-Ledger*, March 24, 1974; David F. Belnap, "Title Fight Shakes Up Caracas," *Los Angeles Times*, March 21, 1974; Patrick Kehoe, "When George was King: Foreman vs Norton 29 Year Anniversary," SecondsOut, secondsout.com/legends/legends-update/when-george-was-king-foreman-vs-norton-29-year-anniversary; Thomas Hauser, "Bob Sheridan: The Voice of Boxing," SecoundsOut, secondsout.com/columns/thomas-hauser/bob-sheridan-the-voice-of-boxing; R. Smith, "Referee Is a Boy's Best Friend."

13. Norman Unger, "Foreman's Strength Hurts Gate Appeal," *Chicago Defender*, March 30, 1974; "Joe Louis Inspired Foreman's Victory," *Houston Post*, March 27, 1974; "Foreman Stops Norton for 2nd-Round TKO," *Miami Herald*, March 27, 1974.

14. Larry Merchant, "Destructive Force," *New York Post*, March 27, 1974.

15. Jerry Izenberg, *Once There Were Giants: The Golden Age of Heavyweight Boxing* (New York: Skyhorse, 2017), 93; David F. Belnap, "Fight Itself Was Shortest Battle of a Hectic Day," *Los Angeles Times*, March 27, 1974; R. Smith, "Referee Is a Boy's Best Friend"; Dave Anderson, "Foreman Retains Title by Stopping Norton in 2:00 of Second Round," *New York Times*, March 27, 1974; "Brutal Foreman Smashes Norton for TKO in 2nd," *Miami Herald*, March 27, 1974; "Foreman Had 'A Little Faith,' Norton Forgot Fight Plan," *Chicago Defender*, March 28, 1974; Jerry Izenberg, "George's Way," *Newark Star-Ledger*, March 27, 1974.

16. "Foreman TKOs Norton in 2d," *Newark Star-Ledger*, March 27, 1974; Anderson, "Foreman Retains Title."

17. Daniel, "Foreman Supreme," 6; William H. Heath, "Tax Squabbles Delay Champ's Venezuela Exit," *Miami Herald*, March 29, 1974; "Foreman, Norton Held in Caracas over Taxes," *New York Post*, March 28, 1974; Foreman interview; Hoffer, *Bouts of Mania*, 139.

18. AEC to SSDC, "Secretary Schultz Travel Schedule," March 26, 1974, "Fight over the Fights," March 26, 1974, "Penultimate Fight over Fights," March 27, 1974, "The Fight Goes On," March 29, 1974, and "Ambassador's Response to Video Techniques, Inc.," May 10, 1974, all in CFPF, RG 59, NARA-AAD; Anderson, "Caracas Caper"; "Taxes Bite Champ for 300G's," *Chicago Defender*, April 4, 1974; "Foreman, Norton Still Unable to Leave Caracas," *Houston Post*, March 29, 1974; "Norton on Way Home—Foreman Still in Caracas," *New York Post*, March 30, 1974; "Foreman Is Still Stalled in Caracas," *New York Times*, March 30, 1974; Don King,

"Foreman OK'd Zaire Fight in 'Frisco Parking Lot at Midnight," *Ring*, October 1974, 6–7; Vic Ziegel, "The Hustler," *New York Post*, March 26, 1974; Ray Collins, "Foreman-Ali for $5 Million," *Houston Post*, March 27, 1974; "Tax Bill Paid in Venezuela; Fighters Free," *Newark Star-Ledger*, March 29, 1974; Jack Newfield, *Only in America: The Life and Crimes of Don King* (New York: Morrow, 1995), 53–54; George Foreman and Joel Engel, *By George: The Autobiography of George Foreman* (New York: Villard, 1995), 101–103; Foreman interview.

19. Anthony Marenghi, "No Doubts Now—Dynasty is Born" and "Africa Dents U.S. Boxing Monopoly," *Newark Star-Ledger*, March 27 and 28, 1974; "Houston Dims as Site for Foreman-Ali Go," *Houston Post*, March 29, 1974; Hoyt Basset, "Punch Lines," *Ring*, July 1974, 30; Sam Taub, "What, in Heaven's Name, Is a Zaire?," *Ring*, July 1974, 10; Loubet, "As Nat Loubet Sees it," *Ring*, September 1974, 5; George Girsch, "Foreman a Man without a Country," *Ring*, September 1974, 20–21.

20. Nat Loubet, "As Nat Loubet Sees it," *Ring*, August 1974, 5; AEC to SSDC, "Possible Advantages in a Taxation Treaty with Venezuela," April 1, 1974, CFPF, RG 59, NARA-AAD.

CHAPTER 10: TO THE MOUNTAINS OF THE MOON

1. Sam Taub, "What, in Heaven's Name, Is a Zaire?," *Ring*, July 1974, 10; Jerry Izenberg, "Does Ali Have a Chance," *Sport*, September 1974, 22–32. Norman Mailer's research notes for *The Fight* are available in the NMC. For American popular-culture references to Central Africa in the first half of the twentieth century, see *Stanley and Livingstone*, dir. Henry King and Otto Brower (20th Century Fox, 1939); Joseph Conrad, *Youth: A Narrative, and Two Other Stories* (London: Blackwood and Sons, 1903), 49–182; Vachel Lindsay, *The Congo, and Other Poems* (New York: MacMillan, 1915), 2–20.

2. "Foreman 'Rolls' with Punches," *Chicago Defender*, April 20, 1974; Dan Daniel, "Foreman May Challenge Dempsey's Power but Not Charisma," *Ring*, July 1974, 6, 40; Charley Rabinowitz, "NY, NY," *Ring*, July 1974, 30; Dan Daniel, "Foreman Favored in Betting but Action Is Slow for Zaire Bout," *Ring*, August 1974, 6–7; Gary Smith, "After the Fall," *Sports Illustrated*, October 8, 1984, 68.

3. Nat Loubet, "As Nat Loubet Sees It," *Ring*, November–December 1974, 5; Dan Daniel, "New York Boxing in Jeopardy as Greatest Title Fight in History Is Set for Africa," *Ring*, September 1974, 6–7; Nat Loubet, "As Nat Loubet Sees It,"

Ring, August 1974, 5; Red Smith, "On to the Congo with Dick's Monster," *New York Times*, March 28, 1974. For more on the nature and tax status of Risnelia, see AEK to SSDC, "Taxes—Ali Foreman Fight," October 15, 21, and 25, 1974, CFPF, RG 59, NARA-AAD.

4. Dan Daniel, "Foreman Supreme after 2nd Round KO over Norton," *Ring*, June 1974, 6; Jack Newfield, *Only in America: The Life and Crimes of Don King* (New York: Morrow, 1995), 54–56; Mark Kram, "The Fight's Lone Arranger," *Sports Illustrated*, September 2, 1974, 30–34, and "There Ain't No Others Like Me," *Sports Illustrated*, September 15, 1975, 33–43; Murray Goodman, "John of the Fighting Dalys Not in African Venture as One-Shot," *Ring*, October 1974, 58; Thomas Hauser, *Muhammad Ali: His Life and Times* (New York: Simon & Schuster, 1991), 263–264; R. Smith, "On to the Congo"; "Foreman, Ali to 'Sign Up' Today," *Chicago Defender*, May 15, 1974.

5. Goodman, "John of the Fighting Dalys," 58; "Irked Foreman Rips Ali's Suit at Dinner," *New York Times*, June 23, 1974; Oppenheimer quoted in Len Giovannitti and Fred Freed, *The Decision to Drop the Bomb* (New York: Coward-McCann, 1965), 328.

6. "Foreman Plays Smart, Ignores Word Battle," *Chicago Defender*, May 16, 1974; "Foreman-Ali Ballyhoo Starts," *Baltimore Sun*, March 28, 1974; "Foreman's Day Spoiled; Ali Says He's Sorry," *Chicago Defender*, June 25, 1974.

7. Interviews with George Foreman, in possession of the author, cited as Foreman interview; George Foreman and Joel Engel, *By George: The Autobiography of George Foreman* (New York: Villard, 1995), 104.

8. Dave Anderson, "Broken Glasses at the Waldorf," *New York Times*, June 24, 1974; "Clothes Rip, Dishes Spill as Foreman, Ali Clash," *Baltimore Sun*, June 24, 1974.

9. Anderson, "Broken Glasses at the Waldorf"; Andrew R. M. Smith, "Sculpting George Foreman: A Soul Era Champion in the Golden Age of Black Heavyweights," *Journal of Sport History* 40, no. 3 (2013): 466; Foreman interview.

10. "Clothes Rip, Dishes Spill"; "Irked Foreman Rips Ali's Suit"; Foreman interview.

11. Foreman interview; "Clothes Rip, Dishes Spill"; "Irked Foreman Rips Ali's Suit"; "Foreman's Day Spoiled"; "Sports News Briefs," *New York Times*, June 27, 1974; Anderson, "Broken Glasses as the Waldorf"; Mailer notes, NMC.

12. "Foreman's Day Spoiled"; "Sports News Briefs," June 27, 1974; Anderson, "Broken Glasses as the Waldorf"; "Ali Opens Fight Camp," *Chicago Defender*, July 20, 1974; Dick Jerardi, "Just Three Young 'Zealots' at Deer Lake, Hanging with Ali,"

Philadelphia Inquirer, June 5, 2016; "Foreman, Ali to Attend Africa Benefit," *New York Times*, August 27, 1974; "Foreman, Ali, Frazier Stage Benefit Bout," *Chicago Defender*, August 28, 1974; Matthew Piper, "The Champ Was Here: Ali Sparred at the Salt Palace, Met Third Wife at Salt Lake Airport," *Salt Lake City Tribune*, June 4, 2016; Foreman interview.

13. Randy Neumann, "Ali-Foreman Fight in Africa: Public Relations vs. Pugilism," *New York Times*, August 18, 1974; "Ali Prays in Preparation for Foreman," *Chicago Defender*, August 31, 1974; Mailer notes, NMC; Lindsay, *The Congo*, 3. "Mountains of the Moon" is an ancient term for an East African mountain range assumed to be the source of the Nile.

14. Jim Murray, "Zaire's Symbol a Boxing Glove," *Los Angeles Times*, October 27, 1974; Jerry Izenberg, "The Scene," *Newark Star-Ledger*, October 28, 1974; Peter J. Schraeder, *United States Foreign Policy toward Africa: Incrementalism, Crisis, and Change* (New York: Cambridge University Press, 1994), 79–80. Photographs of the billboards can be seen in the MAC.

15. Schraeder, 67–83; Michael G. Schatzberg, *Mobutu or Chaos? The United States and Zaire, 1960–1990* (Lanham, MD: University Press of America, 1991), 15–33; Jeanne M. Haskin, *The Tragic State of the Congo: From Decolonization to Dictatorship* (New York: Algora, 2005), 42–47.

16. Haskin, *The Tragic State of the Congo*, 45–49; Schatzberg, 34–38; Schraeder, *United States Foreign Policy*, 81; Lewis A. Erenberg, "Rumble in the Jungle: Muhammad Ali vs. George Foreman in the Age of Global Spectacle," *Journal of Sport History* 39, no. 1 (2012): 90; AEK to SSDC, "Mobutu Speech Marks 7th Anniversary of MPR," May 20, 1974, CFPF, RG 59, NARA-AAD; Essolomwa Nkoy ea Linganga, "Hommage à Mobutu," *Elima*, September 13, 1974; Gerard J. DeGroot, *The Seventies Unplugged: A Kaleidoscopic Look at a Violent Decade* (New York: Macmillan, 2011), 320.

17. Mavomo Nzuzi Zola, "Enfin, un Nouveau Stade du 20 Mai," *Salongo*, September 23, 1974; American Embassy Monrovia to SSDC, "Tolberts May Be Financial Backers of Cultural Festival in Zaire," October 30, 1974, CFPF, RG 59, NARA-AAD; Kalonji Kabasele Muboyayi, "Kinshasa est prêt pour abriter la grande explication Ali-Foreman," *Elima*, September 7, 1974; "Le festival de Kinshasa," *Elima*, September 16, 1974.

18. "Mailer Press Kit," NMC; AEK to USIS, "NY Times Articles on Zaire," June 28, 1974, and "Zairian Visa for Newsweek's Andrew Jaffe," July 24, 1974, both in CFPF, RG 59, NARA-AAD; M. M. Drake Jr., ed., *George Foreman Muhammad Ali*

Championship (Milwaukee: Pro-Form, 1974), 5, available in "Boxing Programs," JSRC.

19. Foreman interview; Jeremy Rich, "Zaire for Jesus: Ford Philpot's Revivals in the Democratic Republic of Congo, 1966–1978," *Journal of Religion in Africa* 43, no. 1 (2013): 4–28; Kenneth Lee Adelman, "The Church-State Conflict in Zaire," *African Studies Review* 18, no. 1 (1975): 102–116; Richard Hoffer, *Bouts of Mania: Ali, Frazier, Foreman, and an America on the Ropes* (Boston: Da Capo, 2014), 146–148; Jerry Izenberg, *Once There Were Giants: The Golden Age of Heavyweight Boxing* (New York: Skyhorse, 2017), 96–97.

20. Foreman interview; Aloys Kabanda, *Ali/Foreman: Le combat du siècle à Kinshasa, 29–30 Octobre 1974* (Sherbrooke, QC: Namaan, 1977), copy in NUAC; Kalonji Kabasele Muboyayi, "George Foreman: 'Si Dieu le veut, je crois que je vais mettre Ali K.O,'" *Elima*, September 13, 1974; "Foreman Insists He is Ready for Title Bout," *Jet*, October 17, 1974, 51; "Ali: 'Je battrai Foreman et son chien!,'" *Elima*, September 15, 1974; SSDC to AEK, "Muhammad Ali," June 10, 1974, CFPF, RG59, NARA-AAD; Norman Mailer, *The Fight* (1975; repr., New York: Vintage, 1997), 44–45.

21. John Hollis, "Physicals Day for Title Bout Belongs to Ali," *Houston Post*, October 28, 1974; Grant Farred, "When Kings Were (anti-?)Colonials: Black Athletes in Film," *Sport in Society* 11, nos. 2–3 (2008): 240–252.

22. Mailer, *The Fight*, 156–157; AEK to USIS, "Ali-Foreman Entourage in Kinshasa for Fight Preparations" and "Ali-Foreman Fight Preparations," both May 8, 1974, CFPF, RG 59, NARA-AAD; Dan Daniel, "September 25, at 3 A.M., Scheduled for Foreman-Ali Championship Fight in Zaire," *Ring*, July 1974, 8–9.

23. AEK to USIS, "Accreditation of Journalists for Ali-Foreman Fight," July 11, 1974, CFPF, RG 59, NARA-AAD; Jesse Kornbluth, "Muhammad Goes to the Mountain," *New Times*, September 6, 1974, clipping in NMC; "Ali: 'Je battrai Foreman'"; "La Tension Monte à Kinshasa," *La Semaine*, October 20, 1974; Nat Loubet, "Did Fight Game's Evil Eye Hex Foreman-Ali?," *Ring*, December 1974, 6–7, 43; Dan Daniel, "Ring Detective Explains Zaire Cut Eye Ploy, the Foreman Need for Delay," *Ring*, February 1975, 8–9; Jerry Izenberg, "Awake and Sing" and "Smiling Time," *Newark Star-Ledger*, October 25 and 27, 1974; Hoffer, *Bouts of Mania*, 153; see also Muhammad Ali, *The Greatest: My Own Story*, with Richard Durham (New York: Random House, 1975), and the Howard Bingham Tape Collection, both available at the MAC.

24. Foreman interview; John Brooks, "Bio-rhythms: Will They Decide the

Future for Ali, Foreman, Evel Knievel—and You?," *Argosy*, September 1974, clipping in NMC; Malonga Bouka, "George Foreman blessé par son sparring-Partner Mc Murry [*sic*]" and "Le combat Foreman-Ali reporté au 22 ou 29 octobre 1974," *Elima*, September 18 and 19, 1974; "George Foreman sérieusement blessé à l'oeil," *La Semaine*, September 22, 1974; Loubet, "Fight Game's Evil Eye," 6–7; Odimba Dinavo, "Le Combat reporté au 22 ou au 29 octobre" and "Panorama des sports," *Salongo*, September 18, 1974; Jerry Izenberg, "Fight Now Set for Oct. 23d—if Foreman's Ready," *Newark Star-Ledger*, September 18, 1974.

CHAPTER 11: I DON'T RUN 'CAUSE I DON'T HAVE TO

1. Norman Mailer, *The Fight* (1975; repr., New York: Vintage, 1997), 19–26.

2. Interviews with George Foreman, in possession of the author, cited as Foreman interview; George Plimpton, *Shadow Box: An Amateur in the Ring* (1977; repr., New York: Lyons & Burford, 1993), 228; Mailer, *The Fight*, 20–29. The International Association of Sporting Press filed a letter of protest against the censorship exercised by the Zairois government; see AEK to USIS, "Zairian Media Account of Letter of Protest from International Association of Sporting Press," October 5, 1974, CFPF, RG 59, NARA-AAD.

3. AEK to SSDC, "Ali-Foreman Faces Possible Postponement," September 17, 1974, CFPF, RG 59, NARA-AAD; Larry Merchant, "No Problem," *New York Post*, September 27, 1974; Thomas Hauser, *The View From Ringside: Inside the Tumultuous World of Boxing* (Wilmington, DE: Sport Media, 2003), 88–93; Larry Merchant, "Our Man Is Barred from Zaire," *New York Post*, October 24, 1974; AEK to SSDC, "Revised Hotel and Restaurant Section of DSP-23," November 11, 1974, and "Ali-Foreman Fight," July 26, 1974, both in CFPF, RG 59, NARA-AAD.

4. Thomas A. Johnson, "Many Opt for Zaire Vacation Without a Fight," *New York Times*, September 20, 1974; Al Harvin, "For Tourists in Zaire, There's Still a Music Festival," *New York Times*, September 18, 1974; *When We Were Kings*, dir. Leon Gast (Das Films, 1996); *Soul Power*, dir. Jeffrey Levy-Hinte (Antidote Films, 2008); Jerry Izenberg, "High and Dry," *Newark Star-Ledger*, September 26, 1974; Thomas A. Johnson, "Music Fete in Zaire Has Poor Box Office, but Makes Big Hit," *New York Times*, September 9, 1974; AEK to SSDC, "Zaire 74 Festival," September 25, 1974, CFPF, RG 59, NARA-AAD.

5. Plimpton, *Shadow Box*, 251.

6. Foreman interview; Thomas Hauser, *Muhammad Ali: His Life and Times* (New York: Simon & Schuster, 1991), 415–416; Mailer, *The Fight*, 24, 63–64; "Foreman Stays Silent," *New York Post*, October 24, 1974.

7. Plimpton, *Shadow Box*, 242–250; Mailer, *The Fight*, 83; American Embassy Niamey to SSDC, "American Journalists in Niger," September 4, 1974, and AEK to USIS, "Mobutu Criticizes 'Certain Foreign Journalists' for 'Lies,'" September 24, 1974, both in CFPF, RG 59, NARA-AAD.

8. Plimpton, *Shadow Box*, 270–273.

9. Plimpton, *Shadow Box*, 233–234, 270–271; AEK to SSDC, "Behind the Scenes of the Ali-Foreman Postponement," September 18, 1974, "Request for US Government Assistance to Festival of Zaire 74," September 7, 1974, and "Ali-Foreman Fight Situation Settles Down," September 19, 1974, all in CFPF, RG 59, NARA-AAD.

10. AEK to SSDC, "Foreman Press Conference," September 27, 1974, CFPF, RG 59, NARA-AAD; George Plimpton, "They'll Be Swinging in the Rain," *Sports Illustrated*, September 30, 1974, 38–43; Odimba Dinavo, "Foreman a renoué avec les entraînements," *Salongo*, October 1, 1974; Leonard Lewin, "The Zaire Man: It's No Hustle...Honest," *New York Post*, October 16, 1974; Malonga Bouka, "Foreman 'porté disparu' à N'Sele," *Elima*, September 25, 1974; Foreman interview.

11. Mailer, *The Fight*, 60–61, 82–94; AEC to AEK, "Ali-Foreman Fight Preparations," May 10, 1974, CFPF, RG 59, NARA-AAD.

12. AEK to SSDC, "Ali-Foreman Match," October 15, 1974, and "Message from President Ford to Mobutu," October 30, 1974, both in CFPF, RG 59, NARA-AAD; Plimpton, *Shadow Box*, 238–240; Mailer, *The Fight*, 98.

13. "Foreman Solid Choice over Ali," *Newark Star-Ledger*, October 29, 1974; "Champ Betting Pick, Ali African Favorite," *Houston Chronicle*, October 29, 1974; Mailer, *The Fight*, 113; John Hollis, "Physicals Day for Title Bout Belongs to Ali," *Houston Post*, October 28, 1974; Kitemona N'Silu, "Les journalistes parlent du super-combat de Kinshasa," *Elima*, October 29, 1974; George Plimpton, "Breaking a Date for the Dance," *Sports Illustrated*, November 11, 1974, 23; Phil Pepe, "Logic: Foreman; Sentiment: Ali," *New York Daily News*, October 29, 1974.

14. Plimpton, *Shadow Box*, 314–315, and "Breaking a Date," 24–25; Mailer, *The Fight*, 94. Mailer's notes are available in the NMC.

15. Foreman interview; "Un arbitre noir américain pour le combat Ali-Foreman?," *Elima*, September 14, 1974; Hauser, *Muhammad Ali*, 419; Mailer, *The Fight*, 147–149.

16. Plimpton, *Shadow Box*, 230–232; Jim Murray, "Foreman's Edge: He's Had More Fights at 4 a.m.," *Los Angeles Times*, October 29, 1974; Mailer, *The Fight*, 44–48, 147–149.

17. *The Greatest*, dir. Tom Gries (Columbia, 1977); Mailer, *The Fight*, 141–142, 156–157; Bondo Neama, "Le combat du siècle s'est déroulé dans les meilleures conditions," *Salongo*, October 30, 1974; AEK to SSDS, "Foreman-Ali: The Final Round?," October 30, 1974, CFPF, RG 59, NARA-AAD; Jim Murray, "Going to Market," *Los Angeles Times*, October 28, 1974; Plimpton, *Shadow Box*, 310–314, 334–355; Moaka Toko, "Une nouvelle victoire du Mobutisme," *Elima*, October 31, 1974.

18. Hauser, *Muhammad Ali*, 273; Mailer, *The Fight*, 169–170.

19. Plimpton, *Shadow Box*, 322; Foreman interview; Muboyayi Mubanga, "Dick Sadler: 'C'est l'excès de confiance qui a battu George Foreman," *Salongo*, October 31, 1974; Mailer, *The Fight*, 173–176; Jerry Izenberg, "Sting like a Bee," *Newark Star-Ledger*, October 30, 1974; George Kimball and John Schulian, eds., *At The Fights: American Writers on Boxing* (New York: Penguin, 2011), 219; Plimpton, *Shadow Box*, 315–317, 323.

20. Skop Myslenski, "Ali Flattens Foreman in 8th to Regain Title," *Los Angeles Times*, October 30, 1974; Dundee quoted in Mailer's Notes, NMC; Hauser, *Muhammad Ali*, 276.

21. Mailer, *The Fight*, 151–152, 186–190; a transcript of the broadcast is available in the NMC; Dan Daniel, "Ring Detective Explains Zaire Cut Eye Ploy, the Foreman Need for Delay," *Ring*, February 1975, 8–9; Foreman interview.

22. Plimpton, *Shadow Box*, 324; *The Greatest*, dir. Gries; Izenberg, "Sting like a Bee."

23. Mike Jay, "Ali Has Nothing More to Prove," *New York Daily World*, October 31, 1974.

24. Stanley Crouch in *Muhammad Ali: Through the Eyes of the World*, ed. Mark Collings (London: Skyhorse, 2001), 92; *The Greatest*, dir. Gries; "Un K.O. retentissant et historique pour le super-combat du siècle," *La Semaine Africaine*, November 10, 1974.

25. "After the Fight, the Rain Came . . . and Came," *Los Angeles Times*, October 30, 1974; "Foreman-Ali: the Final Round?," AAD; Mailer, *The Fight*, 219; Hauser, *Muhammad Ali*, 279.

CHAPTER 12: YOU GOT TO HAVE A BOSS

1. George Plimpton, *Shadow Box: An Amateur in the Ring* (1977; repr., New York: Lyons & Burford, 1993), 314–316; Jack B. Bedell, "George Foreman in Zaire," *Hudson Review* 62, no. 2 (2009): 259; Norman O. Unger, "Foreman Stocks Up on Excuses," *Chicago Defender*, February 4, 1975; "Foreman Suggests He Was Drugged," *New York Times*, February 3, 1975; George Foreman and Joel Engel, *By George: The Autobiography of George Foreman* (New York: Villard, 1995), 117; interviews with George Foreman, in possession of the author, cited as Foreman interview.

2. Foreman interview; Foreman and Engel, *By George*, 117–119.

3. Foreman interview; Foreman and Engel, *By George*, 122–125.

4. Foreman interview; Foreman and Engel, *By George*, 128; "Foreman Back, on Ali-Wepner Card," *Chicago Defender*, January 21, 1975; "Foreman Fight," *Baltimore Sun*, January 27, 1975; Gerald Eskenazi, "Lyle Bout Dropped; Ali Suggests Wepner," *New York Times*, January 7, 1975; Norman O. Unger, "Norton vs. Bonavena, Foreman Quits," *Chicago Defender*, February 3, 1975; "Muhammad Ali Opens Training Camp for Mar. 24 Title Bout," *Atlanta Daily World*, February 28, 1975; Dan Daniel, "The Chuck Wepner Miracle," *Ring*, April 1975, 6–7; Thomas Hauser, *Muhammad Ali: His Life and Times* (New York: Simon & Schuster, 1991), 300–304; "Louis Says Boxing Will Die When Muhammad Ali Quits," *Jet*, January 2, 1975, 56.

5. Red Smith, "The Year the Golden Egg Cracked," *New York Times*, December 22, 1974; Gordon S. White Jr., "Ali Receives Hickok Award," *New York Times*, January 15, 1975; "Ali Gets Hickok Belt and Wepner," *Chicago Defender*, January 15, 1975; "Ali in Jamaica Talking of Foreman," *New York Times*, January 1, 1975; "See Foreman Rematch in Four Months, Says Ali," *Chicago Defender*, February 24, 1975; Dan Daniel, "Boxing World Over Waits for Ali to Quit Hibernation," *Ring*, March 1975, 20, and "Ali-Foreman Title Fight to Be held in New Orleans?," *Ring*, April 1975, 8–9; Dave Anderson, "The Purple Blemish," *New York Times*, May 18, 1975; Dan Daniel, "Ali vs Frazier With Arab $ Support," *Ring*, July 1975, 12–13; Dave Anderson, "The King of Boxing Promoters," *New York Times*, April 28, 1975; Foreman interview.

6. "Foreman Keeping Busy as Actor; Waits to Meet Ali," *Jet*, March 20, 1975, 47; "Television," *Jet*, February 27, 1975, 66; "Foreman Debuts in 'Let's Do It Again,'" *Atlanta Daily World*, October 10, 1975; "Star Tracks," *People*, April 21, 1975, 58; Foreman interview.

7. Foreman and Engel, *By George*, 128–129; Randy Roberts, *Jack Dempsey: The*

Manassa Mauler (1979; repr., Urbana: University of Illinois Press, 2003), 265; Thomas Hauser, "Jack Dempsey Revisited," SecondsOut, secondsout.com/usa -boxing-news/usa-boxing-news/jack-dempsey-revisited.

8. "Foreman Is Serious about His Five Foes," *Chicago Defender*, April 24, 1975; "Foreman, in Playful Mood, Defeats Five Foes Handily," *New York Times*, April 27, 1975.

9. "Foreman Rolls Past 'Five,' to End his 'Good Guy' Image," *Chicago Defender*, April 28, 1975; "Foreman, in Playful Mood."

10. Dan Daniel, "Foreman's Confidence Gone, Former Champion's Circus Turns into Burlesque," *Ring*, July 1975, 16–17; Randy Gordon, "It's About Time," *Cyber Boxing Zone Journal*, June 1998, cyberboxingzone.com/boxing/box6-98 .htm#randy; Foreman and Engel, *By George*, 129–130; Norman O. Unger, "Foreman to End 'Good Guy' Image," *Chicago Defender*, April 29, 1975; Cyclops, "TV View: The Dubious Charm of Media Brats," *New York Times*, May 11, 1975; Nat Loubet, "As I See It," *Ring*, August 1975, 5; "Foreman Rolls Past 'Five'"; "Foreman, in Playful Mood"; "Foreman: 'I Fight for my Daughter,'" *Jet*, May 15, 1975, 62–63.

11. "Foreman Sounds like Ali, Changes Nice-Guy Image," *Miami Herald*, May 4, 1975; "Foreman Rolls Past 'Five'"; Anderson, "Purple Blemish."

12. Jack Welsh, "Editorial," *Boxing Illustrated*, April 1975, 6; "Ali Announcing His Retirement," *New York Times*, June 23, 1975; Dave Anderson, "Bugner Bout My Last: Ali" and "People Who Need People Don't Retire," *New York Times*, June 24 and 25, 1975; "Ali Outpoints Bugner and Keeps Title; Champion Decides to Continue Career," *New York Times*, July 1, 1975.

13. Andrew R. M. Smith, "Revisting the Thrilla in Manila: Boxing's Golden Era 40 Years Later," *Sport in American History*, October 1, 2015, https://ussport history.com/2015/10/01/revisiting-the-thrilla-in-manila-boxings-golden-era-40 -years-later; James K. Boyce, *The Philippines: The Political Economy of Growth and Impoverishment in the Marcos Era* (Honolulu: University of Hawaii Press, 1993), 8, 303–338; Albert F. Celoza, *Ferdinand Marcos and the Philippines: The Political Economy of Authoritarianism* (Westport, CT: Praeger, 1997), 39–72; Mark Kram, *Ghosts of Manila: The Fateful Blood Feud between Muhammad Ali and Joe Frazier* (New York: HarperCollins, 2001), 168–188; Richard Hoffer, *Bouts of Mania: Ali, Frazier, Foreman, and an America on the Ropes* (Boston: Da Capo, 2014), 177–187; "Ali Makes Frazier Bout Official," *New York Times*, July 18, 1975; Dave Anderson, "Magellan to MacArthur to Muhammad," *New York Times*, September 23, 1975; Dan Daniel, "Brenner Invites King to Rent Garden, but His Fights Must Merit Arena," *Ring*, November, 1975, 18–19, 46.

14. Foreman interview; *Ring*, May 1976, cover; Foreman and Engel, *By George*, 130–133; George Foreman, *God in My Corner: A Spiritual Memoir*, with Ken Abraham (Nashville: Thomas Nelson, 2007), 47.

15. "Ali Makes Frazier Bout Official"; Dan Daniel, "George Foreman, Forgotten World Heavyweight Champ," *Ring*, November 1975, 6–7; Daniel, "Brenner Invites King," 18–19, 46.

16. "Riessen in W.T.T., Sight Unseen," *New York Times*, March 22, 1975; "Foreman's S. African Tour Set after Request Is Met," *Jet*, April 24, 1975, 59; "Mixed Audience for Foreman in South Africa," *New York Times*, March 25, 1975; "Television," *New York Times*, August 6, 1975; Eric Allen Hall, *Arthur Ashe: Tennis and Justice in the Civil Rights Era* (Baltimore: Johns Hopkins University Press, 2014), 205–206. For more on Ashe and activism, see Eric Allen Hall, "I Guess I'm Becoming More and More Militant: Arthur Ashe and the Black Freedom Movement," *Journal of African American History* 96, no. 4 (2011), 474–502.

17. Daniel, "Brenner Invites King," 18–19, 46; *New York Daily News*, October 30, 1975, front page.

18. Foreman and Engel, *By George*, 132–133; Thomas Rogers, "Foreman Ready for Comeback," *New York Times*, October 14, 1975; Shirley Norman, "Ken Norton Speaks Following KO of Lovell," *Ring*, April 1976, 10–11; Anderson, "Purple Blemish" and "You Got to Have a Boss," *New York Times*, November 16, 1975.

19. Foreman interview.

20. Pat Putnam, "Sweet Science, Indeed," *Sports Illustrated*, February 2, 1976, 18; Red Smith, "The Fighters Took a Little Longer," *New York Times*, January 26, 1976; "Foreman's Off-the-Canvas Win over Lyle Spurs Talk of Frazier Rematch," *Boxing Illustrated*, May 1976, 14; Lester Bromberg, "Does Television Need Boxing," *Ring*, June 1977, 6–7, 46; Bill Rhoden, "Tuning Up for Ali," *Ebony*, March 1976, 66; Foreman interview.

21. "Foreman Shakes Rust; Aims for Title," *Baltimore Sun*, January 26, 1976; Dan Daniel, "King, on Prowl, Tests Macao Gambling Funds for Hong Kong," *Ring*, January 1976, 8–9; Smith, "Fighters Took a Little Longer"; Dave Anderson, "Coopman Not in Ali's Plans," *New York Times*, February 18, 1976, 57; Mark Kram, "One-Nighter in San Juan," *Sports Illustrated*, March 1, 1976, 14–17; "Millionaires Ali, Frazier Spend It All in Ending Ring's Greatest Saga," *Boxing Illustrated*, January 1976, 10; Dave Anderson, "The Friendly Lion of Flanders," *New York Times*, January 8, 1976; "End of an Era, Ali Plans Finale," *Boxing Illustrated*, July 1976, 7–8.

22. Andrew R. M. Smith, "Blood Stirs the Fight Crowd: Making and Marking Joe Frazier's Philadelphia," in *Philly Sports: Teams, Games, and Athletes from*

Rocky's Town, ed. Ryan A. Swanson and David K. Wiggins (Fayetteville: University of Arkansas Press, 2016), 127; Rhoden, "Tuning Up for Ali," 66; "Ali-Norton Fight Sought for Shea," *New York Times*, February 22, 1976; Foreman and Engel, *By George*, 135–136; "Sports News Briefs," *New York Times*, March 9, 1976; "Foreman, Frazier Will Fight in May," *New York Times*, March 16, 1976; Dave Anderson, "The Most Thing Is, I love to Fight," *New York Times*, March 18, 1976; Red Smith, "Homeless Fight," *New York Times*, April 23, 1976; Gerald Eskenazi, "Nassau Coliseum Beats City on Frazier-Foreman Fight," *New York Times*, April 28, 1976; John Ort, "Foreman Drives Frazier into Retirement with KO in Five," *Ring*, September 1976, 46; Robert H. Boyle, "Smokin' Joe Burns Out," *Sports Illustrated*, June 28, 1976, 68–71; Red Smith, "Man Here Hooked on Fight Game," *New York Times*, May 28, 1976; "Foreman Back in Heavyweight Forefront," *Boxing Illustrated*, November 1976, 14–17; Foreman interview; "Heavens to Betsy and by George! Have Foreman and Frazier Wigged Out?," *People*, June 7, 1976, 24; Gerald Eskenazi, "The Heavyweights Return and the City Recaptures a Glow," *New York Times*, June 4, 1976; Michael Katz, "Eager Foreman Tilts at Skyscrapers," *New York Times*, June 11, 1976.

23. Boyle, "Smokin' Joe Burns Out," 68–71; "Foreman Back in Heavyweight Forefront," 17; Ort, "Foreman Drives Frazier," 27, 46; Prentis Rogers, "Smokin' Joe Blown Away by Foreman's Powerful Punches," *Atlanta Daily World*, June 20, 1976; "Day after the Battle," *Atlanta Daily World*, June 29, 1976; Red Smith, "New Script, But . . . ," *New York Times*, June 16, 1976.

24. Jerry Izenberg, "At Large," *Newark Star-Ledger*, June 11, 1976; Mike Katz, "Foreman Faces Long Wait for Title Shot," *New York Times*, June 17, 1976; Ort, "Foreman Drives Frazier," 46.

25. "Steinbrenner Sent 'Gift' By Perenchio," *New York Times*, May 15, 1976; Foreman and Engel, *By George*, 137; "The Dethroning of a 'King,'" *Boxing Illustrated*, October 1976, 52–55; "Foreman, King Unite," *New York Times*, July 9, 1976; Hauser, *Muhammad Ali*, 333–335; Les Brown, "Network Regains Interest in Boxing," *New York Times*, August 14, 1976; Mark Kram, "Elemental, If Not Exactly Artistic," *Sports Illustrated*, October 25, 1976, 28–29; "Foreman Back in Heavyweight Forefront," 14–17; Eskenazi, "Heavyweights Return"; Katz, "Eager Foreman"; "Exclusive Ring Interview with Ken Norton," *Ring*, January 1976, 6–7; Katz "Foreman Faces Long Wait."

CHAPTER 13: A GANGSTER'S GAME

1. "Foreman Fights Today," *New York Times*, August 14, 1976; John Ort, "Foreman KO's LeDoux; Ward Ices Merritt," *Ring*, November 1976, 16; "Foreman KO's Frenchman," *Atlanta Daily World*, August 17, 1976; "Foreman-Dennis Heavyweight Bout Slated for TV," *Atlanta Daily World*, October 8, 1976; Neil Amdur, "Dennis Says He Knows Way to Beat Foreman in Bout Tonight; Duran Meets Rojas" and "Foreman, Duran Score Knockouts," *New York Times*, October 15 and 16, 1976.

2. John Ort, "Foreman and Duran KO Outclassed Opponents," *Ring*, January 1977, 16–17; Amdur, "Dennis Says He Knows"; "Ali-Norton III a Dull, Drab Disappointment," *Boxing Illustrated*, February 1977, 8–17; Steve Cady, "Ali Scoffs at Rematch, Urging Norton to Beat Foreman First," *New York Times*, September 30, 1976; Mark Kram, "Not the Greatest Way to Go," *Sports Illustrated*, October 11, 1976, 36–43.

3. Dave Anderson, "Show Ali a Close-Up of Foreman," *New York Times*, October 5, 1976; "Ali-Norton III," 14–16; Cady, "Ali Scoffs at Rematch"; Kram, "Not the Greatest," 37; "Ali-Norton #3," *Ring*, December 1976, 64; Neil Amdur, "King Bids High for Norton-Foreman Bout," *New York Times*, October 17, 1976; Tony Kornheiser, "Ali Sees a Foreman (and Bobick) in Future and Changes His Retirement Plan Again," *New York Times*, November 23, 1976; Nat Loubet, "As I See It," *Ring*, March 1977, 5; *Foreman*, dir. Chris Perkel (Triple Threat Television, 2017).

4. Jack Kramer, "The Sports Log," *Boston Globe*, October 22, 1976; Marshall Reed, "Fighter of the Year," *Ring*, March 1977, 8–9; "The Man Who Will Be King, Again," *Boxing Illustrated*, January 1977, 7; Arthur Rembert, "Fight of the Year," *Ring*, March 1977, 10; "Foreman-Lyle Pier Six Brawl Was 1976's Best Fight of All," *Boxing Illustrated*, March 1977, 17; Trudie Loubet, "Round of the Year," *Ring*, March 1977, 12; "Lyle-Foreman Fourth Nearly Changed Course of Heavyweight History," *Boxing Illustrated*, March 1977, 17, 36; Gordy Peterson, "Foreman Pounds Out Agosto in Four," *Ring*, May 1977, 19; "Foreman to Fight Agosto This Weekend," *Atlanta Daily World*, January 20, 1977; "Foreman Signs Pact with ABC Sports," *Atlanta Daily World*, November 4, 1976; George Foreman and Joel Engel, *By George: The Autobiography of George Foreman* (New York: Villard, 1995), 138; interviews with George Foreman, in possession of the author, cited as Foreman interview.

5. Red Smith, "The Legend Himself Is Back," *New York Times*, December 22, 1976; Mark Kram, "Keeping the Fight Game Afloat," *Sports Illustrated*, January 3,

1977, 20–23; Jack Newfield, *Only in America: The Life and Crimes of Don King* (New York: Morrow, 1995), 100.

6. Newfield, *Only in America*, 100–101; Michael Katz, "King's Boxing Course: A No-Star Cast at Sea," *New York Times*, December 22, 1976; "People in Sports," *New York Times*, January 22, 1977.

7. Deane McGowen, "Boudreaux Beats LeDoux; Decision Infuriates Loser," *New York Times*, February 14, 1977; Newfield, *Only in America*, 116.

8. Issues of *Tonight's Boxing Program* are available in the JSRC.

9. Sam Toperoff, "Death of the Don King Tournament," *Sport*, August 1977, 29–30; Newfield, *Only in America*, 102–118; Reg Noble, "U.S. Tournament of Champions a 'King'-Sized Ripoff," *Boxing Illustrated*, May 1977, 42–43; Red Smith, "Homecoming in the Slammer," *New York Times*, March 8, 1977; Jacobson quoted in Newfield, *Only in America*, 120.

10. Kornheiser, "Ali Sees a Foreman" and "Ali-Bobick Is Blocked by Norton-Bobick," *New York Times*, November 24, 1976.

11. "Foreman Pummels Agosto and Stops Him in Fourth," *New York Times*, January 23, 1977.

12. Andrew R. M. Smith, "Blood Stirs the Fight Crowd: Making and Marking Joe Frazier's Philadelphia," in *Philly Sports: Teams, Games, and Athletes from Rocky's Town*, ed. Ryan A. Swanson and David K. Wiggins (Fayetteville: University of Arkansas Press, 2016), 127–145; "If Ali's Retirement Is Real Thing, Foreman Best Bet to Be Heavy King," *Boxing Illustrated*, March 1977, 22; "Heavyweight Division Now Young at Heart," *Boxing Illustrated*, July 1977, 42–43; Nat Loubet, "As I See It," *Ring*, November 1976, 5; Mark Kram, "The Champ Looked like a Chump," *Sports Illustrated*, May 10, 1976, 30–31.

13. Nat Loubet, "As I See It," *Ring*, March 1977, 5; "Foreman-Young Bout Scheduled March 15," *Atlanta Daily World*, March 3, 1977; Marcos Perez, "Young Lacks Punch but Not Confidence," *San Juan (PR) Star*, March 9, 1977; Dave Anderson, "One Head but He Don't Use It," *New York Times*, March 17, 1977; Marcos Perez, "Foreman, Escalera 3–1 Picks," *San Juan (PR) Star*, March 17, 1977; "Heavyweight Division Now Young," 40; Foreman and Engel, *By George*, 143.

14. Foreman interview.

15. Pat Putnam, "Jeemy Young! Jeemy Young! Jeemy Young!," *Sports Illustrated*, March 28, 1977, 22; Foreman interview; Marcos Perez, "Foreman Vows Early Finish for Young," *San Juan (PR) Star*, March 11, 1977.

16. Putnam, "Jeemy Young!," 23; "19th Hole: The Readers Take Over," *Sports Illustrated*, April 11, 1977, 108; Pat Putnam, "Boxing Classics: Jimmy Young vs.

George Foreman," The Sweet Science, March 6, 2005, thesweetscience.com/news /articles/1767-boxing-classic-jimmy-young-vs-george-foreman.

17. Daniel Drosdoff, "George—Fans Swayed Verdict," *San Juan (PR) Star*, March 19, 1977; Putnam, "Jeemy Young!," 22–23; Dave Anderson, "Young Floors Foreman in 12th and Wins Unanimous Decision," *New York Times*, March 18, 1977.

18. Putnam, "Boxing Classic"; "King Wants an Ali Bout in Havana," *New York Times*, March 19, 1977.

19. "Foreman Muffs Chance for Ali Rematch," *San Juan (PR) Star*, March 19, 1977; Putnam, "Boxing Classics."

20. "Foreman Leaves Hospital," *San Juan (PR) Star*, March 20, 1977; Putnam, "Jeemy Young!," 23; John Ort, "The Experts Ask: What Now, George Foreman?," *Ring*, June 1977, 10–11, 42; Putnam, "Boxing Classics"; Gary Smith, "After the Fall," *Sports Illustrated*, October 8, 1984, 68–69; "Foreman Says He's Quitting," *New York Times*, May 9, 1977; Prentis Rogers, "Rogers' Two Cents," *Atlanta Daily World*, May 12, 1977.

21. "Photo Essay: A George Foreman Retrospective," *Ring*, August 1977, 18–23; Putnam, "Boxing Classics"; Gerald Eskenazi, "Nassau Coliseum Beats City on Frazier-Foreman Fight," *New York Times*, April 28, 1976; Randy Gordon, "It's About Time," *Cyber Boxing Zone Journal*, June 1998, cyberboxingzone.com/boxing /box6-98.htm#randy; Nat Loubet, "As I See It," *Ring*, September 1977, 56; Foreman interview.

22. Foreman Rehires Sadler as Pilot, Drops Clancy," *New York Times*, April 20, 1977; "George Foreman Marries 1972 Miss Black Teenage America," *Ebony*, November 3, 1977, 22–23; Foreman interview.

23. Mike Katz, "A TV Scandal Overshadows Ali," *New York Times*, December 18, 1977; Loubet, "As I See It," September 1977, 56; Toperoff, "Don King Tournament," cover, 35; "ABC Suspends Telecasts of Boxing Tourney," *Baltimore Sun*, April 17, 1977; Dave Brady, "ABC Suspends U.S. Boxing Championships," *Washington Post*, April 17, 1977; "ABC Halts Boxing Telecasts Pending Probe," *Philadelphia Inquirer*, April 17, 1977.

24. Michael Katz, "Is the Involvement of TV Networks Helpful or Harmful to Pro Boxing?," *New York Times*, May 24, 1977; Red Smith, "Jim Farley, the Man in the Middle," *New York Times*, April 22, 1977; Dave Anderson, "Only the Boxers Change," *New York Times*, April 24, 1977; Steven A. Riess, "Only the Ring Was Square: Frankie Carbo and the Underworld Control of Boxing," *International Journal of the History of Sport* 5, no. 1 (1988): 29–52; Dave Anderson, "The TV Squeeze on Leon Spinks," *New York Times*, March 9, 1978; Jeffrey T. Sammons, *Beyond the*

Ring: The Role of Boxing in American Society (Urbana: University of Illinois Press, 1990), 137–175; Dave Anderson, "A Miracle for St. Francis of Palermo," *New York Times*, November 3, 1977; Red Smith, "Blinky Is More Sad than Angry," *New York Times*, March 15, 1978; State of New Jersey Commission of Investigation, Organized Crime in Boxing: Final Boxing Report (Trenton, NJ: December 16, 1985), 3. For an in-depth exposé of boxing under the IBC in the 1950s and early 1960s, see Barney Nagler, *James Norris and the Decline of Boxing* (New York: Bobbs-Merrill, 1964).

CHAPTER 14: JESUS RODE ON A JACKASS

1. Gary Smith, "After the Fall," *Sports Illustrated*, October 8, 1984, 72; Thomas Hauser, *The Black Lights: Inside the World of Professional Boxing* (New York: Mc-Graw-Hill, 1986), 212; Michael Katz, "Shavers, Holmes Matched in 'Elimination' Bout," *New York Times*, February 23, 1978.

2. Interviews with George Foreman, in possession of the author, cited as Foreman interview; "Ex-Champion Loses Bout in Area Court," unidentified newspaper clipping, GFBF, HPL; "Fighter George Foreman Tells of Religious Decision," *Los Angeles Times*, April 16, 1977. Thanks to Michael Gillespie for sharing recollections of Foreman's street preaching in Houston.

3. Foreman interview; Jon Verboon, "Ex-Boxing Champ Arrested in Tomball as He Preaches," *Houston Chronicle*, January 18, 1980; "Rob Meckel, "Ex-boxer Foreman Arrested at Church Revival," *Houston Post*, January 18, 1980; "Dream Lands Ex-Champ Foreman in Texas Jail," *Jet*, February 14, 1980, 52; "Foreman Accepts a Draw in Texas Revival Arrest," *Jet*, March 6, 1980; "George Foreman Tells Council He Wants to Preach on Streets," *Houston Chronicle*, February 28, 1980.

4. Foreman interview; Bill Rhoden, "The Champ Who Gave Up Millions for God," *Ebony*, April 1978, 42; "Ex-Champion Loses Bout," GFBF, HPL; "Judge Dumps Foreman's Charges against Minister," *Jet*, September 10, 1981, 8; Karen Gilmour, "Ex-Champ Says Preacher Assaulted Him," *Houston Chronicle*, July 5, 1981.

5. George Foreman and Joel Engel, *By George: The Autobiography of George Foreman* (New York: Villard, 1995), 153–154, 168–174; "George Foreman Tells Council"; "Television," *New York Times*, April 30, 1980; G. Smith, "After the Fall," 62–80; Foreman interview.

6. James Slater, "Ali to Foreman: Please Come Back and Beat Ken Norton for Me," East Side Boxing, June 16, 2016, http://www.boxing247.com/boxing-news/ali-foreman-please-ken/57817.

7. Nat Loubet, "As I See It," *Ring*, January 1978, 5, 42; Thomas Hauser, *Muhammad Ali: His Life and Times* (New York: Simon & Schuster, 1991), 350–362; Michael Katz, "Holmes Reaches Top on Courage in 15th," *New York Times*, June 11, 1978; William Nack, "The Future Is Soon," *Sports Illustrated*, March 10, 1980, 26–31.

8. Dave Anderson, "The Maps Boxing Scandal," *New York Times*, February 1, 1981; James F. Clarity, "Harold Smith: Man and His Money Remain a Mystery," *New York Times*, February 8, 1981. For more on the MAPS scandal, see Dean Allison and Bruce Henderson, *Empire of Deceit: Inside the Biggest Sports and Bank Scandal in U.S. History* (New York: Doubleday, 1985).

9. William Nack, "The Champ Who Would Be Champ," *Sports Illustrated*, September 22, 1980, 74–84; *Muhammad and Larry*, dir. Bradley Kaplan and Albert Maysles (ESPN Films, 2009); William Nack, "A Sad Show for Smokeless Joe," *Sports Illustrated*, December 14, 1981, 22–23; "Smokin' Joe Battles to a Draw," *Pittsburgh Post-Gazette*, December 4, 1981; William Nack, "Not with a Bang but a Whisper," *Sports Illustrated*, December 21, 1981, 26–29.

10. Nack, "Future Is Soon," 26; A. J. Liebling, *The Sweet Science* (New York: North Point Press, 2004), 4; George Vecsey, "Cosell Says 'I've Had It,'" *New York Times*, December 6, 1982; Dave Kindred, *Sound and Fury: Two Powerful Lives, One Fateful Friendship* (New York: Free Press, 2006), 249–250; George D. Lundberg, "Boxing Should Be Banned in Civilized Countries," *Journal of the American Medical Association*, January 14, 1983, 250; Hauser, *Black Lights*, 24, 109; Nack, "Not with a Bang," 27; Ferdie Pacheco, *Tales from the 5th St. Gym: Ali, the Dundees, and Miami's Golden Age of Boxing* (Gainesville: University Press of Florida, 2010), 235–236; Richard O. Davies, *The Main Event: Boxing in Nevada from Mining Camps to the Las Vegas Strip* (Reno: University of Nevada Press, 2014), 200–210.

11. Leo Zainea, "Foreman Gives Tokens of Gratitude to LBJ Library," *Austin American-Statesman*, September 30, 1983; "Ex-Champ George Foreman Donates Title Belt, Robe To Job Corps, LBJ Library," *Jet*, November 21, 1983, 30; Tom Allan, "Nebraskaland Honoree Unveils Trust Fund" and "Foreman Admits to Fear Before First Frazier Fight," *Omaha World-Herald*, February 27, 1983. Letters between Foreman and Lady Bird Johnson, as well as the text of Foreman's dedication speech, are available in the reference file "Foreman, George," LBJL.

12. Jack Newfield, *Only in America: The Life and Crimes of Don King* (New York: Morrow, 1995), 144, 167–177; Davies, *Main Event*, 202; "Don King's Control Grows," *New York Times*, May 15, 1983.

13. "Sports People," *New York Times*, June 20, 1984; Dave Anderson, "Advice From Ali Is an Aid for Breland," *New York Times*, July 30, 1984; G. Smith, "After the Fall," 72; Dave Anderson, "Zaire Memories 10 Years Later," *New York Times*, October 30, 1984; "Like Mt. Olympus," *Jet*, October 29, 1984, 48; "Brown to Portray Foreman in Film," *Jet*, January 3, 1980, 56; "Boxer Foreman Lands Recording Pact," *Jet*, January 31, 1980, 60; Frank Deford, "The Rocky Files (a Rerun)," *Sports Illustrated*, June 7, 1982, 70; "Reader's Rap," *Jet*, September 29, 1977, 4; "19th Hole: The Readers Take Over," *Sports Illustrated*, October 22, 1984, 140; George Vecsey, "Foreman Fights from Pulpit," *New York Times*, November 17, 1982; Jack Gallagher, "Foreman Shows the Colors Again," *Houston Post*, July 39, 1984.

14. Foreman interview; G. Smith, "After the Fall," 70–80; Foreman and Engel, *By George*, 183–198.

15. Foreman and Engel, *By George*, 200–203; Budd Schulberg, "The Second Coming of George Foreman," in *Sparring with Hemingway, And Other Legends of the Fight Game* (Chicago: Dee, 1995), 227–228; Timothy O'Brien, "Fortune's Fools: Why the Rich Go Broke," *New York Times*, September 16, 2006; Foreman interview.

16. G. Smith, "After the Fall," 70, 79.

17. Foreman interview.

18. Foreman interview; Earl Gustkey, "George Foreman Joines the Comeback Parade," *Los Angeles Times*, August 30, 1986; "Sports People," *New York Times*, August 31, 1986; Phil Berger, "Saloon Champion Swings for Pro Title," *New York Times*, December 4, 1986; "Names in the News," *Los Angeles Times*, January 14, 1987.

19. Foreman interview; Phil Berger, "Tyson Wins W.B.C. Championship," *New York Times*, November 23, 1986; Dave Anderson, "Tyson Era is Now," *New York Times*, November 24, 1986.

20. Foreman interview; Diane Vaughan, *The Challenger Launch Decision: Risky Technology, Culture, and Deviance at NASA* (Chicago: University of Chicago Press, 1996), 12–14.

21. Foreman interview; "George Foreman," OTOHP, transcript of interview, January 16, 2013; "Newswire," *Los Angeles Times*, February 21, 1987, and February 28, 1987; Richard Hoffer, "Michael Spinks May Have Outsmarted Himself by Going

After Cooney," *Los Angeles Times*, March 1, 1987; Jeff Masa, "Foreman's Comeback Opponent Finally Approved," *Sacramento Union*, March 3, 1987; Steve Kennedy, "Foreman's Foe Not Used to Being Knocked Down," *Sacramento Union*, March 6, 1987; Jeff Masa, "Plodding Foreman Pummels Zouski," *Sacramento Union*, March 10, 1987; Dave Anderson, "Foreman's Second Wind," *New York Times*, February 26, 1987.

CHAPTER 15: MAN OF LA MANCHA

1. Interviews with George Foreman, in possession of the author, cited as Foreman interview; "Sports People," *New York Times*, March 12, 1987; *Foreman*, dir. Chris Perkel (Triple Threat Television, 2017).

2. Phil Berger, "Foreman Is Fighting His Waistline and Critics," *New York Times*, February 3, 1988; Richard Sandomir, "A Pitchman with a Punch," *New York Times*, January 21, 2000; George Foreman and Joel Engel, *By George: The Autobiography of George Foreman* (New York: Villard, 1995), 235–242; Jack Newfield, *Only in America: The Life and Crimes of Don King* (New York: Morrow, 1995), 254–281; Jose Torres, *Fire and Fear: The Inside Story of Mike Tyson* (New York: Warner, 1989), 30; "Today's Sports," *New York Times*, June 26, 1988; "Foreman Come Back to Caesars," *Las Vegas Sun*, February 4, 1988; Alan Goldstein, "There's No Sign of Armistice in War Between Promoters Arum, King," *Baltimore Sun*, August 21, 1988; "Drug Report on Cooper," *New York Times*, June 16, 1989; Richard Woodbury, "A Slugger and a Dream," *Time*, July 24, 1989, 8; Foreman interview.

3. Neil A. Wynn, "Deconstructing Tyson: The Black Boxer as American Icon," *International Journal of the History of Sport* 20, no. 3 (2003): 99–114; Phil Berger, "Fighting-Trim Tyson Hunkers Down," *New York Times*, February 19, 1989; Bruce Keidan, "Foreman KO's Cooney in Second Round," *Pittsburgh Post-Gazette*, January 16, 1990; Richard Hoffer, "Still Hungry after All These Years," *Sports Illustrated*, July 17, 1989, cover, 60–74; Foreman and Engel, *By George*, 243; Foreman interview. For discussions of "rapsploitation" film and culture, see Kimberley Monteyne, *Hip Hop on Film: Performance Culture, Urban Space, and Genre Transformation in the 1980s* (Jackson: University Press of Mississippi, 2013).

4. Keidan, "Foreman KO's Cooney"; "The Circumference Factor," *Sports Illustrated*, August 7, 1989, 11; "Foreman, Tyson May Have Title Fight in China," *Seattle Times*, June 2, 1989; Robert McG. Thomas Jr., "China Said to Offer $25 Million for

Tyson-Foreman in Beijing," *New York Times*, June 2, 1989; "Tyson vs. Foreman in Beijing?," *Miami Herald*, June 3, 1989; "Chinese Troops Storm Square, Fire on Crowd," *Seattle Times*, June 4, 1989; Phil Berger, "Promoter's Novel Approach to Financing a Fight," *New York Times*, July 5, 1989. Thanks to Joe Cortez for discussing his life in boxing, from Spanish Harlem to Las Vegas.

5. Berger, "Promoter's Novel Approach"; Foreman interview.

6. Newfield, *Only in America*, 282–283. For a complete analysis of the Tyson-Douglas fight, see Joe Layden, *The Last Great Fight: The Extraordinary Tale of Two Men and How One Fight Changed Their Lives Forever* (New York: St. Martin's, 2007).

7. *42 to 1*, dir. Ben Houser and Jeremy Schaap (ESPN Films, 2018). For the state of Japan's economy at the time of the Tyson-Douglas fight, see Christopher Wood, *The Bubble Economy: Japan's Extraordinary Speculative Boom of the '80s and Dramatic Bust of the '90s* (New York: Atlantic Monthly Press, 1993), and Koichi Hamada, Anil K. Kashyap, and David Weinstein, eds., *Japan's Bubble, Deflation, and Long-Term Stagnation* (Boston: MIT Press, 2011).

8. Ron Kantowski, "For Big George, This Could Be the Big One," *Las Vegas Sun*, June 15, 1990; Foreman interview; Frederick C. Klein, "The Long Arms of the Champ," *Wall Street Journal*, September 28, 1990; Jeff Ryan, "Beers with ... George Foreman," *Sport*, August 1990, 24.

9. Phil Berger, "Holyfield Flattens Douglas and Takes the Title," *New York Times*, October 26, 1990; "Holyfield Lines Up Foreman Bout," *New York Times*, October 12, 1990; Foreman and Engel, *By George*, 243.

10. John Helyer, "Pay-Per-View Aims for Boxing Knockout," *Wall Street Journal*, January 24, 1991; Jerry Izenberg, "Future Shock Meets the Big Green Machine," *Newark Star-Ledger*, April 11, 1991.

11. Randy Roberts, *Joe Louis: Hard Times Man* (New Haven, CT: Yale University Press, 2010), 252–256; Thomas Hauser, *Chaos, Corruption, and Glory: A Year in Boxing* (Wilmington, DE: Sports Media, 2005), 104–105; "Top 100," *Sport*, June 1987, 26, June 1988, 24, June 1989, 76, and June 1990, 68; "From Edison to Marconi to TV," *Ring*, March 1972, 40; Jeff Ryan, "Boxing's '80s," *Sport*, October 1989, 76–77.

12. W. H. Stickney Jr., "Foreman's Dreams of Preaching, Fighting Coexist," *Houston Chronicle*, April 18, 1991; Mickey Herskowitz, "No Matter Who Wins, George Already Has," *Houston Post*, April 15, 1991; Jerry Izenberg, "Foreman Wants a Miracle—and a Lot of Cheeseburgers," *Newark Star-Ledger*, April 17, 1991; Ed Fowler, "Foreman Lives His Life to Excess," *Houston Chronicle*, April 19, 1991;

W. H. Stickney Jr., "Foreman-Holyfield Notes," *Houston Chronicle*, April 19, 1991; Chris Thorne, "Foreman Looks to Cap Comeback," *Newark Star-Ledger*, April 19, 1991; Jerry Izenberg, "Atlantic City Happy Times," *Newark Star-Ledger*, April 19, 1991; Joanne Lipman, "Foreman Wins Fight by KO with Sponsors," *Wall Street Journal*, April 23, 1991; Izenberg, "Future Shock."

13. Foreman and Engel, *By George*, 245; Kenny Hand, "Fight of the Ages Proves Just That," *Houston Post*, April 20, 1990; Frederick C. Klein, "Heavy Leather and Hard Breathing," *Wall Street Journal*, April 22, 1991.

14. Budd Schulberg, "Foreman-Holyfield: The Bigger They Are, the Harder They Don't Fall," in *Sparring with Hemingway, And Other Legends of the Fight Game* (Chicago: Dee, 1995), 232–237; "Holyfield-Foreman Round-by-Round," *Newark Star-Ledger*, April 20, 1990; "Round by Round," *Houston Post*, April 20, 1990.

15. Glen Macnow, "'Battle of Ages' Is King of the Moneymakers," *Philadelphia Inquirer*, April 25, 1991; Pat Putnam, "No Joke," *Sports Illustrated*, April 29, 1991, 22–27; "Foreman's Dream Close to Reality," *Houston Post*, April 20, 1990; Chris Thorne, "Foreman as Big a Winner as Holyfield," *Newark Star-Ledger*, April 21, 1990; Lipman, "Foreman Wins Fight"; Jerry Izenberg, "Big George's Real Victory," *Newark Star-Ledger*, April 21, 1990; Ann Hodges, "George Foreman, HBO Sign Entertainment Pact," *Houston Chronicle*, July 18, 1991; *Foreman*, dir. Perkel; Foreman interview.

16. Schulberg, "Bigger They Are," 232; "Foreman to Retire after June 7 Match," *New York Times*, April 8, 1993; David Theis, "Hail, George," *Houston Post*, June 10, 1993; Royce Feour, "Big George: Second Career Also Successful," *Las Vegas Sun*, June 6, 1993; Jerry Izenberg, "Mr. Foreman: Exit Smiling," *Newark Star-Ledger*, June 7, 1992; Laurie M. Grossman, "Dorito Chips Get More Ad Spending, Little Less Garlic," *Wall Street Journal*, April 22, 1992; Kevin Goldman, "Networks Parade Their Works in Progress," *Wall Street Journal*, March 25, 1993; Foreman interview.

17. Royce Feour, "Morrison: My Fists Will End Foreman's Career," *Las Vegas Sun*, June 5, 1993; Chris Thorne, "Morrison Hopeful He Can Cause the Final Retirement of Foreman," *Newark Star-Ledger*, June 7, 1993; Dean Julpe, "Foreman's on the Light Side," *Las Vegas Sun*, June 7, 1993; "Boxing Writers Poll," *Las Vegas Sun*, June 6, 1993; Dean Julpe, "Arum Angered by Commission," *Las Vegas Sun*, June 2, 1993; Chris Thorne, "Morrison Ends Foreman Career," *Newark Star-Ledger*, June 8, 1993; Chris Thorne, "Morrison Game Plan Paid Off," *Newark Star-Ledger*, June 9, 1993.

18. David Zurawik, "Foreman Takes on New Role as 'George' in ABC Sitcom,"

Baltimore Sun, July 26, 1993; Foreman and Engel, *By George*, 251–253; Jack Rejtman, "Hold the Mustard; Hot-Dog Sales Drop," *Wall Street Journal*, July 8, 1993; Bruce Pascoe, "Battered Holyfield Has No Complaint," *Las Vegas Sun*, April 23, 1994.

19. Foreman and Engel, *By George*, 253–255; "Foreman Group Files Lawsuit," *New York Times*, August 16, 1994; "Judge Gives Foreman Green Light for Bout," *New York Times*, August 21, 1994; Foreman interview.

20. Foreman interview; Fred Liscum and Jeffrey W. East, *Floods in Southeast Texas, October 1994*, report prepared for the US Geological Survey (US Department of the Interior, January 1995); Richard Hoffer, "Ko'd," *Sports Illustrated*, November 14, 1994, 22; Dean Julpe, "Foreman Approaching This Fight with a Fury," *Las Vegas Sun*, November 3, 1994.

21. Foreman interview; Ed Odeven, "George Foreman Reflects on Bouts in Japan, Interactions," *Japan Times*, November 30, 2018; Chris Thorne, "Here's Title Bout with New Wrinkle . . . Foreman's Age," *Newark Star-Ledger*, November 2, 1994; Jerry Izenberg, "Head Games in Gomorrah," *Newark Star-Ledger*, November 3, 1994; Dean Julpe, "This Is No Time for Friendly Chat," *Las Vegas Sun*, November 1, 1994; Chris Thorne, "Moorer's Willing to Give Up Laughs but Not His Title," *Newark Star-Ledger*, November 3, 1994; Kevin Goldman, "Catch a Falling Star: Big Names Plummet From List of Top 10 Celebrity Endorsers," *Wall Street Journal*, October 19, 1994; Hoffer, "Ko'd," 21–22.

22. Jerry Izenberg, "Jackpot! Jackpot!," *Newark Star-Ledger*, November 6, 1994; Doug Mitchell, "Pow!," *Houston Post*, November 6, 1994; Odeven, "George Foreman Reflects." Everlast made a series of customized trunks for Foreman when he was heavyweight champion, and some included a large emblazoned "GF" on the left leg, which he wore against Norton and Ali. The pair he chose for Moorer did not have initials on the leg, and his only title defense in the 1970s while wearing plain shorts was the Roman fight.

23. Foreman interview; Izenberg, "Jackpot!"; "Foreman-Moorer Round by Round," *Las Vegas Sun*, November 6, 1994.

24. Izenberg, "Jackpot!"; "Foreman-Moorer Round by Round."

25. Hoffer, "KO'd," 20–23; Foreman and Engel, *By George*, 256–257; Izenberg, "Jackpot!"; Chris Thorne, "Foreman Jars Moorer in 10th to Regain Title," *Newark Star-Ledger*, November 6, 1994; Foreman interview.

26. Dean Julpe, "Age Wins Out in a Beauty," *Las Vegas Sun*, November 7, 1994.

EPILOGUE

1. Interviews with George Foreman, in possession of the author, cited as Foreman interview; David E. Engen, "The Making of a People's Champion: An Analysis of Media Representations of George Foreman," *Southern Communication Journal* 60, no. 2 (1995): 141–150; James T. Patterson, *Restless Giant: The United States from Watergate to Bush v. Gore* (New York: Oxford University Press, 2005), 310–313; Jan Reid, "Big," *Texas Monthly*, February 1995, 156.

2. Greg Hassell, "Win Adds to Foreman's Marketability," *Houston Chronicle*, November 9, 1994; "Television," *New York Times*, April 16, May 14, May 16, 1995, March 27 and June 12, 1996; Leonard Moon, "The Return of Big George," *Houston Newspages*, December 8–14, 1994; Reid, "Big," 155–156; Foreman interview.

3. "Foreman Victory Helps Increase Boxer's Endorsement Potential," *Houston Newspages*, November 10–16, 1994; Doug Mitchell, "Plethora of Options Face Foreman," *Houston Post*, November 7, 1994.

4. Foreman interview; Gerald Eskenazi, "A Triumphant Whitaker Moves to Claim Next Title," *New York Times*, March 5, 1995; "WBA Ruling Takes Foreman's Title Away," *Houston Post*, March 5, 1995; Dean Julpe, "Schulz Warms to Media Glow," *Las Vegas Sun*, April 20, 1995; Chris Thorne, "Foreman Wins . . . but Few Believe It," *Newark Star-Ledger*, April 23, 1994; Nat Gottlieb, "Over-the-Hill Foreman has a Shill in Merchant," *Newark Star-Ledger*, April 25, 1995; Dean Julpe, "King George Is Saved," *Las Vegas Sun*, April 24, 1995; Tom Friend, "Foreman Gets Last Laugh, and He Knows It," *New York Times*, April 24, 1995.

5. Jerry Izenberg, "The Night the Calendar Moved," *Newark Star-Ledger*, April 24, 1995; "IBF Orders a Foreman-Schulz Rematch," *New York Times*, June 4, 1995; Chris Thorne, "Arum Wants Title Tournament," *Newark Star-Ledger*, April 23, 1995; Jerry Izenberg, "Tough Talk in the Emerald City," *Newark Star-Ledger*, April 20, 1995; "Foreman Giving Up Title," *New York Times*, June 29, 1995; Friend, "Foreman Gets Last Laugh"; "Lucrative Bout Awaits Foreman," *Las Vegas Sun*, April 28, 1995; Timothy Smith, "Foreman Subpoenaed in Corruption Investigation," *New York Times*, April 3, 1999; "Arum Details Payoff Proposal in Trial of IBF's Founder," *New York Times*, June 6, 2000.

6. Julie Sloane, "Gorgeous George," *Fortune Small Business*, June 1, 2003; Hal Sundt, "A Tale of Two Grill Masters," *Inventors Digest*, May 2015, 19–24; Foreman interview. For best-seller lists, see *New York Times*, June 17, 1995, and *Wall Street Journal*, June 21, 1995.

7. Foreman interview; George Foreman, *God in My Corner: A Spiritual Memoir*, with Ken Abraham (Nashville: Thomas Nelson, 2007), 156–157; Sloane, "Gorgeous George"; Sundt, "Tale of Two Grill Masters"; Hulk Hogan, *Hollywood Hulk Hogan*, with Michael Jan Friedman (New York: Simon & Schuster, 2002), 252–254; Richard Sandomir, "A Pitchman with a Punch," *New York Times*, January 21, 2000.

8. Sundt, "Tale of Two Grill Masters"; Sloane, "Gorgeous George."

9. David Como, "July 11, 1996: Bowe vs. Golota I," The Fight City, July 11, 2018, https://www.thefightcity.com/july-11-1996-bowe-vs-golota-i-riddick-bowe-andrew-golota-mike-tyson-lennox-lewis-riot-madison-square-garden; Corey Erdman, "What It's like to Commentate on a Boxing Match When a Riot Breaks Out," Vice Sports, March 17, 2017, https://sports.vice.com/en_uk/article/ezeaea/what-it39s-like-to-call-a-boxing-match-when-a-riot-breaks-out-uk-translation; Thom Loverro, "20 Years Ago, Riddick Bowe and Andrew Golota Fought in a Fight No One Won," *Washington Times*, July 11, 2016; Sloane, "Gorgeous George."

10. Andrew Pollack, "Foreman and Morrison Earn the Right to Fight Again," *New York Times*, November 4, 1996; Ed Schuyler Jr., "Retirement Talk is Probably Just Talk," Associated Press, April 25, 1997; Timothy Smith, "Foreman Looking for Who's Next," *New York Times*, April 28, 1997; Sherri Day, "George Foreman Adds Steak to the Sizzle," *New York Times*, March 4, 2003; Sandomir, "Pitchman with a Punch"; Timothy Smith, "Briggs Wins, Crowd Boos and Foreman Says He Likely Won't Box Again," *New York Times*, November 23, 1997; Steve Springer, "Foreman Promoters Launch Protest," *Los Angeles Times*, November 30, 1997; Timothy Smith, "Foreman Takes His Cheeseburgers to Go," *New York Times*, November 24, 1997.

11. Patrick McGeehan, "Salton Pays $137.5 Million for George Foreman's Name," *New York Times*, December 10, 1999; "What's News: Business and Finance World-Wide," *Wall Street Journal*, December 10, 1999; Sam Walker, "George Foreman's Endorsement In Perpetuity Nets $137.5 Million," *Wall Street Journal*, December 10, 1999; Sloane, "Gorgeous George"; Sundt, "Tale of Two Grill Masters"; Michael Bamberger, "Mining Woods for Gold," *Sports Illustrated*, September 25, 2000, 27; Foreman interview.

12. Sloane, "Gorgeous George"; Foreman interview.

13. Foreman interview; Stephanie Frederic, "TV Land's Family Foreman," *Los Angeles Sentinel*, July 24, 2008.

14. Foreman interview; Rick Porter, "Tuesday Final Ratings: 'Better Late Than Never,' Everything Else Unchanged," *TV By the Numbers*, August 24, 2016, "Tues-

day Final Ratings: 'America's Got Talent' Adjusts Up," *TV By the Numbers*, August 31, 2016, "Tuesday Final Ratings: 'America's Got Talent' Adjusts Up, 'Better Late Than Never' Adjusts Down," *TV By the Numbers*, September 8, 2016, and "Tuesday Final Ratings: 'America's Got Talent' Adjusts Up, 'Better Late Than Never' Down," *TV By the Numbers*, September 14, 2016.

15. Foreman interview; Rick Joe Otterson, "TV Ratings: 'Better Late Than Never' Finale Hits Season High," *Variety*, February 6, 2018.

16. *Foreman*, dir. Chris Perkel (Triple Threat Television, 2017); Bill Baldowski, "Foreman at Sage Summit: 'Never Stop Fighting,'" *Northside Neighbor*, May 11, 2017.

17. Nathan Rush, "Foreman Talks Boxing, Business, and TV Stardom," Athlon, https://athlonsports.com/life/george-foreman-talks-boxing-business-and-tv -stardom; Bud Schulberg, "Foreman-Holyfield: The Bigger They Are, the Harder They Don't Fall," in *Sparring with Hemingway, And Other Legends of the Fight Game* (Chicago: Dee, 1995), 232; Robin Finn, "Breakfast of Champions," *New York Times*, December 26, 1997; Sandomir, "Pitchman with a Punch"; McGeehan, "Salton Pays $137.5 Million"; Day, "Foreman Adds Steak"; Dave Anderson, "The Search for Tomorrow's Somebody," *New York Times*, April 17, 2004, and "Four Heavyweight Champs Is the Same as None," *New York Times*, December 13, 2004; Foreman interview.

Index

ABC (broadcasting network): radio, 30; television, 3, 7, 56, 78, 124, 126–127, 131, 212, 213, 215, 222, 224–225, 230, 232, 234–236, 246, 269, 271; *Wide World of Sports*, 78, 145–146, 205–206, 217

Abdul-Jabar, Kareem, 60, 210

Addie, Johnny, 82–83, 105

Alcindor, Lew. *See* Abdul-Jabar, Kareem

Ali, Muhammad, 3, 8–9, 30, 36–37, 48, 59–60, 71, 75–77, 85–87, 100, 103, 128, 139–140, 208, 211, 214, 223, 233, 241–247, 260, 264, 266, 294; and Foreman, 101, 107, 133, 155–157, 160–161, 165–173, 177–184, 187, 190–200, 203–207, 212, 216, 219, 221–222, 229, 234, 273; and Frazier, 4, 93–98, 104, 106–107, 117, 120–123, 125–127, 144–147, 208–210; and military draft, 43–45; and Nation of Islam, 36, 93, 107, 169, 171, 186, 221;

and Norton, 133, 136, 141, 143, 149–150, 158, 217, 220, 227–228

Amateur Athletic Union (AAU) Boxing Tournament (1968), 50–54

Anderson, Dave, 171, 294

Andrews, Mays, 83

Arledge, Roone, 222, 235

Arum, Bob, 71, 127, 210, 223, 242, 246, 257–258, 262–263, 266, 270, 272, 278, 284

Astrodome, 71, 109, 113, 138, 143, 162, 247

Atlantic City Convention Center, 263–264, 266

Atlas, Teddy, 274, 276–277

Berbick, Trevor, 244–245, 251

Berger, Phil, 257

Better Late Than Never, 8, 291–292

blaxploitation, 100, 258

Bobick, Duane, 227–229

Boehm, Michael, 285–287